The technique of special effects cinematography

The library of communication techniques

The technique of special effects cinematography

Raymond Fielding

Focal Press
London & Boston

Focal Press
is an imprint of Butterworth–Heinemann

PART OF REED INTERNATIONAL P.L.C.

First published 1965
Second edition 1968
Third edition 1972
    Reprinted 1974, 1977, 1979, 1982, 1984
Fourth edition 1985
    Reprinted 1987, 1990

British Library Cataloguing in Publication Data

Fielding, Raymond
    The technique of special effects cinematography.
    –4th ed.–(The Library of communication
    techniques. Film)
    1. Cinematography – Special effects
    I. Title   II. Series
    778.5'345   TR858
    ISBN 0-240-51234-0

Library of Congress Cataloging-in-Publication Data

Fielding Raymond.
    The technique of special effects cinematography.
    (The Library of communication techniques)
    Bibliography: p.
    Includes index.
    1. Cinematography – Special effects.   I. Title.
    II. Series
    TR858.F5   1985   778.5'345   85-4417
    ISBN 0-240-51234-0

Composition by Genesis Typesetting, Laser Quay, Rochester, Kent
Printed and bound by Hartnolls Ltd, Bodmin, Cornwall

Contents

Contents

Contents

Color plates

Plates 1 to 8 located between pages 176 and 177.

To Carole

Preface

The contributions of the visual-effects cinematographer have always been valued highly within the theatrical motion-picture industry. Because of his work, film producers have been able to endow their pictures with considerable 'production value' which the budget could not otherwise sustain. They have realized enormous savings in time and in set-construction costs and, even more important, their films have displayed the stylistic touches and polish which we have come to associate with the high-budget, theatrical product.

In past years, so long as the more complicated visual effects techniques were practiced solely within the major studios of the theatrical film industry, there was no need for a textbook such as this. Knowledge and experience in the art proceeded from master to apprentice. Even between different major studios, an unnecessary amount of secrecy surrounded such work.

Since the Second World War, however, nearly all of the internal visual-effects units which used to operate within the major studios have been closed down and their place taken by independent special-effects organizations who serve numerous clients. During this period, there has been explosive growth of both independent feature film production and of non-theatrical film production. A whole new generation of film-makers has appeared who work outside of the major-studio system, oftentimes with quite modest budgets. It is for these people in particular that this textbook is intended.

This book, the first of its kind in the English language, is designed to provide a basic familiarity with professional visual-effects processes currently in use throughout the world. Specifically, it is designed for the production cinematographer who wishes to acquire facility in executing these techniques. However, I hope that writers, directors and producers throughout the film industry will also find the information useful.

I have proceeded upon the assumption that the reader has a more than casual familiarity with standard cinematographic procedures, and that it is not necessary to describe or re-state the fundamental facts, practices and nomenclature of professional motion-picture production. At the same time, there is a limit to how much technical detail can be built into a book of this size. Almost any one of the several chapters easily could have been expanded into a full-length treatise. Accordingly, I have attempted to develop the description of each class of visual-effects technique to the point where a competent cinematographer could proceed to develop his or her own particular practices and applications.

In assembling the illustrations for the text, every effort has been made to select the best quality of photographs available to illustrate particular points. In some cases, however, the quality of reproduction has suffered, particularly in making photo-enlargements from 16 mm and 35 mm prints, some of which were two and three generations removed from the original negatives.

Patents

In those rare cases in which I have known a special-effects process to be 'protected' by patent, I have indicated this. In most cases, however, the really important processes were never patented at all, or, in those cases in which they were, the patents have long since expired.

As for the patents which remain in force, their validity is questionable. It is a relatively easy matter to secure a patent, but the test of its validity is always in the courts, and in the history of cinematography few effects patents have been held enforceable. Whether this is for the good or the bad depends upon one's point of view, but the reasons for this turn of events can be seen clearly.

In the first place, most effects techniques are based upon well-known optical and mechanical principles, none of which is patentable in itself. In many cases in which enthusiastic inventors (including myself) have developed a 'new' process, they have discovered that it was introduced and described many years earlier, even though it may not have been commercially exploited.

Second, it is difficult to monitor the use of a particular process, inasmuch as its use, if well-executed, is not apparent in a production. Indeed, one of the reasons why secrecy prevailed for so many years in the theatrical film industry's effects departments was that workers in each of the many studios so often infringed on each other's patents. Significantly, most of the important patents in the early days were pooled and made freely available to the entire industry.

Finally, even assuming that the use of a process could be accurately monitored and a patent enforced, there are so many other different ways of achieving the same result, which are not patented, that it is neither sensible nor necessary for a producer to pay license fees in order to secure a particular effect.

In making these points, I hope that my comments will not be interpreted as an attack upon the traditional theory of patent protection, but rather as a realistic appraisal of circumstances prevailing in a particular field of technology.

R. F.

Preface to the fourth edition

Exactly 20 years have passed since the first edition of this text appeared, in 1965. During this period, I have been deeply gratified by the enthusiasm with which it has been received and used in professional film-making circles.

I have had the pleasure of hearing from cinematographers, directors, engineers, and students throughout the world. Some of these required additional information about special-effects processes. Many wished to communicate to me their own unique experiences in the field. All of them had valuable suggestions to make for enlarging and improving the book.

More than a decade has passed since the last revision, and, although many techniques remain the same, significant advances have been made in particular areas. This is especially the case with front-projection and traveling-matte techniques, and with the introduction of computers and motion-control hardware into the visual-effects workshop.

This fourth revision introduces new information in nearly all chapters. 130 new illustrations have been added, many of them illustrating feature films which are currently in release. The bibliography has also been enlarged considerably.

A technical text is never finished, however; it is merely refined somewhat with each revision. I look forward to receiving further comments from the same film-makers and students who responded to earlier editions, as well as from new friends who are making the book's acquaintance for the first time.

R. F.

Acknowledgements

Anyone who writes about special-effects procedures is indebted to the hundreds of cinematographers, engineers, and inventors who developed the technique upon which this specialized art rests. Most of these people are not only unheralded, but, in many cases, completely forgotten. I am at least privileged to acknowledge the assistance given to me by many contemporary workers in the motion-picture industry, as well as by writers, editors, producers and manufacturers' sales representatives, some of whom provided illustrations for the text, others of whom read the manuscript and made suggestions for its improvement. These included Walter Beyer (Universal Studios), William Byers (Filmeffects of Hollywood), Dominick Capano (SOS Photo-Cine Optics), Terry Chostner (Lucasfilm, Ltd.), Charles Clarke (Twentieth Century-Fox), James Danforth, Norman Dawn, Andrew Delio (Film Opticals, Inc.), Linwood Dunn (Filmeffects of Hollywood), Richard Edlund (Industrial Light and Magic), Harrison Ellenshaw (Walt Disney Studios), Roy Field (Field Films, Ltd.), Arthur E. Gavin (American Society of Cinematographers), Douglas Fries (Fries Engineering), Wally Gentleman (Synergy Studios), Jeff Giordano (Century Precision Cine/Optics), Jack Hall (Producers Service Corp.), Sol Halprin (Twentieth Century-Fox), Warren Hamilton (UCLA), Bill Hansard, Gerald Herschfeld (MPO-Videotronics, Inc.), Joseph Hiatt (Universal Studios), Dave Inglish (Walt Disney Studios), N. Paul Kenworthy, Jr. (Kenworthy Snorkel Camera Systems, Inc.), John Kiel (Photo-sonics, Inc.), Jaakko Kurhi (J-K Camera Engineering), J. F. Lorence, Jr. (Mitchell Camera Corp.), Eustace Lycett (Walt Disney Studios), Alan C. Macauley (SOS Photo-Cine Optics), Kenneth MacGowan (UCLA), James Martin (National Film Board of Canada), Norman Martlew (The Rank Organization), E. B. McGreal (Producers Service Co.), Dennis Muren (Industrial Light and Magic), Beaumont Newhall (George Eastman House), Richard Patterson (American Society of Cinematographers), Zoran Perisic (Courier Films), W. E. Pohl (Technicolor Corp.), Badia Rahman (UCLA), David Samuelson (Samuelson Group), Hal Schieb (Cinema Research Corp.), Charles Staffell (The Rank Organization), John Stears (Pinewood Studios), Mrs. Katherine Stenholm (Bob Jones University), Roy Stewart (Stewart Film Screen Corp.), Donald

Acknowledgements

E. Stults (Pioneer Marketing Corp.), Harry Teitelbaum (Hollywood Film Co.), Robert Troy (Oxberry Corp.), Petro Vlahos (Vlahos-Gottschalk Research Corp.), Robert Wagner (Ohio State University), R. T. Watkins (Assoc. of Motion Picture Producers), Don Weed (Filmeffects International), and Edward Wilette (Oxberry Corp.).

I gratefully acknowledge the permission granted by the Journals of the Society of Motion Picture and Television Engineers, the American Society of Cinematographers, and the British Kinematograph, Sound and Television Society to republish certain diagrams appearing in their publications.

Finally, I am indebted to Carole Fielding, who, once upon a time, left a comfortable job as my secretary to become my long-suffering but patient wife, and who not only aided materially in the editing and preparation of this book but also suffered, with me, through the usual vicissitudes of authorship. It is to her that this book is dedicated.

1

The techniques available

Nearly always, in the course of professional film production, the need arises for certain kinds of scenes which are too costly, too difficult, too time-consuming, too dangerous, or simply impossible to achieve with conventional photographic techniques.

These scenes may call for relatively simple effects, as when optical transitions such as fades, wipes and dissolves are used to link different sequences together. Or, they may be much more demanding, as when a city must be seen destroyed in an earthquake, when a non-existent, multi-million dollar building must be shown as part of a live-action scene, when actors on the sound stage must be shown performing in locales which are hundreds or thousands of miles distant, when pictorially uninteresting shots must be artistically 'embellished' through the addition of clouds, trees and architectural detail, or when fantastic events which contradict the physical laws of nature must be shown upon a screen in order to satisfy the demands of an imaginative script-writer.

Nature of special effects

The solution of these and many other problems of similar magnitude calls for the application of a set of non-routine photographic techniques, which, for the purposes of this text, we refer to as 'special-effects cinematography'. Broadly speaking, special-effects work falls into two categories – photographic effects (sometimes termed 'visual effects', 'optical effects', or 'process cinematography') and mechanical effects. In this book we treat only photographic effects.

Special-effects procedures are as infinitely varied in their application as the kinds of production problem which can arise, for each effects assignment is a new one, and is different in its peculiarities from every other one that has been done before.

It is this variety of problems and solutions which renders the field so interesting; it is the same variety which also makes the work of the special-effects cinematographer so complicated. There are few rules, if any, and mistakes are common. The tools of the art can range from simple, inexpensive devices which can be held in the hand, to extremely costly machines weighing a ton or more. The length of time spent on an effects shot can range from a few minutes to several weeks. In the end, only familiarity with the tools and techniques of the field will provide the right solution for a particular problem, and only a certain amount of experience will provide consistently professional results.

The techniques classified

The techniques which are available can be classified in a number of different ways. Basically, they can be described as being:

1. In-the-camera effects, in which all of the components of the final scene are photographed on the original camera negative.
2. Laboratory processes, in which duplication of the original negative through one or more generations is necessary before the final effect is produced.
3. Combinations of the two, in which some of the image components are photographed directly on to the final composite film, while others are produced through duplication.

Viewed in this fashion, the various techniques can be categorized in the following manner:

1. *In-the-camera techniques*
    A. Basic effects.
        1. Changes in object speed, position or direction.
        2. Image distortions and degradations.
        3. Optical transitions.
        4. Superimpositions.
        5. Day-for-night photography.
    B. Image replacement.
        1. Split-screen photography.
        2. In-the-camera matte shots.
        3. Glass-shots.
        4. Mirror-shots.

2. *Laboratory processes*
    A. Bi-pack printing.
    B. Optical printing.
    C. Traveling mattes.
    D. Aerial-image printing.

3. *Combination techniques*
    A. Background projection.
        1. Rear projection.
        2. Front projection.

This classification is necessarily oversimplified, for techniques in different categories are often used in combination or succession to produce a given visual effect. Thus, miniatures might be combined with live-action through bi-pack printing, or titles added through optical printing and traveling mattes to a composite of live-action and representational art-work which was originally produced by means of a mirror-shot. Also, many particular effects such as optical transitions, image distortions, image replacements, superimpositions and the like can be produced with substantially identical results through *either* in-the-camera or laboratory techniques. Since this is so, it remains to the cinematographer to decide which set of techniques is best suited to a particular assignment.

Choosing the right technique

Four criteria are central to the choice of technique: (1) image quality, (2) flexibility, (3) cost, and (4) the kind of production set-up available.

On the one hand, in-the-camera techniques provide the maximum image quality, inasmuch as they are photographed in finished form upon the original camera negative. Laboratory processes, on the other hand, produce inherently poorer image quality, since they require the duplication of emulsions. Emulsion duplication, whether through contact or optical printing, reduces resolution, increases contrast and increases grain. In practice, this decrease in image quality may be so slight as to be negligible; still, the quality of image can never be as fine as that which is produced in the camera.

For a variety of reasons, but principally because of the economic impact of color television, nearly all motion pictures, in both 16 mm and 35 mm gauges are produced today in color. For all of this, the art of color cinematography remains an imprecise and uncertain one, vulnerable to those various factors which tend to degrade color images at different stages of production.

Workers will wish to experiment with a variety of both camera and duplication emulsions, in order to gain an intimate knowledge of each stock's advantages and limitations. Duplication steps must be kept to an absolute minimum in color work, and the closest kind of liaison between cinematographer and processing laboratory must be maintained.

Theoretically, maximum image quality is always to be desired in cinematography. However, in special-effects work, this ideal must be balanced off against the flexibility of a technique. As the word is used here, flexibility refers to the extent to which a technique allows the cinematographer and director to control the timing relationships of action which appears in different components of the shot. It refers to the speed and convenience with which the shot can be executed, relative to the number of crew members who are tied up by the shot. Finally, it refers to the ability of the director to correct errors which occur during photography of the shot, and to experiment with different combinations of image components.

Flexibility

Generally speaking, in-the-camera techniques are rather inflexible. The timing of any live or mechanical action which occurs in the shot must be perfectly executed. The spacial relationships of the various image components must be precisely determined, as must any exposure, contrast or color-balance matches. Once captured on film, these variables cannot be altered at a later time. Since in-the-camera effects are made during on-stage production time, the entire cast and crew are tied up until their completion. Finally, if an error is made during the shot's photography, there is no way to correct it, short of re-photographing the entire scene. The analogy which comes to mind here is that of the director who 'cuts in the camera'. It *can* be done, but it had better be perfect!

By contrast, laboratory processes which involve the duplication of emulsions are almost infinitely flexible. Since all of the image manipulations or replacements are produced by re-printing one or more strips of film, the ultimate amount of control is provided over the timing of action and the balance of exposure and color values which appear in the various image components. Unlimited experiments can be made and, should an error occur, it is a simple matter to go back to the original production footage and start the printing steps all over again. Finally, much less 'on-stage' time is required to secure the required footage. Once this basic footage is shot, the remaining manipulations are conducted at leisure, far away from the sound-stage and by relatively few workers.

Generally speaking then, laboratory processes are much more versatile than in-the-camera techniques. There are some exceptions: when in-the-camera techniques such as glass- and mirror-shots are used for image-replacement purposes, they allow great precision and convenience in the determination of spacial relationships between image components. The effect of the final composite can be seen by the director and cinematographer at the time that the shot is made, merely by looking through the camera's eyepiece, whereas when laboratory processes are employed, only an educated guess can be made as to how the separately photographed components will look when they are combined. This is an important consideration when working with directors or producers who do not understand what the special-effects cinematographer is capable of achieving, and who are loathe to entrust any part of the visualization or execution of a sequence to another individual. Finally, in-the-camera shots are returned from the laboratory the following day, together with the production 'rushes', at which time they can be immediately viewed and appraised. By comparison, an effects shot which is produced in the laboratory may be days or weeks in preparation.

Relative costs

The third and fourth criteria – those of cost and operational circumstances – are closely related; together, they usually constitute the determining factors in the use and selection of particular special-effects techniques.

On the face of it, in-the-camera techniques always appear less expensive than laboratory processes. The equipment which is used is inexpensive and the shot can be made by the regular production crew. For example, *insofar as equipment is concerned*, a split-screen shot can be done in-the-camera at practically no cost. If the same shot is executed in the laboratory with an optical printer, it requires expensive apparatus plus the labor of the specialists who operate it.

The point that must be borne in mind, however, is that the cost of equipment is only one of a variety of costs that figure in a motion-picture budget; indeed, it is generally a relatively minor factor. Most of a production's expenditure goes on *labor* – for the energy, the experience and the talents of the crew and the cast. A sizeable percentage of the budget also goes into sound-stage rental or over-head fees. In the business of film production, as perhaps more than in any other kind of business, time is money, and any kind of on-stage operation which ties up the cast, the crew and stage space for prolonged periods of time is inherently wasteful.

Many of the in-the-camera techniques are quite time-consuming. Although they require very little equipment, their successful execution takes so much on-stage time for set-up, rehearsal and shooting that the saving in equipment cost is more than offset by the delay they cause in the production schedule. For this reason, only the simplest of in-the-camera techniques, such as overcranking, undercranking, optical diffusion and day-for-night photography are ever employed on a major production.

For low-budget production, on the other hand, in-the-camera techniques may be found quite feasible. Working with longer shooting schedules, smaller crews and lower overhead costs, a small production organization can afford to employ glass-shots, mirror-shots, and certain types of in-the-camera superimpositions and matte shots. This is particularly practical when one or more members of the production team have an interest in special-effects cinematography, and the time to develop their individual skills.

Even in the case of low-budget production, however, many effects are more cheaply executed if achieved in the laboratory rather than on the sound-stage. Of course, laboratory processes require expensive equipment. In years past, low-budget 16 mm producers either had to conduct their special effects through in-the-camera techniques or eschew them altogether; they simply could not afford the costly investment which was necessary to set up their own special-effects facility.

Outside contractors

In recent years, however, with the spectacular growth of both 16 mm non-theatrical production, and the film-for-television business, scores of independent special-effects organizations have sprung up throughout the world to meet the needs of the impecunious producer who cannot afford to operate his own effects shop. Today, it is possible to contract virtually every kind of special-effects work to outsiders. Further, these service organizations will handle only so much of the special-effects assignment as the producer desires. In some cases, as with matte shots or optical printing, the producer may wish to execute much of the work with his own crew, and

Special-effects techniques – their cost and operational characteristics

Type of process	Complexity of operation	Relative cost for purchase, lease or construction of equipment	Relative speed of sound-stage operations	Relative cost to have the service performed by a contractor	Experience required for execution	Relative length of time required for execution including all steps	Amount of sound-stage space tied up, beyond normal
I. In-the-camera							
A. Basic effects	Little	Nil	Fairly rapid	Low, if available	Little	Minutes	None
B. Image replacement							
1. Split-screen	Moderate	Nil	Slow	Low, if available	Moderate	Minutes or hours	None
2. In-the-camera shots	Considerable	Low to medium	Very slow	Quite high if available	Considerable	Days	None
3. Glass-shots							
a. Painted mattes	Considerable	Low	Very slow	Quite high	Considerable	Days	Slight
b. Photo mattes	Moderate	Low	Slow	High	Moderate	Hours	Slight
c. Transparencies	Little	Low	Fairly rapid	Low, if available	Little	Minutes	Slight
4. Mirror-shots	Moderate to considerable	Low	Slow	High, if available	Moderate to considerable	Hours	Moderate
5. Aerial-image photography	Moderate	Medium	Medium	?	Moderate	Hours	Slight
C. Miniature	Considerable	Low to high	Extremely slow	Moderate to very high	Considerable	Days, weeks or months	Moderate to considerable
II. Laboratory processes							
A. Bi-pack printing							
1. Painted mattes	Considerable	High	Fairly rapid	High	Considerable	Days or weeks	None
2. Photo mattes	Moderate	High	Fairly rapid	Medium	Moderate	Days or weeks	None
B. Optical printing	Moderate	Extremely high	Not required	Low to medium	Moderate	Hours or days	None
C. Traveling mattes	Considerable	Medium to high	Fairly rapid	High	Considerable	Days or weeks	None
D. Aerial-image printing	Moderate	Extremely high	Fairly rapid	Low to medium	Moderate	Days	None
III. Background projection							
A. Rear projection	Considerable	Extremely high	Slow	Medium to high	Considerable	Days for preparation; hours on stage	Considerable
B. Front projection	Moderate	Medium to high	Slow	Medium to high	Moderate	Days for preparation; hours on stage	Moderate

then send the footage out to the laboratory for completion. In other cases, as with background projection, he may wish to turn the entire operation over to the outside group.

Facilities for 16 mm

Significantly, it is only within the last few years that special-effects processes have become practical for 16 mm production, and that suitable equipment has been manufactured for the smaller gauge. Previously, the 16 mm producer who did not shoot his effects in-the-camera had to first photograph them in 35 mm and then reduce to 16 mm dupe negative for release. Today, with the exception of traveling mattes, there is hardly a single special-effects technique which is not employed in 16 mm production. And, many of the effects which were previously achieved through traveling mattes are now produced with far better quality in 16 mm through aerial-image printing.

Increasingly, too, 16 mm producers are investing in certain minimum pieces of special-effects apparatus which allow for a considerable range of in-plant work. The purchase of a basic process camera, for example (or modification of an existing production camera for bi-pack, rotoscope operation) provides the film-maker with a tool with which a tremendous range of effects can be achieved. Producers who have more money to spend and who do a great deal of animation work may wish to invest in an aerial-image/animation-stand complex. The initial cost is high, but this single piece of equipment permits virtually every type of animation and special-effects assignment encountered today.

In the end, experience and common sense provide each particular production team with a working philosophy which assigns certain effects to the stage and others to the laboratory. The chart opposite sums up the costs and operational characteristics of the various techniques; all of the comparisons are relative, of course, and must be interpreted with respect to the size, production volume and specializations of each individual organization.

2

Camera equipment

In the chapters which follow, the specialized pieces of equipment which are involved in the different effects processes are described in detail. Basic to all effects work, however, are the various types of camera used. These can be classified as being either (a) production cameras, which are used to photograph the basic footage to be manipulated (Figs. 2.1 and 2.2) and (b) process cameras, which are employed in the laboratory for the final printing stages (Fig. 2.3).

Both production and process cameras can, in turn, be described with reference to the following five essential components: (a) a light-tight box, (b) a power drive, (c) an optical system, (d) a viewfinding system and (e) an intermittent movement.

Fig. 2.1, part 1. A popular studio production camera, the Golden Panaflex, manufactured by the Panavision Corporation. Studio cameras typically feature a wide variety of high-quality lenses, a precise pilot-pin movement, reflex viewing and numerous accessories.

Fig. 2.1, part 2. Another highly-regarded studio production camera, the Arriflex BL-3, which features an unusually compact coaxial magazine.

Fig. 2.2. A production camera designed by Fries Engineering Co. expressly for special-effects cinematography. The basic camera is a re-built 35 mm Mitchell 'High-speed Standard', to which a 'through-the-lens' reflex viewfinder has been added. A video tap in the camera's optics allows for off-camera viewing of the shot on a video monitor while the scene is being photographed. Film clips of already-photographed shots can be mounted on registration pins within the optical system to allow for line-up of shots. A computer-controlled follow-focus system is available for motion-control photography.

Fig. 2.3. The Acme 35 mm process camera, designed for photography and/or bi-pack printing in the effects laboratory. This view shows the 'swing-up' reflex viewfinder, variable shutter control and footage/frame counter.

The light-tight box

The light-tight container, in which the raw stock is housed, through which it travels, and in which it is stored after exposure, can take a variety of forms. Most commonly, the bulk of the film is housed in externally-mounted, detachable magazines, conventionally of 1000 ft capacity for 35 mm production, or 400 ft for 16 mm work. Ordinarily, these are of the double-chamber type, the forward section containing the unexposed film, the rear chamber containing the exposed (Fig. 2.4). A few cameras employ coaxial magazines, the feed and take-up reels being mounted next to each other.

Fig. 2.4. A conventional 1000 ft two-chambered magazine for the 35 mm Mitchell camera. Raw stock is stored in the left-hand chamber, exposed film in the right.

Process cameras always employ external magazines, as do most production cameras. However, a few 35 mm production cameras and a wide variety of 16 mm cameras store their raw stock within the body of the camera, in lengths ranging from 100 to 400 feet.

For certain types of effects work, an external 'bi-pack' magazine is used which has four chambers. The upper two contain the raw stock, the lower two a processed color master or a processed color negative (Fig. 2.5).

Fig. 2.5. A four-chambered, 35 mm Mitchell magazine designed for bi-pack photography or printing. For printing purposes, raw stock is stored in the upper left chamber and is taken up into the upper right. Color fine-grain positive is stored in the lower left chamber and is taken up into the lower right. The capacity of any one chamber is 400 ft.

One or more footage counters are always incorporated into the camera to indicate the amount of footage photographed and the amount of raw stock remaining. For special-effects work, these counters should be calibrated in both feet and frames.

Power drives

The power drives which operate motion-picture cameras can be (a) hand-cranked, (b) spring-driven or (c) electrically motor-driven. Hand-crank drives are obsolete for production purposes today. Spring-wound drives are commonly used for hand-held cameras and for certain types of portable 16 mm equipment. By their nature, they are incapable of driving more than short lengths of film through the camera, and, unless equipped with speed-regulating governors, are inclined to move the film through the intermittent movement at varying rates of speed.

Electrical motor drives of the following types are available for nearly all professional cameras:

'Wild' or variable-speed motors. This motor can be operated over a wide range of speeds by adjusting a built-in variable rheostat. Some models incorporate a tachometer which gives an exact indication of speed. 'Wild' motors, if well built and maintained, are fairly accurate instruments, ordinarily not varying more than ±1 frame per second (fps). Even this slight amount of variation in speed renders them unsuited for double-system sound recording. Hence, wild motors are used for sequences which are shot silent, and to which sound will be added later.* Depending upon its design, a wild motor can be operated from either DC or AC power sources, and at a variety of voltages.

Synchronous motors. For many kinds of 'double-system' sound recording, it is essential that both the camera and sound-recording equipment turn over at exactly the same and constant rates of speed. For such purposes, a synchronous motor is employed which takes its timing cue from the 50 or 60-cycle alternating current which is provided throughout most parts of the world. When provided with such an alternating current, these motors will turn over at exactly 24 frames per second.

Some synchronous motors are built to operate at higher or lower speeds; however, they are not variable in speed unless some sort of supplementary clutch system is incorporated to allow for the transfer of power.

Interlock/Selsyn motors. Ordinary synchronous motors will operate at a constant 24 frames per second, but only after they have overcome the inertia of the moving parts in the camera or recorder and are operating 'up to speed'. At this point, in conventional sound-recording practice, synchronism is established on both action and track by means of clapper sticks or other mechanical aids.

For certain kinds of special-effects work, however, it is required that two or more motors turn over at precisely the same speed *from start*. For such purposes, so-called Selsyn, 220-volt, three-phase interlock AC motors are employed, all of which are electrically interconnected. One of the motors in the circuit serves as a drive motor, sending out electrical signals to the other 'slave' motors. This set of motors is first interlocked electrically, so that their rotors are similarly positioned, relative to their stators. As the rotor shaft of the drive motor begins to turn over, the shafts of the other motors turn at exactly the same rate of speed, through 10°, through 30°, through 90°, and so forth. With such motors, it is certain that the

---

* There are certain types of portable, double-system camera and sound-recording outfits in use today in which the camera motor generates a pulse-sync signal to the magnetic tape in the recorder for subsequent synchronous transfer. These systems can be run off DC power packs. These are not true synchronous motors, however; the system with which they are used provides synchronization of action and track.

intermittent movements of two separate cameras, or the movements of a camera and a projector will be exactly synchronized from the very first frame. As will be described in later chapters, these motors are essential to rear-projection work in which the relationship of camera and projector-shutters must be permanently fixed.

Stepper motors. A stepper motor is a DC-powered device which takes 'instructions' in the form of power impulses. The impulses cause the rotor of the stepper motor to move in one or more discrete intervals, to any point or points in its 360° revolution. By attaching several motors to pan and tilt, dolly and crane mechanisms, it is possible to cause the camera to move, with both precision and repeatability, across the sound-stage floor, towards and away from, above, below, and to one side of objects which are being photographed. Such a capability for controllable and repeatable camera movements has many applications in so-called 'motion control' cinematography, which is described in Chapter 13.

Stop-motion motors. Stop-motion or single-frame motors are build so as to expose only a predetermined number of frames of film (ordinarily one frame) with each operation of the motor switch or button. Oftentimes, a synchronous motor is used to power this kind of drive, thus ensuring identical shutter exposures from frame to frame. A clutch system may also be added to the system to allow for different shutter speeds. This kind of motor is essential for animation work, as well as for most kinds of optical, aerial-image or bi-pack printing procedures. Process cameras are equipped with motors which are capable of both stop-motion and continuous drive.

Stop-motion motors are also used for 'pop-on' and 'pop-off' effects, and for so-called 'pixilation' sequences, in which objects or actors move abruptly from position to position, thereby creating a novel or stylistic effect.

Time-lapse motors. If a stop-motion motor is operated at intervals which are greatly extended beyond 24 frames per second, movement in the scene will be tremendously accelerated. The effect can be used for novelty, or for scientific and educational purposes. In practice, an intervalometer is attached to a stop-motion motor, and is set to provide whatever exposure interval is appropriate to the shot.

Optical systems

A wide selection of high-quality lenses is available in varying focal lengths and relative apertures for all production and process cameras. The uses to which these optics are put to solve conventional photographic problems are so well known that they do not need reiteration here.

For effects work, the highest-quality optics should be employed, as free from color-cast, distortion, spherical and chromatic abberations and curvature of field as possible. The duplication of emulsions, which is so necessary to most special-effects processes, so compromises image quality as it is that the best possible image should be produced at the start.

Most production cameras employ rotating mounts for focusing purposes. Some process cameras, on the other hand, use a bellows assembly for focusing. The lens does not rotate; rather, it is moved towards and away from the film plane by means of a rack-and-pinion movement. This latter system is somewhat to be preferred, since it more nearly guarantees coincidence of the mechanical and optical centers of the lens throughout all of its longitudinal movements.

Viewfinding systems

Whatever the kind of camera, some means must be provided whereby the operator can accurately view and compose the scene that he is photographing. There are many different kinds of viewfinder employed for motion-picture work, each with its own peculiar applications:

1. Monitoring viewfinders.
2. 'Through-the-lens' viewfinders.
   Rack-over.
   Reflex – type 1.
   Reflex – type 2.
   Focal plane.

Monitoring viewfinders

These types may be built into the body of the camera or may be temporarily attached to the outside of the camera or blimp. They incorporate their own optical system and produce their monitoring images either through virtual-image optics or by producing a real image upon a small, ground-glass screen.

When any kind of external viewfinder is used, parallax differences occur between the field of view photographed by the film and that which is viewed by the operator. This is inevitable, because the viewfinder is not located along the optical axis of the taking lens. For conventional motion-picture production, these differences in parallax are not so great that an experienced cameraman cannot learn to adjust to them. For special-effects work, however – particularly with those techniques which involve image replacement – it is absolutely essential that the viewfinder show the exact field of view which is being photographed. For such purposes, some sort of 'through-the-lens' viewfinding system is required.

Rack-over viewfinders

The first of these systems, the 'rack-over' viewfinder, requires that the box of the camera (which holds the intermittent movement and the film) be physically moved a few inches along a rack-and-pinion movement until a special, supplementary viewfinder (the eyepiece) is brought directly into line with the optical axis. The image cast by the lens is formed on a piece of ground-glass within the 'through-the-lens' viewfinder. By looking through the eyepiece, the cinematographer and director can view the scene exactly as it will appear on the screen.

Once the focusing and composing of the shot has been completed, the camera box is then racked back to taking position, with the raw stock aligned behind the lens (Fig. 2.6). During photography, the 'through-the-lens' viewfinder is useless, and so the external monitoring viewfinder is used by the operator to view the scene. Most rack-over systems move the camera box laterally; one or two cameras, however, pivot the camera box so that it moves in an arc – the effect is the same in either case.

Fig. 2.6, part 1. Rear view of the 35 mm Mitchell 'Standard' production field camera, showing the rack-over through-the-lens optical system in operation. Here, the eyepiece is positioned directly in line with the lens, allowing for viewing of the field of view as it will be photographed.

Fig. 2.6, part 2. By turning a handle, the entire body of the camera is shifted left, bringing the negative raw stock into position for exposure. During photography, an external viewfinder is mounted to the left of the camera for monitoring purposes.

Reflex viewfinders

Through-the-lens focusing may also be accomplished by means of a reflex viewfinder, of which there are two types. The first of these is usually found on a process camera. The turret housing of the camera and design of the lens are such as to allow room between the lens and the aperture for a movable prism. For composing and focusing purposes, the prism is swung in front of the film so as to reflect the image 90° to one side, where it is formed on a piece of ground-glass and viewed through a magnifying eyepiece (Fig. 2.7). Once composing and focusing are completed, the

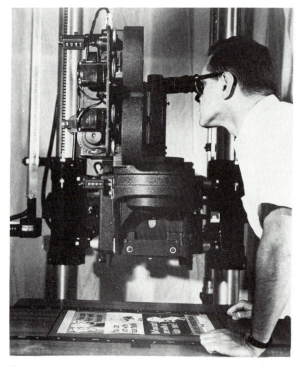

Fig. 2.7. A typical reflex viewfinder in operation. In this case, the Oxberry process camera is mounted vertically on an animation stand, with the art-work below it. Note the torque-motor drives to the left of the magazine which power the take-up spools within the magazine chambers

prism is swung out of the way and light from the lens passes directly back to the film. This kind of system does not allow for the viewing of the field of view during photography; however, since the shots which are made with a process camera are nearly always fixed shots, there is no need for a monitoring viewfinder. Some process cameras are available with either rack-over or reflex finders. Nearly always, the reflex finder is to be preferred. It has very little mass and causes no vibration during its operation which would be likely to misalign the camera – this freedom from misalignment is crucial because of the high magnifications at which the process camera's optical system often operates.

There is a second type of reflex finder which is found on certain makes of production camera. It employs either a beam-splitter or a rotating, segmented mirror/shutter between the lens and the film. The system allows the operator to view the exact field of view *during the progress of the shot*, as well as during the preliminary focusing. Cameras such as the Arriflex, the Eclair, the Panaflex and the Mitchell Reflex employ such a system (Fig. 2.8).

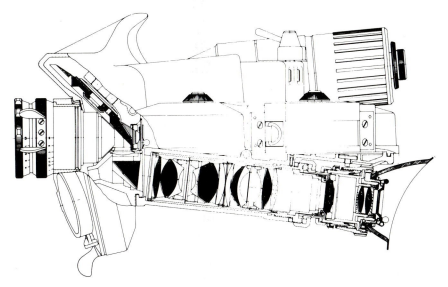

Fig. 2.8. A schematic diagram of a type of reflex viewfinder which allows for continuous through-the-lens viewing during photography. This particular design is used in the 16 mm Arriflex camera.

Focal-plane viewfinders

Finally, the image can also be focused and composed upon a piece of film or ground-glass set into the focal plane of the intermittent movement. This system requires that the area behind the film, which is ordinarily occupied by the pressure plate, be opened during focusing. The image which is cast on to the film or ground-glass at the focal plane may then be viewed either (a) from the side of the camera, by means of a right-angle prism and eyepiece assembly, or (b) straight-back, at the rear of the camera, by means of a supplementary 'boresight' optical system. Focal-plane viewing offers the maximum amount of accuracy in composing and focusing. Because of its inconvenience, however, its use is usually restricted to alignment procedures when the camera is used as part of an optical printer or animation-stand assembly.

There is a variation of focal-plane focusing work which works in reverse, and which is frequently employed in several kinds of matte-shot techniques. A master positive of a scene is inserted into the intermittent movement of a process camera and a right-angle prism or mirror is mounted behind the cut-out pressure plate. A lamp-house assembly is attached to the side of the camera. The light from this lamp house is reflected 90° by the prism, passes through the master positive and the lens system, and is allowed to strike a matte-board easel where an enlarged, projected image of the frame is formed. The exact character and field of view of the projected frame may then be appraised, matte lines can be drawn on the easel, and a variety of image replacement manipulations can be undertaken. These techniques are described in Chapter 6. The entire lamp-house and prism assembly is often referred to as a 'rotoscope' and the projection process as 'rotoscoping'.

One or another type of 'through-the-lens' viewfinder is essential for most kinds of special-effects cinematography, both on the sound-stage and in the laboratory. Without such a viewfinder, most effects work is simply not worth attempting.

Video taps

In recent years, some production cameras have been designed or retrofitted to incorporate a so-called 'video tap', a small video camera which 'intercepts' the image formed by the film camera's lens and sends that image to a video monitor off-camera, where the camera's field of view can be seen during photography. The image on the video monitor may even be recorded on video tape for subsequent replay and examination. The design of the video tap varies from one camera to another. In most cases, a pellicle is inserted into the optical system of the camera. During photography, most of the image-forming light passes *through* the pellicle and exposes the film. However, a portion of the light is reflected at 45° *off* the surface of the pellicle and is picked up by the lens of the 'video tap' camera. In a few systems, the video-tap camera picks up the image from the mirror-silvered, front surface of the rotating shutter blades. Each system has its advantages and disadvantages. Video taps have many applications in special-effects cinematography. These are described in Chapter 13.

The intermittent movement

The intermittent movement (or simply, 'the intermittent' or 'the movement') is the last essential component of any motion-picture camera. Taken as a whole, this assembly consists of (1) a pull-down claw, (2) a rotating shutter, (3) a sprocket drive, and (4) some sort of registration system.

The pull-down claw engages the perforations of the raw stock and advances the film, frame-by-frame, as it moves in between the aperture plate and the pressure plate. This motion is intermittent; that is, after a frame of the film is positioned behind the aperture plate, the claw withdraws and moves up to engage the next frame's perforations. During this period, a synchronized, revolving shutter rotates so that its opening

Fig. 2.9. A Vistavision-format 'Empireflex' camera designed by the Industrial Light and Magic group for use on Lucasfilm Productions. The pin-registered intermittent movement pulls eight perforations of 35 mm film across, sideways, with each stroke of the claw. The camera is capable of high-speed photography and is computer-controlled. At left, the camera's blimp. At right, the camera's electronic control unit. (Courtesy of Lucasfilm, Ltd.)

Fig. 2.10. Rear view of the ILM 'Empireflex' camera. The case of the camera is constructed of carbon-fiber material. The tripod-mounted pan head which is shown here is servo-motor-controlled.

passes in front of the aperture plate, allowing exposure of the frame. Once the opaque portion of the shutter again interrupts the light from the lens, the claw pulls the next frame of film into position. In a professional camera, the shutter's aperture is variable, ranging from fully-closed to its maximum aperture. For most cameras, the maximum aperture is about 170°; however, in some special designs, it may be as great as 235°.

The upper and lower sprocket-drive assemblies feed film to the intermittent movement and maintain the 'Latham loops' above and below the aperture plate.

Registration methods

Finally, some sort of registration system is required to ensure that each frame of film is positioned, or 'registered', behind the aperture plate in exactly the same position as every other frame, relative to the perforations.

At its simplest, registration accuracy is provided by a spring-loaded pressure plate (and/or tension plates or buttons along the edge of the aperture plate) which hold the film in position once the claw has disengaged the perforations. Assuming that such a movement is well-designed and is in good repair, it is satisfactory for much conventional work. The pressure which is exerted upon the film may be quite heavy, as with a 'tight gate', or relatively light, as with a 'loose gate'. Both types of gates have their respective advantages and disadvantages. However, a loose gate is not too well suited for special-effects cinematography – at least not for those techniques which involve image replacement through multiple exposures or multiple printings. Loose gates are inclined to allow a certain amount of film movement, backwards and forwards along the optical axis. This is particularly pronounced at higher-than-normal operating speeds. This movement may not be sufficient to throw the picture noticeably out of focus, but it is great enough to cause magnification changes in the image. Should such a piece of film be re-exposed or re-printed, the matte line which separates image components may become visible and the different sections of the composite may weave towards and away from one another. A tight gate more nearly guarantees that the film will remain in the focal plane during all exposures and at all camera speeds. However, tight gates must be kept meticulously clean, for the smallest bit of grit will gouge out pieces of emulsion and cause severe scratches.

A minimum registration accuracy is necessary for *all* motion-picture photography. Without it, the projected image would jump or weave around the screen in a very distracting manner. For special-effects cinematography, these minimum standards are extremely high. Although a simple pull-down claw will provide fairly accurate registration, most professional production cameras and all special-effects equipment employ a much more precise 'pilot-pin' system.

There are two major pilot-pin movements in use throughout the world today. Named after the manufacturers who first introduced them, they are known as the Mitchell movement and the Bell & Howell movement.

The Mitchell intermittent

The Mitchell movement is shown in Fig. 2.11. As the double pull-down claw withdraws from the perforations and swings upward, a pair of pilot pins move inward and enter into another pair of perforations. For 35 mm work, one of the pins is 'full fitting' and completely occupies its perforation. The other pin is machined so that it fills its perforation

Fig. 2.11. A 35 mm Mitchell intermittent movement for the high-speed model. The pull-down claw, which is seen at the bottom of the movement, sweeps downward, alternatively engaging and releasing the film's perforations as it pulls each frame into position. The double-pronged pilot-pin bar, directly above it, moves straight in and out. A slot which is cut into the aperture-plate assembly allows for the insertion of focal-plane mattes.

vertically but allows a microscopically small amount of play horizontally. The two pilot pins remain inserted in the perforations while the frame of film is exposed, following which the pins withdraw and the pull-down claw re-engages the film and pulls the new frame into position. A similar movement is found in many other highly-respected cameras, such as those made by the Ariflex and Panavision Companies. Most production cameras employ two pilot pins, registering perforations on each side of the film. A few cameras employ only a single registration pin.

The Bell & Howell intermittent

The Bell & Howell movement is illustrated in Fig. 2.12. This intermittent design features *fixed* pilot pins which are an integral part of the aperture plate. During operation, the film is held away from the pilot pins while the pull-down claw moves a new frame of film into position. At this point, the film is pushed on to the pins, the shutter opens and the exposure is made.

Fig. 2.12. A 16 mm Bell & Howell-type intermittent shuttle movement with fixed pilot points. The entire assembly is easily removed from the camera. Movements of this sort are used in the Acme and Oxberry process cameras.

The film is then pulled off the pins, and the claw resumes its pull-down cycle. The Bell & Howell shuttle is the oldest precision pilot-pin design in the film industry. It survives, virtually unchanged, today, and is found in such process cameras as the Acme and Oxberry.

For any type of special-effects cinematography in which multiple exposures or multiple printing are required, a pilot-pin movement is essential. Without it, the different elements of the composite image will weave or jiggle against one another and the illusion of the scene will be ruined. Either the Mitchell or Bell & Howell movement is satisfactory for such work, although the Bell & Howell is generally preferred. It has fewer moving parts and is less likely to get out of adjustment. It is easier to load, particularly for bi-pack operations. Because of the fixed position of its pins, it is inclined to register film to finer tolerances. Finally, the Bell & Howell movement can be easily removed from the camera and replaced with another assembly with different pilot-pin or aperture positions.

Checking registration accuracy

Even the best intermittent movement will fail to meet special-effects standards if it is not properly cleaned and maintained, however. Worn or misadjusted pins will deform the perforations and compromise registration accuracy. A sure sign of such wear is the presence of emulsion 'dust' within the movement, caused by abrasion of the perforations by the claw or pilot pins.

A simple but effective test for registration accuracy can be conducted by mounting the camera firmly on a tripod or optical bench and double-exposing a cross-hatched chart. The chart is first photographed at about half the regular exposure. With the shutter closed, or the lens covered, the film is then re-wound to start position and the camera is moved very slightly on the diagonal, so that the image of the chart is shifted out of position on the film, relative to that of the first exposure. A second exposure is then made of the same chart, again at half regular exposure. When the developed test film is projected on to a large screen, the accuracy of the movement is revealed in the extent to which the double-exposed set of lines weave towards and away from one another (if both sets of lines move uniformly in the same directions, it is because the projector's movement is faulty). By special-effects standards, there should be no discernible weaving or jiggling of the lines, towards or away from one another, when the film is projected on to a conventional, full-size screen. Sometimes, specially-drawn charts are used for such purposes, in which the varying increments of distance between lines is specified. By examining the film under a microscope, it is then possible to measure and specify the registration tolerances of the movement.* The intermittent movements which are used in process cameras should also be capable of accepting and accurately registering bi-pack loads, in which two strips of film are run through the camera simultaneously, their emulsions in contact.

Registration procedures

Even for in-the-camera effects, a high standard of registration accuracy is essential. For laboratory processes, however, in which a number of separately photographed strips of film are successively printed to combine various image components, the very highest registration precision is required. Without it, the matte lines which separate components will become visible, images will weave or jiggle against one another, and color fringing will become apparent. To achieve these high standards, certain registration procedures must be followed throughout the entire duplication process.

We have already spoken of the pilot pins which are used to register film, and of the two major types of intermittent movements which are employed today. One discovers, however, that these two movements register film in different perforation positions, relative to the aperture.

Pilot-pin positions

Assuming that we were to view a piece of raw stock *from lens position* after it has been loaded into the intermittent, we find that the pilot pins of the 35 mm Bell & Howell camera movement engage the perforations directly above the frame; those of the Mitchell movement directly below the frame. In each case, the full-fitting pin is located to the left of the frame, next to

---

* A. C. Robertson, 'A method of measuring the steadiness of motion-picture cameras', *JSMPTE*, January 1959, p. 21; L. J. Wheeler, 'Apparatus for measuring unsteadiness in motion picture cameras', *Brit. Kinematography*, October 1958, p. 102

the sound track, and the loose-fitting pin to the right. When optical printer projector heads are used for effects work, the registration positions (above or below the frame) are ordinarily reversed. As seen from lens position, the Bell & Howell projection movement registers below the frame, the Mitchell above it. For 16 mm work, double-perforated film is ordinarily registered below the frame, with the large pin located to the left of the frame, the smaller pin to the right. Single perforated 16 mm film is registered vertically, the large pin ordinarily engaging the perforation at the bottom of the frame, the smaller pin registering two perforations higher. The 35 mm registration positions are shown in Fig. 2.13.

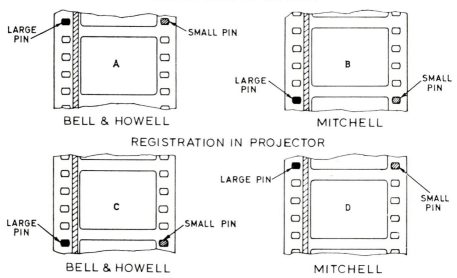

Fig. 2.13. Registration positions for Bell & Howell (A, camera; C, projector) and Mitchell-type (B, camera; D, projector) movements in cameras and projectors. The view presented is that which is seen from lens position, emulsion towards the viewer. (JSMPTE.)

Parenthetically, it should be noted that 35 mm pilot-pin systems are designed to be used with emulsions which have negative (so-called 'Bell & Howell') perforations. Negative perforations have curved sides, as contrasted with positive print perforations (so-called 'Kodak Standard'), the sides of which are straight and parallel to one another (Fig. 2.14).

There are other types of perforations, such as the Dubray-Howell and Cinemascope perforations. For the moment, however, these are employed mainly for certain types of colour or wide-screen release prints, and are not of immediate concern to the special-effects cinematographer.

The full-fitting pilot pin is designed to fill the negative-type perforation exactly. Original negatives, master positives and fine grain duplicating negatives, which are used for 35 mm effects duplication must always have negative-type (Bell & Howell) perforations. If stocks with positive-type perforations are employed, the pilot pins will not fit properly. As a consequence, registration accuracy will be compromised.

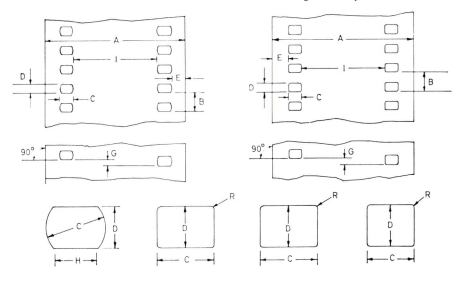

FILM	ASA STAND	ASA DIMENSIONS, INCHES									
		A	B	C	D	E	G	H	I	L	R
35mm BH 1870[1]	PH 22 34	1377	·1870	·1100	0730	079	<·001	082	·999	18·70	
35mm BH 1866[2]	PH 22 93	1377	·1866	·1100	0730	·079	<·001	082	·999	18·66	
35mm KS 1870[3]	PH 2236	1377	1870	1100	0780	·079	<·001		999	18·70	·020
35mm DH 1870	PH 22 1	1377	·1870	·1100	0730	·079	<·001		·999	18·70	·013
35mm CS 1870	PH 22·102	1377	·1870	·0780	0730	·086	<·001		1·049	18·70	013
TOLERANCE ALLOWED ±		·001	·0005	·0004	·0004	002			·002	·015	

[1]'LONG PITCH' NEGATIVE ; [2]'SHORT PITCH' STANDARD NEGATIVE; [3]STANDARD POSITIVE
NOTE : DIMENSION 'L' IS THE LENGTH OF ANY 100 CONSECUTIVE PERFORATION INTERVALS

Fig. 2.14. Types and sizes of 35 mm perforations. For special-effects work, so-called 'negative' or 'Bell & Howell' perforations are used for all duplication stages. In conventional 16 mm practice, negative and positive perforations are identical. (DUPONT.)

Matching printer and camera

All special-effects duplication is performed with either step-contact or step-optical printers. Unlike a continuous printer, a step printer provides pilot-pin registration. A typical step-contact printer is shown in Fig. 2.15. Step-optical printers are discussed and illustrated in Chapter 7.

Whenever duplication steps are carried out in the preparation of an effects shot, it is essential that registration positions be preserved throughout the *entire* operation. By using the same perforation positions throughout each of these many steps, microscopic irregularities in the size or position of the perforations are minimized. These irregularities can result from either manufacturing errors or shrinkage.

For example, if a Mitchell camera is used for photography of the original strips of film, the film will be registered below the frame. When the master positive is struck off, an intermittent movement must be used in the step printer which also registers the film below the frame. If the master positive is then used in a process camera for bi-back printing, the process camera's

Fig. 2.15. The Model 37C Acme 35 mm Registration Step Contact Printer, with Bell & Howell automatic additive-color lamphouse. This particular model is designed for 35 mm work and has a capacity of 2000 ft. The additive-color lamphouse system provides virtually unlimited control over the color balance of the resulting print.

movement must also register below the frame. If the master positive is used in an optical printer with traveling mattes, then the mattes, should be originally photographed with an intermittent movement which also registers below the frame.

In practice, this means either that all pieces of duplicating equipment must be standardized or that a set of replaceable intermittent movements with different pin positions be kept on hand. The latter of these alternatives is the most common. Nearly all step printers and process cameras employ Bell & Howell movements, which are instantly interchangable. A complete set of such movements would provide (a) different pin positions above and below the aperture, (b) different positions of the large and small pins; (i.e. to the right or left of the frame), (c) different sound-track positions, and (d) different size apertures.

A great deal of special-effects work is accomplished during original photography with either a full silent aperture, or with a Vistavision aperture in an 8-perforation-pull-across movement, or on 65 mm negative with any number of possible aspect ratios. The use of such larger-than-normal formats during the preliminary stages provides finer image quality in the composite. It also allows for convenient flipping of the emulsion position during optical printing, since the sound track is not present.

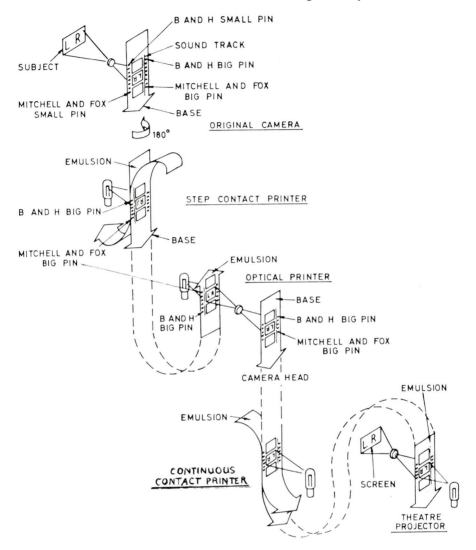

Fig. 2.16. A schematic representation of a typical series of duplication steps for a special-effects shot. Following original exposure in the camera (top), the processed color negative is flipped around for contact step-printing (center). The resulting processed color fine-grain positive is inserted into the optical printer, 'heads-up', and is re-photographed on duplicating color negative raw stock in the process camera (center). The dupe color negative which results is then printed in a continuous-contact printer (bottom), producing a color positive which can be projected onto a screen (bottom right). Note the changes of registration position (above and below the frame) and pin positions (left and right) which occur during this series of operations. (JSMPTE.)

The really meticulous worker will see that not only the above or below-the-frame registration is preserved throughout duplication, but also the relative positions of the large and loose-fitting pins. For example, when a camera negative is printed onto a master positive, in a contact-step printer, the negative is flipped around to allow for emulsion-to-emulsion contact. Accordingly, the position of the large and small pins on the step printer should be reversed from left to right, compared to that of the camera's intermittent. Fig. 2.16 demonstrates a series of pin-position relationships for a typical operation.

Occasionally, it becomes necessary to change registration positions, above or below the frame, from one strip of film to another. Assume, for example, that a background scene is photographed with a Bell & Howell-type movement, but that the positive print from it must be used in a background projector with a Mitchell-type movement. In a case such as this, the master positive would be made on an optical printer rather than a contact printer, and the pin positions would be reversed optically.

Registration accuracy will be greatly improved if the many emulsions which are used in the printing operations are suitably stored, both before and after development, so as to prevent shrinkage or expansion due to changes in temperature and humidity. Most film manufacturers recommend a temperature of 50°F and a relative humidity of 50 per cent for such purposes.

Finally, depending upon the type and brand of film stock employed, the conditions under which the film has been stored, and even the parts of the world in which one works, it may be found necessary to test sample strips of raw stock for dimensional stability. Some workers have custom-built their own equipment for the precision measurement of perforation and film-width dimensions. In this manner they insure that the raw stock they select for photography will have been manufactured to the highest standards of accuracy. (See *American Cinematographer*, Sept. 1979, p. 892.)

In the last few years, Estar-based film stocks have been widely used in special-effects circles for traveling-matte work in which repeated passes through the camera and the optical printer are required. These Estar-based materials suffer substantially less shrinkage, and are far more dimensionally stable than acetate-based stocks – a consideration of special importance in the use of 8-perforation-pull-down formats.

Reviewing the entire duplication process, then, the following factors will be found most important in determining registration accuracy: (1) The use of a quality pilot-pin movement in all cameras and printers, (2) The stability with which production and process cameras are mounted during photography, so as to prevent vibration, (3) The preservation of pilot-pin positions, above and below the aperture, through all duplication stages, (4) Consistency in the positioning of the full and loose-fitting pins through all duplication stages, (5) The proper storage of film stocks, before and after development, to reduce dimensional changes to a minimum, and (6) The reduction of duplication stages to the bare minimum which is required for a particular effect.

Assuming that all of these factors operate optimally throughout the entire duplication process, a resulting overall registration accuracy of ±0.0002 inch is possible.

Extended discussions of the problems and techniques involved in achieving registration accuracy will be found in the professional literature cited in the bibliography of this book, in the section titled 'Registration procedures for special-effects cinematography'.

3

Glass-shots

One of the most frequent tasks to which effects cinematography is put is the replacement of selected portions of a particular scene with an entirely different kind of visual detail. The aim, in such cases, is usually either the pictorial enhancement of the final image or the saving of set construction costs.

The need for image replacement

For example, the script may call for long and medium shots of a hotel, a building, a palace or a department store, in front of which sync-sound action takes place. In many such cases, the type of building which the producer and director envisage may not be available in real life. More commonly, a situation arises in which it is not feasible from the standpoint of sound recording quality or production efficiency to photograph extensive sync-sound sequences on location. Assuming that the budget permits, this problem may be solved by building a complete set of the desired building, which conforms in every respect to the imaginations of the creative team. The set is built on the sound stage, where isolation, controlled lighting and proper acoustics are available for the best production quality.

The cost of constructing a complete hotel-front, palace or store-front is fairly high, however, and also wasteful, inasmuch as all of the foreground sync-sound action is performed in front of only the first floor of the building. In order to save construction costs, the special-effects cameraman and his team are usually called in at this point to devise a method whereby only the first floor of the building is built on the stage but, in the finished long shot, it appears as an integral part of a complete four- or five-story structure.

Image replacement may be used to solve a variety of other problems. A demanding production schedule may force a location camera crew to photograph outdoor action against barren skies on dull, overcast days; the special-effects cameraman may be required to add attractive clouds in the sky area. The same production company may find itself photographing action in front of a generally attractive landscape, but in the background of which a tree may be 'improperly' situated for appropriate compositional balance. The effects cameraman may be asked to remove the tree, or to reposition it. The effects cameraman and his associates may also be required to provide landscape detail which is not even present at the locale, such as a mountain range, a setting sun, or a distant building.

Such problems nearly always involve 'image replacement' in their solution – the use of one technique or another to add missing pictorial detail or to create more attractive detail than appears in the real scene. Among the many effects processes which allow for this kind of manipulation are glass-shots, mirror-shots, in-the-camera matte shots, bi-pack printing, traveling mattes, optical printing, and aerial-image printing. In this and the following chapter, we deal with the simplest of these techniques – those of glass-shot and mirror-shot photography.

Nature and origin of the glass-shot

The term 'glass-shot' is taken from the nature of the process itself. A large sheet of glass is mounted in front of a camera which has been set up and focused upon the scene to be altered. An artist paints appropriate representational image upon portions of the glass. The images obscure and replace certain visual components of the real scene. By viewing the emerging composite through the camera's eyepiece, the artist blends the real and artificial visual elements together, developing appropriate perspective, tonal, and density relationships as he goes along. When

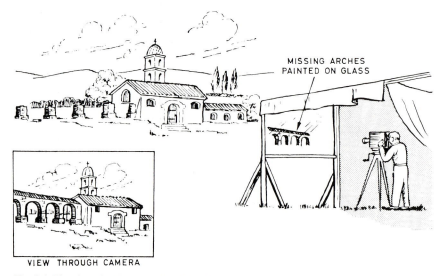

Fig. 3.1. The glass-shot is one of the oldest of visual-effects techniques, apparently first employed in sophisticated fashion by Norman Dawn in 1907 for his production of *Missions of California*. Replacement details are painted on a sheet of glass which is positioned between the camera and the live-action set. (Adapted from a sketch drawn from memory by Norman Dawn.)

completed, the complementary visual components from the real scene and from the painted images are photographed simultaneously with one pass of the raw stock through the camera (Figs. 3.1 to 3.4).

The origins of the glass-shot process are obscure. One of the first film-makers to develop the technique for professional work was the veteran cameraman-artist-director, Norman Dawn. Dawn first employed this process for still photography in 1905, and for motion-picture production in 1907. Over the years which followed, he became one of the film industry's most frequent and skilful practitioners of the art and introduced it to many other workers in the field. During the 1920s and 30s, the glass-shot became a favourite technique of the special-effects camera crew. Even today, it is occasionally used in the theatrical industry, although it has been largely supplanted by other, more versatile processes which are described later in this book.

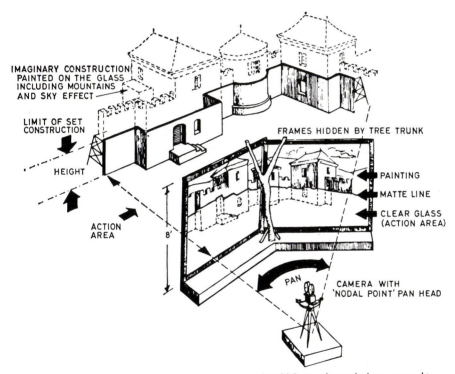

IMAGINARY CONSTRUCTION
PAINTED ON THE GLASS
INCLUDING MOUNTAINS
AND SKY EFFECT

LIMIT OF SET
CONSTRUCTION

FRAMES HIDDEN BY TREE TRUNK

HEIGHT

PAINTING

MATTE LINE

CLEAR GLASS
(ACTION AREA)

ACTION
AREA

8'

PAN

CAMERA WITH
'NODAL POINT' PAN HEAD

Fig. 3.2. A somewhat more complicated glass-shot, in which two glass paintings are used to add architectural detail to a one-story set. A tree trunk is positioned to mask the junction of the two glass panels. (JSMPTE.)

Despite its fall from favor in the theatrical film industry, however, variations of the glass-shot process remain of real interest to the low-budget, non-theatrical film maker because of their simplicity and low cost. In the following section we examine, first, the conventional painted glass-shot, and second, a much less expensive variation which employs photographic cut-outs or transparencies.

Glass paintings

In its original and most costly form, a glass-shot requires the services of a highly-skilled artist with a flair for representational painting, and a mastery of perspective rendering. Skill in such work is not easily gained and many otherwise fine artists do not find it possible to master this kind of assignment.

During consultation with the director, the cameraman, and the art director, the artist prepares projected sketches of the composite scene as it will appear on the screen. Still photographs of the existing location background, or the partially-built sound stage set (photographed from final camera position) and are often provided as a point of departure. The area in which the actors will perform is decided upon by the director – once set, this cannot be easily changed.

If a location scene is involved, the time of day at which the shot will be made must be carefully pre-determined, so that shadows which are painted into the images on the glass will match the direction and angle of those which fall on objects in the background. On the day on which the glass-shot is to be made, time must be provided for the artist to prepare the glass painting *before* that brief period arrives when sun angles and shadows in the real and painted elements match one another. Once the painting is completed, the composite shot must be taken within a reasonable length of time, or the sun's position will change, relative to the earth's surface, and the shadows and texture of the painting will no longer match that of the background. Happily, such problems are not involved in sound-stage work, where the lighting can be controlled.

The artist

The entire success of a painted glass-shot depends upon the skill and experience of the artist, who works with a variety of media and materials. Oftentimes, a base layer of white tempura is laid onto the glass, onto which other media are then laid. Unused and unwanted areas of the white tempura can be either washed off or scraped off. Glossy, oil-based paints are frequently used for the painting, as these produce high-saturation colors which photograph well.

Occasionally, a glass-shot is painted on to a sheet of stiff, opaque, compo-board. Upon completion of the painting, the unpainted portions are cut away with a knife or other tool, thus allowing for photography of the live-action scene through the cut-away section. The use of compo-board allows the artist to use chalks instead of paints. Some artists find that chalks lend themselves particularly well to this kind of work, since they allow for very subtle blends between the art work and live-action components.

The artist must be capable of rendering a highly representational image which matches the subject matter, the size and spatial relationships, the tone and hues, the densities, and the textures of the live-action scene with which the painting is being combined.

In some cases, the artist will produce a 'soft' blend of visual elements, as, for example, when a mist-shrouded mountain-top is added to a landscape or when continuous tones or colors in the middle foreground of the live-action set are blended with those of the painting. In other cases, as when adding additional floors to a one-story sound-stage set, the artist will fit the painted and real elements together at particular architectural junction points or divisions – usually at the edges of the sound-stage set, along its mouldings. A glass-shot composite will appear particularly convincing when portions of the painted image are made to appear to be partially obscured by features of the real background scene. This requires, from the artist, a nice eye for spacial and parallax relationships.

Detail and aerial perspective

Obviously, perspective lines which are present in the real scene must be accurately carried forward into the painted element. This matching of linear perspective depends not only upon the nature of the live-action scene, but also upon the focal-length of lens employed on the camera. In addition, the detail perspective and the aerial perspective of the scene must be taken into consideration. When we look at a real cityscape, for example, nearby buildings are perceived as being finely detailed, with individual bricks or ornamental 'gingerbread' clearly seen. When we shift our glance to buildings which are situated at progressively greater and greater distances, however, we perceive less and less detail. Finally, at great distances, we see only the gross form or outline of the buildings. The density or color saturation of nearby buildings also decreases with distance, due to atmospheric haze; far-off buildings appear a neutral or light grey, and strong colors become pastel in appearance.

All of these characteristics of detail and aerial perspective which we experience in real life must be duplicated by the artist in preparing his glass painting. If certain objects in the painting are supposed to be located at a great distance from the foreground, then an amount of haze which is appropriate to the real scene has to be introduced into the painting. Similarly, the detail which is painted into distant objects has to be decreased, together with their densities and/or color saturations.

If color cinematography is involved in the shot, additional technological problems arise, due to the general unpredictability of contemporary color emulsions in recording the colors in nature and the colors in pigments as the human eye sees them. Experimentation with different pigments, and preliminary exposure tests will nearly always be necessary before the production take can be made with confidence.

It is essential that a camera with a 'through-the-lens' viewfinder be used. This can be either of the rack-over or reflex type, so long as it is accurate. Any discrepancy in viewing and taking positions, no matter how slight, produces parallax differences which make it impossible for the artist to accurately 'jigsaw' the visual components together.

Preparing the painting

In beginning his work, the artist usually roughs-in guide-points or an outline of the painted area. Sometimes this is done on the *reverse* side of the glass with brush or grease pencil. Once the painting on the *front* surface

34

Fig. 3.3, part 1. Earliest known surviving photograph of a glass-shot set-up, made in 1908 by pioneer cameraman Norman Dawn while shooting footage in Tasmania. The painted element, a rooftop, can be seen on the sheet of the glass. A canvas cover prevents reflection of the camera by the glass. The resulting composite is seen in the accompanying photograph. The technique was used here to reconstruct an historically important building which was partially destroyed. Although this photograph was taken more than 70 years ago, the set-up shown is identical to that which is used today.

Fig. 3.3, part 2. The resulting glass-shot composite. This is an enlargement from the original 1908 nitrate print.

Fig. 3.4, part 1. For an exterior shot in the production of *Flame in the Wind*, the top of a monastery gateway is added by means of a glass shot. Here, the artist adds the finishing touches to the painted element. The glass panel, which is about 3 × 4 ft in size, is supported in a wooden frame. Although considerable skill on the part of the artist is required, the investment in equipment and materials is minimal.

Fig. 3.4, part 2. The finished composite of painting and live action. (Unusual Films, Bob Jones University.)

of the glass is finished, the guide-points and outline can then be removed with a suitable solvent. This process of outlining can be greatly accelerated if the artist has an assistant to aid him. The artist can look at the scene through the camera's eyepiece and instruct the assistant in the placing of guide points, and in the rendering of the outline. Without an assistant, the artist must constantly run back and forth between the sheet of glass and the viewfinder, roughing-in outline markings and then correcting them accordingly. Even after the outline is complete and the painting begun, regular sightings through the eyepiece are necessary to ensure a satisfactory blend of the different visual elements.

As the painting nears completion, the artist and/or cameraman will ordinarily wish to make a series of test exposures which are either sent off to the laboratory or which are 'slop-test-processed'.

Only short lengths of test footage, a foot or so in length, are necessary. After processing, these negative test strips are examined to determine whether the different visual components are fitting together properly and whether the photographic densities of the painting and background areas match. It takes a little experience to 'read' negatives, rather than positives, but this skill comes with time and is something every competent cinematographer should be capable of, anyway.

For black-and-white photography, density matches can also be checked with a Polaroid-Land camera, providing that a panchromatic Polaroid film stock is selected whose color sensitivity is similar to that of the motion-picture raw stock.

For color photography, if a 'soft' blend is made between painting and background (i.e. in which a particular hue in the painting merges with an identical hue in the background), the matching of color values may be quite critical. Apart from extensive experience and experimentation, nothing short of laboratory processing and printing of the color test strips will ensure a proper match on such assignments. Motion-picture color emulsions *can* be 'slop-tested' with black-and-white chemicals – naturally, this destroys the color values of the test strip, but it does tell the cameraman/artist whether the components are being fitted and blended together properly, and whether the densites of the real and artificial elements match one another. Polaroid color film can also be used in a Polaroid camera to provide a rough indication of color matching; however, a good deal of experimentation is necessary before the cameraman learns to interpret the manner in which Polaroid film records different hues, and to relate this to the characteristics of the color stock being used in the motion-picture camera.

Photographing the glass-shot

Since the glass-shot composite is photographed in one pass through the camera, registration accuracy is not the problem that it is with other composite processes. A pilot-pin movement is by no means essential, and very nice results will be achieved with a conventional pull-down-claw movement. Even if a certain amount of weave and jiggle is present in the intermittent movement, the visual elements on the glass and in the background area will be *equally* affected by the registration inaccuracies – they will weave in the same direction, and at the same time, rather than against one another.

Rigid mountings

It is necessary, however, that both the camera and the sheet of glass be rigidly mounted – the first on a sturdy tripod, the second in a well-supported wooden or metal frame (Fig. 3.5). If either the camera or the glass painting vibrate or weave during the shot, either with respect to each other or to the background, the composite picture is ruined. The

Fig. 3.5. Glass paintings can be mounted either on separate stands or on supports attached to the camera. This convenient rig is used at the National Film Board of Canada for glass, transparency and mirror-shots.

camera tripod should be of massive construction and should be tied down to the stage floor with chains. For exterior work, a wooden platform can be provided – either elevated or set at ground level – on which both the camera and glass frame can be mounted. As an alternative, hollowed wooden stakes can be driven into the earth, into the openings of which the spiked ends of the tripod legs can be set. A fourth stake can be driven into the ground directly below the centre of the tripod, and a chain and turnbuckle attached to hold the tripod steady against the earth. The frame which holds the sheet of glass must be made equally secure from vibration due to wind or ground movements.

Avoiding atmospheric effects

Care must also be taken to avoid atmospheric disturbances during the shot such as fog, dust, heat waves, rain and mist. The illusion of the composite is compromised if these environmental peculiarities appear in the live-action area and not in the painted scene. A typical problem arises

38

Fig. 3.6, part 1. Another exterior glass shot, partially completed for the production of *Auto de Fe*. The art director is in the midst of blocking in and painting details upon the sheet of glass which will not only add set detail, but will also block out the buildings and bleachers in the background.

Fig. 3.6, part 2. The finished composite glass shot: a square in Seville, Spain, recreated on a college campus in South Carolina. (Unusual Films, Bob Jones University.)

when horses, wagons, or automotive vehicles are driven over dusty roads in the live-action part of the scene. As the dust passes behind the painting, it disappears, creating a very curious effect – all the more so when the painted element is supposed to appear to be located *behind* the live-action area.

Lighting

The glass painting must be illuminated with sufficiently high light levels so that its brightness matches that of the background scene. For location work, if the direction of the sun allows, raw sunlight may sometimes be used for this purpose. Otherwise, artificial lights have to be employed: 45° lighting from each side, as is employed in most photographic copying, does the job nicely.

Because of the high ambient-light levels which are common in exterior photography, it is usually necessary to isolate the camera and the sheet of glass from excess reflected light. Otherwise, the image of the camera, the camera operator, and any other bright objects behind the camera will be reflected off the transparent surface of the glass and will be picked up by the lens. The amount of isolation necessary depends on the location of the glass-shot assembly, the size of the glass sheet, and the size of the transparent areas left on the glass after the painting is completed. Often, a tarpaulin can be suspended over the assembly to provide this kind of isolation. In other cases, it may be necessary to mask the entire work area. Fortunately, this is not so acute a problem on the sound stage, where lighting can be controlled, and where the off-set ambient light level is generally quite low.

Depth of field

Because of the proximity of the glass element to the camera, fairly small relative apertures, running anywhere between $f/11$ and $f/22$, are usually necessary to hold focus on both the painting and the background. The variables which are involved include (a) the size of the painting, (b) the distance of the painting from the camera, (c) the distance of the painting from the background action, (d) the focal length of lens employed on the camera, (e) the gauge of the raw stock, (f) the speed of the raw stock, and (g) the illumination levels produced at the glass and in the background.

The size of the glass painting can vary considerably. Some which have been used in the theatrical industry have been as large as 6 × 8 ft. At the other extreme, excellent results can be achieved – particularly in 16 mm work – with paintings as small as 16 × 20 in. The 16 mm cameraman enjoys a major advantage over his 35 mm colleague here, since 16 mm lenses offer a greater depth of field than 35 mm lenses for a given field of view. Shorter-than-normal lenses in either gauge naturally provide greater depth of field, an advantage which must be balanced against the likelihood of peripheral distortion, peripheral vignetting, lowered contrast, and the decreased resolution which can afflict many of the less expensive lenses. This author has used a 10 mm retrofocus lens on 16 mm cameras for glass-shots, with good results. Such extremely short focal-length optics

Fig. 3.7, part 1. For a scene from the production of *Flame in the Wind*, it was found desirable to insert ceiling detail by means of a glass shot. This photograph shows the live-action set as it actually appeared, with the lights and scaffolding at top center as it would have otherwise appeared in the shot.

Fig. 3.7, part 2. Here, an artist prepares the glass painting which carries the beamed ceiling detail. The live-action foreground component can be seen beneath the painted section.

Fig. 3.7, part 3. The finished composite blends live-action set detail with the painted ceiling element, thereby achieving great economy in set construction costs, and increasing the production value considerably. (Unusual Films, Bob Jones University.)

produce an almost infinite depth of field, even at relatively large apertures. They also require a closer camera position relative to the live-action set. This changes the perspective of the shot, which may or may not be tolerable, depending upon the nature of the scene.

All of the variables involved must be taken into consideration during the planning stages. Standard charts and tables which provide depth-of-field, hyperfocal-distance, and angle-of-view data should be consulted by the cinematographer, art director and glass-shot artist so as to arrive at just the right combination of aperture-distance-size relationships for a satisfactory composite shot. Ideally, the depth of field will be sufficient to render both the painting and the live action sharply focused. If, however, one or the other *must* be favored, then focus will ordinarily be set to favor the live action which is seen through the glass sheet. The reasoning involved here is that the painted element is usually designed to appear as part of the far background scene and so, as in normal cinematography, more likely than the foreground to be softly focused.

Camera movements

One of the advantages of the glass-shot over many of the other processes described in this book is that the camera may be panned and tilted during photography of the composite. These movements require, however, that the camera be mounted on a specially-designed tripod or dolly head which positions the nodal point of the lens exactly at the pivot-point of the pan or tilt (Fig. 3.8). If this precaution is not taken, then displacement of the camera lens causes the painted and live-action elements to go out of register and to appear to 'slide' against one another. Obviously, too, the

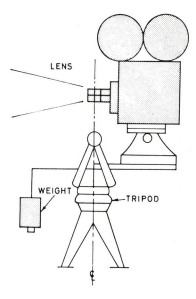

Fig. 3.8. The camera can be panned and tilted across glass-shot paintings provided that it is mounted with the fulcrum point of the pans and tilts located at the nodal point of the lens. This diagram shows one type of nodal-point mount. Alternatively, adaptor plates are available for some of the studio gear-heads which position the camera in similar fashion.

painting must be large enough to accommodate whatever camera movements are attempted.

If the painted element is supposed to appear to be located *in front* of the live-action scene, it is sometimes possible to execute a dolly movement towards or away from the glass. This may be done either by physically moving the camera or by using a zoom lens. The success of this kind of shot depends upon the nature of the composite and the extent of the dolly or zoom movement. In many cases, differences of field of view and parallax-motion may be too apparent to render these movements feasible. Moving the camera one foot towards the glass produced a tremendous change in the field of view of the painting, but virtually none in the background live-action scene.

Photo-cut-out glass-shots

Despite its relative simplicity, the painted glass-shot requires the services of a highly skilled and experienced artist. Even in the major theatrical film centres, there are relatively few people who specialize in this sort of work. The conventional process, for this reason, is not too practical for low-budget producers. Using the principle of the glass-shot, however, many of the same effects can be achieved at a very low cost by substituting large, cut-out photographic enlargements for the paintings.

The use of photographic cut-outs requires that many of the previously-described operations be reversed. As we have seen, a glass painting is 'custom-built' to fit an existing landscape or partially-constructed set. In contrast, when photographic cut-outs are employed, it is necessary that the live-action component be staged to match the peculiarities of the photograph; in this respect, the variation is far less versatile than the conventional process.

Photo-cut-outs work best when natural 'apertures' are present in the still photograph, within which the live-action scene can be staged – apertures such as doors, windows, balconies, hallways and the like. Photo-cut-outs can also be used to good advantage to add ceiling detail, roof-tops, and distant landscape detail. They are *least* suitable when subtle blends of continuous tones must be made between the glass-shot element and the live-action scene.

In practice, a still photograph is first made of the scene to which the live-action element will be later added. This still-photo scene should conform, pictorially, as nearly as possible to the character of the live-action insert – in subject-matter, scale, perspective effects, tonal relationships, field of view, and angle of view. Ideally, a 4 × 5 inch view camera will be used for this work. It produces a large negative which can be subsequently enlarged with a minimum of grain and a maximum of resolution. It also allows for the swings, tilts and shifts of lens board and film which are necessary for perspective manipulation in still photography.

A 16 × 20 inch photographic print is produced by conventional projection printing. This is mounted, either with cement or dry-mounting tissue, on to stiff cardboard or composition board. The section of the enlarged photograph in which the live action is to be inserted is then cut out with a knife, scissors or other tools. Photographs can also be mounted on a glass support, if desired, in which case the live-action area is removed before mounting.

The photo-cut-out is mounted in a frame in front of the camera, and the live-action set is arranged to match the cut-out's configurations. Just as with conventional glass shots, the camera and cut-out must be stabilized against vibration, both with respect to each other and to the live-action scene beyond.

Since the photo-cut-out is prepared ahead of time, the execution of the final composite shot is much more rapid than with paintings. Nevertheless, time must be provided for alignment of the camera, the photo-enlargement, and the set pieces – an operation which is just as critical as with paintings. Much of this set-up time can be reduced through pre-planning of the components' positions by the cinematographer and the art director. Standard reference works, such as the *American Cinematographer Manual*, provide the angle-of-view and depth-of-field tables required for this work. For a given overall size of the photo-enlargement, a given size of the cut-out opening, and a given focal-length of camera lens, all of the other variables involved can be determined: the distance from the cut-out to the set and the actors, the height and width of sets behind the actors, the configuration of set pieces which are supposed to match the contours of the cut-out area in the photo-enlargement, the relative aperture of the camera lens, and the illumination levels for the photo-cut-out and the live-action set.

Generally, the final composite will be most conveniently and convincingly made when the division line is positioned along a sharp architectural junction (as along the edges of a doorway or window), or when the immediate area of the division line is darkened off into shadow.

Happily, since there is no sheet of glass involved in this variation, there is no danger of contaminating the composite image with reflections. For this reason, isolation of the camera and photo-cut-out is not necessary.

Glass-shot transparencies for cloud effects

For exterior cinematography, it is usually desired that attractive clouds be included in the scene, either for pictorial or dramatic enhancement. Assuming that clouds are present in the sky at the time of production, the tonal contrast between white cloud and blue sky can either be photographed as the eye perceives it, or can be accentuated through the use of filters.

Many occasions arise, however, in which the production crew assembles on location, only to find a complete absence of cloud formations above them. When this occurs, the production company must either spend valuable time waiting for clouds to appear and properly position themselves, or must shoot the scene against a barren and cheerless sky. No amount of overall filtering will render a white sky darker, not can it add clouds which are not there.

It *is* possible, as we shall see later, to add cloud effects to a scene long after it has been photographed, by means of matte-shot, aerial-image, and optical-printing techniques. It is also possible to execute a conventional painted glass shot which will serve the same purpose. All of these are fairly complicated processes, however, and may not fit within the budget allotted to the production. What is required for low-budget work is a system which allows for the addition of artificial cloud detail at the time that the shot is originally made, and with a minimum of cost and delay.

The Clarke process

Such a system was developed in the early 1940s by Charles Clarke of Twentieth-Century Fox who subsequently received an Academy Award for this contribution. The process was patented by Fox Studios, but the patent is not enforced. The Clarke process utilizes a 16×20 in or 20×20 in glass-base photographic positive transparency, the bottom section of which is completely clear and the upper section of which shows cloud detail of one sort or another. This diapositive plate is positioned in front of the camera in such a manner that the division between the cloud scene and the clear section is placed along the horizon. The live-action scene, which is staged in the lower portion of the field of view, is photographed without modification, through the clear section of the glass plate. The sky area of the scene, which occupies the upper portion of the field of view, is photographed through the positive cloud image of the transparency.

The barren sky of the real scene serves as a printing light which is modulated by the different densities of the cloud and sky images on the plate. In those areas of the transparencies in which clouds appear, there is little or no density, and light from the sky passes through unimpeded, thus producing a relatively heavy density on the negative raw stock in the camera. In those areas of the diapositive in which a medium-gray or dark

Fig. 3.9, part 1. Typical glass-shot composites for cloud effects. Several of the scenes show before- and after-effects. (Charles Clarke.)

sky has been recorded, the density of the image impedes light from the sky, thus producing a relatively low-density image on the negative. A positive print from the camera negative will, therefore, show a composite of live-action in the lower portion of the picture, and white clouds against a medium- or dark-gray sky in the upper portion (Fig. 3.9). The whitest 'clouds' in the composite will have the same relative brightness as the real sky above the live-action scene; they cannot be any brighter, of course,

Fig. 3.9, part 2. Different cloud plates are used to provide entirely different kinds of pictorial and emotional effects. The middle plate suggests a peaceful, mid-summer scene. The heavily filtered sky in the bottom plate produces a much more dramatic and emotionally charged effect.

because it is the real sky which is being used to provide the 'printing light' for the composite.

If much use is to be made of this process, a fairly large selection of cloud plates should be prepared with different types of clouds, different degrees of contrast between cloud and sky, and different placements of the horizon. Later, on location, this variety will allow for just the right choice of cloud effect for a particular landscape.

Fig. 3.9, part 3. Configuration and placement of clouds must match the foreground scene. Cloud area (top and middle) extends straight across the frame. At bottom a diapositive cloud plate has been selected and positioned to allow the masts of the ship to extend upwards into the transparent cloud. (Charles Clarke.)

The cloud photograph

The original cloud photographs can be made on any size of negative, although larger formats will naturally produce finer-grained positives. For black-and-white work, the enlarged transparencies are produced in the still-photo darkroom through conventional projection printing. By means of 'dodging', the image of the sky can be very gradually blended off at the

Fig. 3.10. Camera set-up for simple but effective transparency shot for cloud effects. If a great deal of work with this technique is anticipated, it is worth building a portable stand on which to mount the glass plates.

division line between the upper and lower portions of the plate. Providing that the barren sky of the real scene is sufficiently milky to produce 'white' clouds, the process can also be used for color cinematography. All that is required is that the silver image of the sky area be toned blue.

For each cloud photograph which is selected, a set of three plates should be made, with the horizon line placed at centre, at one-third of the distance from the top of the field of view, and at one-third from bottom. The cloud plates should also provide a variety of configurations of the horizon line, so that irregular contours in the real-life landscape can be accommodated. Few landscape or cityscape scenes present a completely flat horizon. Buildings, trees, telegraph poles, steeples, mountain peaks and the like nearly always punctuate the dividing line between earth and sky. So long as an object in the landscape is positioned *within* the transparent area of a cloud, it will be clearly and brilliantly rendered, just as if the cloud were located *behind* the object (Fig. 3.9). However, if such an object is allowed to extend upwards into the sky area of the transparency, it will appear noticeably darker, from the point of the division line upwards. These irregularities in landscape contour can be accommodated through the use of plates in which low-flying clouds are positioned along the division line of the transparency.

Actors against the sky

Actors may be photographed against this artificial sky, either in long-shot, medium-shot, or close-up, providing that the face and figure of the actor is positioned *within* the area of a cloud (Fig. 3.11). For close-ups, however, the actor must remain relatively immobile, lest his face or figure pass into the denser sky area of the transparency, and become noticeably darkened. If changes of field, from long-shot to close-up, are anticipated, then a variety of plates of the same cloud photograph should be made – one

Fig. 3.11. Cloud plates can also be used with actors in the scene, providing their faces and figures remain within areas of the upper frame which are filled with clouds.

showing the entire, cloud-filled sky, a second with a somewhat more restricted view of the clouds, and a third showing a single, large cloud mass against a relatively small area of sky. If different angles of view are to be shot with this process, the original cloud scene should be photographed so as to provide head-on, 45°-left, and 45°-right backgrounds. This matching of angle and field from shot to shot will provide pictorial continuity when the various shots are cut together, later, by the editor.

It is also possible to pan the camera, providing (1) that an oversized plate is employed, and (2) that the camera is mounted with the nodal point of its lens positioned exactly at the pivot-point of the pan. For these shots, the cloud diapositive should be printed on flexible photographic film rather than glass, so that it can be bent into a curve which matches the circular arc of the pan.

As with painted or photo-cut-out glass-shots, the relative apertures which are required to hold focus will ordinarily range from $f/11$ to $f/22$, depending upon the size of the transparency and the many other factors which have already been mentioned. For 35 mm photography, 16×20 in diapositives are most convenient. For 16 mm work, 11×14 in plates will suffice, particularly with shorter-than-normal focal-length lenses. The transparency either can be positioned in a frame, independently of the camera, or can be mounted in a specially-built matte box. Ideally, the matte box or space which separates the lens and the plate will be surrounded with an opaque fabric cover, thus eliminating reflections off the surface of the diapositive.

Should the cameraman discover that the highlights on the clouds do not match the angle of the sun and of the shadows upon the landscape, it is a simple matter to reverse the cloud plate in its matte box. The plates can also be reversed for the purposes of compositional balance.

If, for a given cloud-plate composite, the brightness of sky and foreground does not balance, a proper match can be gained by positioning a segmented neutral-density filter either in front of the lens or in the focal plane of the intermittent, thereby darkening the brighter portion of the composite.

Multiplane glass-shots

By its nature, the glass-shot lends itself to multiplane photography, wherein two or more sheets of glass, each bearing painted images, are

Fig. 3.12. A combination glass-shot and mirror shot, designed to produce an 'outer-space' scene of the moon and the earth against a star field. A miniature of the moon is suspended against a dark blue backing, and can be seen *behind* the camera. Sheets of glass are stacked in multiplane fashion, at right, bearing paintings of (a) foreground whisps of clouds, (b) a view of the earth, and (c) a distant star field. A beam-splitting, semi-transparent sheet of glass (center) is positioned between the camera and the sheets of glass. Angled off at 45°, it reflects the miniature of the moon, while the camera also shoots *through* the beam splitter to photograph the stacked sheets of glass bearing the various painted image elements. If the shot remains on the screen for very many seconds, it may be desirable to move the foreground sheet of glass, which bears the whisps of clouds, very slowly past the camera. (From the filming of *One From the Heart,* Zoetrope Studios.)

photographed simultaneously in 'stacked' positions, the further glass paintings being photographed through the clear areas of the nearer sheets.

Quite realistic representations of clouds can be produced in this fashion and integrated with background detail of star fields, moon, planets, and the like (Figs. 3.12, 3.13 and 3.14). Being vaporous, clouds which are painted on the closest sheet of glass allow for the camera to photograph detail on the back sheets *through* the clouds, as well as those around them. Miniatures of airplanes and the like can be positioned behind the glass sheets, as can full-field paintings. By moving the various glass paintings relative to each other and to the camera, additional realism can be introduced into the shot, especially if the appropriate motion parallax which exists between the various moving images is reproduced.

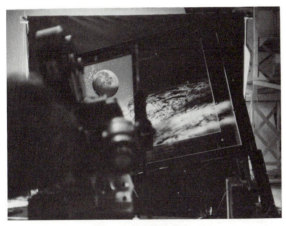

Fig. 3.13. A view of the previous set-up from behind the camera, showing the pick-up of the miniature moon by the beam-splitter.

Fig. 3.14. The finished composite, achieved by combining both glass and mirror-shot techniques.

Solid paintings on foreground sheets of glass can often be combined in a very realistic fashion with paintings, miniatures, still photographs and other detail in the background. Some of the most striking shots of the airship *Hindenburg*, flying over New York City for the Universal production of *Hindenburg*, were produced by means of glass paintings created by artist Albert Whitlock.

A device sometimes called a 'roundee-roundee' can be used to support the glass painting (Fig. 3.15). It is capable of being rotated smoothly, at various speeds, through 360°. For Stanley Kubrick's production of *2001: A Space Odyssey*, the illusion of a fountain pen floating freely in mid-air within a commuter's space ship was created in this fashion. The pen was attached lightly to the glass support and made to turn slowly through several degrees as the background of the space ship set was seen through the glass. The shot ends when a 'stewardess' plucks the fountain pen out of mid-air; which is to say, off the surface of the glass support.

Fig. 3.15. A 'roundee-roundee' glass support for a painted space ship. The sheet of glass upon which the painting is laid can be rotated through 360° as well as moved through yaw and pitch motions relative to the camera. Background detail is photographed through those portions of the glass not covered by the painting. In this case, the space ship is painted. However, it is possible to mount a three-dimensional miniature on the surface of the glass as well, thus allowing for lighting from different angles.

The glass-shot: for and against

The glass-shot, in its several variations, offers the following advantages:

1. The equipment costs very little to construct.
2. Because the composite is produced in the camera, the 'dailies' are returned the following day, as is normal, rather than being tied up in the effects laboratory for several weeks.

3. Because the composite is produced in the camera, maximum image quality is achieved on the original negative.
4. Only that portion of the set which appears behind and immediately around the actors need be built and lit.
5. The director and cameraman may line up and view the composite during the period that it is photographed. Precision in alignment is assured, and all of the personnel involved know exactly what the finished scene will look like.
6. There is no increase in grain when zooms are produced with this technique.
7. A conventional pull-down claw movement can be used. Pilot-pin registration is not necessary.
8. The colors of the pigments laid by the artist onto the glass support are more likely to photograph as he sees them than they will in processes such as bi-pack and optical printing, which require several steps in the duplication of the color film.

The technique displays, however, the following disadvantages:

1. The actors are restricted to particular areas of the composite; should they move elsewhere, they will disappear.
2. Even though expensive sets are not required, the services of an entire production company may be tied up for some time while the glass element is painted and aligned, and while 'slop-tests' are made. If a large and expensive crew is involved, its cost may greatly reduce the savings realized in set construction.
3. If the glass image is to be painted, the services of a highly-skilled and experienced artist must be employed.
4. Exterior shots must be made within a limited period of time, before the movement of the sun produces shadows on the landscape which do not match those of the painting.
5. If an error in lighting balance, compositional placement, or action timing occurs, the composite which results cannot be corrected – at least, not without recourse to other, expensive remedial processes.

4

Mirror-shots

Mirrors are used for all sorts of useful ends in motion-picture production: to bounce light into inaccessible sections of the set; to provide wide-angle views in restricted areas when the camera cannot be pulled back and when short focal-length lenses cannot be profitably employed; to increase the size of projected backgrounds while using long focal-length projection lenses (see Chapter 10); and to provide extremely high- or low-angle shots on small stages.

Mirrors can also be used to solve particular problems in special-effects cinematography. Like glass-shots and other in-the-camera effects, mirror-shots produce maximum image quality on the original negative, they allow the director to see the finished composite at the time that it is photographed, and they require relatively little equipment to execute.

Superimpositions

If a partially transparent mirror is placed in front of the camera and angled off 45° or so, relative to the optical axis of the lens, then art work or live-action which is staged at one side of the camera will be picked up and superimposed over the main image of the set (Fig. 4.1). The effect is that of a 'phantom' or 'ghost' image, in which background detail is seen *through* the superimposed image; it is identical in appearance to the effect which is produced through double-exposure and double printing.

The semi-transparent mirror may take a variety of forms, the cheapest and most common of which is a thin sheet of ordinary plate glass. Other types of 'beam-splitters' include semi-metallized, 'two-way' mirrors and pellicles, both of which are described in Chapter 11.

Mirror-shots can be used for a variety of superimposition purposes. 'Ghostly' figures can be added to live-action scenes, titles can be 'supered' over background images, and special pictorial detail of a semi-transparent nature can be added for dramatic or compositional purposes.

In most cases, mirror-shots are much to be preferred over double-exposure. In the first place, double-exposure – whether performed in the camera or through subsequent optical printing – requires the use of

Fig. 4.1, part 1. Sound-stage set-up for a superimposition mirror-shot. A sheet of plate glass is set at 45° to the camera's optical axis and reflects a transparent image of the performer, who is posed to one side in front of a black drape.

Fig. 4.1, part 2. The camera simultaneously photographs the sound-stage set beyond the beam-splitter and the reflected transparent image of the performer. (UCCLA.)

high-quality intermittent movements, lest the ghost image and the background scene weave and jiggle with respect to each other. Mirror-shots, on the other hand, offer the maximum possible registration accuracy, even with simple claw movements, since the two visual elements are photographed simultaneously on the same negative. Should intermittent weave be introduced by the movement, both the real and superimposed images will weave in synchronism, rather than against one another.

In the second place, double-exposure work involves a critical determination of exposure balance between the background and phantom images. Since the two components of a double-exposure are photographed at different times, the technique does not allow for the viewing of the composite prior to processing. Exposure balance, therefore, becomes a speculative sort of business. If the ghost image is too brightly exposed, it will be 'burned in' a solid white, thus destroying the transparent effect. Blurring at the edges of the superimposed image, halation, and overall fogging of the background scene may also occur. If, on the other hand, the exposure of the superimposed detail is too light, then its dramatic or artistic effect will be lost. In either case, the whole two-step procedure must be repeated. In contrast, mirror-shots allow for a precise balance of exposure values; the final effect can be seen through the camera's viewfinder at the time that the composite is photographed, and the cameraman can easily detect and correct any imbalance in the brightness ratio. As a further check on exposure balance, test footage can be shot in the camera and 'slop-test-processed', or test photographs can be shot with a Polaroid still camera before the production take is made.

A third advantage of the mirror-shot over double exposure is the precision it provides to the director in arranging spacial relationships between superimposed and background detail, and in synchronizing action which occurs in the two components. If, for example, a phantom figure is expected to walk up a flight of stairs which appear in the real background set, a second flight of stairs will be built, painted dead black and set up in front of a black backdrop, at 90° to the camera's optical axis. The second set of stairs is positioned so that its configuration, as reflected off the beam-splitting mirror, exactly matches that of the real set. Since neither the black wooden staircase nor the black backing reflect light, neither is recorded on the negative. As the 'phantom' actor walks up and down this second set of stairs, his figure is superimposed properly upon the real set pieces of the background. Alignment of the two sets – real and duplicate – is easily achieved by simply viewing the composite through the camera's eyepiece, matching object positions and rehearsing the actor until the desired illusion is achieved. If the 'phantom' actor is required to react to live-action dialogue or business which occurs in the 'real' set, he may do so with relative ease and with a maximum of precision.

Mirror-shots may also be used to add pictorial detail of a transparent nature. For example, a director might find himself shooting a church interior, into which he would like to have a dramatic ray of sunlight pass from the upper windows, through the interior of the building, and on to the floor or altar below. Such an effect *could* be added later through bi-pack or optical printing, but only at considerable expense. Using the mirror-shot technique, however, it is a simple matter to position an ordinary blackboard next to the camera, and, with white chalk, to draw upon it the particular kind of sunbeam effect that is desired. The same technique can be used to add a spotlight effect to a scene of a theatre's stage, or to add dramatic lighting effects of any sort to a middle-key or low-key scene, the only precaution being that actors must not be allowed to appear to be standing *in front* of the beam of light – they must always be positioned so as to appear to pass behind or within it. If it is necessary to place actors in the foreground of such a shot, then they must remain out of the area of the beam entirely.

Two-way mirrors can be used to introduce a base-level light into the shadows of a scene. The mirror is angled off at 45° from the optical axis of the camera so as to reflect a white or colored card (or a white card illuminated by colored light), below or to one side of the camera. This technique has little effect upon the highlights, but adds density to the shadow areas of the negative. If white light is used, the effect simply is to lower contrast. If a low intensity of colored light is used, the technique adds a subtle tint to the scene. For an evening, day-for-night shot, for example, a very faint bluish tint can be added to the shadows in this manner, rather than by filtering the set lamps, which tint *both* the shadows and the highlights. If the intensity of the reflected light is increased further, an overall hazy or foggy effect can be imparted to the scene. If a small amount of smoke is produced off-camera and picked up by the mirror, the smoke can be placed within the scene, by reflection, where one wants it. This technique avoids the necessity for laying down real smoke or fog over the entire set.

Mirrors can also be used to multiply images in a scene. Sometimes this is done quite obviously, for a surreal effect (as with the multiple images of Charles Foster Kane in one of the last scenes of *Citizen Kane*). In other cases, it is done to multiply or 'repeat' certain features of the set. For the 'Lake of Fire' scene in *Dragonslayer*, mirrors were set into apertures in the set of the subterranean cave in such as manner as to reflect real fire which was created in the foreground of the set. In the finished shot, there appeared to be additional fires burning in distant grottos and passages of the cave which could be seen through the holes and tunnels in the set. The technique not only made an already large set look larger, but also saved costs and prevented hazards which might have been involved in the creation of additional real fires on stage.

Mirrors have also been used to 'repeat' *generalized* image details in selected areas of the screen. In a recent television commercial, it was desired to give the effect that an automobile was floating through the air, a few feet off the highway. A mirror was suspended in the field of view of the camera in such a manner as to reflect a blurred section of the highway which was actually several feet to one side of the vehicle. Since one section of the highway looks very much like another, the two blurred images blended perfectly together, and the wheels and axles of the automobile were made to disappear.

Finally, mirrors can be used to safeguard the crew and equipment from hazards which arise in filming certain kinds of shots. It is possible, for example, to create the impression of an automobile or railroad locomotive driving directly into the camera by placing the camera off to one side, at 90° to the line of the vehicle's passage, and filming the moving vehicle as it is seen in a fairly large mirror set at 45° to both vehicle and camera. The camera's field of view is adjusted so as to fall within the mirror's area, and the automobile or locomotive is allowed to actually hit the mirror. The effect, as seen on the screen, is startling! (Fig. 4.2).

Image replacement

Just as glass-shots are used for the purpose of replacing unwanted or unattractive visual detail with more suitable images, so may mirror-shots be employed. For this purpose, a conventional (non-transparent) mirror is used, its reflecting surface being positioned so as to occupy a portion of the

Fig. 4.2. Mirrors are ideally suited for photography of hazardous action. For the television-film production of *Cosmos*, it was desired that a locomotive be driven directly into the camera. Rather than risk the loss of a 'dedicated camera', a large mirror was positioned at 45° to the train tracks and to the optical axis of the camera, the latter of which was positioned several feet to one side of the tracks. In the finished film, the train is allowed to run directly into the mirror, and, by reflection, into the camera! (Courtesy *American Cinematographer.*)

field of view, and thus allow for the simultaneous photography of detail in both the live-action scene, which is located *beyond* the mirror, and the replacement detail, which is reflected *off* the mirror (Fig. 4.3).

Mirror-shots are more versatile than glass-shots for this work; at least, with respect to the kinds of visual detail that can be added. Not only may art-work and still photographs be used to replace portions of the set, but also miniatures and full-scale live-action scenes. Mirror-shots also minimize the depth-of-field problem which is inherent in glass-shot photography. When a mirror is used in any scene, sharp focus of the reflected image is secured at a distance equal to the *sum* of the distances from the camera to the mirror, and from the mirror to the reflected objects. The effect is to move the point of focus of the reflected detail much closer to that of the directly-photographed scene. Also, inasmuch as focus is secured on the reflected object, rather than on the surface of the mirror, the mirror's edge is softened, and the fitting together of the 'real' and reflected images is made more convenient.

For best results, the mirrors which are used for this kind of work should be front-silvered. A conventional mirror is likely to produce double images, since light which strikes it is reflected off both the front and rear surfaces of the glass. If a back-silvered mirror must be used, its glass should be as thin as possible and free from internal, retracting flaws.

For image-replacement work, three different mirror-shot techniques are available – the first two relatively simple, the third rather more complicated.

Fig. 4.3. A Schüfftan-shot. The camera picks up the full-scale, live-action component as it is reflected off the silvered area of a mirror. Simultaneously, the camera photographs either art work, miniatures or (as shown here) a rear-projected image, seen *through* the clear sections of the mirror, blending the two elements together. The sketch is adapted from the original Schüfftan patents.

Straight-edge division

If the junction between the 'real' and reflected scenes occurs along a straight edge in the set – such as the moulding of a door, wall, or ceiling – then the edge of the mirror is visually positioned along this line and a composite is produced which is similar in appearance to a split-screen shot (see page 81). If the join is neatly made and if the perspective and set detail of the two components match, a convincing illusion is produced.

Nearly always, this technique is employed when the division line extends straight through the entire frame, either vertically or horizontally. It is possible, of course, to cut a mirror so that its configuration matches irregular set lines in the background. It is even possible to insert such a mirror into the *middle* of the background scene by suspending it with tin wires; the wires, like the edges of the mirror, will be thrown out of focus and rendered invisible. This is tricky work indeed, however, and can best be accomplished with the third method, described below.

Shadowed division

In those cases in which convenient, straight-edge lines are absent in the directly-photographed set, the area which surrounds the division line in both background and reflected scenes is allowed to fall into deep shadow or total darkness (Fig. 4.4). Alignment in such cases is relatively easy, since the junction line is rendered invisible. Understandably, this technique works best with low-key scenes.

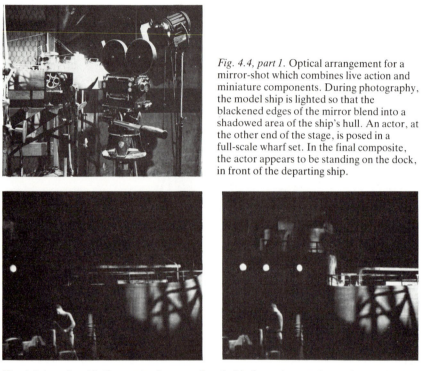

Fig. 4.4, part 1. Optical arrangement for a mirror-shot which combines live action and miniature components. During photography, the model ship is lighted so that the blackened edges of the mirror blend into a shadowed area of the ship's hull. An actor, at the other end of the stage, is posed in a full-scale wharf set. In the final composite, the actor appears to be standing on the dock, in front of the departing ship.

Fig. 4.4, parts 2 and 3. Composite shots, produced with the equipment shown above. The shot gains in realism when seen in motion, the ship being produced continuously behind the actor as it moves from left to right, next to the dock. These photographs are enlargements from a 16 mm negative.

Irregular contours

It may sometimes be desired that the reflected image be placed *within* the primary field of view and that its edges follow irregular contours in the real set beyond. In the solution of such problems, an entirely different kind of technique is employed.

First, a mirror which is large enough to totally fill the field of view of the lens is positioned in front of the camera and angled off 45°. Second, selected portions of the silvering are completely removed, thus revealing the desired portions of the real set which are seen beyond, through the transparent glass. Third, the art-work, miniatures, or live-action detail which is being used to replace portions of the main scene is positioned at 90° to the camera's optical axis, where it is picked up and reflected off the now selectively-silvered mirror. Assuming that the real and replacement images are properly aligned with respect to the modified mirror, a convincing composite will result.

Schüfftan-shots

Such a composite is usually called a 'Schüfftan-shot', after the German film technician, Eugen Schüfftan, who was most responsible for its development. Schüfftan-shots were widely employed throughout the theatrical film industry in the 1930s, particularly in Germany and Great Britain; since then, the technique has been almost entirely replaced by *post-facto* laboratory processes. Properly executed, the Schüfftan-shot is useful, convincing, and inexpensive, thus rendering it of interest to low-budget producers. Like other types of glass- and mirror-shots, it provides maximum image quality on the original negative and allows the production personnel to view the finished composite at the time that it is made.

The technique is by no means a simple one, however, and requires a good deal of trial-and-error experimentation before confidence and consistently predictable results can be gained.

In practice, there are at least two different methods by which a Schüfftan can be executed. The first, just mentioned, requires that the silvering be removed from certain sections of the mirror. The second employs a partially-transparent beam-splitter in conjunction with complementary opaque masks.

Silvering removal

The basic Schüfftan process calls for the complete removal of portions of the reflective coating. First, the area of the mirror through which the scene beyond will be photographed is determined. The outline of this area is scraped away from the mirror's silvering. The scraping can be done with any sharp-pointed or sharp-edged instrument, although care must be taken to avoid scoring the glass surface. Once the outline has been scraped away, the area within it can be removed with nitric acid on a swab.

Front-silvered mirrors work better than rear-silvered mirrors with this technique. They eliminate double reflections, their silvering is easier to remove from the glass support, and they are more conveniently reached during the outlining phase. Because the coating of a front-silvered mirror is a fragile thing, however, soft gloves should be worn while working with it to avoid abrading it, or leaving acid-sweat stains from the fingertips on its surface.

Using this technique, the determination of the outline area is always something of a problem. First, the cameraman finds that he cannot see any of the scene *beyond* the mirror until some of the silvering has been removed. Should a major error be made in the outlining phase, it may be necessary to replace the mirror and to begin all over again. In the second place, the plane of the mirror is nowhere the lens' plane of focus, which means that any scoring tool or indexing device which is placed against the surface of the mirror will appear greatly out of focus, and therefore not too much help in determining the position of the division lines. In the third place, since the mirror is set at a more-or-less 45° angle, relative to the lens' axis, an optical 'keystoning' effect results which distorts the actual shape of the outline and renders its determination more difficult than in glass-shot work, where the replacement element is photographed head-on.

To facilitate the outlining process, the camera, mirror and reflected art-work or miniatures are first permanently aligned. By sighting through the camera's viewfinder, the cameraman may now see where the division lines should occur. Assuming that a front-silvered mirror is employed, and is mounted fairly close to the camera, it may be possible for the cameraman to reach around and scrape away the outline while he views the scene through the eyepiece. At this time, the surface of the mirror *can* be brought into sharper focus by stopping down the lens and increasing the depth of field, provided the image magnification is not markedly altered by changes in relative aperture, as can occur with some lenses.

Fig. 4.5, part 1. Equipment used for the photography of Schüfftan-shots. A partially-transparent, partially-reflective mirror is mounted in front of the camera at 45° to the optical axis, allowing for simultaneous photography of image components which are located both dead ahead and 90° to the right of the camera. At the front and side of the assembly, sheets of thin plate glass are mounted in wooden frames. Complementary masks are positioned on the sheets to obscure and transmit various sections of the composite.

Fig. 4.5, part 2. The camera photographs the 1/6 scale miniature directly through the front mask, and the live-action component off the two-way mirror. For the composite shot shown in this series of photographs, the performer was positioned about 20 ft behind the camera which took this picture.

If the cameraman cannot reach the front-silvered mirror from camera position, he may wish to have the outlining performed by an assistant, while he views the emerging composite through the viewfinder and gives appropriate instructions.

Two-way mirror

A much less complicated, but equally effective, variation of the Schüfftan process employs a partially-transparent ('two-way') mirror, or a pellicle, either of which will both reflect and transmit light. In this variation, the entire, partially-reflective coating is left intact. However, complementary masks are positioned (a) between the mirror and the live-action set, and (b) between the mirror and the reflected art-work or miniatures (Fig. 4.5).

The masks are made of opaque sheets of paper or card, out of which the complementary areas of the composite are cut with scissors, a knife, or other tools (Fig. 4.6). Assuming that the masks are of identical size and are positioned so that they register, optically at a 1:1 ratio, then the female counter-mask can be quickly prepared by tracing its outline with pencil from the first mask.

Fig. 4.6, part 1. The complementary masks are set into place, the one at left passing light from the live-action set, the one at right passing light from the miniature. The white card at the back of the unit is for illustration purposes only; it was removed during actual photography.

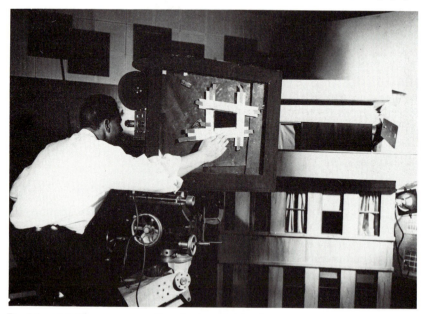

Fig. 4.6, part 2. The cameraman aligns the rig containing the camera and two-way mirror, and adjusts the complementary masks so as to pass and reject the appropriate amounts of visual information from the miniature and the full-scale sets.

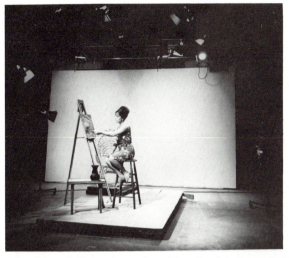

Fig. 4.7, part 1. The performer is positioned at the other end of the sound-stage, in front of an appropriately lighted backing. Note that the live-action scene is staged in reverse, the image being flipped around, from left to right, by the mirror optics during photography. (Badia Rahman.)

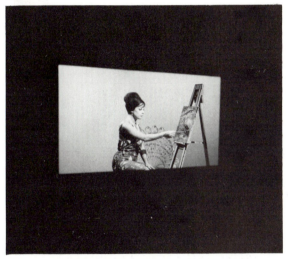

Fig. 4.7, part 2. Live-action component, with miniature unlighted. The actress is positioned about 30 ft away from the miniature.

The mask which stands between the mirror and the full-scale set holds back all visual detail *except* that area in which the actors perform (Fig. 4.7). The complementary mask, on the other hand, obscures from the reflection of the art-work *only* the area into which the live-action is being inserted (Fig. 4.8).

This method is much cheaper and simpler than that previously described. First, the 'destruction' of the mirror's surface is not involved; it is the mask, rather than the mirror, which is altered. The outline of the insert can be determined either by drawing the division lines on to the surface of the opaque card or by punching small pin holes through it. Either of these will be seen superimposed over the reflected image. Once the contours of the outline have been established, the insert area can be cut from the mask. (Inaccurately-placed pin holes can be covered with black tape.) If a major error ruins the mask, it is a simple and inexpensive matter to replace the card with another and to start again.

Fig. 4.8, part 1. Miniature and backing, with live-action area unlighted.

Fig. 4.8, part 2. Test composite, using Schüfftan set-up shown in Fig 4.5. For a 16 mm camera, relative aperture is $f/4$ using a 10 mm retrofocus lens. Light levels are 640 footcandles on miniature, 120 footcandles on live-action. (Badia Rahman.)

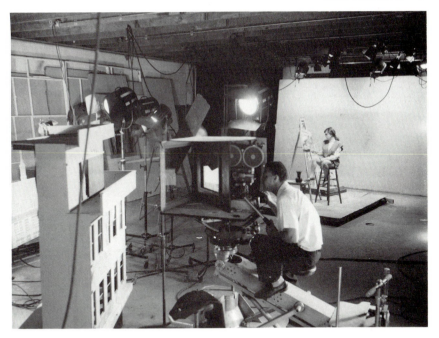

Fig. 4.9. Overall view of sound-stage operations for the previously illustrated composite

Alignment of masks

Using this technique, the cameraman can more easily view the complete composite as it develops. Even before the complementary masks are prepared, the reflected art-work and the full-scale, live-action set can be visually aligned – superimposed upon one another by the beam-splitter.

As additional advantages, each of the two masks faces its scene head-on; therefore, optical keystoning of the outline area is avoided. And finally, each of the two masks, although not located at the plane of focus of the lens, is certainly much closer to it than is the mirror. This means that guide lines for the outline can be drawn in sharper focus and with greater accuracy on the masks than they could be on the surface of the mirror.

An additional technique is employed by some workers as an aid in alignment and outlining – it is a tedious procedure, but one which provides the maximum accuracy and versatility in executing such a shot. The camera, mirror, and art-work are permanently aligned, and a few feet of film are shot of the reflected image. The film is 'slop-test-processed', quickly dried, and inserted into the intermittent movement of the camera. A rotoscope-type prism and lamp house (similar to that described in Chapter 6) is inserted into the camera and the image of the negative is projected through the lens system of the camera. In those cases in which the silver coating is removed from the mirror, a piece of paper is placed over the mirror and the image of the art-work is cast upon it. The division lines are drawn on to the paper, the paper is cut with scissors, and the scraping of the silver proceeds, using the configures paper as a guide. When masks are used with a beam-splitter, on the other hand, the projected image is simultaneously reflected off the beam-splitter on to the mask which faces the art-work, and transmitted through the beam-splitter on to the mask which faces the full-scale set. Working from this projected image, it is an easy matter to draw the division lines on to either of the masks, following which the outline area can be removed with scissors, and a tracing made from it directly on to the counter-mask.

Also, using the rotoscope projection device, once the mask which faces the live-action scene has been cut, the image of the negative test strip can be projected through the mask and across the sound stage; the position of this projected image, as it falls across set pieces, can be used as a guide in positioning the components of the full-scale scene.

Planning the set-up

Obviously, in any type of Schüfftan-shot, a good deal of planning must go into each set-up, so that the different components will properly match. Depth of field, relative aperture, illumination levels and component distances must be pre-determined with the assistance of conventional optical data charts. If paintings, photographs or miniatures are employed for the reflected component, their perspective and scale relationships must be appropriate to the full-scale set. If, on the other hand, a reflected live-action insert is combined with a directly photographed live-action scene, then the scale of the reflected set can be properly established by varying its angular position and distance, relative to the position of the mirror. By employing more than one mirror, additional visual components located on both sides of the camera, can, of course, be combined.

Throughout this description, we have assumed that it is the art-work or miniatures which are reflected and the full-scale set which is photographed directly. In many cases, however, it will be found more convenient to reverse this procedure (Figs. 4.4 and 4.8). On reflection from the mirror, however, the image is reversed from left-to-right. This means that the art-work, miniatures, or live-action which make up this component must be drawn, built, or staged in reverse, or that a second mirror must be employed to return the reflected element back to its normal appearance.

Pans and tilts across the composite image are possible, providing that the camera is pivoted at the nodal point of its lens. Dolly or zoom shots, on the other hand, are not usually practicable.

Over the years, individual workers have developed their own special equipment for working with this process, including (a) segmented mirrors, whose surface is composed of numerous reflecting particles, the positions of which can be mechanically changed to conform to particular outlines, (b) special frames which allow for rapid alignment, and (c) supplementary optical systems which provide for sharp focus on reflected objects which are placed relatively close to the mirror.

Some mirror-shot techniques

Mirrors lend themselves to a variety of other effects, all of them suited to low-budget production. Most of these applications are well known and need only be mentioned in passing here.

Image fragmentation and multiplication

For novelty or subjective-camera purposes, a basic image can be fragmented and multiplied any number of times. The effect is similar to that which is produced by a kaleidoscope, and may be either weird or amusing, depending upon its use. To produce the effect, the image which reaches the lens is passed through a set of refracting prisms or a three- (or more) sided assembly of mirrors. In its simplest form, an image fragmenter may be constructed of three 2 × 4 inch mirrors, fitted together within a tube in the shape of an eqilateral triangle. With the tube placed over the camera lens, objects which are photographed through it are multiplied several times, the size and placement of the images depending upon the length of the mirrors and the diameter of the tube. Increasing the number of mirrors increases the number of images; modifying the geometric shape which is described by the joined mirrors alters the placement of the images. The same effect can be gained by using a commercial image fragmenter similar to that shown in Fig. 4.10. These devices usually incorporate prisms rather than mirrors.

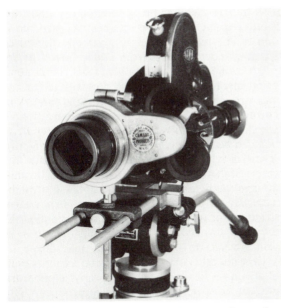

Fig. 4.10. The Camart prismatic image fragmenter. Depending upon the choice of prism used, from four to seven multiplications of an object will be produced. By turning a crank, the images can be rotated. Another, similar, device rotates a single image around its own center, clockwise or counter-clockwise, through a full 360°, if desired. (Camera Mart, Inc.)

Water reflections

By extending a single mirror outward from the camera, beneath the lens, objects photographed above and beyond the mirror are reflected, upside-down, in the lower portion of the scene. The illusion which results may be naturalistic, in which case the directly-photographed scene appears to be reflected from a pond of water or a rain-soaked pavement. The effect may also be rendered completely surrealistic.

Mirrors are also sometimes used in a tray of water to increase the brilliance of the reflection for scenes in which an actor's face is to appear to be reflected from a body of water. An interesting problem arises whenever a subjective-camera shot is made across water of an actor or object reflected in it. In real life, the reflected image appears upside-down. Should it be desired that the reflection be seen right-side-up, however, then the camera should be inverted during the shot. The picture which results is naturalistically impossible, but dramatically effective, and very few members of the audience will notice the inconsistency.

Image distortions

A number of weird and amusing manipulations of conventional scenes can be gained by reflecting the image of the scenes off a highly-polished ferrotype tin. By twisting the tin, elongations, compressions and disintegrations of the image are produced which are quite surrealistic in appearance, being similar to the view one gains by looking into the trick mirrors which we find at amusement parks and arcades. A particularly grotesque effect results when the ferrotype tin is gradually bent into compound curves, thus fragmenting portions of the image into separate components.

Examples of the clever and involved uses to which both refracting and reflecting optics can be put are seen in Francis Thompson's film, *New York, New York*, in which the beauty and chaos of a great metropolitan city are interpreted by surrealistic alterations of familiar city scenes.

Another type of distortion can be produced by photographing an actor's figure off the surface of a mirror which is mounted horizontally within a pan and is covered with water. So long as the surface of the water is calm, there is no indication to the audience that the actor is not being photographed conventionally. By tapping the edge of the pan, however, ripples are formed on the water's surface which gradually distort and break up the actor's features.

Some workers have used silvered mylar film for unusual distortion effects. If the mylar film is stretched taut, it reflects the scene, or parts of it, normally. Since the film is quite flexible, however, any number of interesting distortions of the set or of performers can be introduced by a slight amount of twisting, or by simply touching the mylar film from behind. It is even possible to make a particular part of the image disappear by altering the topology of the film's silvered surface. Manipulations such as these can be accomplished either during principal photography or during post-production, at leisure. During post-production, for example, one can set up a rear-projection screen and cast onto it the scene which is to be altered. One then positions a mylar pellicle at 45° to the screen and to the camera, the latter being positioned off to one side at 90° to the screen. With such a rig, gentle pressure can be brought to bear upon the back of the silvered mylar film during the re-photographing of the rear-screen image, and all manner of extraordinary alterations to the image can be produced, one of which is a 'swallowing up' of image details, and a 'spitting out' of them in a different part of the frame.

Dissolves and wipes

For a very low-budget work, where bi-pack contact or optical printing cannot be afforded, certain types of in-the-camera dissolves and wipes can be produced with mirrors.

For wipe effects, a mirror is hinged at its edge and mounted in front of the camera lens with the pivot point of the mirror placed at one side or the other of the field of view. By staging the incoming scene at 90° or so to one side of the lens axis, and swinging the mirror in and out of the frame, a serviceable wipe is produced. The same effect may be gained by sliding the mirror along a grooved support, across the field of view. Unlike optical printing, these techniques produce maximum image quality on the original negative and require virtually no investment for equipment. However, they require a fairly large stage area in which to set up the different scenes, and perfect performances and synchronized action in each of the two components.

Using such a set-up as this, a very violent kind of wipe can be produced by simply shattering the mirror, thus destroying the reflected scene and allowing direct photography of the set beyond. A thin, back-silvered mirror can be used for such work. The pattern of the break can be pre-determined by scoring the front surface with a glass cutter. Fracture of the glass can be accomplished by producing torsion along the edges of the mirror by twisting it in its frame, or by striking it a sharp blow on one of its edges. Because of the speed with which this effect is executed, its appearance will be greatly enhanced if the shot can be taken in slow motion.

In those rare cases where titles are superimposed over sound-stage live-action by means of semi-transparent mirrors, a set of two mirrors can be mounted in front of the lens, each at 45° to the optical axis, but facing in opposite directions. Each of these beam-combiners pick up the image of its own set of title cards. By dimming or brightening the lights which illuminate each set of cards, fades and dissolves between titles can be produced.

5

In-the-camera matte shots

Despite the usefulness of the glass- and mirror-shot processes and their special suitability for low-budget production, their previously described limitations have always been keenly felt in professional film circles. Ever since the introduction of the glass-shot in 1907, a need has been felt for more versatile image-replacement techniques which could be performed in the laboratory *after* the principal photography had been completed. Such *post-facto* techniques would allow for: (1) the rapid and economical photography of the basic scene, as in conventional practice, (2) the subsequent alteration of the basic image at leisure, and with a maximum of artistic control, and (3) the opportunity to leave the design and choice of replacement images until the last stages of production, thus allowing for adjustment to any changes of the film which may occur during editing stages.

Over the years, a number of *post-facto* laboratory techniques have been developed which meet these needs: bi-pack contact printing, optical and aerial-image printing, and background projection. In this chapter, we describe a technique which followed the glass-shot and preceded bi-pack contact printing. For lack of a better term, we shall refer to it as the 'in-the-camera matte shot'. Although it is an awkward and sometimes expensive process, it does, like all in-the-camera techniques, provide the maximum image quality, and so is especially popular in contemporary feature-film production.

History of the process

Like the glass-shot, the in-the-camera painted matte shot was a technique employed by the veteran cameraman, Norman Dawn, who first used it as early as 1911. Of course, certain types of in-the-camera matte and split-screen shots had been employed by film makers long before 1911. In conventional earlier practice, part of the image which was recorded by the camera was obscured during first exposure by a 'matte' – an opaque card or plate inserted into the external matte box or the intermittent movement of

Fig. 5.1. A nineteenth-century composite photograph. As with most 'modern' photographic techniques, composite photography can be traced back almost to the beginnings of the art. By the late 1850s, exceptionally fine 'combination shots' were being produced by leading still photographers. As many as ten or more separately-photographed pictures, or fragments of pictures, were trimmed and pasted together in a pre-determined pattern to produce a compositionally 'perfect' print. This beautiful combination shot, entitled 'When the Day's Work is Done', was made by Henry Peach Robinson in 1877. (International Museum of Photography at George Eastman House.)

a camera – so as to prevent the recording of certain portions of a set or scene. During a subsequent exposure, a 'counter-matte', whose outlines conformed exactly to those of the matte, was similarly inserted, and a new scene was exposed and fitted into place with the rest of the already-recorded image (Fig. 5.2).

Although effective when properly executed, this type of matte shot is generally unsuited for professional production. The process is time-consuming, requiring that the same camera and matte-box assembly be employed for both shots, the first scene being shot in one locale, the camera moved, and the second exposure being made in the second locale. Moreover, the success of the shot is always uncertain. If the matte inserts are not precisely matched and aligned, or if the exposures of the two scenes are not properly balanced, the shot is ruined – the whole process has to be repeated and both scenes have to be re-staged.

In 1911, Dawn introduced a more practical variation of the split-screen technique which successfully overcame these limitations. It also provided for far more sophisticated manipulation of the image components.

Fig. 5.2. In-the-camera matte shots have been with us since the earliest days of the motion picture. In Edwin S. Porter's 1903 classic, *The Great Train Robbery*, a railroad locomotive and cars are matted into the window area of the railway station set, as they pull into the station yard outside. Here, the matte line is hard-edged and follows the lines of the window. The perspective is off a bit, but the effect on the screen is quite good – especially for 1903.

Photographing the live component

To execute an in-the-camera matte shot of the sort which Dawn developed, a large sheet of glass is mounted in front of the camera, just as is done in the glass-shot. However, instead of painting the new, artificial images upon the glass, the artist 'mattes out' the area of the new image by brushing opaque black paint on to the surface of the glass sheet, the edges of the paint conforming exactly to the blend-line ('matte line') which serves as a boundary between the real scene (photographed through the glass) and the new image components which will be added at a later time. The painting of the black matte on glass can be accomplished fairly rapidly, following which the first exposure, with performing actors in the foreground, can be made.

Once this first shot has been made, a partially-exposed negative results, on which only the live-action portion of the scene has been recorded. Since the painted black matte in front of the camera neither reflects nor transmits light, those portions of the negative which record the matte area are not exposed (Fig. 5.4).

Immediately after the first exposure has been made, and while the camera and glass matte are still set up in the same position, an additional 50 to 100 ft of film are photographed on the same roll. This extra, non-production footage will be used later for test purposes at the time that the artificial-image elements are added.

Fig. 5.3. Exterior shot photographed with a binocular-patterned matte.

Fig. 5.4, part 1. In-the-camera matte shot for the MGM production of *See Here, Private Hargrove.* The first exposure, with the upper section of the sound-stage matted out.

Fig. 5.4, part 2. The second exposure with ceiling detail added by the matte painter. (Norman Dawn.)

76

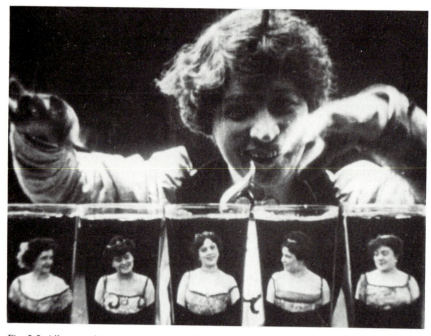

Fig. 5.5. All matte shots require either double exposure in the camera, or double printing in the laboratory. In some such shots, performers or objects are posed in front of black backings and are 'matted' into soft-edged dark areas of a previously-exposed film, by means of double exposure, in-the-camera. Here, five women, reduced in scale by photographing them at a distance, are matted into their positions within glasses of water in the 1907 Pathé novelty short subject, *The Enchanted Glasses*. Today, less costly and time-consuming methods would be used to achieve the same effect. Despite the cruder methods employed here, however, this early trick film displays real technical virtuosity. (James Card Collection, International Museum of Photography at George Eastman House.)

Fig. 5.6. Different matting techniques can be used to produce in-the-camera split-screen shots. Here, mattes are being positioned in the camera's external matte box. Those which are inserted from the side bisect the frame vertically; those from above, horizontally. Specially-cut mattes, with irregular contours, can also be inserted into these slots.

Once the live-action scene and test footage have been photographed, the magazine of the production camera, containing the partially-exposed but as yet undeveloped roll of film, is set to one side, preparatory to transferring it to a second camera, back at the effects laboratory. The exposed negative (sometimes referred to as a 'held' negative) will be refrigerated if extensive delays in its subsequent exposure are anticipated, in order to prevent color changes in either the exposed or unexposed portions of the film, and shrinkage or expansion of the emulsion or base.

The laboratory camera is mounted on a lathe bed which in turn is set on a metal or cement base, this massive support being designed to reduce camera vibration. The laboratory camera is aimed towards an easel to which art board is attached, and on which the replacement images are to be drawn (Fig. 5.7).

The laboratory camera may be either a process camera or a modified production camera. If a process camera is used, the reflex viewfinder usually incorporates a separate set of registration pins which match the position of the pins in the intermittent movement (Fig. 5.8). If a conventional production camera is employed, it must be altered to permit insertion of a right-angle prism and a magnifying eyepiece behind the intermittent movement's pressure plate, the back section of which has been removed. By means of such viewfinding systems, it is possible to view an

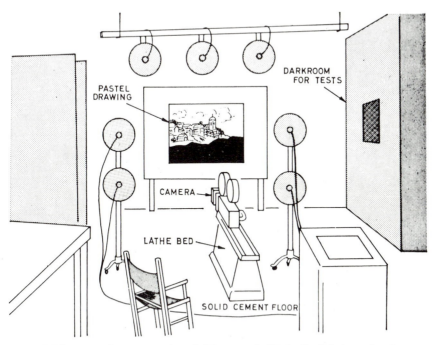

Fig. 5.7. Diagrammatic representation of a laboratory facility for final photography of in-the-camera matte shots. The camera is mounted on a vibration-free base and is focused on an easel which holds the art board upon which matte lines are drawn and the painted scene is rendered. The lower half of the painting shown in this sketch, which represents the area occupied by live-action, has been matted out with black paint.

image of any art-work on the easel as it is cast by the lens on to the developed test negative which is registered either in the camera's intermittent movement or on the pins within a process camera's reflex viewfinder. (Alternatively, if a process camera is employed, a rotoscope lamp house can be attached which projects the image of the test negative on to the easel.)

Fig. 5.8, part 1. All process cameras allow for the registration of a piece of test negative or color positive within the reflex viewfinder. Here, the viewing eyepiece of the Acme camera is swung open, revealing the ground-glass screen and supplementary registration pins. When the internal prism is swung into viewing position and a strip of negative or positive film is registered within the viewer, art-work on the easel is viewed on the ground-glass, superimposed over the test footage. The relationships of these different image components is exactly the same as if they were viewed within the movement itself.

Fig. 5.8, part 2. The Oxberry camera, with a piece of black-and-white master positive registered within its reflex viewfinder.

Preparing the matte-board

In the darkroom, a couple of feet of the extra test film are cut out of the roll of production footage in the camera and processed. A frame of this strip of processed negative is then registered in the camera's viewfinding system. The easel (or 'matte-board' or 'copy-board') in front of the camera is now illuminated with artificial light, and its image focused through the lens system and superimposed onto the processed test negative.

The edge of the matted-out area produced during the first exposure (which is clear on the negative) is now traced on the surface of the matte-board with light pencil. If a rotoscope lamp house is used to project the negative's image, the matte line can be easily traced on the matte-board so as to follow the contours of the unexposed area. If, on the other hand, the image of the matte-board painting is to be viewed through a frame of the test negative in the viewfinding system, then it will usually be found useful to employ an assistant. The cameraman/artist views the superimposed image while the assistant traces the matte line according to his instructions.

Once the matte line has been traced, the lower portion of the matte-board is painted in solid with black paint, thus creating a counter-matte which covers exactly the same area of the picture as the original live-action component. Alternatively, the painting is made on glass which is front-lighted and photographed against a black backing.

With the black counter-matte completed, a skilled matte painter now begins painting in the appropriate landscape or architectural details in the clear area of the matte-board, developing proper perspective, density and tonal relationships between live action and painted elements as he goes along. The demands upon his skill are just as great here as in the glass-shot process, except that he may work at leisure, without having to worry about holding up the work of the entire production crew.

As the painting on the matte-board progresses, the accuracy with which the matte lines are aligned and the artistry with which the live-action and painted elements are matched can be checked, step-by-step, by viewing the image of the matte-board painting superimposed onto the developed, first-exposure negative in the camera aperture.

Photographing the matted image

With the painted element completed, the negative test strip is removed from the intermittent movement, and the roll of previously-exposed but still undeveloped production footage in the magazine is threaded into the camera. Two or three feet of the remaining test footage at the end of this roll are then exposed in the camera, thus providing a composite exposure of the live-action and painted elements. During this test, several different exposure values can be tried for matching purposes. The short composite test strip is then cut out of the roll in a darkroom and processed. By examining the developed negative, and the wedge tests made from it, the artist/cameraman can determine, first, which exposure value is appropriate for the matching of densities, and second, whether the matte-line blend has

Fig. 5.9. Typical early in-the-camera composites created by pioneer cameraman Norman Dawn. *Part 1*: A scene from Thomas Ince's *The Eye of the Night* (1915–1916). Matte line extends across the frame beginning just above the first story of the nearest house.

Fig. 5.9, part 2. Matte shot from Rupert Julian's *Beasts of Berlin* (1939), all detail from the roofs upwards being painted.

Fig. 5.9, part 3. Three-element matte shot for Dawn's production of *The Adorable Savage* (1920). Foreground water was photographed at Santa Catalina Island. Middle foreground was built and photographed on the Universal back lot. The background of trees is painted.

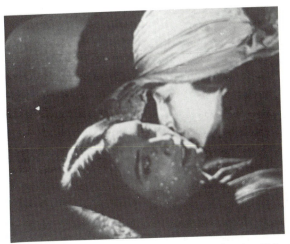

Fig. 5.10. A very difficult in-the-camera matte shot, in which actress Dorothy Phillips kisses her own cheek in a double role in *The Right to Happiness* (1919).

been properly executed. Any necessary changes in matte-line position or in the painting itself can be made at this point, and, if necessary, additional lengths of test strips can be exposed, processed, and examined. If time is available, a photo enlargement can be made from this composite test negative and critically appraised.

Finally, once the proper matching of visual elements has been achieved in the test footage, the entire roll of production footage is re-wound to start position and run through the camera, producing the final composite of the live action and the painted replacement images (Fig. 5.12).

Some workers expose the production negative used for the live-action component an extra half stop or so, which allows them to print down later for rich blacks. Some workers use an emulsion such as Eastman's type 5247 for both the production negative and, later, the photography of the matte painting and the printing of the color master. Others use a duplicating color-negative stock for final printing of the negative and photography of the painted matte. And still others employ black-and-white separations for

Fig. 5.11, part 1. For the 1937 production of *The Prisoner of Zenda*, it was required that actor Ronald Colman play a double role, as King Rudolph V and as a visiting Englishman. Colman plays opposite himself in several scenes by means of double-exposed split-screen shots. Here cameraman Jack Cosgrove lines up the first half of the shot. The camera photographs the scene through an oversized matte-box, one half of the shot being obscured and, hence, not exposed.

Fig. 5.11, part 2. During first exposure actor Colman plays the imposter (right). Only the right-hand side of the screen is exposed during this first take. Colman reads his lines with director John Cromwell (left).

Fig. 5.11, part 3. The resulting exposure shows Colman playing the part of the imposter. Director Cromwell is not in the shot.

Fig. 5.11, part 4. After first exposure, the film is rewound in the camera to 'start' position. During second exposure, the previously-exposed section of the frame is masked off, and the left-hand section is revealed. This time, a recording of the actor's voice is played back from the first take and Colman performs his part and reads his lines with his 'alter ego'.

Fig. 5.11, part 5. Assuming that a great many technical requirements are met, a perfect composite of the two exposures results, with the actor performing a dual role with himself both on the screen and on the sound track.

the final photography/printing of the composite. In the end, as with any art, personal experience and preference will determine procedures.

If desired, of course, more than two image components may be 'matted together', and any combination of elements may be used – live action, painted art-work, miniatures, or photographs (Fig. 5.12). If art-work is used for the replacement image, a variety of media may be used for the drawing, depending upon the artist's wishes. Oil-based paints are the preferred medium for such work, although water-colors, charcoal, pastel chalks and pen and ink have also been used from time to time.

A typical-size glass support for a matte painting is 2½ × 6 ft, while masonite supports have been built as large as 4 × 8 ft. The aspect ratio of the painting must, of course, match that of the production. Generally speaking, small paintings should be avoided, as the brush strokes may show in the finished composite. This ability of contemporary color films to resolve fine detail must be kept in mind, especially as manufacturers continue to improve their products.

Fig. 5.12, part 1. Although in-the-camera matte shots are time consuming and difficult to execute, many of today's film makers employ them to achieve maximum image quality. For a Canadian Film Board production, it was required that historical events which centered around a particular building be re-created dramatically. Starting point for the sequence was this contemporary print of the original building.

Fig. 5.12, part 2. The first story of the set is built on the sound-stage.

Fig. 5.12, part 3. The first component of the scene is photographed as an in-the-camera matte shot, the upper portion of the frame being obscured with an external matte.

Fig. 5.12, part 4. A painting of the upper part of the building is prepared with the lower half matted out. This painting is now re-exposed onto the re-wound, original camera negative, producing a partially-completed composite. Some areas of the roof and behind the windows in this painting have been left opaque, however, in anticipation of a third exposure which will add a fire effect.

Fig. 5.12, part 5. From the perspective of the matte painting, a small model of the roof and upper window section is built, ignited and photographed.

Fig. 5.12, part 6. A master positive of the fire effect is printed in bi-pack with the still-undeveloped camera negative, thus accomplishing the third and final exposure. The fire effect is shown here superimposed over the painting alone.

Fig. 5.12, part 7. The final composite – a combination of full-scale, live-action foreground, matte painting and miniaturized fire effects.

Fig. 5.12, part 8. Another composite of the same scene, lighted and painted for a daylight effect.

Precautions against failure

When the in-the-camera matte-shot technique is used, many of the precautions involved in glass and mirror-shot photography will also apply during the original, on-set exposure. Both the camera and the sheet of glass must be stabilized against vibration, lest matte-line weave be introduced at this stage. In addition, high-quality, pilot-pin movements must be used in both the production and laboratory cameras, since two or more passes through the camera are involved in the process. Ideally, the same camera or the same intermittent movement would be used for each step. In any case, the registration position of the pilot pins should be identical for all exposures.

Isolation of the camera and the glass sheet from light may be necessary to prevent reflections off the transparent sections of the glass. Also, as little light as possible should strike the glossy black paint of the matted area, lest this reflect some light and produce a density on the negative.

Placing the matte

Each worker who uses the in-the-camera matte-shot technique will have to determine for himself at what distance the black, external matte must be placed away from the camera's lens in order to produce the desired effect. Ordinarily, the glass or masonite matte is located close enough to the lens during the first exposure so as to be rendered slightly out of focus. The soft matte line which is thereby produced is more easily blended with the painting than is a hard edge. It is also usually desirable to produce a soft matte line on the painting during the second exposure. Naturally, the camera's lens must always be sharply focused upon the painting. Therefore, in order to 'fuzz-off' the matte line during second exposure, the painting must be provided by the artist with a soft edge. Alternatively, the

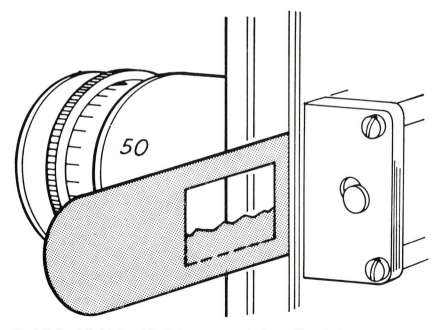

Fig. 5.13. Specially-fabricated focal-plane mattes can be inserted into the intermittent movement. A complete set of mattes would provide vertical, horizontal and quarter-cut bisections, as well as binocular and telescope patterns. The matte shown here was hand-cut to fit a particular kind of scene. (Norman Dawn.)

black counter-matte which blocks out the previously-photographed live-action can be painted on to a separate glass sheet, rather than on to the surface of the art board. This glass matte is then positioned a few inches in front of the painting and its matte-line edge is allowed to be rendered suitably out of focus.

Some workers have dispensed with the external matte entirely during the first exposure by employing individually-cut focal-plane mattes which are inserted into the intermittent movement of the camera. Such a matte is shown in Fig. 5.13. Its aperture is exactly the same size as is that of the film frame. Since it is not actually in contact with the film, however, its matte edge is rendered slightly out of focus, which is desirable. The matte which is shown in Fig. 5.13 was made of thin fibreboard material and was cut with a pen-knife in about one minute. Such work is extremely difficult, however, and requires considerable skill and experience, not only because of the small size of the matte but also because it has to be cut upside-down and reversed, right-to-left, so as to match the inverted image formed by the lens. Very few people are capable of mastering this technique.

In-the-camera matte: for and against

Historically, the in-the-camera matte shot has passed in and out of favor, depending upon the type of production film stocks being used. It provides greater flexibility and control than is possible with glass- or mirror-shots, and was used for many years in the theatrical film industry for black-and-white cinematography. From the early 1930s onward, with the introduction of high-quality black-and-white duplicating stocks, it was, for

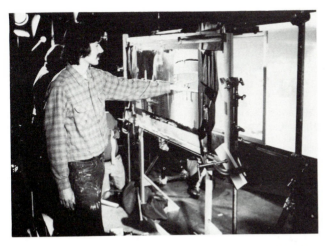

Fig. 5.14. Matte board set-up for Lucasfilm's production of *The Empire Strikes Back*. Matte painting supervisor Mike Pangrazio inspects the painting prior to photography. Several sheets of glass-mounted paintings are stacked in multiplane fashion. The last painting is of whisps of clouds which are made to move slowly across the frame, behind the buildings. A live-action shot of actress Carrie Fisher will be inserted by rear projection into the area to which Pangrazio is pointing. (Courtesy of Lucasfilm, Ltd.)

a while, largely replaced by bi-pack printing, which was based upon the same principles but offered still greater flexibility, lower cost, and greater predictability. Still later, when the film industry converted almost wholly from black-and-white to color cinematography, the in-the-camera matte shot returned to favor, it being the only process of its kind capable of producing a composite color image in which the grain, resolution, acutance, hue and saturation were not degraded. In such productions as *2001, Star Wars, Close Encounters of the Third Kind, The Empire Strikes Back*, and many others, the in-the-camera matte shot was used to produce composite images of extremely high quality.

Still more recently, a few matte artists have begun to work again, in color, with the bi-pack printing method described in the next chapter. It is conceivable that as color stocks – production, internegative, and interpositive – are made still more sophisticated, and as matte artists learn to work comfortably and effectively with these stocks, the bi-pack printing approach may again replace the in-the-camera shot.

In summary, the in-the-camera matte shot process has the following advantages over the glass- and mirror-shot techniques:

1. Set-up time for the first exposure is far more rapid; the production company is not tied up during production while the artist paints the scene.
2. Once the black/glass matte has been prepared, the first exposure can be made at any time of the day. For location work, this means that the cameraman/artist need not worry about the matching of sun and shadow positions, since these will be matched during preparation of the painting at a later time.
3. The replacement images are added to the live-action scene long after the first exposure has been made. This second step can be conducted at leisure, by relatively few technicians.
4. Addition of the replacement images may be delayed until the very last stages of production, thus allowing for last-minute changes in the nature or style of the replacement scene.
5. Since all exposures are produced on the original negative, the maximum image quality is produced on the screen.

Despite its great advantages over earlier techniques, the in-the-camera matte shot nevertheless displays the following limitations:

1. Although set-up time is much faster than with glass and mirror-shots, it still involves expensive delays while the glass matte is mounted, painted and aligned. The painting of the black matte usually requires the services of an experienced artist or draftsman. Isolation of the glass matte from light is generally necessary to prevent reflections – this requires still further delays before the shot can be made.
2. If, during second exposure, any unexpected circumstance should interfere with the operation of the camera or the lighting equipment, the composite may be ruined. A film jam, the burning-out of a lamp, fluctuations in the line voltage or a momentary power failure could destroy a valuable shot and necessitate an expensive re-shooting of the live-action scene.

3. There is no room for experiment in the replacement of images. Once the second exposure has been made, the composite is permanently set, and cannot be re-done or corrected.
4. Although far more versatile than glass and mirror shots, the in-the-camera matte shot requires more elaborate and expensive equipment, including pilot-pin movements in both the production and laboratory camera, and some kind of provision to allow for superimposition of the imaged art-work on to the test negative.
5. The camera cannot be panned or tilted unless very elaborate 'motion-control' machinery is used, similar to that described in Chapter 13.

6

Bi-pack contact matte printing

In the previous chapter, a variety of 'in-the-camera' painted matte shots were described, all of which required successive re-exposure of the original negative. Although excellent image quality results from such work, the awkwardness and expense of the technique has never made it very popular with schedule-conscious, low-budget producers.

Back in the days of black-and-white cinematography, once high-quality duplicating stocks became available, offering relatively fine grain, medium contrast and high definition, a different and far more flexible matte-shot process was introduced – that of bi-pack contact matte printing. In its day, for black-and-white work, bi-pack printing virtually replaced in-the-camera matte shots. With the conversion of the film industry to color, however, and the rather unpredictable and often disappointing character of color-film duplication, film makers returned to the in-the-camera technique for the best-quality work.

Still more recently, dramatic improvements in color-film technology have again rendered bi-pack printing feasible for high-quality work, and an increasing number of special-effects workers are returning to this technique, enjoying its many advantages.

In this chapter, we shall describe the process as it is used for black-and-white production. Then we shall discuss its application to contemporary color cinematography.

The bi-pack process

In contrast to the 'in-the-camera' matte shot, for which all of the image manipulations and replacements are performed upon the original negative, bi-pack printing allows for such work to be done from master positives which have been struck from the negative. In this manner, the risk of failure which always attends re-exposure of the irreplaceable negative is avoided, as is the necessity for the time-consuming creation of a matte on a sheet of glass at the time and place of the original photography.

The principle of matte printing is as follows. The original negative, containing certain image components which we wish to transfer to the finished scene, is printed to a master positive on a step-printer. The master positive is then threaded into a process camera in bi-pack fashion, with a roll of fine-grain duplicating negative raw stock. The master positive is placed directly behind the aperture plate and the dupe negative behind the master positive, both strips in contact, emulsion-to-emulsion (Fig. 6.1).

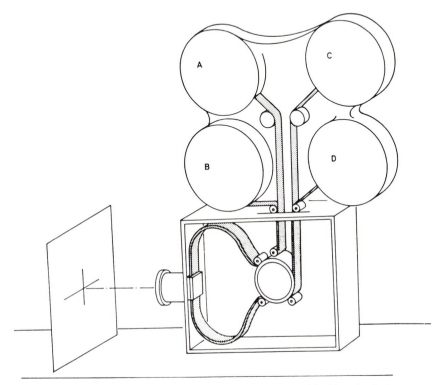

Fig. 6.1. A simplified, cut-away sketch of a process camera, loaded for bi-pack printing. Duplicating color negative stock is loaded into chamber A. A color master (positive) is loaded into chamber B. The exposed dupe negative is taken up into chamber C, the color master into chamber D. The two strips pass through the intermittent movement, emulsion-to-emulsion, with the raw stock to the rear.

A white matte-board is set up on a rigidly-mounted easel in front of the process camera and the lens is focused on the board. So long as the entire white matte-board is adequately and evenly illuminated, the camera will function as a step-printer, printing a dupe negative from the entire frame area of the master positive. If, however, selected areas of the matte-board are blackened with ink or paint, then those areas, as imaged by the optical system, will not provide light to print sections of the master positive on to the dupe negative.

If, as a second step, a counter-matte is prepared which matches the contour of the original blackened area exactly, but in which the black and the white areas are reversed, and if the dupe negative is re-wound in the camera and again run through the intermittent movement, this time by itself, then art-work which has been painted over the white area of the counter-matte will be optically fitted into place with the live-action image which was printed on the first run from the master positive.

This process may be used to combine the desired visual elements of the master positive with either hand-drawn scenes or still photographs. It can also be used to combine several different live-action shots. For really complex effects, any number of different visual elements – live-action, miniatures, paintings and still photos – may be matted together so as to build a finished representation of reality which, of course, does not actually exist anywhere (Fig. 6.2).

Fig. 6.2. A non-existent cityscape, created through bi-pack matte printing. Only the live-action foreground is three-dimensional and contains full-scale set pieces. The upper section is painted, the matte line bisecting the frame horizontally just above the first story of the buildings.

Equipment

Ordinarily, a specially-designed process camera will be used for bi-pack printing, although modified production cameras can sometimes be used. Whatever one may wish to call such a piece of equipment, it is in fact both a camera and a contact step-printer. On the one hand, it employs an optical system, by means of which art-work or still photographs can be imaged upon a fine-grain dupe negative, and, on the other hand, a bi-pack magazine and suitable intermittent movement to allow for contact printing of selected image components on to the same dupe negative from one or more rolls of master positive.

Among the more versatile of such instruments are the Acme and Oxberry process cameras, both of which have accessories designed to suit them for matte printing (Figs. 6.3 and 6.4). In addition, the Bell & Howell 'Standard' can be satisfactorily modified for such work, as can the Mitchell 'NC', although considerable engineering is necessary in the latter case.

Fig. 6.3. The Acme process camera, with bi-pack magazine mounted.

Fig. 6.4. The Acme camera with rotoscope lamp house attached.

Fig. 6.5. For rotoscoping operations, the pressure plate is removed and a right-angle mirror attached behind the intermittent. Light from the lamp house is reflected off the mirror, passes through the color master and is focused by the camera lens onto the art-board easel.

Both the Acme and Oxberry cameras are designed to accept an accessory lamp house (Figs. 6.4 and 6.5) which, together with a right-angle prism or mirror located behind the cut-out pressure plate opening (Fig. 6.6) allows for the projection of a frame of master positive through the optical system of the camera and on to a matte-board easel or animation-crane table-top. Such a facility is necessary to allow the cameraman or artist to trace the matte lines that are required. (In some circles, the lamp house and prism assembly is referred to as a 'rotoscope'.) In the event that a production camera is modified for such work, attention will have to be paid in the design of the lamp house to incorporate efficient condensers and heat-absorbing elements to avoid overheating and buckling of the master positive in the movement.

Professional process cameras will ordinarily provide not only single-frame but also continuous projection of the master positive on to the matte-board to allow for fast monitoring of the entire run of film, as well as for complicated frame-by-frame matte-line changes, if desired. Ordinarily, the pressure plates will be changed between single-film and bi-pack operations, thus providing the proper amount of pressure to the bi-pack load during contact printing. The design of the pressure plate varies from

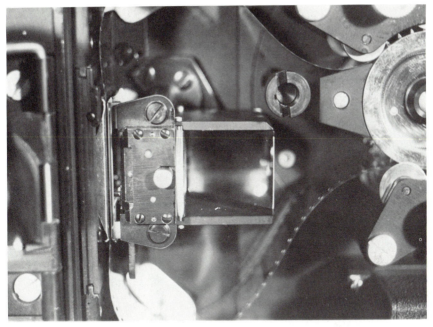

Fig. 6.6. The Oxberry process camera, with magazine removed, its door opened and a rotoscope lamp house attached. Note the lens mount, which moves straight in and out on a bellows extension.

camera to camera, some employing a varying number of rollers, others using a set of raised buttons on the surface of the plate.

The Acme and Oxberry process cameras are available in both 16 mm and 35 mm gauges. In addition, current models of these cameras make provision for interchangeable intermittents, sprocket drives and magazines, thus allowing the single instrument to be used for either gauge. The interchange of parts is rapid and can be accomplished without complicated tools (Fig. 6.7).

Procedures

At least eight steps are involved in bi-pack printing, although many variations in technique are possible during any one of these steps:

1. Photography of the live-action negative(s).
2. Processing of the negative.
3. Printing of a master positive from the negative.
4. Projection ('rotoscoping') of the master positive and drawing of the matte lines.
5. Preparation of the matte, counter-matte and/or art-work.
6. Printing of the master positive to the dupe negative – 1st run.
7. Photography of the matted art-work on to the dupe negative – 2nd run.
8. Processing of the composite dupe negative.

Fig. 6.7. Both the Oxberry and Acme process cameras are designed to accept either 16 mm or 35 mm gauge films, by interchanging intermittent movements, sprocket drives, lenses and magazines. Here, removal of the 35 mm sprocket drive and movement from an Oxberry camera is shown. The exchange of parts is made rapidly and without special tools.

Photographing the live action

As a first step, the live-action component of the scene is photographed with a production camera, the intermittent movement of which must be as steady as that of the process camera which is to be used for the printing. A pilot-pin movement of some sort is essential, as is consistency with the process camera in registration positions.

Rigidity of the production camera is of great importance since even the most accurate of intermittent movements will be compromised if the camera vibrates during photography of the original scene. Vibration and jiggle are particularly likely to occur when the tripod is mounted on a parallel or other support some distance from the earth, and correspondingly greater care must be taken to insure the stability of the mount. Chains should be used on the tripod whenever possible.

Although not ordinarily a problem, care must be taken to avoid heat waves across the field of view, lest their absence in sections of the finished composite becomes apparent. The same prohibition applies to dust, smoke, fire, rain and other atmospheric effects. If such effects *are* present, they must be duplicated in the matted-in image, and to exactly the same degree.

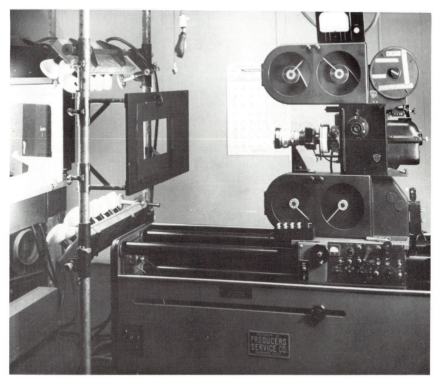

Fig. 6.8. A typical horizontally-mounted bi-pack printing set-up, using multiple easels. The photographing instrument is an Acme matte-shot printer. It serves the same function as the previously described process camera, but is designed differently. Note that provision is made for tri-pack operation, if desired, thus allowing for mattes to be used within the intermittent movement, as well as on the easels, during printing operations.

As would be expected, low-speed, fine-grain films, normally exposed, will be found best for such work. For color cinematography, the best possible color balance between light source and film must be achieved during the initial photography. Attempts to correct color-temperature mismatches during printing stages will be frustrated by the natural tendency of the duplication process to degrade color values still further.

Processing the negative

Unless experimentation is intended, processing the negative will be normal.

The master positive

A master positive is struck from the negative at the laboratory. This must be done on a step-printer, the registration position and pin locations of which conform to those of the production and process cameras. The process camera itself can be used as a step-printer, the only disadvantage being that it operates at a relatively slow speed. Consistency in the timing of the master positive from day to day is much to be desired, of course, since accurate determination of the final, bi-pack printing exposure depends upon it.

The matte lines

With the timed master positive in hand, the fourth step may now be executed in the special-effects laboratory. For this and all subsequent steps, the process camera is mounted on a lathe bed, cement pedestal or optical bench of sufficient weight and rigidity to dampen vibration of the camera during its operation (Figs. 6.8 and 6.9).

The master positive is inserted, heads down, into the intermittent movement of the process camera, the rotoscope lamp house is installed, and a typical frame is projected on to the white matte-board. This should be done at maximum aperture to allow for convenient drawing of the matte lines. Whether the lens should be sharply focused at the time that the matte lines are drawn depends entirely upon the particular type of shot being made and the type of matte or counter-matte being employed. The cameraman must remember that when a master positive and dupe negative

Fig. 6.9. Bi-pack printing can also be conducted with the camera mounted vertically, providing that a really sturdy support is employed. This massive Oxberry animation stand is ideal for such purposes. Vertical mounts provide for horizontal positioning of the art-work and mattes, which may be convenient for the artist.

are run through the camera in bi-pack, maximum sharpness of print will always occur no matter how the lens is focused, inasmuch as the two films will always be in contact. An out-of-focus lens will produce a soft matte edge, however, which is ordinarily desired for the blending of closely-matched detail and continuous tones. When two or more live-action components are matted together from several strips of master positive, the matte lines can be 'fuzzed' out of focus during each run. On the other hand, when art-work is used as a replacement element, and is photographed directly on to the dupe negative, the lens must obviously be focused sharply on the matte-board during that run.

The need for soft *vs* hard matte edges and the extent of their softness are factors which vary from assignment to assignment and which can only be gauged by experience. In any event, should it be desired to soften the matte lines by racking the lens slightly out of focus, it is important that the matte lines be originally drawn on the easel board with the lens in the appropriate out-of-focus position. Due to magnification changes in the projected image which occur when the lens is racked in or out, the position of the matte lines can be accurately determined only if it is drawn with the lens in its final operating position. Some workers run a piece of clear 35 mm stock through the intermittent in bi-pack with the duplicating negative during photography of the painted art-work. This eliminates the possibility of a change in the relative sharpness and position of the matte-line edge in the finished composite due to displacement of the dupe negative during the second exposure.

The matte lines having been drawn, the matte and the counter-matte must now be prepared. At this point, various different techniques present themselves.

Preparing traced mattes

The tracing technique requires the use of translucent art paper which is registered on the matte-board easel by means of an animation peg bar, the paper having been pre-punched to fit it (Fig. 6.10). Various brands of peg bars and punches, manufactured for the film and graphic arts trades, are available for such purposes (Fig. 6.11).

Once the matte lines have been drawn, the sheet of paper is removed from the easel and placed on an animation light box – a tracing glass which is illuminated from below. A peg bar, mounted next to the tracing glass, allows for the re-registration of the sheet. Another sheet of paper is placed in register over the first and a careful tracing of the matte line is made on the second sheet. These two sheets comprise the materials from which the matte and counter-matte will be made.

Assuming, for example, that two live-action shots are to be matted together, then one of the sheets will be inked in solid above the matte line and the other below it (Fig. 6.12).

The mattes which result are complementary and will be used in whatever sequence the printing of the different rolls of master positive demand. Obviously, if more than two live-action elements are being matted together, an equal number of mattes will be required.

Fig. 6.10. The matte-board easel can take a variety of forms. This very elaborate unit is found on the Oxberry animation stand. (The same unit could be mounted vertically for use with a horizontal camera mount). Like most animation-board compounds, this one allows for North-South, East-West and rotational movements of the art-work. A light box is mounted below a sheet of glass which is set into the center of the table's surface. This provides rear illumination for either the tracing of mattes or for final photography. Although this kind of unit is essential for animation work, it is far more elegant than is usually used for bi-pack printing. (See Fig. 5.14 for a view of a typical matte-painting easel.)

Fig. 6.11. The Type 81 Oxberry three-hole punch for animation cells and mattes.

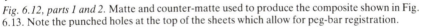

Fig. 6.12, parts 1 and 2. Matte and counter-matte used to produce the composite shown in Fig. 6.13. Note the punched holes at the top of the sheets which allow for peg-bar registration.

If, instead of matting only live-action shots together, we intend to matte live action and art-work together, then one of the sheets of paper becomes the 'canvas' on to which oils, watercolors or chalks will be laid to create the hand-drawn component. The lower part of such a painted matte will be inked in solid black so as to prevent exposure of the dupe negative in that area.

Should it be desired, transparent animation cels, suitably inked, can also be used for mattes. The use of cels is to be recommended in the matting-together of live-action and still photographs, the photographic prints being registered beneath the partially-opaque cels.

Although the tracing technique is widely used, its numerous shortcomings will become immediately apparent to practitioners of the art.

Accuracy in the registration of the sheets is critical, both with respect to each other and to the projected image from the master positive. The matte lines must be traced with great care so as to ensure an absolutely snug fit of the visual elements – the precision required here is far greater than in regulation animation work. A grade of paper must be selected for the matte sheets which will take the application of watercolors, oils and other media without buckling or warping the matte lines out of true.

Most annoying of all, however, is the difficulty which workers often encounter in producing a true, all-absorbing black matte which will not reflect some light back into the optical system of the camera.

Because of the rather high light levels employed in bi-pack printing, any paint except the deepest black will reflect a considerable amount of light, thus washing out matte areas with flare or contaminating them with unwanted images from the master positive. Those individuals who intend to use the tracing technique will wish to experiment with a variety of black paints and inks, both glossy and dull, to achieve maximum absorption of light. Because of their high saturation, oil-based paints are generally favored for both the blackened area and for the images of matte paintings.

All of these problems may be avoided through the use of a second kind of matte which, for lack of a better term, may be called the 'cut-out' or 'paper-doll' matte.

Preparing cut-out mattes

To produce such a matte, the master positive is projected in the usual fashion on to a sheet of opaque, white paper. Following the drawing of the original matte line, the paper is bisected (or otherwise shaped to conform to the design of the matte) by cutting with a pair of scissors or a knife. Once the paper has been cut, one of the portions will be retained, the other discarded, the choice depending upon the particular assignment at hand. If two live-action scenes are being combined from master positives, then either of the cut-outs can be used on the easel – the choice is inconsequential. If, on the other hand, a painting is to be matted to live action, then the cut-out which corresponds to the painted area is retained and becomes the support on to which the oils, pastels or other media are laid. However the case may be, the cut-out matte which is retained is re-aligned upon the easel, either with a registration peg bar or by eye.

The easel which we employ for cut-out mattes differs from that which was used for traced mattes, in that the central portion of the board over which the cut-out matte is placed is transparent plate glass. Beyond this easel, and capable of being viewed through the glass by the process camera, another easel is set up and is lit separately (Fig. 6.8). Upon this second board, large white or black sheets of paper will be mounted at appropriate times.

The principle of the cut-out matte technique is probably now apparent to the reader. If the white matte which is mounted on the forward easel is illuminated while the second easel is not, then the cut-out reflects the light necessary to print through selected areas of the master positive on to the dupe negative. During the second run through the camera, the lights on the front easel are extinguished. A large sheet of white paper is mounted on the second easel and is properly illuminated. The camera now prints the second master positive with light reflected from the second easel. However, since the optical system is focused on the front easel's cut-out matte, which is opaque, the matte's edges determine the configuration of the area printed from the master positive. Providing that the easels are rigidly mounted, the matte line will be maintained in exactly the same place for both exposures. Since black inks are not used to matte-out different areas of the scene, there is no possibility of unwanted reflections causing print-through or flare.

To produce a soft matte edge on a matte painting, it is possible to mount the painting on the *rear* easel, and a white cut-out matte on the forward one. By varying the distance of the matte from the painting, varying degrees of matte-edge softness can be achieved.

Naturally, this technique requires that each easel be completely isolated from the light which falls upon the other. Spill light must be carefully controlled, and it will probably be found necessary to cover the second easel with a large sheet of black paper during the period that the front easel is illuminated. Also, the cut-out matte must be truly opaque so as not to transmit light from the second easel during the re-exposure of the dupe negative. In the selection of white matte paper, a compromise will ordinarily be reached between opacity and thickness. Workers will wish to examine some of the thin white art papers, such as flock paper, which are backed by intensely black surfaces. These are sufficiently opaque to prevent transmission of light while thin enough to be easily cut with scissors.

A variation of the cut-out matte technique employs a sheet of plate glass on to which a white distemper or acrylic is painted and allowed to dry. After the matte lines have been drawn, the distemper surface serves as a medium on to which oil-based paints are applied in preparing the replacement art-work. As a final step, any unpainted sections of the distemper 'canvas' are removed by scraping or with a solvent. The remaining printing procedures are identical to those already described.

Sometimes, the support on to which the art-work is painted is a photographic enlargement of the master positive. This is produced by projecting the master positive on to photo-enlarging paper, which is then developed and fixed. Either a negative or positive image can be produced, depending upon whether the original negative or a master positive is used for projection. This technique has the advantage of providing the matte artist with a visual guide for the continuation of perspective lines and the matching of tone, contrast, color and texture between the live-action and the painted components.

Printing the dupe negative

The printing of the dupe negative from the master positive may now be conducted. To illustrate, we will assume that we are matting two live-action sequences together (Fig. 6.13). Specifics of the technique which follow will vary from worker to worker and from assignment to assignment. The details which are given here are intended only to suggest one possible sequence of operations in given circumstances.

First, 6 ft leaders are attached to both of the master positives, care being taken that their frame lines match those of the leaders at the point of the splice. Start marks are made on the leaders exactly 3 ft from the first frame of action; a symmetrical, full-frame pattern, together with a dead-center punch mark, will be found to be of real help to the camera operator in aligning the bi-pack strips and in loading them into the intermittent movement. Since there are four possible frame-line positions for any

Fig. 6.13, part 1. First printing for a bi-pack matte-shot combining two live-action scenes. The original background, which contained trees and shrubbery, has been removed.

Fig. 6.13, part 2. Second printing, adding background detail on the UCLA campus, photographed from the top of a ten-story building.

Fig. 6.13, part 3. Final composite. The mattes used for this shot are shown in Fig. 6.12.

particular 35 mm frame, the positioning of the sync mark in a consistent manner is essential – failure to do so will result in out-of-register composites. Compared with 35 mm, the alignment of 16 mm stock is a relatively simple matter.

After cleaning, the first master positive, wound on a core, heads down and emulsion-out, is loaded into the lower left hand chamber of the bi-pack magazine. It is taken up into the lower right-hand chamber. The dupe negative, wound emulsion-in, moves from the upper left chamber to the upper right. The magazine is designed so that, when properly loaded, the master positive is positioned in front of the dupe negative, emulsion-to-emulsion (Fig. 6.1).

The sync marks are aligned and centered in the intermittent movement. Final alignment can be checked by opening the shutter of the camera while the pilot pins are engaged and looking through the lens back into the intermittent.

The symmetrical pattern of the sync marks will indicate whether the two strips of film are aligned with each other and whether they are properly set into the intermittent with respect of their frame-line positions.

The intensity of light required for the final printing of the composite depends to a great extent upon the type of negative used in the process camera as a duplicating material. For best results, a standard duplicating negative stock should be used. Such emulsions offer panchromatic color sensitivity for the natural reproduction of painted mattes, exceptionally fine grain, and a relatively linear sensitometric response over a wide range of exposures. They are, unfortunately, quite slow in speed and will require rather high light levels, particularly when printing through the master positive. The effective speed of such a stock depends, in turn, upon the kind of processing which it receives at the laboratory. Exposure tests will have to be performed by the individual cameraman with the co-operation of the laboratory technicians before the effective speed can be determined.

Because of the high light levels, slow camera speeds and wide apertures which follow from the use of standard duplicating negative materials, some workers prefer to use a fine-grain production emulsion which, no matter how slow by conventional standards, is many times faster than a duplicating negative stock. It is argued that the increased convenience and speed of operation which follows from the use of such higher-speed production emulsions more than compensates for their inherently greater graininess.

If the use of production stocks is anticipated, it is essential that close co-operation, considerable experimentation and rigid standardization prevail between the cameraman and the laboratory since these stocks are in no sense intended for printing applications.

Once the cut-out matte has been aligned and mounted on the easel, the first printing of the dupe negative can be made. The appropriate easel is evenly illuminated, while the alternate board is darkened and isolated from ambient, 'splash' light. The bi-pack pressure plate is inserted into the movement and the lens is checked to see that it is racked out-of-focus to an appropriate extent. All other obvious steps having been taken, the camera is turned on and the first printing of the dupe negative is made (Fig. 6.14).

Detailed, accurate records of the many variables which operate in this process should be kept throughout the run; if re-takes become necessary, the exposure records provide point-of-departure data for changes and corrections. All operations, instruments and techniques of measurement must be standardized. Once optimum conditions have been established, any changes in procedure must be accomplished one-by-one so as to determine its exact effect upon the finished product.

Should the cameraman lose control of the process through carelessness in measurement, in operating technique or in record-keeping, the whole business of determining and specifying variables must begin all over again.

Fig. 6.14, part 1. First printing of a scene which is supposed to have been taken in a railway terminal. The full-scale foreground area has been photographed and the upper section of the frame matted out.

Fig. 6.14, part 2. The final composite. The artist and effects cinematographer have matted in a painted ceiling and wall. Some detail has also been added to the roofs of the railway carriages.

Adding the matted work

Following the first printing, the shutter of the camera is closed, the master positive and dupe negative are re-wound within the camera and the master positive is removed. If only live-action sequences are being matted together than the second roll of master positive is loaded into the magazine and its sync mark aligned within the movement with that of the dupe negative. If, on the other hand, a painted or photo matte is used, then only the dupe negative will pass through the camera on the second run. In this case, a change in pressure plates will be necessary and the lens will have to be focused sharply on the art-work.

The lighting of the easels is alternated, with care being taken throughout the process to avoid disturbing the positions of the matte, the easels, the camera or the bench and mounting assembly.

The shutter having been re-opened, the second run is now made, thus completing the composite printing of the dupe negative (Fig. 6.14). In the event that more than two picture areas are matted together, then additional exposures will, of course, be necessary.

The matching of exposures between the first and second runs is more of an art than a science, since so much depends upon the subject-matter of the master positives or painted mattes and their respective transparencies or reflectances. Also, the effective speed of the dupe negative is greatly increased during the photography of the painting or photo matte, inasmuch as the light no longer passes through a master positive before reaching it. Ordinarily, cameramen will attain considerable proficiency through experience in estimating exposures.

For real convenience, however, the cameraman will provide himself with some sort of 'slop-test' facility, either in the camera room itself or nearby, wherein rapid processing and inspection of test sections of the negative can be conducted. The ability to 'read' negatives properly is one which many motion-picture cameramen will have to cultivate. 'Slop-tests' of color emulsions may also be conducted using black-and-white processing chemicals. The color values will be destroyed, but the relative densities of the different components will become immediately apparent, as will the match of matte-line positions.

Lacking the convenience of 'quick-and-dirty' processing, the cameraman can make a series of three or more bracketed-exposure runs which will allow for half or full-stop increments in the exposure of the dupe negative during the second part of each run.

Processing the composite

Laboratory processing of the composite negative constitutes the eighth and final step in the bi-pack printing process. The need for intimate liaison between cinematographer and laboratory has already been stressed; only through extensive tests can optimum exposure and processing conditions be determined. Ordinarily, the processed composite will be expected to print around mid-point on the scale of printer lights. Optimum contrast, however, remains pretty much a matter of personal taste. As a point of departure in conducting tests, it is suggested that cameramen specify a development gamma ranging between 0.60 and 0.70 for black-and-white stocks.

Special techniques

Bi-pack printing methods can be adapted to a variety of techniques, according to the nature of the result required.

Photo mattes

Just as with glass-shots, it is possible to use photo cut-outs for image replacement in cases where the budget does not allow for the services of a skilled matte painter. Those areas of the photographic enlargement in which live action is to be inserted are cut away with scissors or knife, the photograph is mounted on the front easel and the printing procedures are the same as for any other kind of cut-out matte. Properly executed, this technique is very effective and costs only a fraction of the expense involved in matte painting.

Moving-camera mattes

In the previous chapter we laid a fair amount of emphasis upon the fact that the camera may not move either during the photography of the original action or during the printing of the dupe negative. This is an oversimplification. Like everything else in special-effects work, nothing is impossible providing one has sufficient time, energy and budget available. For those demanding producers to whom no expense is too great, at least one very complicated method allows us to deal with either the accidental or purposeful panning and tilting of the production camera during the original take.

With the master positive inserted into the intermittent movement and the rotoscope unit attached, the *entire* strip of film is projected, frame by frame, on to the matte-board and as many mattes are prepared as are required by the original camera movement. Cut-out mattes can be used for this purpose, but they must be registered on peg bars rather than by eye.

The sequence in which the mattes are used must be accurately determined and repeated for each of the printing runs. Computing from zero position at the start of the master positive, the appropriate frame-counter numbers should be penciled in the corners of the mattes so as to ensure their proper arrangement during the different printing stages.

With the dupe negative and master positive loaded into the intermittent, the first printing is accomplished using a different matte for each frame in which movement occurs. The same mattes, registered in the same sequence, are used for the second run. Naturally, the movement of the pan or tilt in the second master positive strip must correspond fairly exactly in speed, acceleration, deceleration and direction to that of the first strip or the two image components will 'slide' against one another. If the shot does not run too long or present overly intricate movements, discrepancies in perspective and motion parallax will not be too apparent.

In the event that a painting is to be employed in a moving-camera shot, it is necessary to prepare an oversized 'full-frame' painting and to photograph it during the final printing run using suitably inked animation cels to progressively cover or reveal it. The painting must be moved a proper distance behind the cels with each change of matte. These movements are best plotted and executed on a standard animation compound with north-south, east-west movements (Fig. 6.10). Naturally, such movements cannot accurately duplicate original pan-and-tilt movements of the production camera, both of which cause changes in perspective as well as in motion parallax. As is the case with glass-shot pans, the best results using this method would be obtained if the production camera were originally mounted with the fulcrum point of the pan and tilt movements centered at the nodal point of the optical system. In this way, perspective and parallax motion would be minimized.

As an alternative method, painted mattes can be used in moving-camera shots by photographing them first on separate negative with appropriate camera movements, and then, printing a master positive from it. The master positive of the painting is used in the final matte printing just as if two live-action scenes were being matted together.

Some of the film industry's special-effects organizations have constructed motion-control devices which provide virtually identical camera movements during both the original photography and the subsequent printing steps. Positions of the production camera, in its pan-and-tilt movements, are sensed by servo or stepper motors which transmit signals to a computer memory. Later, during bi-pack printing, the same signals are re-transmitted to an identically-geared, motor-driven camera mount which moves the process camera in the same fashion during photography of the painted art-work. Such a device allows for extremely complicated moving-matte effects (as distinguished from traveling mattes). Equipment such as this can be rented. Only an organization with considerable financial and engineering resources and the expectation of extensive use of such equipment would be justified in fabricating it, however.

Hand-drawn traveling mattes

Where the story calls for some really complicated effects in which props or set pieces, such as falling rocks or masonry, are required to envelope or partially obscure actors, it will be necessary to animate the painted image components and to prepare accompanying animated traveling mattes, cel by cel and frame by frame. The same animation technique can be used to add birds, falling water, wave action, distant lights, background figures and other atmospheric background action to a live-action scene. This animation of art-work and accompanying traveling mattes will also be necessary in combining live-action and moving cartoon figures. Such combinations are frequently used today for novelty effect in the production of television commercials.

The animation techniques employed here are, in themselves, not much different than for regular animation save that the size, perspective and movement of animated objects or figures must always be synchronized and integrated with that of the live action. The bi-pack printing technique employed in photographing such composites differs from the ordinary to the extent that hundreds of animation paintings are photographed during the second run through the process camera instead of only one single piece of art-work. Also, of course, those sections of the white matte-board in which the animated art-work appears must be progressively obscured and revealed during printing of the master positive, by means of an equal number of transparent cels on which black matte silhouettes have been drawn to match the movements, configurations and positions of the cartoon figures – a hand-drawn 'traveling matte'.

The preparation of such a traveling matte is a tedious and expensive business. Fortunately, this labor can be avoided by using animation cels in exactly the same way we use cut-out mattes in conventional matte printing, the only requirement being that the inked and painted areas of the cels be completely opaque.

Let us assume, for example, that a cartoon figure is to be added to a live-action scene. For the first run through the process camera, with the master positive and dupe negative in bi-pack, the cels bearing the cartoon drawings are successively registered, frame-by-frame, on the front easel. It is the rear easel which is illuminated, however, so that only the area surrounding the cartoon figure is printed through from the master positive to the dupe negative. After the first run, the dupe negative is re-wound and run through the camera again, this time by itself. Using the same animation cels in the same order, the forward easel is now illuminated while the rear board is darkened. The desired composite of cartoon figures and live action results. As usual, extensive preliminary tests for exposure and color balance will be necessary.

Titles

Titles are added to live-action scenes in much the same fashion as cartoon figures. The titles are inked or hot-press-printed on transparent cels which are then registered on the forward easel. If desired, a 'drop shadow' can be printed on to a second cel and registered behind the first. The first exposure, in bi-pack, is illuminated with light from behind the easel, thus printing through the live-action, but leaving the title area unexposed. During the second run, only the dupe negative is exposed and the title cel is illuminated from the front.

Optical transitions

Virtually all of the transitional effects which are more generally achieved through optical printing can also be realized with bi-pack printing. These include fades, dissolves, wipes and superimpositions. The procedures are identical to those of optical printing and are described in Chapter 7. The techniques differ only in that one involves optical reproduction, the other contact. In both cases, master positives should be used for the printing of fades and dissolves.

Wipe effects are particularly convenient to make through bi-pack printing. Whatever the kind of wipe that is desired, a series of cut-out mattes will be prepared and punched so as to properly register on the peg bar of the easel. During the first run, the mattes are lit from the front, their different configurations being successively photographed so as to progressively vary the light passing from the master positive to the dupe negative. The dupe negative is then re-wound, the front light is extinguished and the white card behind the easel is illuminated. The outgoing master positive is replaced with the incoming one. A second exposure is made, in bi-pack, with the same set of cut-out mattes being successively registered in the same order as for first exposure. The speed of the wipe can be varied by increasing or decreasing the number of mattes, as well as by photographing each matte two or more times.

Alternatively, a simple horizontal wipe can be produced by imaging a single cut-out matte which bisects the frame vertically, during both of the bi-pack printing steps. This requires the use of a movable, calibrated camera carriage on the lathe-bed support. The operator moves the camera laterally across the bed so that the image of the vertical, cut-out matte is made to progressively obscure or reveal the frame, and thus provide light for the printing of the master positive to the dupe negative. Naturally, both runs through the camera require *precisely* the same camera positions, relative to the cut-out matte on the easel and to the particular frames which are being printed.

The more complicated wipe effects, such as those illustrated in Chapter 8, will require animated male and female mattes which are hand-drawn on registered sheets of paper.

Matte printing from negatives

Contradicting the almost universally applicable principle of always executing optical and bi-pack printing effects from master positives, it is nonetheless possible to do matte printing using the original negative in the process camera. This variation in technique offers a marginal advantage to educational and industrial producers who photograph their pictures in 35 mm and then reduce them for a 16 mm release. If, as is ordinarily done, master positives are employed in the process to print a dupe negative, then the dupe negative which results will have to be re-duplicated to a second 35 mm master positive and then reduced to a 16 mm dupe negative, at which point it can be intercut with the other reduced 16 mm production negative. On the other hand, by performing 35 mm matte printing from the original production negatives, a composite master positive is produced which can then be reduced directly to a 16 mm dupe negative. A full generation of duplication is thereby eliminated and a considerable increase in image quality is achieved.

This variation in technique is feasible only when live-action scenes from production negatives are being matted together. If still photographs or paintings were used, it would be necessary to work from negative images of these which would raise too many other problems to be really practical. The other prohibition which applies here concerns the production of fades and dissolves, neither of which can be satisfactorily achieved except by printing from master positives to dupe negatives.

Conventional traveling mattes

The conventional traveling-matte system, as described later in this book, is ordinarily considered a technique of optical printing. Nonetheless, it is possible to create such effects through bi-pack printing, providing that it is not required that the *background* image move.

Of the many systems available for the production of traveling mattes (see Chapter 8), one is selected which will provide, first, a master positive of the actor with a black surround, and, second, a matte which is opaque in the area of the actor's image and clear in the surround.

The master positive of the actor is loaded into the process camera in bi-pack with the dupe negative, the optical system is focused on an illuminated white matte-board, and the first exposure is made. An image of the actor has now been printed through to the dupe negative, but inasmuch as the surround was opaque on the master positive, no image yet exists around the actor on the negative. The bi-pack load is re-wound and the master positive of the actor is replaced by the matte in which the actor's silhouette is opaque and the surrounding area is clear. The process camera is now focused upon a photograph or painting against which the moving actor is to be matted. During the second printing, the image of the photograph or art-work prints through the clear surround of the traveling matte, but not through the opaque actor's silhouette. Properly executed, a convincing composite results.

In practice, such a technique must take varying emulsion positions into consideration. The matte which is produced must have a suitable emulsion position to allow for contact printing with the dupe negative.

Special applications

The applications of bi-pack printing are so varied as to defy attempts to list and categorize them. So long as actors are not required to pass from one matted area into another, the process allows the director and set designer to realize, on film, anything their imaginations and the budget will allow. The description of a few obvious applications must suffice.

Addition of set components

The addition of painted ceilings to partially-completed interior sets (Fig. 6.15), the alteration of certain features of existing architectural detail (Fig. 6.14), and the addition of extra stories to one-story buildings (Figs. 6.17 and 6.19), probably constitute the most common uses to which bi-pack printing is put. These operations can reduce set construction costs considerably. In particular, the addition of ceilings by means of matte printing also allows for rapid lighting and superior sound recording, neither of which are usually possible when real ceilings are used.

For the most convincing effects, all of these assignments will require the services of a skilled matte painter, the replacement components being hand-painted to match the character, perspective, texture and tonal values of the particular set involved (Figs. 6.17 to 6.23). Sometimes, still photographs of appropriate ceiling or architectural detail can be specially photographed with an appropriate choice of angles and lenses to match the live-action scene fairly exactly. In cases such as these, it will be found best to shoot the set components head-on and thus avoid complicated perspective effects, to use natural breaks in the existing set as matte-line divisions, and to avoid showing the edges of sets. Still photographs can also be used quite effectively to provide views of a landscape or other background detail which is seen through windows or open doors of the set, providing that the actors are not required to pass in front of these apertures.

Fig. 6.15, part 1. Sound-stage preparations for a scene to which a painted ceiling is to be added through bi-pack printing.

Fig. 6.15, part 2. The completed scene with ceiling added. Apart from the considerable savings in set-construction costs, this technique allows convenient sound-recording. The microphone can be suspended anywhere in the original shot above the matte line.

Addition of clouds

In those unfortunate cases where the director of photography has found it necessary to photograph location or back-lot action against a barren, unattractive sky, clouds may be added later through different matte-printing techniques (Fig. 6.24).

The first of these is the conventional, successive-run printing which has been previously described. A master positive is prepared of the foreground action; this is matted together with scenes of clouds on still photographs,

Fig. 6.16, part 1. A matte-shot set-up at Pinewood Studios. From the front, one sees the matte painting which provides detail in roof tops and background. The live-action component is being provided by a projector, left. In order for the artist to see the live-action image, a diffusion screen is introduced at the plane of the glass sheet onto which the painting is applied. Subsequently, the painted and live-action components can be fitted together either through (a) a combination of painting and rear projection (usually made in two separate passes through the camera), (b) bi-pack printing, or (c) optical printing. The gauge of the camera is 65 mm, and the projector's is variable 65/70 mm.

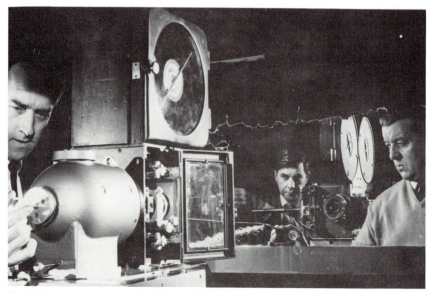

Fig. 6.16, part 2. Reverse angle of the set-up shown in the previous illustration. The 65/70 mm projector, left, has been brought abnormally close to the matte painting for demonstration purposes, and the diffusion screen onto which the live-action foreground element is projected is not shown. (The Rank Organization.)

Fig. 6.17. The late British visual-effects worker, Les Bowie, at work on one of several matte paintings for *Superman*, for which work he won an Academy Award. Of all the effects techniques available, matte painting is notably dependent upon the skill, experience and talent of a relatively small number of artists throughout the world who specialize in this kind of work.

paintings or master positives – the latter of which will ordinarily be used when the clouds are required to move.

If much work of this kind is anticipated, it would be worth building a library of photographed or hand-drawn cloud backgrounds which would offer different kinds of meteorological conditions and dramatic effects. Contrast filters can be used at the time that the cloud plates are shot to provide a variety of sky tones, while under-cranking of the motion-picture camera will increase the apparent speed of clouds.

Some care is necessary with this technique in blending together the skyline of the foreground and the cloud images. The most convincing blend will result when the matte-line area is clear of clouds and sky tone in both of the matted sections. When this is the case, the matte line should be drawn just above the landscape or cityscape detail so as to bisect a clear, density-free area of the sky. As is the case with clouds added through glass-shot techniques, close-ups and medium close-ups of actors can be combined with cloud backgrounds providing that the body of the actor remains within the main configuration of the cloud behind him.

A second matte-printing method may also be used to add clouds to foreground action, providing that the sky area in the master positive is absolutely clear and free of an image. This technique requires only one pass through the process camera.

An extra-sized painting, still-photograph print or diapositive is prepared, the top portion of which carries the image of clouds against an appropriately darkened sky, and the lower portion of which is dead-white. This photograph or painting is positioned so that the clear area near the middle blends naturally into the equally clear area just above the

Fig. 6.18, part 1. A common assignment – adding stories to a building which has been partially constructed on the sound-stage or back lot. Here, only the first story of what purports to be a large government building has been built and the top portion of the frame matted out during first printing.

Fig. 6.18, part 2. A test for the complete shot, with the upper section of the building added by the matte painter. The still-visible matte line will have to be removed. Paintings are usually used for this type of shot, but still photographs or miniatures can also be composited with full-scale, live-action shots.

foreground of the master positive. Inasmuch as the bottom part of the still photograph is dead-white, it provides an evenly-reflected light source to print the foreground part of the master positive to the dupe negative. As for the upper part of the cloud plate, the cloud image set against the darkened sky will print through the clear portion of the master positive, thus producing the composite.

Fig. 6.19, part 1. Components of an elaborate matte shot from the Twentieth Century-Fox production of *In Old Chicago* (1938). Only the first story of the full-scale building has been finished off. Here the crowd of extras is moved straight towards the artificial lake.

Fig. 6.19, part 2. The same extras are directed into the right-hand section of the frame and photographed on a separate piece of film, from the same camera position.

Control and correction of production lighting

The amount of care and attention which ordinarily goes into motion-picture lighting is far greater than in still photography, not merely because the camera and the actors are required to move, but also because of the inability of the cinematographer to correct the processed motion-picture negative for errors in lighting balance or accent. Mistakes do occur, however. Whereas the still photographer need only repair to his darkroom to exercise a number of controls during the projection printing process to

Fig. 6.19, part 3. The crowd is re-assembled and, for the third take, moves into the left-hand part of the picture.

Fig. 6.19, part 4. The final composite. The original group of extras has been multiplied three-fold and burning miniatures, properly scaled to match the foreground perspective, have been matted in above the first floor of the buildings. (All photos, Kenneth MacGowan Collection.)

rectify his errors, the motion-picture director of photography may have to re-shoot the whole scene.

Readers with experience as still photographers are doubtless familiar with the variety of techniques employed during the enlargement process to coax the best out of a recalcitrant negative. Overexposed areas are 'burnt in', while thin shadow areas are 'dodged'. Sky tone is darkened, particularly near the top of the frame and in the upper corners, while over-bright 'practical' lights (street lamps, lighted windows, neon lamps, etc.) are reduced in intensity. The objective of all these techniques is to

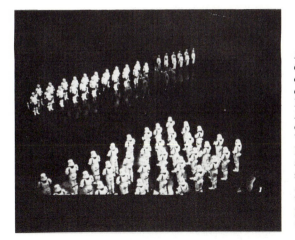

Fig. 6.20, part 1. Another example of the multiplication of crowds through visual-effects technique. For Lucasfilm's production of *The Return of the Jedi*, the story called for the arrival of Darth Vader and his associates at the Death Star station, where they are met by hundreds of Empire soldiers in military formation. Altogether, about 70 extras were posed appropriately and photographed here, as Vader and his officers walk past.

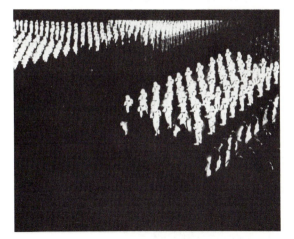

Fig. 6.20, part 2. The matte artist has added several hundred more soldiers, fitting them into their appropriate places within the frame.

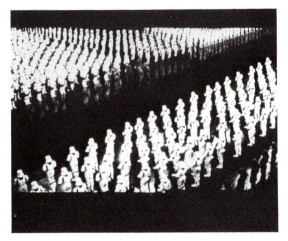

Fig. 6.20, part 3. The finished composite – a crowd scene with superlative production value, created at a fraction of the cost which would otherwise be involved with conventional photography. (Courtesy of Lucasfilm, Ltd.)

Fig. 6.21, part 1. Live-action components of a partially-constructed, full-scale set, photographed on the second stage.

Fig. 6.21, part 2. Final composite, with sections of the boat and harbor detail added by the matte painter. (Jack Rabin Studios.)

balance the tonal values in the scenes artistically and to correct carelessness in the original lighting and photography.

In motion-picture production, when the importance and value of an already-photographed but improperly-lit scene warrants the additional effort and expense, the same types of image manipulation as are used in still photography can be achieved through matte printing. The question which must be answered by the producer is whether it is possible to re-shoot the same scene, and, if so, whether it would be cheaper or more expensive to do so rather than to make the necessary corrections in the special-effects laboratory.

If it is decided to correct the scene through bi-pack printing, a master positive is struck from the production negative and is projected in normal fashion on to the matte-board. Assuming that we begin with a clean, white

121

Fig. 6.22, part 1. Re-creating a nineteenth-century Canadian street scene. First, a crowd of extras was photographed on the back lot from an elevated angle.

Fig. 6.22, part 2. A glass-painting of surrounding city detail. During the first printing, this painting was front-lit against a black background so that only the painted surround was recorded on the duplicating negative.

Fig. 6.22, part 3. During the second printing, a master positive of the live-action was printed onto the dupe negative. The glass painting, lit from behind, provided a printing light for the central live-action component, producing this composite.

Fig. 6.23, part 1. First exposure of a matte shot, with actors performing in a rowing boat chocked up on wood blocks, next to a studio building. The upper right portion of the shot has already been matted out.

Fig. 6.23, part 2. Painted component, with live-action matted out.

board, then over-bright areas in the original scene (i.e. insufficient highlight density in the master positive) can be held back and corrected by darkening the matte paper in those areas with pencil or charcoal. Sky tones can be selectively darkened through shading, or selected portions of the image can be rendered totally black, if desired, by using inks or paints. Such a technique comes in handy for darkening or replacing objectionable signs or other detail in long shots. It is even possible to remove and replace signs on *moving* vehicles providing the producer has the budget to afford frame-by-frame animation of a traveling matte.

For such a darkening of highlght areas, only one run through the camera with the master positive and dupe negative in bi-pack will be necessary.

Fig. 6.23, part 3. Painted and live-action composited. The lower section of the frame has been left clear to allow for addition of foreground detail.

Fig. 6.23, part 4. Final composite. A live-action shot of water has been matted into the foreground scene.

For the brightening of *shadow* areas, however, two runs are necessary. Either an animation cel can be prepared which is totally black except for the area of the projected master positive which needs brightening, or a cut-out matte can be made which is opaque except for the scissored-out matte area. Following the first run of the master positive and dupe negative through the camera using a blank-white matte-board, both strips are re-wound to start position and the master positive is removed. The dupe negative is then re-exposed again. Only the area which is to be brightened (i.e. made more dense on the dupe negative) will be printed this time, thus effecting a more even and pleasant balance of tonal values in the resulting scene.

Fig. 6.24, part 1. Painted-glass component of a shot designed to show an off-shore view of old Halifax. Printing procedures are identical to those described in the text for cut-out mattes.

Fig. 6.24, part 2. In the final composite, a live-action shot of water has been matted into the foreground area, and clouds have been added to the sky. (National Film Board of Canada.)

Bi-pack printing for color cinematography

Matte printing in color, when properly executed, can be especially effective, offering the same kinds of enhanced realism or increased opportunity for artistic experimentation as with in-the-camera techniques, and at a substantial reduction in time and cost. The ability to make the finished shot and to return the rushes of it to the director overnight, as well as the ability to re-make the composite, over and over, until it is perfect, all make the bi-pack printing process potentially more attractive than in-the-camera techniques for professional production.

Even today, however, the art of color cinematography remains an imprecise one. Even under ideal conditions, the duplication of color emulsions leaves much to be desired, due to losses in resolution and saturation, increases in graininess, and a general unpredictability of the resulting contrast and color balance.

Pigments on matte-boards do not always photograph and reproduce in the same way in which we see them. Extensive tests by artist and cameraman with different kinds of oils, pastels and watercolors will be necessary before confidence can be gained in the use and photography of these media. Special problems will be found in blending continuous colored tones from one matte area into another; whenever possible, matte lines should be drawn so as to sharply separate color values along natural breaks or divisions in the scene. For the printing of live-action components from color positives, the matte paper employed on the easels should be dead white in color, lest it impart an overall cast to the finished composite. Conversely, interesting experimental effects can be secured by purposely printing selected areas of the composite from colored mattes. It is even possible to print black-and-white positives on to color stocks, imparting a desired color to the different components through the selection of appropriate matte-board materials.

The use of 35 mm color negative as a production emulsion necessarily requires the use of an intermediate color positive (or of black-and-white separations) for matte printing. In color cinematography, far more than in black-and-white work, however, the stock which is used for original photography of the live action is not suited for the duplication printing of the color master of the painting, and vice-versa. It follows that one or the other – live action or painted surround – will suffer somewhat in quality when bi-pack printing is conducted in color. In most cases, the live-action component will be favored, which means that an appropriate intermediate color negative will be used in the process camera to print the production negative, and that the same stock will be used for the *original and direct* photography of the painting. Should this be the case, experience will have to be gained in estimating the effects produced by photographing certain hues in the oil-based paints with such a stock. Contrariwise, if the area occupied by the live-action component is relatively small compared with the painted element, it may be found desirable to use a conventional-production color negative, such as Eastman's type 5247, in the process camera, for both the photography of the painting and for the printing of the positive color master.

For all matte printing in color, accuracy in measurements, consistency in operations, standardization of technique, the keeping of meticulous records and a substantial amount of experimentation will be found necessary. The color temperature of the light falling on matte boards should be checked before each run is made to ensure a correct match with the emulsion being used. The well-equipped cinematographer will have a fairly complete set of color-correction filters on hand to make minute adjustments in the balance between light sources and film stocks. As in black-and-white work, it may be found desirable to run the matte-board lights off a voltage regulator. In color cinematography, differences between image elements in both brightness *and* color temperature can result from changes in line voltage. In all cases, the laboratory involved should be consulted for its recommendations.

7

Optical printing

Of all the special-effects tools in the professional film-maker's workshop, few are so versatile, none so frequently used as that of the optical printer. Virtually every film made in 35 mm, as well as many in the smaller gauge, passes through some kind of optical printing before it is complete, if only for its share of optical transitions. In its more versatile applications the optical printer is capable of space, time, and image manipulations which surpass the wildest dreams of Baron Munchausen. No matter how subtle or fantastic an imagined film effect may be, it can usually be realized through some sort of optical printing.

Surprisingly, many directors in both the theatrical and non-theatrical film industries have never seen an optical printer or watched it operate. Fewer still have a clear understanding of its principles and an appreciation of its capabilities for dramatic and pictorial embellishment.

Fundamentals of the process

In principle at least, there is nothing complicated about optical printing. In the early days of nineteenth-century photography, long before the Talbotype and other negative-positive contact-printing processes were introduced, optical printing provided the *only* means for producing copies from an original photograph. Even today, as with the Polaroid-Land system, a certain amount of printing is still done optically.

In still photography, the equipment used for such work is relatively simple. Assuming, for example, that we wish to copy an 8 × 10 inch positive transparency optically, we place the transparency in front of a light box, mount a conventional view camera on a tripod in front of the transparency, compose and focus the positive image on the camera's ground glass, balance the intensity of the light-box illumination with the lens aperture and shutter speed, insert the film, and make the exposure. What we have done, obviously, is to take a picture of a picture. The copy negative which results may now be printed conventionally in contact with a positive paper or transparency print. (If there were any good reason for doing so, it would even be possible to print the positives optically from the copy negative, tedious and time-consuming though it would be compared with contact printing.)

Assuming, in the previous example, that the selection of lens system, negative emulsion, exposure-illumination balance, and processing procedures are all appropriate to the copying job at hand, then a reasonably faithful copy of the original photograph is produced. Assuming, further, that the combination of film size, camera distance, and focal length of lens provide a 1:1 magnification, then the image recorded on the negative in the view camera is exactly the same size as that of the original transparency. By changing these variables, we may reduce the size of the original photograph so that it occupies only a portion of the 8 × 10 copy negative. Conversely, by changing the distance from the camera to the transparency and racking the optical system farther out, we may select only a portion of the original picture and magnify it to fill the entire 8 × 10 copy negative.

This example which has been provided represents optical printing at its simplest. Unfortunately, the process by which we record and reproduce photographs in *motion* involves so many other variables that optical printing for the cinema is rendered a vastly more complicated and expensive business (Fig. 7.1).

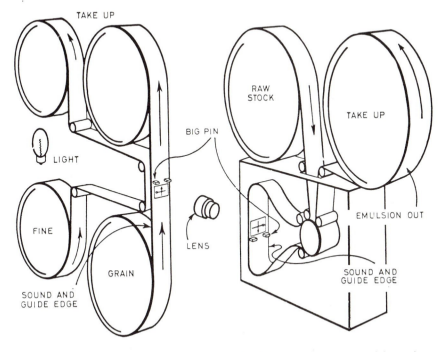

Fig. 7.1. The optical printer, diagramatically simplified. The process camera, at right, copies a color master (positive) in the printer head (sometimes called a 'projector head'), at left. In this sketch, the printer head is loaded in bi-pack for traveling-matte work, two strips of film passing through the movement at the same time. Note the reversal of pin positions from one intermittent to the other, and the dirction of film travel in the printer head ('heads up').

In the first place, we are copying not one but thousands of transparencies on to an equal number of copy negatives, the positive and negative images in each case being recorded continuously on flexible, perforated ribbons of film.

Secondly, both the positive transparencies and the copy negatives are in motion, relative to the camera, the optical system, the light box, and to each other. It is necessary (for conventional work) that as each positive transparency is replaced by a new one, so must a new copy negative be produced to record it, frame by frame, foot by foot.

Thirdly, it is imperative that the positions of images on both the positive transparency and the copy negative be maintained with great precision from frame to frame, relative to the perforations on both strips of film. In the copying of a still photograph, inasmuch as each picture is a unique and isolated creation, the exact position of the positive image as it is cast by the lens on to the copy negative is relatively unimportant from a technical point of view. In the optical printing of motion pictures, however, no single frame of picture stands alone, but exists only as one of several thousand other frames which immediately precede and follow it. Any variation in image registration between the transparency and copy negative films or in

Fig. 7.2. The Acme-Dunn printer – the first commercially 'mass-produced' optical printer. Manufactured for the armed forces during World War II, and introduced to the professional film industry shortly after the end of that war, it remained the industry standard for many years. The machine was designed by Linwood Dunn and Cecil Love, and won a technical Academy Award in 1944. This early Model 103 featured a single projector head. Many of these fine machines are still in operation throughout the world.

the relationship of the different images on each strip of film with respect to each other, will compromise the illusion of the motion-picture presentation – if it is bad enough, it will totally destroy it. Not only must intermittent movements of the highest quality be employed for both the positive transparency and the copy negative, but the machinery and transport systems through which they pass must be of massive construction, rigidly mounted, so as to reduce vibration.

Fourthly, unlike the large 8×10 transparency used in our earlier example, a motion-picture frame is relatively tiny. Because of its small size, special printing lenses are employed to secure 1:1 copying. Still higher magnifications require the use of extension tubes or bellows to 'rack-out' the lens from the camera. Such extensions may involve considerable light losses compared to conventional optical systems. These light losses, together with the need for shutter speeds far more rapid than are common in still photographic copying, demand the production of high light levels in our light box. Also, because of the small size of the transparency and the extent to which the optical system must be modified to produce even a 1:1 magnification, highest-quality optics are required in the design and operation of the printer.

Obviously, optical printing for the cinema is a considerably more formidable operation than that encountered in still photography. The equipment is difficult to design and expensive to construct. Very few small producers will ever find the means to build or purchase such a machine. Fortunately, however, there are numerous optical-effects organizations throughout the world which service the needs of the impecunious producer. By amortizing the cost of such equipment over a number of years and among their many customers, these firms are able to provide optical printing at reasonable rates. Optical printers can also be leased on a monthly or yearly basis.

The uses to which such machinery can be put depend entirely upon the particular design of the printer and the accessories which are used in conjunction with it. For this reason, it will be necessary to describe the apparatus in some detail before its applications can be considered.

Equipment availability

Reflecting the relatively small market, only a very few manufacturers fabricate optical printers for the professional trade. Their products are available for purchase or rental throughout the world, however, in both 35 mm and 16 mm gauges.

Perhaps the best-known and most popular of these brands are the Acme and Oxberry printers (Figs. 7.3 and 7.4). The Acme printer is sold by Hollywood Film Enterprises of Los Angeles. The Oxberry machine is available for sale or lease from the Oxberry Division of the Richmark Camera Co. of New Jersey. Other respected optical printers which have been manufactured and sold to the trade within recent years are those of the Pioneer/Trebes organization of Burbank, California and BHP of Chicago (Figs 7.5 and 7.6). In addition, many extremely fine optical

Fig. 7.3. A modern Acme step-optical special-effects printer, the Model 1002, employs two printer heads, aerial-image optics, electronic stepping motor drives, microcomputer follow focus on both aerial and main optical systems, tilting movements on camera and aerial image projector, and additive or subtractive lamp houses. The Acme printer is distributed by the Hollywood Film Company.

Fig. 7.4. Another modern dual-projector-head optical printer, the Model 7600 by Pioneer/Trebes Corporation, featuring an all-electronic drive system, automatic follow-focus, stepping-motor drives, and interchangeable 16/35 mm movements.

Fig. 7.5. The highly regarded Oxberry step-optical printer. This Model 5111-00 is designed principally for 1:1 and 2:1 printing. Massively built to reduce vibration, the weight of such a basic machine is about 1500 lb.

Fig. 7.6. Another excellent make of optical step-printer, manufactured and distributed by the BHP Corporation of Chicago. This is the Model 6212, featuring electronic dissolve, automatic camera zoom, and modular electronic drive system.

printers have been custom-built for particular studios or optical-effects houses, and are one-of-a-kind machines not available elsewhere.

All such machines are splendid designs. All, in their various models, offer substantially the same versatility in operation. All are quite expensive.

Whatever the brand or design employed, however, any optical printer intended for professional work incorporates a number of components which provide both for quality optical duplication and for flexibility of operation.

The process camera

The process camera has already been described in earlier chapters. For optical printing work, it must offer the highest-quality registration of film strips. Fixed pilot-pin movements which provide for registration tolerances in the order of ±0.0001 inch are employed. These movements must be capable of accepting both bi-pack and single-film loads without re-adjustment, and the camera must be capable of taking either two or four-chamber magazines. Because of the relatively high magnifications employed for such work, a reflex-type of viewfinder is most commonly used since it has less mass and produces less vibration in operation than a rack-over viewfinder. For unusually precise alignment in composing and focusing, provision is sometimes made for removal of the pressure plate in the intermittent movement and for focusing directly on ground glass or on the film itself, with a supplementary optical system. Other features of the process camera, which have been previously described, should also be provided, including a dissolving shutter, continuously variable from 0° to 170°, and provision for supplementary registration pins in the reflex viewer.

'Projector' or printer head

The master positive which is to be copied passes through mechanism called a 'projector' head or printer head (Fig. 7.7). Both terms are used synonomously in this chapter. Actually, the term 'projector' is a misnomer inasmuch as there is ordinarily no projection involved in optical printing, the only lens system involved being that of the process camera (except in aerial image printing. See page 232).

The intermittent movement of the printer head is a fixed pilot-pin design which must be manufactured to the same precise tolerances as that of the camera (Fig. 7.8). The back of the movement, ordinarily occupied by a pressure plate, is permanently removed so that illumination is allowed to strike and pass through the master positive from the rear.

Feed and take-up magazines, together with appropriate loop-forming sprocket drives, provide for 1000 ft single-film, 200 ft bi-pack, or 100 ft tri-pack operations. Film is fed and taken up automatically, usually by geared or torque-motor drives. The projector does not ordinarily incorporate a shutter, inasmuch as exposure control and dissolve

Fig. 7.7. Printer head on an Acme Model 102 optical printer. As with the camera, a Bell & Howell-type movement with fixed pilot pins is employed. Here, the printer head is loaded in bi-pack for traveling-matte work.

operations are conducted with the camera's equipment. Like the camera, the projector may be operated forward or reverse and at a variety of speeds.

Equipment support and movements

Both the process camera and the printer head are mounted on a massive support designed to provide precise movements of the components relative to one another and to reduce vibration during operation.

The camera is mounted on a small lathe-bed, the carriage of which is driven along rails by a worm-gear lead screw, towards and away from the projector (Fig. 7.9). In some models, the camera carriage may also be moved laterally and vertically, as well as being tilted through several degrees off the horizontal (Fig. 7.12).

Fig. 7.8. Intermittent movement and condensing optics in the printer head of a BHP optical printer. This particular machine allows the operator to view the entire width of the color master, including the edge numbers, so as to facilitate selection and positioning of particular frames in the projector-head aperture.

The projector head is usually attached to the printer by means of a dovetail plate assembly. This plate is part of a compound-movement mount which allows for vertical, lateral, and small tilt movements of the projector. In some models, the projector may be removed from the printer and replaced by another head of a different-gauge film. In such models, the camera can also be replaced for different film size requirements, allowing for 35 mm/35 mm, 16 mm/35 mm, and 35 mm/16 mm copying (provision for reduction to 8 mm or enlargement to 65 mm is also available). In other designs, this multi-gauge versatility is achieved by replacing only the intermittent movements, sprocket assemblies and magazines rather than the entire camera and projector.

Either micrometer-type, dial gauges or LED digital electronic counters are provided on the printer to indicate exact positions of the process camera, the printer head, the lens assembly, and the various accessories, to average tolerances of ±0.001 inch. (A few custom-built printers have achieved a precision in component positioning of ±0.0001 inch.) These controls are crucial to the daily business of 'line-up', whereby the particular configuration and position of the various components is produced by a technician each time a different printer operation is begun. The line-up of

Fig. 7.9. Projector head and camera of a typical optical printer. Both the camera and its bellows-extension lens can be moved towards and away from the printer head on geared mounts. Micrometer gauges indicate positions of the various components. (BHP Corporation.)

Fig. 7.10. Acme camera, with its door open, on a Model 6213 BHP optical printer.

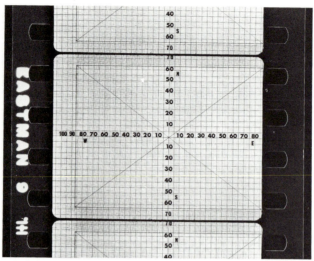

Fig. 7.11. An example of the high-resolution images produced by modern optical printers and their lenses is this film-clip image of a lens-test 'target'.

Fig. 7.12. On many optical printers, the process camera can be tilted through several degrees on its optical axis. This Model 102 Acme optical printer allows for up to 35° tilts, clockwise or counter-clockwise, electronically programmed.

the printer for a complicated series of shots can take as long as an hour or more.

The entire camera and projector assembly is rigidly mounted on a heavy metal base which houses the electrical controls, circuitry and motors. The combined weight of base and components may reach nearly a ton, but the resulting loss in portability is more than compensated for by the freedom from vibration which is achieved. Typical dimensions of a basic optical

Fig. 7.13. Some printers, such as this Oxberry, allow for tilts of *both* the camera *and* projector, through several degrees.

printer are approximately 6 ft in height, 5½ ft in length and 2½ ft in depth, although multi-headed printers are much larger. The working space between camera and projector averages about 26–28 inches on most printers, leaving room for installation of large anamorphic lenses and special optical accessories.

Motor drives

Power for the camera, printer head and related accessories is often provided by motors located in the base of the printer, and delivered to the components by gear, shaft, and chain-linked drives. Some of the newer designs dispense with mechanical linkages by replacing them with solid-state electronic components, and by powering the camera and printer heads, the optical system, and the various accessories directly with separate stepper motors. Such a design eliminates most mechanical backlash and vibration, and generally makes for greater speed, simplicity, and efficiency in operations. Modern printers such as these are frequently controlled by computers, the software of which allows for repeatable, motion-control of all moving parts of the printer. These computers can be made to generate hard-copy count-sheets of the various moves and operations. With their use, a 'line-up' procedure which might take an hour under ordinary circumstances can often be executed automatically by the computer within minutes.

Both camera and printer may be operated forward or reverse, in the same or contrary directions, at speeds ranging from 2½ to 40 ft per minute. By viewing the film through the camera's reflex finder during rewinding, the entire assembly can be used as a sort of moviola for the rapid selection of particular frames. Both camera and projector drives may be disengaged to allow for manual operation if desired.

Separate drives provide power for the automatic focus and diaphragm controls and for accessory mechanical traveling-matte and optical-distortion accessories mounted in the projector head, or between camera and projector.

Fig. 7.14. A typical console for optical-printer operations. The Acme Model 1002.

Controls

Located on the front of the optical printer are various controls by means of which an almost infinite number of effects can be executed (Figs. 7.14 and 7.15). Switches provide for forward and reverse operation of camera and projector, either in the same direction with respect to one another, or in different directions. In the case of a computer-controlled printer, instructions are entered by means of a keyboard.

Fig. 7.15. Control panel of the Pioneer/Trebes printer. Increasingly, the operation of modern optical printers is microcomputer-controlled.

Rewinding in either forward or reverse directions is controlled typically by a single lever, the amount of pressure on it determining the speed of the film.

Skip-frame switches allow for the photography of every second, third, fourth, and other combination of frames in the projector while the camera runs continuously; conversely, the projector may be operated continuously while the camera skips frames. Multiple printing of selected frames in the projector by a continuously-running camera may also be achieved in any number of combinations through appropriate circuit switching. Both camera and projector may be pre-set to start or stop together or separately at any particular footage and frame count.

The automatic dissolving shutter of the camera is also operated from the console, producing fades and dissolves from 8 to 128 frames in length. Shorter or longer dissolves, as well as special non-linear dissolves, can be executed manually or through special programming of the machine (Fig. 7.16).

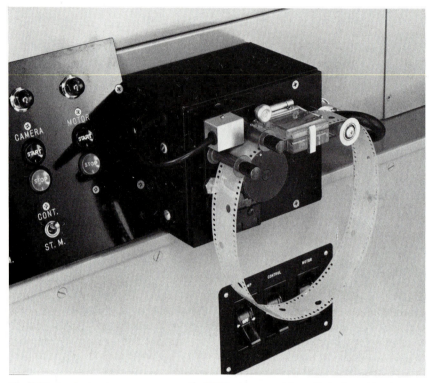

Fig. 7.16. An electronic programmer on the BHP printer provides unlimited combinations for skip-frame and multiple-frame printing, and for different lengths of fades and dissolves. Operations are programmed by punching holes in a continuous loop of 35 mm film.

Additional controls operate the accessories, the automatic lens diaphragm, and the follow-focus mechanism of lens and camera. The vertical and lateral movements of both projector head and camera lens are ordinarily adjusted manually, although they can be computer-controlled.

Frame and footage counters are positioned throughout the equipment, indicating both magazine and sequence footage counts for camera and projector, cumulative footage for the entire printer, and special footage counts for automatic stop-start operations.

Optical system

Various focal lengths and optical designs are available for different types of printing requirements. Whatever the characteristics of the lens system employed, the quality of optics must be the best obtainable. Because of the magnifications involved, high-resolution lenses should be employed which are relatively free of spherical aberration, coma and curvature of field. Inasmuch as color emulsions will be frequently copied, the same lenses should be free of chromatic aberrations, chromatic difference of magnification, and noticeable color cast. If oversized, Vistavision-type formats are to be used in the printer, care must be taken to select lenses which are capable of covering the increased size of the format with high resolution. Some lenses employed for optical printer work are capable of resolving 180 lines/mm without distortion.

Typical lens designs recommended' for different types of printing requirements include the following:

For 1:1 copying – a 103 mm $f/2.8$ Printing Ektar or Nikor.
For blow-up or reduction copying – a 90 mm $f/3.5$ Printing Ektar or Nikor.
For zooms and variable magnification work – a 100 mm $f/4.5$ Printing
 Ektar or Nikor.

Several manufacturers make high-quality lenses suitable for optical printing. Ektars and Nikors are cited as examples here because they are standard equipment on many optical printers.

Either tubes or bellows extensions may be used to 'rack-out' the camera lens for variable magnifications. Fixed-focal-length printing lenses are usually employed when the printer is intended for more or less permanent service at particular magnifications: 1:1, straight reduction, or straight blow-up printing. For work of a more complicated nature, the lens is mounted on a bellows extension or in a movable tube. Printer lenses are focused by being moved straight in and out, rather than by rotation. This kind of movement guarantees that both the optical and mechanical axes of the lens will be coincident and that the lens may be focused without causing a circular movement of the field around the horizontal axis. A versatile printer will offer magnification ranges from 1:3 enlargement, through 1:1, and down to 4:1 reduction.

Changes in magnification, in focus, and in the selection of portions of the master positive image may be made by racking the lens system towards or away from the printer head, together with appropriate movements of the camera. For continuous magnification changes such as zooms, automatic focusing is provided.

Because of the high magnification involved, any changes in bellows or tube extension reduces or increases the intensity of light reaching the film; accordingly, automatic diaphragm adjustments are made by the printer to compensate for varying lens extensions. Both the automatic diaphragm and focus adjustments may be disengaged and operated manually for out-of-focus effects if desired.

The lens mount at the forward end of the bellows is of a compound movement type and allows not only for longitudinal movements towards and away from the projector, but for vertical and lateral movements as well. Micrometer dial-type gauges indicate lens movements in the order of ±0.001 inch (Fig. 7.18). A few custom-built printers, such as those used at ILM for Lucasfilm Productions, move the projector head relative to a fixed lens position, rather than the other way around.

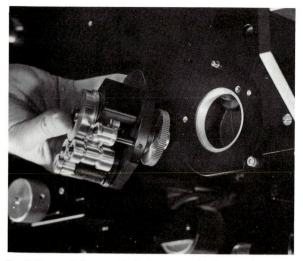

Fig. 7.17, part 1. Some optical printers provide for easy interchangeability of sprocket drives and intermittent movements so as to allow for either 16 mm or 35 mm operation. The sprocket unit shown here is part of a BHP printer.

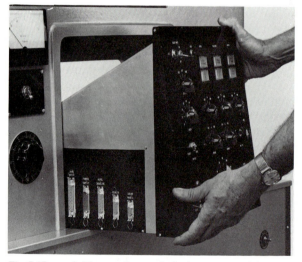

Fig. 7.17, part 2. Most modern optical printers are modular in design. Here, the entire electronic control module is removed in one piece for either repair or replacement.

Lamp house

A fairly high intensity of controlled light is required to illuminate the master positive during printing operations. This is provided by a standard pre-focus bulb, ranging in size from 300 to 1000 watts, mounted in the lamp house which is situated directly behind the projector head (Fig. 7.19). A condenser system produces a collimated, high-intensity, evenly-illuminated field of light over the entire frame area. Some condenser

Fig. 7.18. Lens assembly on an Oxberry printer. Controls allow for longitudinal, vertical and lateral movements of the lens. Dial gauges indicate exact positions of the lens to tolerances of ±0.001 in. Relative aperture is automatically adjusted as the lens is racked in and out.

Fig. 7.19. Lamp-house assembly on a Model 102 Acme printer. Slots in the lamp housing allow for insertion of neutral density or color-correction filters. The lamp house takes a standard Tru-focus C13D lamp. The voltage of the printing lamp is regulated by a voltage stabilizer, voltmeter and variable transformer built into the printer.

systems produce an oval spot of light which more nearly conforms to the dimensions of the film frame than a round one. Standard condensing optics usually incorporate a ground-glass diffusion element to provide evenness of illumination. Some printers, however, employ specially-designed achromatic condensers, corrected for spherical aberrations, coma, and chromatic aberrations, which may be used without a diffusing glass, thereby producing a considerably greater output of light. The use of such condensers produces very high light levels at the projector's film plane, despite the relatively low size of bulbs employed. A light meter and a set of special probes are provided with some printers by means of which footcandle levels can be read at the film plane of either the projector or the camera.

A blower system mounted below the lamp house, and heat-absorbing filters located in the condensing optical system, reduce the amount of heat delivered at the film plane of the projector, an important function in those cases when a single frame of master positive must be held in the projector's intermittent for a prolonged period of time.

Fig. 7.20. A variety of accessories are offered for all makes of optical printers which speed operations and extend the versatility of the equipment. This model 900 Film Gate Photometer allows for direct reading of both white-light illuminance and color primaries at the film gate, by means of a probe. The device assists operators in judging the proper printer exposure and color balance for particular runs of the equipment. Since the light is measured directly at the film gate at regular intervals, this system permits compensation for faded filters, changing light sources, variations in print stock, and numerous other conditions. (Hollywood Film Company.)

Fig. 7.21. An inexpensive, but fully professional, optical printer for 16 mm work, manufactured by J-K Camera Engineering, Inc. Projector head, right, and camera, left, can be operated in synchronism or independently of one another, in forward or reverse modes. Maximum synchronous speed is 50 frames per minute. With a 50 mm lens on the camera, the rig is capable of an image magnification and reduction range of from 1:4 through 4:1. Exposure is controlled with either neutral density filters or with the diaphragm of the camera lens. The printer head features a fixed-pin registration movement.

Fig. 7.22. This one-of-a-kind 16 mm to 35 mm optical printer was made from an antiquated projector and camera, pieces of wood, and scraps of tinker-toy metal, by technicians at the British Film Institute. For all of that, it is fully professional, and has performed admirably in the salvage printing of rare footage for the National Film Archive.

Provision must be made for proper adjustment of the bulb within the lamp house with respect to the position of the filament and its reflection by the lamp house's spherical mirror. The entire lamp-house assembly must be designed for operations with color emulsions. A voltage regulator is usually employed in the circuitry together with a variable transformer; together, they ensure consistent and exact color temperatures for the printing of modern color stocks. The voltage at which the lamp house bulb operates is assumed to be a fixed value in normal operations. All variations in exposure are achieved by inserting neutral-density filters into the light source or by varying the camera shutter opening, camera speed, or relative aperture.* Attempts to control exposure by varying the lamp house voltage affect the color temperature of illumination and will necessarily compromise the quality of the optical print; any distortions of color temperature which may be *desired* can be achieved, subtractively, by inserting the appropriate filters into the optical system.

Alternatively, the printer can be equipped with a so-called 'additive' lamp house, within which are operated three separate light sources. The light from each of these is filtered with a different sharp-cutting additive (red-green-blue) filter. By varying individual shutters, which are placed between these three additive light sources and the main condenser system of the lamphouse, an unlimited range of precisely-controlled, repeatable color changes can be introduced into the printer's frame-by-frame operations.

Accessories

A mechanically-operated, traveling-matte device is mounted in front of the projector's intermittent movement and offers wipe-offs in all directions and with any desired softness of edge. Many wipe blades are available and their movement and adjustment is accomplished either automatically or manually, in repeatable frame-by-frame steps. The same device will also accept fixed mattes and counter-mattes of a variety of shapes. The 'wipe-offs' produced by this device should not be confused with 'push-offs' which require movement of the camera or projector head and which are described later.

A flip-lens attachment mounts between the camera lens and the projector head. This consists of a supplementary optical system mounted on gimbals. So long as the attachment's lens is positioned in line with that of the camera, the master positive image is transmitted without distortion. By moving the supplementary lens in its mount, however, it is possible to flip a shot vertically or horizontally on the centre lines of the frame.

An image spin device mounts in place of the projector movement and *mechanically* rotates a single frame of film on the centre of its aperture, clockwise or counter-clockwise. The same effect can be achieved by means of an *optical* spin attachment which, like the flip-lens device, is placed between the camera's lens and the projector head. By rotating this device, it is possible to spin or rock the image without actually moving either the camera or projector.

---

* Exposure adjustments for optical printing are ordinarily made with neutral-density filters. Changes in relative aperture are likely to affect image contrast.

Operating the printer

Unlike the operation of a standard projector, all film passing through the projector head of the optical printer moves 'heads up', passing from the lower magazine, through the intermittent movement, to the upper magazine. In this manner, an erect positive image is presented in proper frame sequence to the camera's optical system (Fig. 7.1).

Fig. 7.23, part 1. This simple optical printer was designed by a film student and an engineering student at the University of Iowa. It employs an old silent 16 mm projector for a printer head, and a 16 mm Arriflex for a camera. The projector's lens has been removed and discarded. An auxiliary lens set midway between the camera's lens and the projector allows for sharp focus upon the film in the projector's gate. A motor control allows either for independent operation of the camera and projector motors, or operation of the two in synchronism. All of the components – printer head, camera, and auxiliary lens – can be moved towards and away from one another on the optical bench support, thereby increasing or decreasing the area of the film in the printer head which is re-photographed. Although the registration accuracy of such a design does not allow for the more complicated 'repeat-run' jobs, much good work can be done with a simple rig such as this.

Fig. 7.23, part 2. Close-up of the auxiliary lens and its mount, showing adjustment controls which allow for East-West, North-South movements.

As with all other special-effects processes which involve duplication, the location of the pilot pins with respect to the aperture must be standardized and maintained from one piece of cinematographic machinery to the next. Any variations in registration-pin position between one strip of film and another can be dealt with, however, by stocking and employing a set of different intermittent movements for both process camera and projector. A complete set will offer not only different pin-registration positions but also different sound-track positions and varying aperture sizes.

Fig. 7.24. Another 'home brew' job, this time built by Industrial Light and Magic Company for LucasFilm's productions of *Star Wars* and *The Empire Strikes Back.* The printer was built solely to blow-up footage of explosions, pyrotechnics, and 'star bursts' on 16 mm film to 35 mm Vistavision format, for use as image 'accents' in selected shots in the feature films. Although something of a 'Rube Goldberg' contraption in appearance, it does the job quite professionally.

By the use of such different movements, the registration characteristics of an original piece of footage may be changed through optical printing to conform to another operational standard. A problem might arise, for example, in which a background plate, shot on a camera with Mitchell-type registration (see page 20), must be subsequently run on a background projector employing Bell & Howell-type registration. In such a case, the negative of the plate (Mitchell registration) is placed in the printer head and copied optically onto a positive in the camera, the latter of which employs an intermittent movement which registers the film above the aperture so as to conform to the Bell & Howell registration to be employed later in the background projector. Alternatively, one could go through a complete generation of duplication by making a master positive from the original negative (Mitchell registration) and then optically printing a dupe negative which is registered above the aperture (Bell & Howell), and from which the positive print for the background projector is struck.

Plotting the printing operations

In even the simplest optical printing operation, a certain amount of planning is necessary to prepare the color masters to determine the sequence and nature of effects, and to programme the printer.

At least two systems are commonly employed to plot and indicate such effects. The first utilizes the 'edge' or 'key' numbers which are printed through to the emulsion of the color master from the original negative (alternatively, the color master's own latent image key numbers can be used, if desired). These key numbers change their last digit with each foot of running footage (Fig. 7.25). Reference to such key numbers provides a

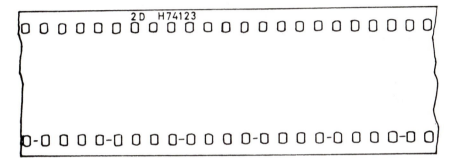

Fig. 7.25. Negative and master positive stocks in both 35 mm and 16 mm gauges carry edge numbers ('key numbers'), the last digit of which changes with each running foot. These allow for precision in plotting and programming optical-printer operations. The letter(s) preceding these numbers identify the type of raw stock. The small black dashes at the lower edge of the frame indicate frame separations, every four perforations, on 35 mm stocks. These are useful, while threading film into the camera and printer heads, in preserving frame-line and pin positions. (Eastman Kodak.)

foolproof way in which to designate exact stop-start maneuvers in even the most complicated kind of optical printing. If desired, special runs of 'code numbers' may also be sequentially printed with ink on color masters, the last digit changing with every foot as in the case of key numbers. Fig. 7.26 shows a typical optical-effects order sheet which employs key numbers.

A second method for plotting printing operations depends upon running footage and frame counts computed from a start position which is punched or drawn on leader attached to each roll of film which passes through the printer. A 'bar sheet' is prepared which indicates the desired manipulations of frame sequence and image for each strip of film ('A' roll, 'B' roll, etc.).

Either kind of optical order form may be employed, depending upon the preferences of the laboratory and the film-maker. In either case, the dupe negative passing through the process camera will nearly always have a start mark punched into it, to which the camera's footage counter is zero-set, so as to aid the printer's operator in relating the movements of the dupe negative in the process camera to that of the color master strips in the projector head. Whether key numbers or bar sheets are employed, the shots to be printed may be either separated into different rolls or spliced together, heads to tails, with blank leader separating the different shots.

150

Fig. 7.26. A typical optical-effects work order which employs edge numbers

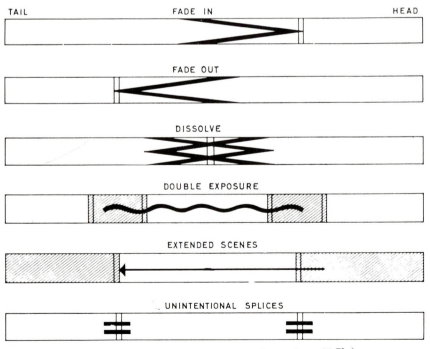

Fig. 7.27. Standard methods of marking workprints to indicate effects. (ACL.)

Depending upon the kind of effect desired, either the editorial staff or the special-effects department will design and lay out the particular effects operations required. In the case of simple transition, such as fades, dissolves and superimpositions, this work is usually performed by the editor's assistant in conformity with grease pencil, cado pen, or scribe marks laid on to the production work print by the supervising editor (Fig. 7.27).

In all but experimental work, optical printing requires the use of fine-grain, high-resolution duplicating stocks for the printing of both color masters and color internegatives. Once the printing operations have been completed, the quality of the resulting image depends entirely upon the skill, care, and consistency of laboratory processing provided. Considerable experimentation will be necessary in setting up new routines and in establishing a working relationship with the laboratory personnel.

The image, space, and time manipulations which are possible through optical printing are so infinitely varied that only a few of its more obvious uses can be suggested here. Once the range and technique of the process are understood, its application to particular problems naturally follows.

Optical transitions

Perhaps as much as 80 per cent of the optical printer's mechanical life is devoted to the preparation of optical transitions: fades, dissolves, wipes, and 'push-offs'. Prosaic and conventional as this type of work may be, it represents the machine's most important contribution to the motion-picture story-telling art. Indeed, some optical printers are built to offer only 1:1 copying and are devoted entirely to this routine chore.

Prior to the perfection of optical printing, all of the simpler transitions had to be done in the camera, while the more complicated ones had to be foregone entirely. The production of a fade-in or fade-out in the camera required that those artistic and dramatic controls over timing, pacing, and emphasis which are properly left to the editor had to be irrevocably executed by the director during the photography of a single shot. Once made, there was no provision for altering or removing the fade. At best, the process was imprecise; at worst, it could negate all of the director's intentions in the putting-together of a complete sequence.

The making of dissolves in the camera was totally impractical for professional work, since it required that both the outgoing and incoming shots be perfectly synchronized by the camera operator, that they occur at exactly the right position for editorial purposes, and that the action be perfectly performed in both shots. If any of these conditions failed to materialize, both of the shots had to be completely re-staged. With the introduction of the optical printer, however, all of these transitions, together with many more intricate ones, have become routine techniques in professional production. (For all 35 mm work, as well as for 16 mm black-and-white productions, virtually all transitions are produced through optical printing. For 16 mm reversal color production, however, transitions are usually made by 'A' and 'B'-roll contact printing.)

The transitionary purposes to which such effects are put are so well known as to hardly require elaboration here. Whereas a straight cut ordinarily suggests a change of view or locale which is instantaneous in time, a dissolve (sometimes called a lap-dissolve) or a 'wipe' suggests a time lapse of relatively short duration. Fades in and out between sequences indicate still longer periods of elapsed time. These effects are conventions which audiences have been educated to accept and understand. The lapse of time in each case is always relative and depends entirely upon the structure of the film, its pacing, and the story line involved.

Fades

To produce a fade with an optical printer, the machine is first adjusted for 1:1 printing ratio. For a two-second fade-in (48 frames), the master positive is re-photographed on to the dupe negative with the shutter of the process camera being full-closed at the beginning of the shot and gradually opening with the copying of each successive frame until the 49th frame and all subsequent ones are copied with full and proper exposure. A fade-out is produced in just the reverse manner.

Dissolves

Dissolves are made by double-printing a fade-in of the incoming shot with a fade-out of the outgoing scene. The master positive of the outgoing shot is first copied on to the dupe negative, the process camera's shutter closing a predetermined degree with each passing frame, and the effect beginning and ending at pre-determined frames as indicated on the editor's work sheet. With the camera's shutter full-closed, the dupe negative is then backed up in the camera to the dissolve's start mark. The master positive of the outgoing shot is removed and replaced with that of the incoming scene. Once the incoming footage is positioned so that its start mark conforms to the editor's instructions, both camera and projector are again set running, this time with the camera's shutter gradually opening, in exactly the same fashion as prevailed in the previous run, until full exposure is given to the incoming shot.

Inasmuch as laboratories charge a running footage fee in addition to a set charge for each effect, some producers try to save money by ordering only the exact footage of the dissolve (plus three or four frames on each side for splicing purposes) and then direct the negative cutter to intercut the dupe negative of the effect with the original negatives of the incoming and outgoing shots. This practice is not to be recommended, inasmuch as the unavoidable differences in grain, contrast, and resolution between the original and the dupe negatives are often apparent on the screen and causes the transitionary footage to 'pop' in and out. If is far better to duplicate the entire incoming and outgoing footage, even though the laboratory cost will be slightly higher. The slight overall degradation in image quality which results is far less noticeable than degradation of the dissolve alone.

Conventional fades and dissolves run from 24 to 48 frames; however, they may be shortened or extended to whatever length pleases the director and editor. At the one extreme, we find exceptionaliy long dissolves of the sort employed by George Stevens in *A Place in the Sun*, some of which ran

15 feet, and more. At the other extreme, we have very short dissolves, sometimes called 'soft cuts', which run between 6 and 12 frames in length. 'Soft cuts' are usually used to take the place of direct cuts when mismatches in action ('jump cuts') occur between shots in the same sequence and when it is neither feasible nor economical to re-photograph the original action. The 'soft cut' is particularly useful in the editing of animal or newsreel footage in which it is often impossible to match action between shots.

If desired, both fades and dissolves may be executed so that the progression of shutter openings from frame to frame is arithmetically linear, each change in shutter aperture, whether increasing or decreasing, being incrementally equal in degrees to the previous change. In producing dissolves, however, it has been found that a smoother, more pleasing effect can be gained if a non-linear progression of shutter openings is used in the mixing of both incoming and outgoing shots. In practice, the various frames of the dissolve are printed with increases and decreases in shutter openings which are not equal to one another. The result is a progression of cumulative densities which allow for a very gradual introduction and elimination of the incoming and outgoing shots (Fig. 7.28).*

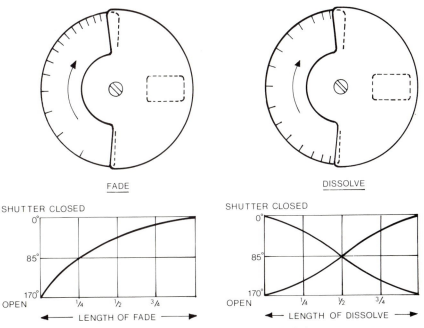

Fig. 7.28. Fade and dissolve curves for the variable shutter of the Oxberry process camera.

Both linear and non-linear dissolves can be easily programmed into the printer's automatic operation, usually by changing a cam in the variable-shutter mechanism. By disengaging the automatic dissolve, special non-linear dissolves may be executed manually.

* The reasoning behind this practice is lucidly explained in a short note by Brian G. D. Salt, entitled 'Mathematics in aid of animation', published in Halas and Manvell, *The Technique of Film Animation* (New York: Hastings House, 1959), pp. 323–28.

Wipes

For transitionary purposes, a wipe serves the same function as a dissolve – the indicating of relatively short lapses of time between sequences. Whereas a dissolve 'mixes' the outgoing and incoming scene together by superimposition, a wipe replaces one scene with another by means of a moving optical edge – straight or configured – which passes through or across the scene, progressively revealing the new scene and removing the old. The effect is illustrated in Fig. 7.29. Movement continues within each component; however, neither of the two images involved in the wipe actually move across the screen – only the optical wipe-edge moves.

Simple wipes may be produced mechanically with the accessory device which is mounted on the optical printer between the camera and the projector head. In practice, the wipe blade is moved across the field of view in synchronism with the frame-by-frame movements of the master positive and dupe negative. For a right-to-left lateral wipe, lasting two seconds (48 frames), the distance which the wipe blade must travel from one side of the frame to the other is divided into 48 increments. The color master of the outgoing scene is copied conventionally by the process camera until the start frame of the wipe is reached, at which point the wipe blade is manually or automatically moved through its 48-step movement, one increment of movement occuring with each change of frame. At its last position, the wipe blade totally obscures the aperture of the printer head.

The dupe negative is then re-wound 48 frames, and the color master of the outgoing shot is replaced with that of the incoming.

For the second exposure, the wipe blade again travels right to left, but this time progressively *reveals* the second shot in its 48-step movement, from a totally obscured aperture at the beginning to a completely revealed one at the end. Naturally, the changes in blade position, from right to left, must conform exactly to those of the first exposure. The positions of the blade can be determined and set to tolerances of about ±0.001 inch on most printers.

Ordinarily, the wipe blades are positioned next to the intermittent movement of the printer head, thus producing a sharp edge. Any degree of softness may be secured, however, by moving the wipe device away from the master positive. Using this device, wipes may be made to move in any direction, vertically and horizontally as well as diagonally. Using two blades, the wipe can be made to proceed from any two sides of the frame towards the middle, or vice versa. More complicated wipes which involve spiralling, expanding, dissolving, exploding, and rolling effects usually require the use of traveling mattes. These are described and illustrated in Chapter 8.

During the 1930s, the wipe gained great popularity in motion-picture circles for its novelty value. In the intervening years, however, it has been so overworked that it is now a cliché. Unlike the dissolve, the wipe is relatively brazen in the performance of its transitionary function. The device is still widely employed in the production of television commercials, trailers, and 'Previews of coming attractions', for which work it is ideally suited.

Fig. 7.29. A simple transitionary wipe.

Used with restraint, the wipe can also be employed effectively in conventional film production. In all cases, the movement and character of the wipe should be appropriate to the action on the screen. A shot of an automobile moving laterally across the screen might be 'wiped' away to the next shot by a wipe-edge which follows behind the car and moves in the same direction. The same technique is frequently used with shots of lifts, in order to bridge the time lapse between floors.

Push-offs

Similar in effect to the wipe, but different in appearance, is the 'push-off'. Whereas the images in a wipe do not move across the screen, those of the push-off do. The incoming shot appears to push the outgoing shot off the screen, just as sliding doors emerge and recede into the frame and wall area of a door. As in the case of the wipe, action *within* the frame continues throughout the effect.

The push-off is achieved by moving the printer head which carries the color master (or, alternatively, by moving the camera or its lens).

During first exposure, the printer head is moved from right to left a given increment of distance for each frame of positive which is printed. The outgoing scene therefore appears to slide leftward, off the screen. During the second pass, the printer head carries the incoming color master image, again from right to left, but this time emerging from the right side of the frame and passing left until it fills the screen entirely. If the movements of the printer head are properly matched during first and second printings, the second scene will appear to push the first off the screen. Push-offs can also move left to right and vertically as well as horizontally.

Frame sequence and direction alterations

One of the assumptions on which all conventional film production proceeds is that the cameras on the set will operate at the same frame rate as the projector in the theatre, thus ensuring a normal reproduction of motion on the screen. During optical printing, however, the original frame rate can be altered so that the action is speeded up, slowed down, reversed or even stopped. The first of these is effected by skip-framing.

Skip-framing

In order to skip-frame the action to twice-normal speed (which is the same effect as originally undercranking the camera at 12 frames per second), the process camera on the printer is set to photograph every other frame of film which passes through the projector's intermittent. In practice, the color master in the projector is set to run twice as fast as the dupe negative in the process camera, the camera's shutter opening only during the registration of alternate frames of master positive.

By further varying the relative speeds of printer head and process camera, time may be compressed still further. If we re-photograph every fourth frame of the color master we speed up the resulting screen action to four times normal, and achieve the same effect as if we had originally undercranked the production camera at 6 frames per second.

This technique allows us to increase the apparent speed of automobiles, trains, aircraft, machines, clouds, waves, fire, explosions, and other environmental phenomena which operate too slowly in the original photography to suit the editorial or dramatic character of a scene. For the purposes of motion analysis in science and industry, time-lapse compressions of a lengthy series of events can be achieved by re-photographing only every 20th, 40th or other sequence of frames. Comedy effects of many sorts can be realized by the same technique, either by increasing the apparent speed of actors two or three times, or by varying the speed of their movements within the same shot – first faster, then slower. For compression effects in which comedy is *not* intended, however, it is best to select scenes in which humans are either not seen or are relatively immobile, inasmuch as even twice normal speed renders normal human behavior ludicrous.

Skip-frame printing can also be used to add realism to the performance of fights, falls, automobile accidents, and other impact action in which the performed event is too hazardous to be executed at normal speed. The producer's stunt-man may take his fall down a flight of stairs at a leisurely and relatively safe speed; by skip-framing the resulting action, a velocity can be achieved which will satisfy even the most demanding director. Using the same technique, 'the fastest gun in the west' can be helped to draw his six-shooter a shade faster than the villain. Whoever controls the optical printer always wins the shootout.

Multiple printing

If, instead of speeding up the action, we find it necessary to slow it down, we may do so by reversing the process just described. By setting the process camera to photograph each frame of the color master more than once, we retard the apparent motion on the screen in proportion to the number of times each frame is repeated. For example, by copying each frame of the color master on three successive frames of dupe negative, we achieve a slow-motion effect similar to that obtained if our production camera had originally operated at 72 frames per second.

As in the case of skip-framing, the slowing-down of action through multiple printing may be used for either editorial or dramatic purposes. Scenes which are too short for the editor's taste can be prolonged to twice their normal length. This can be done even though actors appear in the scenes, since slowness in human locomotion appears much less eccentric than does rapidity. By changing the frame-sequence relationships of process camera and projector within a single shot through multiple and skip-frame printing, automobiles and other moving objects can be made to either accelerate or decelerate, providing the printing multiples used for deceleration do not become so high that jerkiness results.

Multiple printing adds realism to the movement of miniatures which were allowed to operate too fast in the original photography. Similarly, explosions and other very rapid events may be dramatically retarded.

Slow-motion studies of athletic events can be simulated by the same technique, although there are limits to which normally-photographed action can be extended without the technique becoming apparent to the audience. True slow-motion photography produces a greater than normal number of frames in recording a given action, each frame of which presents a slight but noticeable difference in object position. Multiple printing, however, prolongs each of a normal number of frames which were originally photographed at regular camera speed. If a single frame of action is presented to the audience too many times in succession, jerkiness in the overall movement will be noticed, particularly in the presentation of familiar actions. In addition, the grain structure of each image may become apparent.

Special problems arise in the restoration of silent films, originally shot at 16 frames per second, for sound-on-film versions presented at 24 frames per second. Inasmuch as the ratio of frame rates is not that of an even multiple, a mathematically correct conversion would require that successive frames of the original be re-photographed in a 2:1 printing sequence, printing the first frame once, the second frame twice, the third frame once, and so forth. The result is not attractive on the screen, however, since it obviously alters the normal movements of objects in an alternately accelerating and decelerating manner. The best solution in such cases is to rephotograph each frame twice, thus producing a moderate slow-motion effect and increasing the original running time of the production by a factor of one half.

Finally, through special programming of the optical printer, either skip-framing or multiple printing may be used to alter the spacial relationships of objects in motion. Given a scene in which automobiles at a race-track or a flight of aircraft in the sky pass in front of the camera, the intervals between these objects can be extended or compressed. In the race-track scene, we may extend the intervals between cars by double- or triple-framing the view of the track and spectators which is seen after each of the automobiles has passed, thus giving the impression that the first car has a much greater lead than is actually so. In our scene of the aircraft, we may compress intervals by skip-framing footage between planes, thus bringing the aircraft closer together and simulating a tight formation or a hazardously close pursuit. This technique allows for the synchronization of random movements with musical accents. It also provides for the complete elimination of one of a series of passing objects.

Reverse printing

Up to now, we have been assuming that both the process camera and the projector head have been transporting their respective films in the same direction, relative to one another. If, however, these components are run in opposite directions, then the resulting action on the screen will be reversed. In practice, the color master is threaded into the top magazine of the projecor head, tails out, and is transported downward through the intermittent and into the lower magazine, while the dupe negative in the process camera moves forward in conventional fashion. Alternatively, the projector head can be threaded and operated in a normal manner while the process camera is run in reverse, in which case the dupe negative will move from the back magazine of the camera to the front magazine.

The applications of reverse printing, although numerous, are not always apparent to the film maker. The technique should be frequently considered as a solution to special problems which may not be mentioned in the examples which follow.

In the photography of impact action in which automobiles, actors, or objects are required to move rapidly towards the lens of the camers, the original photography of the action is often done with all of the action performed in reverse, for obvious reasons of safety. To simulate an automobile collision, for example, the vehicle is first positioned within a few inches of the lens so that its image fills the screen, and then, during the take, is backed up the street away from the camera. Later, through reverse optical printing, the automobile's apparent movement is reversed and the car appears to bear down upon the audience. Naturally, in the original photography, the automobile will be accelerating for the first few seconds while it is backed away. When reversed through optical printing, this causes an undesirable *deceleration* of the car during its final approach. This deceleration in movement can be overcome by combining the reverse printing of the action with skip-frame compression during the last few feet of footage. The velocity of the car may thus be kept constant or even accelerated during the final two or three seconds before it fills the screen.

By changing the direction of the color master in the printer – first forward, then reverse – while the process camera moves its dupe negative continuously forward, a number of subtle and intricate distortions of action are possible. In the photography of animals, both domestic and wild, their normal behaviour may be manipulated in printing so as to react to the environment in certain ways. If we wish to show a dog rejecting a plate of food, we film it in normal fashion with the animal approaching the food. Later, in optical printing, this footage is allowed to run forward until the animal reaches the plate, at which point the footage is reversed and the dog backs away from the plate – still using the same footage. By reversing a short length of footage within the same scene, it is even possible to make the dog hesitate a moment before finally backing off, assuming of course, that the original scene lends itself to that much manipulation. This technique has been applied with great effect on numerous occasions by the Walt Disney Studio in its 'True Life' adventures, in which normal behaviour is changed so as to suggest anthropomorphic motivations. An example of the extent to which the process may be used is the scorpion square-dance sequence in *The Living Desert* in which random movements of insects were printed backwards and forwards in synchronism with music. Comedy effects may also be achieved in the same fashion. During the Second World War, a hilarious film was made by the British in which Nazi soldiers on parade were made to perform intricate dance motions to the tune of 'The Lambeth Walk'.

A more prosaic application of 'back-and-forth' printing allows us to prolong the screen time of a too-short sequence. Assuming, for example, that a director has 'cut' his camera immediately after an actor's exit through a door, the editor may later find himself with inadequate footage for a dissolve out of the scene. Through optical printing, it is possible to print the frames which remain *after* the actor's exit, backwards and forwards, until a sufficient length of footage is printed to satisfy the editor. Naturally, actors and other moving objects must be absent from the shot so as to avoid cyclic repeats in their movements. In solving such problems, this technique is much to be preferred to 'stop-frame' printing of a single frame, in which the grain structure of the image become apparent.

Stop-frame

If, in the course of multiple printing, a single frame of master positive is re-photographed a sufficient number of times, the effect when shown on the screen will be that of 'freezing' the action. The effect, called a stop-frame or hold-frame, is quite unnatural, of course, but if used judiciously it can serve as a stylistic accent. In one recent non-theatrical production, prominent drivers at an automobile race were introduced to the audience in the midst of their pre-race activities by suddenly stop-framing their movements in close-up while their individual voices were heard on the sound track, commenting upon the coming event. The effect allowed for a total exclusion of extraneous action, the selection of a dramatic pose, and a 'cameo' presentation of each of the competing protagonists. For another film, in which the history of the motion picture is documented, the *absence* of motion is emphasized by gradually slowing down a speeding automobile through multiple printing until, finally, all motion ceases in a stop-frame.

'Pixilation' techniques can also be secured in optical printing, through a combination of skip-frame and stop-frame techniques.

Image modifications and distortions

We have not yet exhausted the possibilities of image manipulation that can be carried out in the optical printer. Many other modifications can be made, from simple double printing to complicated color effects.

Superimpositions (double printing)

Superimpositions of two or more shots are made by successively re-printing the dupe negative from any desired number of different master positives, the relative exposure given to each positive determining its visual prominence on the screen.

Superimposition is most commonly employed in black-and-white films for the 'burning in' of titles over background action. Ordinarily, the background master positive is first copied in its entirety, with a normal printing exposure. The dupe negative is re-wound to start position, and additional positives which bear the white titles against a black background are then successively printed on to it (Fig. 7.30).

For this kind of work, the original title cards are prepared with black letters on a white field and are photographed on a high-contrast positive stock. The positive is developed conventionally, producing white (clear) letters against an intensely black field. It is this original positive strip which

Fig. 7.30. Superimposed titles for feature films. (Film Opticals, Inc.)

is run through the printer head during the superimposition printing process (using the original title positive in this fashion requires that its emulsion position be reversed in the printer head so that the titles will read properly on the screen).

Title footage may be assembled either on different 'A' and 'B' rolls or spliced head-to-tails on the same roll. In either case, edge-number or running-footage counts from a start position must be provided so that the printer's operator will know at what points the titles are supposed to appear, dissolve, and disappear. A smooth transition between titles is achieved by simply lap-dissolving the footage from one title to the next.

Some experimentation is necessary to determine the proper printing exposure to give the titles. An inadequate amount will produce transparent letters through which the background image may be seen. Too much exposure, on the other hand, will blur the lettering and may also contaminate the background scene with light which passes through the black field of the title footage.

Inasmuch as the titles are being 'burned' into the background through double printing, it is not possible to provide a dark 'drop shadow' or to incorporate intricate designs in a color film, since the color of the title usually contaminates that of the background action. If colored or elaborate title effects are desired, traveling mattes, bi-pack printing or aerial image printing should be employed.

For industrial or educational film production, superimposition may be used to add arrows, animated lines, and other graphic attention-directing devices to live action. It may also be employed to give an 'X-ray' view of a mechanical, electronic or biological machine. An automobile engine, photographed from without, can be combined with a cut-away motor block so that the movements of pistons, cam shaft, valves, and other moving parts are seen superimposed over the outside view. A close-up of the human chest, as seen from without, can be combined with animated art-work indicating the action of the heart and the operation of the circulatory system. An ingenious use of 'X-ray' superimposition for dramatic purposes occurs in the Alfred Hitchcock production of *Psycho*, in the last scene of which the image of a skull is faintly superimposed over a close-up of a madman. The image of the skull disappears almost at once and the scene dissolves into the last shot of the picture, that of an automobile being pulled out of a marsh. The superimposition is so subtle and occurs so rapidly as to be almost subliminal, but the psychological effect is startling.

Superimposition is used from time to time to combine a variety of action images for montage, transitionary, hallucinatory, and ghost effects. The technique has become rather clichéd, however, and should be used with restraint. Double printing can also be used to add rain, snow, lightning, or fog to a shot, either to enhance its dramatic values or to hide production or photographic inadequacies. The technique is not entirely convincing, however, inasmuch as it does not allow for precipitation to fall on or behind the actors.

A very specialized kind of superimposition has been used in recent years by Canadian film-maker Norman McLaren to produce a kind of multi-image, strobe-effect, in his brilliant dance film, *Pas de Deux*. For this film, ballet dancers were photographed in a totally black environment, and were lighted with rim lights as they passed through their dance routines. Successive printing of the original footage on to high-contrast stocks produced the maximum amount of separation between the lightly-tinted bodies of the dancers and the black surround. In an optical printer, the separate shots were individually printed, over and over, with the start mark progressively moved a pre-determined number of frames with each printing. The effect upon the screen is an extraordinary one, in which the bodies of the dancers fragment into separate, superimposed phases of movement (Fig. 7.31). In those cases in which the optical printing

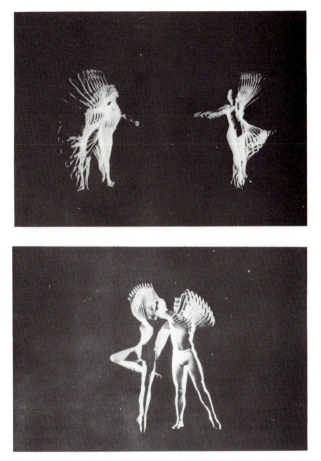

Fig. 7.31. Examples of multiple-image superimpositions for the Norman McLaren film, *Pas de Deux.* In synchronism with the accompanying music, the bodies of the dancers fragment into separate phases of movement, as they move from one position to another, producing an extraordinary strobe effect, and one which is controlled at every point and moment by the director of the film.

operations caused the different printings of a strip of film to superimpose on a static image, the dancers are seen immobile. In other cases, by varying the number of superimpositions, and by varying the number of frames by which each strip film was advanced for successive superimposition printings, the director was able to produce precisely the flow and rhythm of the strobe effect which he desired, and to synchronize it appropriately with the music track. Even more recently, other film makers have used the same technique for colored effects. By printing these superimpositions from a color original on an optical printer which employs an additive color lamphouse, it is possible not only to fragment the shape of the image, but also to break up its color into the additive components of which it is composed. The effect is startling.

Image size changes

If the process camera's lens is moved closer to the printer head than for normal 1:1 reproduction, it becomes possible to select and enlarge only a section of the original frame and to blow it up to full screen size. This may be desirable if the original scene was improperly composed or if it contained irrelevant action or detail. Alternatively, the process camera's lens may be moved in slowly towards the printer from frame-to-frame, thus simulating a 'zoom' into a predetermined field of view. By pulling the lens away from an enlarged section, in contrary fashion, a zoom-out can be produced.

The extent to which zooms and changes in field of this sort can be conducted is limited by the grain structure of the original scene; too great a magnification will cause a tremendous increase in graininess, which is apparent to the audience. Occasionally, as in the production of *The Miracle Worker*, an *increase* in grain is desired for certain stylized sequences. Accordingly, successive duplication, enlargement and reduction of a scene can be purposely conducted to produce this effect.

If the camera's lens is pulled *farther* away from the printer head than for normal 1:1 reproduction, the original scene is reduced in size and occupies only a portion of the screen. By shifting the process camera's lens out of normal position, this reduced image can also be re-positioned on the screen. This technique is useful for the production of complicated double-printing shots, in which several moving images are combined in the style of a collage. It is also used with traveling mattes to insert images into rear-view automobile mirrors, television picture tubes, window apertures, etc.

Rotary movements

Occasionally, we may decide that we wish to spin an image around its centre, either for montage or 'subjective camera' purposes. A newspaper with bold headlines rushes towards the camera, rotating rapidly as it approaches, then slowing to a readable stop and filling the frame. An alcoholic weaves across a room – we see the set subjectively through his eyes, rocking and rolling with his uneven gait. A Navy destroyer steams out to sea. As we cut in closer (on the sound stage) for medium shots and close-ups, the camera rocks and weaves a bit, as if the audience were located on the ship itself. All of these optical printing effects require that the normal position of the master positive be varied by rotating its image optically or mechanically.

If we desire that motion in the scene shall continue as the shot is rocked, then we employ the optical spin attachment. this mounts between the printer head and process camera, directly in line with the lens system. Rotation of the image through full 360° turns, continuously or back-and-forth, may be easily performed, the calibrations on the device allowing for synchronism with the frame-by-frame printing of the footage. By further varying the position of the camera and spin attachment during printing, spiral effects may also be obtained.

If motion in the image is not required during the effect, a mechanical spin attachment may be used instead. This takes the place of the projector's intermittent movement and physically rotates a single frame around the centre of its aperture. Registration pins within the device insure proper matching of image position with the preceding or subsequent footage. By moving the camera at the same time, a spiral effect can be produced.

The use of either optical or mechanical spin devices ordinarily require that the camera lens be racked in closer than normal to the master positive so as to copy only the central portion of the frame. If this is not done, the edges of the rocking or rotating frame will be seen on the screen as the image turns.

'Day-for-night'

Unquestionably, the best quality of 'day for night' work is done in the camera at the time that the scene is originally shot. Sometimes, however, editorial or dramatic considerations require that a normally-photographed daylight scene be converted into a night effect. Some degree of simulation can be achieved through optical printing, although the result is not usually very convincing. Both black-and-white and color stocks can be altered by underprinting and by darkening-off portions of the sky area through graduated neutral-density filters inserted into the printer's optical system. For color work, an overall bluish case can be imparted to the dupe color negative by the use of filters, the blue tint for night effects being more of a dramatic convention than a matter of fact. Unfortunately, the normal flesh tones of the actors are also turned blue, sometimes with macabre results. Really convincing day-for-night alterations require either bi-pack printing or aerial-image printing, both of which allow for the addition of practical lights, the differential darkening of sky tones, and the precise manipulation of object brightness.

Split-screen

All the in-the-camera split-screen shots described earlier can also be executed during optical printing, usually with far more convenience and likelihood of success. Both fixed and movable mattes, together with their counter-mattes, may be inserted into the 'wipe' device, or into the intermittent movements of the process camera and printer head.

Using the wipe device, it is possible, for example, to entirely remove a person or object from a shot. In this case, the same master positive is employed for both exposures. During the first exposure, the wipe blade passes along behind the moving object which is to be eliminated. The wipe blade finally obscures the master positive shortly after the object has left the screen. For the second exposure, the same master positive is reprinted, beginning at the point at which the object or actor leaves the screen. The wipe blade is now moved across the master positive in counter-matte fashion, revealing the image at exactly the same speed at which it was obscured during the first exposure. On the composite, the moving actor will have disappeared entirely. Actually, it is not necessary that the individual or object even leave the screen, provided it moves from one position to another during the shot. This effect requires very precise registration and calibration of the wipe blade to avoid production of a visible optical edge. It also requires the absence of camera movement and a minimum of background motion during the passing of the wipe.

An intricate use of split-screen optical printing was performed by Linwood Dunn some years ago at RKO Studios. A stunt pilot was photographed crashing his plane on the back lot, following which he jumped from the cockpit to the ground and away from the flames which were supposed to envelop the wreck. Unfortunately, the flames did not materialize quickly enough behind and around him to render the shot as dramatic as it might have been. In the optical printer, a split-screen matte was inserted during the first exposure which blocked out most of the plane except those areas in which the pilot moved. During the second exposure, the master positive was advanced considerably so as to show the spectacular flames which the mechanical-effects people had contrived. Using a counter-matte, Dunn combined the second part of the same footage with the earlier portion. On the screen, the pilot is seen to crash his plane, to be almost immediately engulfed by flame, to jump from the fiery wreck, and to just barely escape from the inferno. Here, optical printing produced an illusion which both budgetary limitations and safety precautions would have otherwise precluded.

Any number of multiple images can be combined in varying patterns through the same technique, a full frame from a single master positive being optically reduced and shifted to a particular position on the composite. The effect is commonly used for novelty in musicals, trailers, and television commercials.

It is also used to produce a multi-image effect similar to that obtained by using several projectors, as at the spectacular international Expo presentations. If intelligently planned, these multi-media presentations, synchronized with appropriate narration, music, and sound-effect tracks, are quite effective. The images which appear in different parts of the screen may complement or contrast with each other. Moving images may be combined with still photos, freeze frames, or art-work. The design variations are unlimited (Fig. 7.32).

De-saturation of colored images

Sometimes, for novelty or stylistic purposes, it is desirable that a sequence in a color film be de-saturated while the scene plays upon the screen – that is, that the color be drained out of the image, rendering it a black-and-white scene. For example, in a color production with which the author was associated, a death-bed scene is played in color until the moment when the character dies. At that point, the color drains from the entire image and the rest of the film is played in black-and-white, dramatically accentuating the shock and finality of the event.

To de-saturate a scene the original shot must be filmed in color. A fine-grain, black-and-white master positive is made from the original footage on a step-printer. During optical printing stages, the original color master is copied in conventional fashion with color duplicating stock in the

Fig. 7.32. Split-screen technique is also used to produce multi-image presentations on a single strip of film, rather than by using separate projectors. In this case, the images are of equal size, and are stacked neatly, but of course any number and variety of shapes and positions of the images can be produced. (National Film Board of Canada.)

Fig. 7.33. For multi-image work with the optical printer, an intermittent movement such as this is sometimes used, which allows for a great variety of shapes, sizes and positions of the images, and the maximum amount of accuracy in aligning them during the successive passes of different strips of film through the printer head. Alternatively, traveling mattes can be used to separate and position the different images. (National Film Board of Canada.)

process camera. At the point where de-saturation is intended to begin, the shutter of the process camera is gradually closed, producing a fade-out. The colour positive in the printer head is replaced with the black-and-white master positive, the frame relationships of the two strips being preserved. The color duplicating stock in the process camera is re-wound the length of the fade-out, and the printing operation is begun again, this time with the shutter being gradually opened. The final effect of this operation is a perfectly-registered dissolve between color and black-and-white positives of the same shot. By reversing the process, a black-and-white scene may be suddenly infused with color.

Miscellaneous distortions

Scenes which have been conventionally photographed may be diffused, dissolved, rippled, elongated, shrunk, or fragmented during printing by the introduction of appropriate accessories into the path of the lens system. Diffusion and fog filters are available in a variety of grades to provide optical retouching of actors' faces in close-up, or heavy diffusion for atmospheric 'color'. A ripple glass may be moved continuously through the field of view to produce water-like distortions. Used subtly, it simulates underwater views; used grossly, it can serve as a 'flash-back' or other type of transition. Kaleidoscopic lens accessories fragment the image in a continuously variable pattern for novelty effects, while anamorphic lens accessories can expand or compress images vertically or horizontally. The moving image of the master positive can also be filtered through a texture screen for an unusual etched quality. Such textured shots were used with great success to introduce several of the sequences in David O. Selznick's production of *A Portrait of Jenny*. Finally, for subjective camera purposes, the entire scene can be thrown in and out of focus by simply disengaging the automatic focus and varying the lens position manually.

Salvage techniques

The optical printer often pays for itself solely by salvaging valuable but technically defective footage. The Hollywood industry depends upon this function to such an extent that at least one of the industry's effects groups facetiously refers to itself as the 'Department of Special *Defects*'. The cost of such remedial printing is sometimes inexpensive, sometimes costly, depending upon the nature of the work. In either case, the cost is frequently far less than that of re-shooting the defective scene.

Removal of scratches

The abrasion or other scratching of either negatives or master positives presents a particularly acute problem in optical printing. In order to produce the highest possible illumination at the aperture of the printer head, most printers incorporate a specular illumination and imaging system, which accentuates scratches. The introduction of diffusion into the system minimizes scratches, but lowers the illumination level considerably, thus requiring slower and less economical printer speeds.

Most shallow scratches occur on the film support base, but whether on base or emulsion, the effect of the scratch is to displace or scatter collimated light which passes through the film, casting a shadow of the scratch on to the printing stock. On the positive print, therefore, negative scratches appear white. Shallow scratches on master positive stocks will be rendered white on the dupe negative for the same reason, and black on the final release prints. On the other hand, deep scratches of the negative emulsion which penetrate to the base of the film will be rendered black on positives; deep scratches of the master positive emulsion will appear white on the final release prints.

Two techniques are currently employed for the removal of both emulsion and base scratches. If the abrasions are fairly shallow, they may be partially or completely removed through 'liquid gate' or 'wet-gate' contact, or optical printing. The process requires that scratched footage be momentarily immersed or covered with a transparent fluid during the period when it passes into contact with a duplicating stock or through the intermittent of the optical printer's projector. A fluid is employed which has substantially the same refractive index as the film base and emulsion. The fluid fills in the scratch valleys and allows the light from the lamp house and condensers to pass straight through the film without being displaced by the scratches (Fig. 7.34). Detailed descriptions of the technique are avalable in the professional literature. (See, for example, *JSMPTE*, Sept. 1979, p. 600).

Fig. 7.34. Close-up of a liquid gate attachment for a 16 mm intermittent movement on an Acme optical printer, designed by Eastman Kodak Company. This system is effective in eliminating scratches from worn or damaged film during optical printing. The film is totally immersed in liquid of appropriate refractive index during the brief period that it passes through the intermittent movement. The system shown here looks fairly simple, but is actually supported by very elaborate machinery to which it is attached, which provides pumps, filters, bubble traps, heaters, a vacuum system, and electrical/electronic controls.

In those cases where emulsion scratches are so deep as to penetrate to the film support, liquid-gate printing cannot successfully restore the image. Providing that the scratches run along the edge of the frame, however, it is possible to optically reprint the damaged footage with the lens system of the process camera racked out for high-magnification copying. The effect is to blow up the remaining, unscratched portions of the image to full-frame size. Unfortunately, this increases the grain size of the image and may also unbalance the composition of the original shot.

Changes in screen direction

Occasionally, through error or inexperience, a director may be unfortunate enough to film a close-up or two-shot with his actors facing in the wrong direction for editing purposes. Such a crossing of the 'stage line' leads to abrupt changes in actor position from shot to shot which are likely to disorient the audience. Consistency in screen direction can be restored by optically printing the offending shots with their emulsions 'flipped' in the printer head. The operator simply winds the color master onto its projector spool with the emulsion position reversed, or, alternatively, gives the film a half twist between the magazine and the intermittent movement. Large close-ups with slightly out-of-focus backgrounds lend themselves best to this strategem since the background set, lettered signs, and other recognizable details are also reversed in the process. Should a flipped shot be left on the screen too long, audiences may notice peculiarities in the actors' costumes – suit coats button on the wrong side, breast pockets misplaced, and so on.

'Manufacture of coverage'

Together with improper screen direction, the inexperienced film maker's most common error is in failing to secure adequate coverage for a craftsmanlike job of editing. As a consequence, the editor has to run particular shots interminably, insert artificial cut-aways, or run the risk of jump cuts between poorly-matched shots.

In an emergency, when the budget does not allow for the re-shooting of the scene, medium shots can be converted into close-ups through optical printing by racking the lens of the process camera in towards the master positive. The close-up footage which is produced can be used either to provide variety in editing or to allow the editor to remove other actors or actions from the original image long enough for him to move to a different shot without producing a jump cut. The same technique can also be used in documentary or archival productions when inadequate footage requires that a single shot be repeated two or three times. By manufacturing close-ups, changing their compositions, and changing the screen direction – all from a single shot – the director may be able to convince an audience that they are watching entirely different views of the same subject matter.

Exposure correction

For conventional release printing, continuous-contact printers provide a wide range of printer light adjustments which compensate for a reasonable amount of under- or overexposure of the original. However, in the case of really gross overexposure of the negative or underexposure of reversal stocks, the contact printer may not produce a printable dupe negative. In such cases a satisfactory dupe can often be produced through optical printing.

A much more complicated salvage problem arises when the motor of the production camera fails to operate at a constant speed during original photography, thus producing a continuously varying density of the negative. A similar problem occurs when a take is cut too soon and the camera slows down on still-useful footage, thus gradually increasing its exposure and consequent density. The restoration of such material is a tedious and expensive operation, justifiable only in the case of unusually valuable footage. Salvage through optical printing requires that the overall density of each frame be determined either with a densitometer or with exposure meter probes on the printer and that appropriate changes in shutter opening be made manually, from frame to frame. Several days' work can go into such an assignment, and the cost is so high that many producers will find it cheaper to re-shoot the entire scene.

Frame-line corrections

In past years, particularly in 16 mm, different brands of cameras often registered their films in different positions relative to the perforations. Even today, although all major makes of production equipment have been standardized, certain types of cameras used for instrumentation photography register their images in a wide variety of positions. Because of the lack of space between 16 mm frames, any variation in frame-line position between shots makes the line visible on the screen moving upwards or downwards from shot to shot. The defect is blatant and gives even the most polished production an amateurish appearance.

To correct frame-line positions through optical printing, an oversized aperture is used in the projector intermittent in which the top and bottom frame lines of the picture are visible, as well as portions of adjacent images. The printer head or the process camera is either raised or lowered until the position of the original frame line, relative to the perforations of the film in the process camera, conforms to ASA standards.

Horizon corrections

Even more amateurish than frame-line jumps are the slanting horizons and leaning verticals which follow from improper levelling of the tripod during original photography,

The defect is remedied during optical printing by tilting either the process camera or projector head, or by rotating the image slightly with the optical spin attachment. Since, in either case, the image must be turned around its own centre, it will be necessary to bring the camera lens in closer than normal and to slightly enlarge a less-than-full-frame portion of the original. Otherwise, the edges of the frame will be seen on the screen.

Corrections for camera movement

There may sometimes be unavoidable occasions when valuable footage is rendered worthless because of accidental vibration or jiggling of the camera. For example, in the production of *The Miracle Worker*, a dolly-back from actors on a porch required that the camera car pass over a stretch of rough road. Holes in the road caused unacceptable jiggling of the shot. The footage was sufficiently valuable, however, to justify salvage through optical printing.

The technique involved is tedious and costly, since it usually requires that each frame be rotoscoped on to an alignment chart where changes in image position which are due to jiggling can be plotted from frame to frame. During final optical printing of the shot, the process camera's lens is moved from frame to frame so as to register the image, thus evening-out vibration in the shot. This operation usually requires that a slightly reduced section of the master positive image be enlarged; otherwise, the correcting movement of the process camera's lens would cause it to photograph areas outside of the frame.

Nitrate-to-acetate salvage printing

For several years now, laboratory workers throughout the world have labored to print early nitrate-based silent and sound motion-picture productions onto long-lasting, safety-based stocks. Apart from its great flammability, nitrate film ultimately deteriorates and turns to dust. Thousands of important early films have already been lost forever, and a race is underway to salvage remaining nitrate-based film productions before they, too, disappear.

The principal problem which one encounters in the optical printing of such material is mechanical in nature. With the passing of years, nitrate-based material loses its dimensional integrity, and both shrinks and expands in an unpredictable fashion. Attempts to print the material on conventional contact or optical printers are frequently unsuccessful, simply because the perforations of the shrunken, deteriorating film will not fit the sprockets and registration pins of the printer.

Optical printing laboratories which specialize in the salvage printing of such material employ a variety of intermittent shuttle movements, with a range of varying pin positions, so as to accommodate the perforations of the shrunken film. In the case of footage in which shrinkage has proceeded beyond any kind of conventional printing, optical printers of special design are employed which register each frame of shrunken film relative to a corner of the frame rather than to the perforations of the film.

Equally challenging is the problem of salvaging modern color film productions, in the negatives and prints of which the colors have begun to fade. No matter how advanced the manufacture of color film stocks, the dyes employed are fugitive, and cannot last forever. The techniques employed for the archival storage of color negatives and prints, and for the restoration of faded color footage, are beyond the scope of this book. Suffice to say that, for the moment, the only sure way of preserving color film productions is to make color-separation positives on safety-based film stocks, which can be recombined, at some future time, into full-color dye prints. This process is, unfortunately, very expensive.

Special equipment: double- and triple-head printers

In recent years, several manufacturers have introduced optical printers which incorporate three or four printer heads, the master positives and traveling mattes of which can be all photographed simultaneously (see Figs. 7.36–7.38). In both designs, two projector heads are positioned 'in-line', the film in the rear projector being imaged into the plane of the front projector's aperture by means of aerial-image optics. A third (and sometimes, fourth) projector is offset at 90° to the main optical bench; its film's image is cast into the plane of the front projector's aperture by means of a beam-combiner (see Fig. 7.36). All three projectors can be moved longitudinally, laterally and vertically, with automatic focusing throughout. Some optical printers are modular in design, allowing for

Fig. 7.35. The Model 6211 optical-effects printer by BHP Company incorporates two separate, in-line, printer heads. The aerial-image optical system which separates, the two printer heads focuses the film which passes through the left-hand head into the plane of the film passing through the right-hand head, at which point both strips of film are then photographed simultaneously by the process camera, right. Printers such as this dispense with the heavy-duty motor, gear trains, levers and other mechanical linkages which were used in the past, and replace them all with separate synchronized stepping motors which individually power the camera and printer heads. Such systems eliminate mechanical backlash and vibration, replace several hundred mechanical components with a handful of solid-state electronic ones, simplify the controls, and generally make for a simpler and more efficient operation. They also allow for the use of modular microcomputer control units which can be quickly and easily removed for servicing.

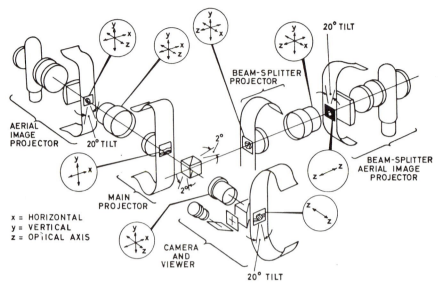

BEAM-SPLITTER
PROJECTOR

20° TILT

AERIAL
IMAGE
PROJECTOR

20° TILT

2°

BEAM-SPLITTER
AERIAL IMAGE
PROJECTOR

MAIN
PROJECTOR

x = HORIZONTAL
y = VERTICAL
z = OPTICAL AXIS

CAMERA
AND
VIEWER

20° TILT

Fig. 7.36. Schematic diagram of the optical system of an Oxberry 1200 series 'quad head' printer.

Fig. 7.37. The Oxberry Model 5117-80 special-effects optical printer, with four separate projector heads – two in-line straight ahead, and two in-line at 90° to one side. Images on film in each of the four heads are all brought to focus in a common plane. Each head is capable of bi-pack operation, allowing for the simultaneous re-photography of eight separate strips of film with one pass through the camera. Machines such as this allow for faster operations and for greater precision in the compositing of numerous strips of film and traveling mattes.

Fig. 7.38. Front view of another model of the Oxberry multi-head optical printer – two projectors in line at left, two offset in-line at 90° in center.

Fig. 7.39. Lens set-up for the one-of-a-kind 'quad' printer built at Industrial Light and Magic Corporation for Lucasfilm's productions of *The Empire Strikes Back* and *Return of the Jedi.* The printer is capable of handling both conventional 4-perforation 35 mm film strips and 8-perforation (sideways, or 'lazy-eight') Vistavision-format film strips. (Courtesy of Lucasfilm, Ltd.)

purchase of a basic single-headed printer and subsequent installation of additional printer heads.

The use of such printers allows the simultaneous printing of multiple strips of film which previously had to be printed separately. The result is an increase in speed of operations and a decrease in intermittent weave due to repeated passes through the printer. Fully equipped, these machines are capable of the most intricate kinds of optical printing and traveling-matte assignments. Not unexpectedly, they are quite expensive.

Plate 1
Top: matte-painting supervisor Mike Pangrazio at work on an in-the-camera painted matte shot for Lucasfilm's production of *Return of the Jedi*. The scene is of the rebel's docking bay. Note the clear areas of glass, into which live-action scenes will be inserted by means of rear projection.
Bottom: finished composite. Full-scale set components and actors have been inserted into the painting at lower right, while miniature space ships against a star field have been added in the area of the open bay entrance at upper rear. (Courtesy of Lucasfilm, Ltd.)

Plate 2
Matte painter Ralph McQuarrie at work on a painting of the landing platform in Cloud City, and the space ship Milenium Falcon, for Lucasfilm's production of *The Empire Strikes Back*. The area in front of the space ship is clear for insertion of full-scale live action by means of rear projection.

Photography of the matte painting by itself, minus the live-action component. A second exposure adds the rear-projected shot of the performers in the foreground.

The final composite, with the actors inserted into the foreground area of the painting. (Courtesy of Lucasfilm, Ltd.)

Plate 3A
A blue-screen traveling-matte shot for Lucasfilm's production of *Return of the Jedi*. Performers Carrie Fisher and Mark Hammel are posed on their 'rocket bike' atop a movable crane on the sound stage, in front of a cobalt blue, rear-illuminated screen. The Vistavision-format camera is also mounted on a crane, and it and the performers can be moved towards and away from each other.

The foreground action shot of Fisher and Hammel. The section of the crane which supports them has been painted blue to match the background screen; in the final composite, it will become invisible.

Below left: female cover-matte of the previous shot. Note garbage matte which removes unwanted miscellaneous equipment in the shot.
Below right: male holdout matte of the same shot.

Plate 3B
Garrett Brown with his Steadicam support for the Vistavision-format camera. For the film's scene in which the performers race their rocket bikes through the forest, Brown *walked* through the forest, at a predetermined pace, around the trees in his path, with the camera running at far less than the usual 24 frames per second.

One of the resulting background plates which was shot by Brown gives theater spectators a first-person, rear-view impression of racing through the forest, just above ground level, at speeds of over 100 miles per hour.

The final composite, showing the performers in their high-speed, death-defying rocket bike race. (All photos courtesy of Lucasfilm, Ltd.)

Plate 4

Top: photography of the miniature set. At the end of a 'Zeus' crane, an Arriflex camera points straight down at the Las Vegas set. A 'pitching lens' assembly at the end of the optical system redirects the field of view horizontally along the line of the set, producing an equivalent height above the pavement of about 6 ft. The technician riding the crane arm takes directions by headset from the special effects supervisor, off sceen, who views the photographed scene on a video monitor.

Bottom: Another view of camera set-up used for photography of the miniature. Technicians in the foreground operate the wires which move the ¼ in scale automobiles along the streets. (All photos from the production of *One From the Heart*. Zoetrope Studios.)

Plate 5
The laying out of the miniature landscape of frozen tundra on the fictional planet of Hoth, for scenes in Lucasfilm's production of *The Empire Strikes Back*. A cardboard cut-out of the 'walker', at lower right, which matches the dimensions of the finished miniature, is used for convenience during construction of the set.

Stop-motion photography of the miniature walkers, one frame at a time. Note the face mask worn by one of the animators to prevent inhalation of particles of the material used to simulate snow on the miniature set.

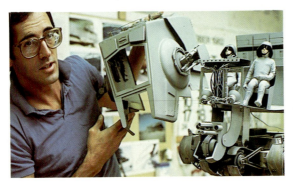

The finished shot of the stop-motion-animated 'walkers'. Laser blast streaks have been added optically.

A model maker adjusts a completed miniature of one of the two-legged walkers from *Return of the Jedi*. Note that the interior of the walker is finished off with miniature figures of its two operators, despite the fact that they are virtually invisible in the photographed scenes.

Plate 6

Early conceptualization of the Rancor monster appearing in *Return of the Jedi*. Following the storyboard sketches, early versions of the creature are first sculpted out of clay. Later, after the design has been fixed, plaster molds of the sculpture will be made, from which the final foam rubber miniature will be constructed.

Painting and touch-up of the finished foam-rubber miniature figure.

The finished Rancor monster, as it appeared in the film. In a crouching posture, the miniature stands a little over a foot high. During final photography, it is operated in real time as a puppet, with control rods extending upward through its feet (All photos courtesy Lucasfilm, Ltd.)

Plate 7

Coppola directs a performer for a test of the Ultimatte system. The performer is posed in front of a cobalt blue screen which is identical to that which will be used in the final traveling-matte shot. For test purposes, her image is picked up by video camera, left, and routed to the Ultimatte compositor for viewing.

Plate 8

Below: the ACES system on stage for production of *The Black Hole*. Camera unit travels across stage on precision rails set into concrete in the stage floor.

Bottom: ACES camera support, right, and model support at left. The model stand is also motion-controlled. (Courtesy of Walt Disney Productions).

8

Traveling mattes

Since the earliest days of the motion-picture industry, technicians have sought a practical way in which to combine a shot of an actor, photographed on the sound stage, with a background scene, photographed elsewhere. Such a process would provide superior sound-recording conditions for the simulation of exterior scenes. It would allow for the convenient and economical incorporation of visual detail which had been recorded in distant locales. It would provide for the photography of hazardous action with relative safety. It would give us the means with which to manufacture an infinite variety of unlikely or fantastic composites.

Over the years, two systems have been developed to allow for just such an effect. The first is background projection. The other is the traveling matte (Fig. 8.1).

Matte shots of several varieties have already been described. None of these allows the performer to move out of his own acting area, however; the moment he attempts to do so, he disappears. Mention has also been made of the 'superimposition' of foreground action over background scenes through double exposure and double printing. Such techniques produce a 'phantom' effect, however, in which background detail can be seen through the body of the actor.

An entirely different process must be used to 'jigsaw' the moving figure of the actor into the background image and to produce a convincing composite, *in motion*. What is obviously required is a type of matte which changes in position, size, and shape from frame to frame – a 'traveling matte', whose silhouette conforms exactly to the shape and movements of the actor, allowing him to move anywhere within the picture (Fig. 8.3).

Two entirely different classes of traveling-matte processes are available to produce this kind of composite. The first is a self-matting technique which is applicable only to black-and-white photography. The second – suitable for either black-and-white or color – is an optical printing process which employs strips of motion-picture film, bearing photographic silhouettes which alternately obscure and reveal foreground and background images during successive printing operations.

Fig. 8.1, part 1. Typical traveling-matte composites. Here, an actress performing on the sound-stage in front of a window frame is combined with an exterior winter scene. (National Film Board of Canada.)

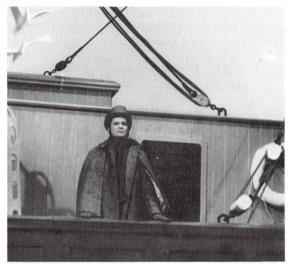

Fig. 8.1, part 2. Seagulls and sky detail composited with a foreground sound stage set.

Fig. 8.1, part 3. Background printer mask for the previous shot. (National Film Board of Canada)

Fig. 8.2, part 1. An actor, photographed on stage, is composited into a sky background. (National Film Board of Canada)

Fig. 8.2, part 2. A shrinking-man effect for a TV commercial. The diminishing figure of the performer is composited into the full-scale scene by traveling-matte technique. (Film Opticals, Inc.)

Fig. 8.2, part 3. A TV commercial in which the coffee appears to overfill the cup without spilling. Traveling-mattes were used to combine separate shots of (a) a coffee cup, (b) black liquid poured into a clear glass cylinder and (c) steam and highlight effects. (Film Opticals, Inc.)

Fig. 8.3, part 1. Traveling-matte technique allows for photography of actors and background detail at different times. The actor is photographed so as to allow for production of a traveling matte of his figure.

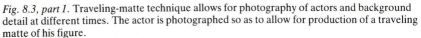

Fig. 8.3, part 2. A background printing mask, or counter-matte, is prepared through step-contact or step-optical printing.

Fig. 8.3, part 3. During composite optical, the separate foreground and background images are combined. This particular shot is a complicated one, involving miniatures, a static matte-painting, a partially-completed full-scale set, a foreground actor and a traveling matte. Creation of the background image is described in Chapter 5. (National Film Board of Canada.)

The Dunning-Pomeroy self-matting process

In the late 1920s, a technique was introduced in the Hollywood film industry by which actors could be photographed on the sound stage, and their images simultaneously combined with background action previously photographed elsewhere. The system was developed by C. Dodge Dunning, and later by Roy J. Pomeroy, and was widely employed until the perfection of background projection. Among the films on which it was used to advantage was the 1933 production of *King Kong*.

The technique required the use of a production camera with a high-quality intermittent movement which was capable of taking two strips of film in bi-pack. Into this camera was loaded a bleached and orange-dyed master positive of the background scene, in contact with a panchromatic negative raw stock. Light from the acting area in front of the camera passed through the base and emulsion of the dyed master positive and struck the negative raw stock behind it. Only the bleached emulsion of the master positive was dyed; that is, the shadow areas were heavily colored, whereas the highlight areas were perfectly clear.

The actor was positioned before the camera and was illuminated with orange-filtered light. Behind the actor, a blank screen was erected which was illuminated only by blue light (Fig. 8.4). In those areas of the master positive which were struck by orange light reflected from the actor's face and costume, the light passed almost equally through both the dyed and clear portions of the master positive, and a colid, conventional image of the actor was recorded on the panchromatic emulsion. On the other hand, in those areas which surrounded the actor, the blue light reflected from the screen provided illumination with which to print the background detail of the master positive through to the dupe negative, the orange dye absorbing

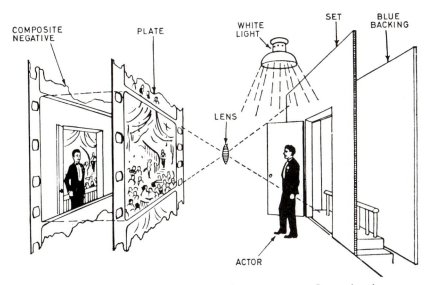

Fig. 8.4. Simplified diagram of the Dunning traveling-matte process. In practice, the composite (dupe) negative and plate are run in bi-pack. (JSMPTE.)

blue light in the shadow portions and transmitting it in the clear highlight areas. Inasmuch as the actor's body obscured the screen directly behind him, the blue light reflected from the screen could not reach those portions of the master positive on which the actor's figure was imaged. Since the blue light was continuously obscured and revealed by the actor's body as he moved across the frame, the performer served as his own matte.

Describing such a process is complicated enough; its execution was infinitely more involved. Excessively high densities in the shadow areas of the master positives had to be avoided lest they produce a 'phantom' superimposition of the actor's image. The bleaching and dyeing of the master positive was a complicated and tedious process, careful determination of hue and saturation being essential. Inasmuch as the two strips of film ran in bi-pack, there was no practical way in which director and cameraman could judge what the finished composite would look like, and be assured that the placement, perspective, and composition of the two components was as it should be. There was no provision for correcting the final composite, short of developing the dupe negative on the spot, examining it, and re-shooting the entire scene. And finally, by its very nature, the process could not be used for color cinematography.

With the introduction and gradual sophistication of background projection technique, the Dunning-Pomeroy process fell into disuse and finally became obsolete. Nonetheless, the principle by which it operated is still of marginal interest. Suitably modified and simplified, the process becomes feasible for certain types of low-budget black-and-white film production. One such modification was introduced by Pomeroy in the late 1920s, which combined the principle of the Dunning process with that of the glass-shot. This technique allows for the combining of foreground action with static background scenes on a single strip of black-and-white negative.

In practice, the master positive of the Dunning process is replaced by a fairly large photographic transparency which is mounted in front of the camera. The actor is positioned between the transparency and a background screen. The transparency has been bleached and dyed orange, the actor is illuminated with orange-filtered light, and the screen is illuminated with blue light. Assuming that short-focal-length lenses and small apertures are employed in order to hold focus on both the actor and the transparency, a reasonably convincing composite results.

By moving the diapositive outside of the camera and changing its form to that of a glass-shot stereo, a number of advantages are gained over the older system. First, the composite may be photographed with any conventional camera, inasmuch as bi-pack operation is no longer required. Second, the photographic transparency is relatively convenient and inexpensive to prepare. Third, so long as the camera and transparency are rigidly mounted, there is no possibility of registration weave between components of the composite – even if an inferior intermittent movement were employed, both the foreground and background images would jiggle in synchronism with one another. Fourth, with the background plate positioned outside of the camera, it is now possible for the director and cameraman to view and compose the complete composite by simply sighting with the 'through-the-lens' viewfinder. Finally, by temporarily substituting a Polaroid-Land camera for the motion-picture equipment, test photographs of the composite can be quickly produced as an aid in balancing foreground and background lighting. This process has much to recommend it to low-budget producers, although a great deal of experimentation is required before consistently good results can be expected.

The traveling-matte principle

Despite their ingeniousness, both the original Dunning-Pomeroy system and Pomeroy's later modification display a number of obvious limitations. The first is unacceptably awkward, the second does not allow for a moving background. Both are limited to black-and-white cinematography, and neither allows for convenient correction of the composite once the foreground action has been photographed.

All of these limitations may be overcome through the use of 'male' and 'female' traveling mattes and counter-mattes – strips of film bearing opaque images which are run in bi-pack with foreground and background color masters or color separations during optical printing.

Let us assume that we already have a traveling matte and a counter-matte in hand, both of which match foreground action photo-graphed on the sound stage. Whatever means we may use to produce it, the (male) traveling matte consists of an opaque photographic silver image recorded against a clear field, on motion-picture film which is identical in width and perforations to the film on which the foreground actor has been photographed. The shape of the opaque mask conforms exactly to the outline of the actor, from frame to frame (Fig. 8.5). The female counter-matte is identical in configuration, but its tones are reversed – the silhouette is clear against an opaque, black field (Fig. 8.5).

We will assume that we wish to combine the shot of our performer with an exterior background, photographed elsewhere. A color master (positive) of the background scene is inserted into the projector (printer head) of the optical printer in contact with the matte, which is opaque in the area of the actor and clear in the surround. The projector and process camera are set running, and the background detail which appears around the actor's matte is copied onto the duplicating color negative during the first exposure.*

The color duplicating negative is rewound to start position, and the color master of the background is now replaced with that of the actor's performance on the sound stage. The matte used during the first exposure is replaced by its female counterpart, which is clear in the area of the actor's figure and opaque in the surround. A second exposure is now made, in which the actor's image is printed onto the dupe negative, thus 'jigsawing' the two components together into one composite. (Alternatively, color-separation positives can be employed for such work.) Assuming many things – that the matte and

---

* Throughout this chapter, the term 'colour master' is used synonymousely with 'color positive'; the term 'duplicating colour negative' is used synonymously with 'color internegative'.

Fig. 8.5, part 1. Components of a typical traveling-matte shot. Here, the live-action foreground is photographed against a color-separation backing.

Fig. 8.5, part 2. The female master or matte master.

Fig. 8.5, part 3. A counter-matte or male matte, step-printed from the image in the previous illustration.

Fig. 8.5, part 4. The background plate.

Fig. 8.5, part 5. The final composite. (All photographs courtesy *American Cinematographer.*)

counter-matte match one another properly, that neither matte has 'bled' excessively during its preparation, that registration-pin positions have been kept consistent in all stages of the operation, that the perforations of the film stocks used have been manufactured to close tolerances, that exposure and contrast of the two images have been properly balanced, and so forth – a convincing composite results (Fig. 8.5).

Hand-drawn traveling mattes

As the reader has probably gathered, the printing of traveling mattes is a complicated business, requiring the highest-precision tools and techniques, consistently applied throughout the operation. Even more complicated are the techniques by which traveling mattes are originally recorded.

Hand-drawn animation provides what is both the most versatile and the most tedious method for the production of a traveling matte. The technique is commonly employed for the addition of animated background detail to live-action scenes – birds in flight, waves, flickering lights, reflections, movement in crowds, and so forth.

In practice, the color master (positive) of the scene to which action is to be added is inserted into the intermittent movement of either a process camera or a matte-shot projector, and the image of a single frame is projected, rotoscope-fashion, onto a matte-board. An animation artist plots the action to be added (e.g. birds flying across the sky) by referring to the projected image of the live-action scene on the matte board. A series of drawings of the birds are produced, appropriately animated for the desired effect. These are transferred with paints to transparent animation cels.

Transferring to film

With the process camera still mounted in the same position as was used for projection of the master positive, the series of animated paintings are now photographed on an appropriate raw stock – black-and-white or color, as the case may be. Each of the separate cels is photographed against a black card, so as to produce self-matting images and to dispense with the later need for a female matte. With the animated art-work photographed, the traveling matte may now be produced on film by either one of two methods.

First, the outline of each of the animation-cel paintings is traced onto punched animation paper and then transferred, in register, to another set of animation cels, on which the outline of the animated action is inked-in solid. This set of matte paintings is then photographed onto high-contrast duplicating stock in the same sequence as prevailed during the photography of the animated art-work, thus producing a traveling matte on film which matches the original drawings. A female matte will not be required during composite printing, inasmuch as the original painted cels were photographed against a black card, and are thus self-matting.

The second method assumes, as is usually the case, that the original animation cel paintings are opaque. That being the case, we can dispense altogether with the tedious tracing process just described. Following the original photography of the animated painting, the cels are re-photographed on high-contrast positive stock. This time, the cels are illuminated from behind, rather than from the front. Since the paints are opaque, light cannot pass through the drawing and a clear outline of the action results on the high-contrast dupe. Since the cels are transparent in those areas surrounding the animated painting, light passes through the clear sections and is recorded as an opaque image on the high-contrast dupe negative.

Once the traveling matte has been photographed, the final composite is made in the optical printer. First, the color master (positive) of the background is copied in bi-pack with the traveling matte. In this operation, the live-action image which appears around the animated art-work is printed to the duplicating color negative. The dupe is rewound to start position, and, during the second exposure, the color master of the self-matting animated art-work is printed.

Hand drawn traveling mattes will also be necessary when actors, or parts of their bodies, pass in front of fixed-outline, matted-in detail, such as a scene on the tube of a television set.

Falling-debris composites

Hand-drawn mattes are also employed for intricate composited in which falling masonry or other objects are required to fall behind, onto, and in front of an actor. In such cases, the falling debris and the actor are photographed on separate pieces of film. (Alternatively, if sufficiently skilled artists are available, the falling objects can be drawn and animated.) The shot of masonry is rotoscoped and a set of matte tracings is prepared which reveals only those parts of the falling objects which are appropriate to the scene. The tracings are transfered to cels, the cels are photographed to produce a traveling matte, and the composite is printed in conventional fashion. In the event that some of the debris is required to fall *behind* the actor, the image of the actor can be rotoscoped over the matte drawings during their preparation, thus allowing the artist to conform the matte to the shape of the actor's body, from frame to frame. In the final composite, the image of the falling masonry will be progressively obscured by the matte, but as if by the actor's body (Fig. 8.6). Alteration of the matte's shape will also be required if the falling objects are expected to crumble or break as they strike portions of the set which are recorded on the background color master. Should a counter-matte be required for final printing, this can be produced by simply step-printing the matte in contact with a strip of high-contrast positive.

As would be expected, considerable planning is necessary in such work to match perspective, motion-parallax, and size relationships between both of the live-action components. The work is quite involved and requires considerable talent and experience for its proper execution.

Wipes

Hand-drawn mattes are also used for the production of complicated wipes, the transitionary function of which is identical to those produced mechanically on the optical printer. By using the traveling-matte process, an almost unlimited number of wipe patterns can be produced, a few of which are illustrated in Fig. 8.7.

The preparation of a traveling-matte wipe is relatively simple. The artist prepared a series of animated wipe drawings on paper, art board, or cels. These are photographed sequentially onto a high-contrast emulsion with an animation or process camera, the length and speed of the moving wipe pattern being determined by the displacement of images between cels and the number of times each cel is photographed. The traveling matte which results is then step-printed in contact with high-contrast duplicating film in

188

Fig. 8.6, part 1. Use of a hand-painted traveling matte to allow envelopment of actors by falling debris in the background plate. Two figures move past a burning hotel building in the 1938 20th Century-Fox production of *In Old Chicago.* The building is, of course, a miniature.

Fig. 8.6, part 2. The hotel explodes and begins to collapse. Note the upper front cornice of the building, which has detached and has begun to fall.

Fig. 8.6, part 3. The hotel collapses. The detached, falling cornice falls onto and in front of the two figures, completely enveloping them. (All photographs Kenneth MacGowan Collection.)

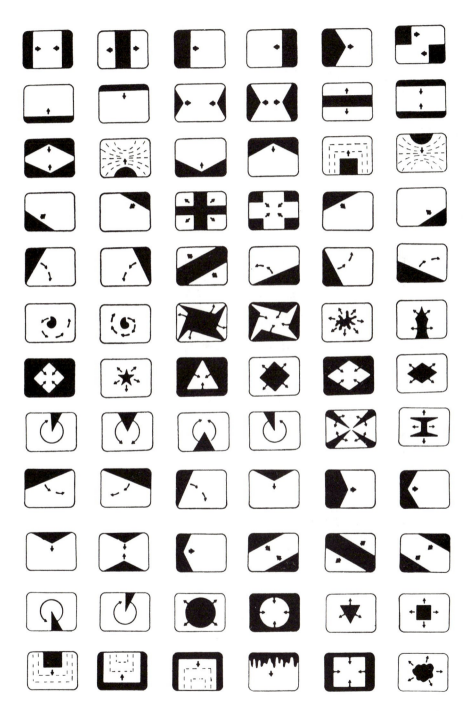

Fig. 8.7. A few of the scores of wipe effects possible with traveling mattes. (Cinema Research Corp.)

order to produce a counter-matte. The final composite-wipe sequence is produced through bi-pack optical printing, as previously described. Once prepared, the traveling matte and counter-matte which are used for a particular assignment can be retained until needed again. In this way, an effects department builds up an extensive collection of wipe effects, the cost of which is greatly diminished once the traveling mattes have been produced.

Traveling-matte inserts

Curiously, the traveling matte is quite commonly used for composite effects in which the matte does *not* move. In such cases it serves to block out certain portions of the original image in a manner which cannot be conveniently done with fixed mechanical mattes on the optical printer. It may be desired, for example, to insert a live-action image into the picture tube area of a television set. To produce the effect, the TV set is photographed as it appears in the scene, on conventional production negative stock, and a color master is prepared which is projected, rotoscope fashion, onto a matte-board. An artist traces the outline of the tube on drawing paper and blocks out its area with black paint. With the process camera or matte-shot projector mounted in the same position, the matte drawing is photographed on high-contrast film stock.

The traveling matte which is produced does not actually move, but provides an opaque, configured image in the middle of the frame which matches that of the television tube on the color master. A female matte is produced through step-printing.

Later, during the bi-pack optical printing process, the color master of the television set is printed during the first run, while an insert of the action is subsequently reduced and positioned on the optical printer so that its scale and composition fit properly into the area of the tube.

Obviously, if anyone in the scene should walk in front of the television set, the image will remain on the screen and will cut their body in two as they pass by. Careful direction of the performers will avoid this problem. If it is absolutely necessary that the performers walk in front of the matted-in image, however, the traveling matte can be hand-drawn to match the position and shape of the actor's body as it intersects the image. For such purposes, a color master of the sound stage scene is rotoscoped onto the matte board so as to provide the animation artist with the outline of the television tube face. Those sections of the actor's body which pass in front of the perimeter of the tube are then outlined relative to the edges of that tube face, frame by frame, onto separate sheets of animation paper. The outlines are then transferred to transparent animation cels and the interior of the outlines are opaqued with black paint. The set of cels which result are photographed, a frame at a time, producing a fixed outline of the television tube, and a traveling matte of the actor's body which moves only within the boundaries of the television tube. A female counter-matte is made, and, in the optical printer, final compositing of the foreground action (which includes the actor's body), and the scene is accomplished, the latter being reduced to the proper scale in the optical printer. It is also possible to accommodate a pan or tilt of the camera by animating position changes of the matte insert area, frame by frame, so that it matches changes in the position of the television set tube during the pan or tilt. However, this is very expensive work, and serves principally as a 'last-resort' method of salvaging 'special defects' in the film coverage of a careless director.

The 'insert' traveling matte is also used to produce various complicated titles in which the letters of the title are seen over a live action scene in the background. The use of traveling mattes for such title effects is especially effective when the titles incorporate elaborate art-work within the body of the title, and 'drop shadows', below and to one side of the lettering. If the lettering of the title is hand-drawn, the artist works with paints upon a transparent cel, incorporating whatever elaboration he desires into the body of the lettering. He also paints a 'drop shadow' with black paint onto either the same cel or a second one which will be photographed in register behind it.

Titles may also be type-printed by 'hot press' methods, in which case two separate cels are always printed. The first bears white letters against the clear field. The second is printed from the same set of type, but with black letters against a clear field. By placing the black-lettered cel behind the white, and shifting the cels out of register, a 'drop shadow' effect is created.

To produce a traveling matte from either a hand-drawn or 'hot press' title, the cel is first photographed with an animation camera. The title is illuminated from the front against a black card, thus recording the highlight detail of the art-work. On a separate, high-contrast stock, the cel is photographed a second time in exactly the same position. This time, the black card is withdrawn and the cel is photographed with illumination from behind, thus producing an opaque photographic matte of both the lettering and its drop shadow. The final composite of title and background action is made through bi-pack optical printing, the self-matting title being printed on the first run; the color master of the background action in bi-pack with its traveling matte, on the second.

All of the hand-drawn traveling-matte effects which have been described here can also be achieved through bi-pack *contact* printing. The technique, which is somewhat different, is described in Chapter 6. If a production organization owns a process camera, bi-pack contact printing may be preferred to optical printing. The cost is lower, since the work is done 'in plant' and the equipment which is tied up is not as expensive. Fewer steps are involved, since the original matte drawings are used during composite printing, rather than traveling-matte strips. Registration and matte-line accuracy are inclined to be better since fewer duplication steps are involved. Finally, the image quality of the compositite is, in some respects, likely to be of finer quality through contact printing than through optical printing.

Photographically-produced traveling mattes

As we have seen, the hand-drawn traveling matte provides the only method of securing certain complicated effects, as well as the cheapest and most convenient method for wipes and 'insert' mattes. For more complicated work, however, in which actors and other foreground objects are to be combined with background action, the hand-drawn matte is not practical. The cost of projecting and tracing an actor's movements onto paper and transferring the matte images to cells would be exhorbitantly expensive for sequences of any length. Instead, a variety of different techniques have been developed which allow for the photographic production of a traveling matte, either at the time that the foreground is photographed, or during subsequent duplication. These are described next.

Single-film systems

As early as the 1920s, technicians were producing traveling mattes for black-and-white composites by first photographing their actors in front of a dead-black backing. The negative of the actor was fully exposed so as to produce a fairly dense image of the performer against a clear surround. After development, the negative was step-printed onto a high-contrast duplicating stock, which in turn, was successively re-printed until sufficient contrast had been built up to produce a traveling matte in which the silver image of the actor was opaque against a clear background.

Providing a black backing was used for the original photography, a counter-matte was not required – the actor's master positive was self-matting. In some cases, however, a white backing was employed, which required slight underexposure of the actor's image and subsequent production of a counter-matte. Sometimes, in an attempt to reduce the number of duplications, the first high-contrast dupe was overdeveloped, or intensified with dyes.

This process was developed and patented by Frank D. Williams. Among the many films on which it was used was the already-cited 1933 production of *King Kong*. For many years, it was the only practical traveling-matte system available. Unfortunately, the effect was not very convincing on the screen. Overdevelopment, intensification, and multiple-duplications of the mattes caused 'bleeding' or spreading of the matte image. When the composite was made, this resulted in a visible matte-line or 'halo' around the actor. The process could be used with color stocks, but the results were even less impressive than in black-and-white.

Color-separation ('blue-backing') systems

A far better traveling matte effect can be produced by employing a negative color emulsion for the original photography, and capitalizing upon the film's ability to record contrasting colors which are intentionally produced in foreground and background areas during original photography.

There are two methods for lighting the shot. In the first, the actor is posed in front of a front-lighted blue flat, the illumination of which is sometimes filtered blue or violet.* Apart from its convenience and low

---

* For such purposes, a cobalt-blue paint is employed, available from several different suppliers. One of these is the 7-K Products Co. of Los Angeles, whose paint for this work is type # SC-71-3-60. A second is the Paramount Paint Co. of Los Angeles, whose applicable paint is Ultra Marine Blue, type # 8580.

cost, this method has the advantage of allowing the shadow which is cast by the actor onto the blue backing or onto the blue-painted floor to be carried into the background scene, if desired.

The second approach to blue-backing photography employs a dye-impregnated translucent screen, illuminated from the rear. Such screens, through which light is *transmitted*, are considered by some to be superior to painted flats from whose surface light is *reflected*, the purity of hue and depth of saturation of the cobalt-blue color of the translucent screen being somewhat greater than that of the painted surface (Figs. 8.8 and 8.9). The actor is lighted conventionally with white light, and photographed on a

Fig. 8.8. A translucent blue screen built at Pinewood Studios for work with Industrial Light and Magic Company on the feature film *Dragonslayer*. The translucent material for the 20 × 20 ft screen was manufactured by the Stewart Screen Company. Rear illumination is provided by approximately 260, 140-watt fluorescent tubes, operating at 220 volts d.c. This unusually intense screen allows for a T-stop exposure of T/20 at 24 frames per second. (Courtesy *American Cinematographer*.)

Fig. 8.9. A rear-view look at the lighting units for a translucent screen used for traveling-matte photography on Robert Wise's production of *Star Trek, The Movie*. Scores of fluorescent tubes and their associated wiring can be seen.

194

Fig. 8.10. Printing steps in the preparation of a conventional 'blue-screen' traveling matte, as described in the text. Illustration A shows the scene as originally photographed on color negative, with the actor posed in front of a blue backing.

color negative stock. The color negative which results is then step-printed in contact with a black-and-white positive which is sensitive only to the blue component of the scene. The result is a black-and-white separation positive in which the background area is clear (Fig. 8.10B).

The color negative is again printed to a black-and-white master positive, this time recording only the red components of the scene. The color-separation positive which results is black in the background area. This positive is then step-printed to a high-contrast dupe, producing a negative image of the actor against a clear field (Fig. 8.10C).

Finally, the blue-filtered positive and the red-filtered dupe negative are optically printed in bi-pack onto a high-contrast black-and-white stock, producing a traveling matte which is clear in the area of the actor and opaque in the surround (Fig. 8.10D). A counter-matte may now be printed from the matte (Fig. 8.10E).

The completed male and female traveling mattes, together with foreground and background color masters (Figs. 8.10F and G), are combined through bi-pack optical printing to produce a composite (Fig. 8.10H).

This description is simplified, in that it does not describe intermediate steps, from color-separation positives, that are often necessary to build up density and contrast in the male and female mattes, as well as special 'cover' mattes which may be required to obscure unwanted highlight areas in the scene which stubbornly resist matting and end up printing-through onto the final composite.

This system is widely employed today and gives fairly good results when properly conducted. If precision and consistency in operations are lacking, however, a matte line results which is just as obnoxious in color as it is in black-and-white. The matte line will assume whatever color is used for the sound-stage backing. In fact, a red backing can be used for satisfactory separation; however, it is easier to separate blue out of the actor's flesh tones than red. Also, if a blue matte line results, it will be far more likely than red to merge into the sky and other areas of the background scene.

Care must be taken to avoid the presence of deep-blue colors in the actor's costume, lest they become transparent on the composite, allowing the background scene to be viewed through portions of the performer's body. Peculiar fringing effects also occur when cigarette smoke, transparent objects, reflections, blurred edges of performers or moving objects and fine mesh materials appear in the foreground. In addition, this system pretty much precludes the photography of highly-polished objects which will reflect the blue backing off their surfaces, thus creating an unwanted secondary matte line. Several years ago, a blue-screen shot made of Julie Andrews for the 20th Century Fox production of *Star* proved impossible to combine with the appropriate background scene during final optical printing stages. A highly-visible matte line surrounded her face which could not be removed by any known remedy. In the end, the scene had to be re-shot, at considerable expense. Veteran visual-effects worker Don Weed worked on the assignment and recalled the frustration which he and his associates experienced with this shot. It was some weeks after the event that he discovered that the make-up man had put a light film of baby oil upon Ms Andrews' face to create an attractive facial 'sheen'. The oil served as a mirror of the cobalt-blue screen behind her, creating *two* edges to her face and a matte line 'halo' which could not be removed.

Another method of producing a traveling matte uses color emulsions in an entirely different way to produce a *black-and-white* composite. The actor is again posed in front of a blue-backing but he is illuminated with orange or yellow-filtered light, as was the case in the old Dunning process. Naturally, the resulting color balance looks peculiar to the eye, but as it is to be used to produce a black-and-white composite, this does not matter. A negative color stock is used for the original photography. The original exposed color negative is printed to a black-and-white positive, with color separation filters which pass the yellow-illuminated foreground but hold back the blue background. This produces a black-and-white master positive which is self-matting.

The same color negative is now printed to a black-and-white stock with color-separation filters which pass the blue background but hold back the yellow-lit foreground. The result is a traveling matte which is clear in the area of the actor but black in the surround. A high-contrast counter-matte is printed from this, producing a clear surround and an opaque foreground image. This counter-matte is used with the background master positive during final composite printing.

Both of these single-film processes offer many advantages. They are relatively inexpensive – at least insofar as the original photography is concerned. Conventional production cameras and lights are employed for the original photography, and the lighting is hardly more critical than for conventional work. Finally, once the original photography is completed, the film can be turned over to a special-effects laboratory for the making of the traveling mattes and the optical printing of the composite.

In ideal conditions, the quality of composite in both systems is good; however, there are limitations in all of the single-film processes described so far. First, since both male and female masks are made from the same color negative, the effect is to render any transparent object in the foreground which is interposed against the blue backing as part of the opacity of the traveling matte, and hence, as invisible in the final composite. This is particularly true of windows, glassware, smoke, and reflections. Semi-transparent materials, such as mesh or hair, acquire a bluish fringe, as do solid objects which are out of focus or blurred through rapid movement. Second, since there is no way in which blue light can be filtered out of the image which is recorded from the foreground, without also altering the record of the background screen, it is essential that primary blue colors be eliminated from costumes and props.

Third, the production of male and female traveling mattes requires several duplication steps, all of which contribute to image bleed and registration error.

Thus, an entirely different kind of process is necessary for the very best quality of work – a process which (1) preserves the image of translucent objects in the foreground, (2) allows for the use of any visible color in costumes and props, (3) minimizes or eliminates duplication steps in the production of the traveling matte, and (4) provides a self-matting image of the foreground action so as to eliminate the need for a counter-matte during final composite printing.

The color-difference process

In recent years, a single-film traveling matte process has been introduced which meets many of these specification. It is called the 'color-difference' system and is available to producers under patent license.

The process was developed by Petro Vlahos for the Motion Picture Research Council, the patents of which are administered by the Association of Motion Picture Producers in Hollywood. Subsequent development of the process for production applications was conducted by Walter Beyer of Universal Studios, W. E. Pohl of Technicolor Corporation, and others.

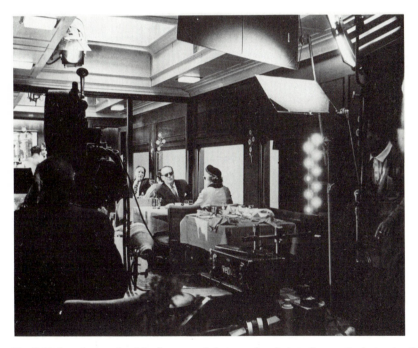

Fig. 8.11. Sound-stage detail for foreground photography of a traveling-matte shot, using the blue-screen, color-difference system. The set duplicates the interior of a railway dining-car, with the rear-illuminated screen mounted just outside the windows. The camera is positioned, left, for a three-quarter shot, to which the background plate will be matched later. A vertical row of lights, part of the several score used to illuminate the screen from behind, can be seen at right. (Courtesy of *American Cinematographer.*)

As with previously-described systems, the color-difference traveling-matte process requires that the actor be posed in front of a blue backing – either a front-lighted flat or a rear-illuminated screen (Fig. 8.11). The system capitalizes upon the fact that if black-and-white separation positives are printed from the camera color negative, the red record will render the blue backing black, and the green record will render the blue backing a dark grey, whereas, of course, the blue record renders it clear (Fig. 8.13).

Fig. 8.12. A scene from the railway dining-car shown in Fig. 8.11, with the moving background detail added.

By performing a rather complicated series of laboratory duplications, a 'synthetic' blue separation is prepared to replace the normal one. This synthetic separation positive of the blue record is also dark in the backing area.

Thus, all three separations can be made self-matting when re-combined with appropriate color-separation filters, during final composite printing of the color inter-negative (Fig. 8.14).

With the original blue-backing converted into a black backing for printing purposes, we eliminate blue fringing around foreground objects and we allow for the realistic rendition of transparent or semi-transparent materials (smoke, mesh, glassware and liquids) in a traveling-matte composite.

The synthetic blue-separation positive is produced by bi-packing the original color negative with the green separation positive and printing with blue (47 + 2b) light. What results is a so-called color-difference matte – a black-and-white image which represents, tonally, the density difference between the blue and green separation positives. If the color-separation matte is now paired with the black-and-white green separation positive, the two films, in bi-pack, become a 'synthetic' blue separation positive, in which (a) the density values of the foreground image are identical to those of the original blue-separation positive, but (b) the original blue backing is now rendered black.

In day-to-day practice, some additional manipulations are also necessary for perfect results. Although the theory of this process sounds good on paper, its consistently good practice requires experimentation and experience. The blue backing which is used on the sound stage is never a 'pure' blue – it always contains traces of green. To remedy this, a special 'cover matte' is prepared and used during final composite printing of the color inter-negative to remove traces of green from the backing. It is also necessary, of course, to prepare a counter-matte to mask the foreground action during composite printing. The preparation of corrective 'cover

Fig. 8.13, part 1. Color-separation positives used with the blue-screen, color-difference system. This is the blue color-separation positive from the color negative. The actors are posed in front of a blue backing which is rendered clear.

Fig. 8.13, part 2. A green separation positive from the same color negative. The background is rendered dark.

Fig. 8.13, part 3. The red separation positive with the backing reproduced as black.

Fig. 8.14. The three-color foreground positive produced from the red, green and 'synthetic' blue color separations shown in Fig. 8.13. Note that the background is now black – self-matting. (Courtesy of *American Cinematographer.*)

masks' and 'counter-mattes' for this system is described in detail in the professional literature.*

The principal limitation of the system is that it cannot faithfully reproduce rich blue or violet colors. And, as with all blue-screen traveling-matte photography, one's camera lenses should be chosen with special care to avoid 'veiling' or flaring of the bright blue background across the whole image, especially when operating which short-focal-length lenses.

Obviously, this is a complicated process, the laboratory operations of which few low-budget producers will execute within their own facilities. The point to be borne in mind is that the *original* photography of foreground action and background plates *can* be conducted by the small producer with conventional production cameras, and the subsequent laboratory operations then completed at leisure by a special-effects service laboratory.

Other single-film techniques

Front-lit/back-lit traveling-mattes

Assuming that an object being photographed in the foreground (such as a miniature) is immobile, so that there is no movement whatever, it is possible to use a so-called 'front-lit/rear-lit' traveling-matte system in which the object is photographed first, with conventional color negative stock, in

---

* A number of techniques are available to coax properly-fitting mattes out of difficult shots. In the case of at least one important feature, workers inserted a glass plate into the optical printer during final composite printing, onto which a thin film of vaseline was spread at the point of matte-line join, in order to blur the matte edges and produce a proper fit.

Fig. 8.15, part 1. Foreground action for a color-difference traveling-matte. The props in the scene have been selected to present detail which ordinarily taxes single-film systems: transparent glass and liquids.

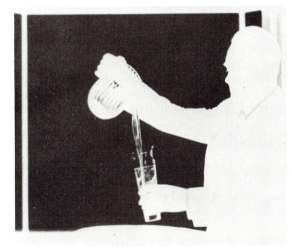

Fig. 8.15, part 2. One of the several mattes used. Limitations of the half-tone printing process prohibit presentation of all the subtly differentiated mattes that are used.

Fig. 8.15, part 3. The final composite. Note the absence of matte-line fringe and the preservation of background detail. (All photos courtesy Technicolor Corporation.)

front of a black background flat. This produces a record of the foreground miniature which is self-matting. A second pass is now made, with black-and-white film stock in the camera, this time with the front light extinguished, and with the black backing replaced by an evenly-lit white screen (or, in a variation, a blue screen). This second exposure produces a female matte from which a high-contrast male matte can be printed, opaque in the area of the object and clear in the surround. The self-matting foreground record and the male traveling-matte may then be used for composite optical printing purposes. Obviously, when using this approach, the foreground object cannot move between takes of the two strips of film, or the images will not fit properly during final composite printing. This limitation pretty well rules out the use of the technique for photographing human beings. It can be used, however, to photograph moving miniatures, providing motion-control equipment is employed, which allows for precisely the same changes in camera and object positions during photography of the two strips of film, in successive passes, from one designated frame to the next. The use of such apparatus is described in Chapter 13.

It is also possible to use the front-lit/back-lit technique by alternately photographing the foreground object and the background matte on *successive* frames of the *same* strip of color negative, processing the exposed film, and then separating out the foreground record and the background traveling matte onto two separate strips of film by means of skip-frame optical printing.

Reverse/negative traveling-matte systems

As we have observed, blue-screen traveling-matte systems pose difficult problems in the photography of miniatures with highly-reflective surfaces, the color of the blue backing being reflected off the object's surface and being recorded as a secondary matte line.

In recent years, a so-called 'reverse' or 'negative' blue-screen traveling-matte process has been employed to solve this problem. First developed by Johnathan Erland, it involves the use of a transparent coating which is applied over the painted surface of the finished miniatures. This coating is invisible under ordinary incandescent light, but fluoresces brightly under ultra-violet light. In practice, using motion-control equipment (see Chapter 13), a so-called 'beauty pass' is first made, in which the miniature is set in front of a black backing, illuminated with incandescent light, and photographed on conventional color negative stock. (Sometimes the incandescent light source is filtered by a Wratten 2B filter to remove excess ultraviolet radiation.) Photographed against a black backing, the image which results is self-matting.

During the second pass of the motion-controlled camera, the miniature is again photographed against a black backing, but is this time illuminated with strong ultra-violet radiation, approximately 360 nanometers in wavelength, causing it to fluoresce brightly at approximately 430 nanometers, which is perceived and photographed as blue light. (A nanometer, sometimes called a millimicron, is one thousand-millionth of a meter.) Depending upon the technique employed, the miniature is photographed with either a high-contrast black-and-white film stock or with color negative stock, the camera lens being filtered to remove excessive ultraviolet light which would otherwise contaminate the image. When processed, this record becomes a male traveling matte, opaque in the area of the miniature and clear in the surround.

Under these circumstances, the miniature becomes a source of illumination *itself*, rather than reflecting the light which is cast upon it. This system allows the traveling-matte photography of highly reflective objects, with specular metallic surfaces or glossy paints. There are many variations and sophistications of the system, which are described in the professional literature.* Patents on the system have been applied for by Apogee, Inc. of Los Angeles. Among the recent feature-film productions which have employed this technique are *Firefox* and *Blue Thunder*.

Multi-film systems

Processes such as the color-difference system, which use a single strip of film in a conventional camera, solve many of the problems involved in the production of traveling mattes. Over the years, however, some studios have used a variety of different 'multi-film' systems, each of which involves the production of the traveling matte *at the same time* that the action negative is photographed. These multi-film systems are complicated and costly, and, for the most part, have been replaced with blue-screen techniques of one sort or another. Nonetheless, they offer good results when properly employed, and they meet all of the previously-mentioned specifications for a versatile and effective traveling-matte system.

All multi-film systems are designed to produce a traveling matte simultaneously with the photography of the foreground action. In the United States, the equipment which is usually employed for this purpose is a 35 mm '3-strip' Technicolor camera (Fig. 8.16). This camera was originally built to record three separate color-separation negatives for subsequent color printing with the Technicolor inhibition dye process. Since the middle 1950s, however, high-quality monopack color emulsions have replaced color-separation negatives as an original recording medium. The Technicolor camera is now obsolete for its original purpose, but can still be used for the production of traveling mattes. In Great Britain, a somewhat similar camera, manufactured by the J. Arthur Rank organization, was designed expressly for traveling-matte work.

Both the Technicolor and Rank cameras employ a beam-splitting prism behind the lens which divides the light entering the camera so that virtually identical images of the scene are passed to two different intermittent movements (Fig. 8.17 and Fig. 8.18). For traveling-matte purposes, one of the movements carries a standard color negative which records the foreground action. The other carries a specially-selected film stock which records the traveling matte of the same action. The two intermittent

* See Johnathan Erland, 'Reverse or negative bluescreen traveling matte process', *JSMPTE*, March 1983, p. 268.

Fig. 8.16. The Technicolor three-strip color camera. Rendered obsolete by the introduction of monopack color negative stocks, the camera is now occasionally used for two-strip traveling-matte photography. Oversize magazines carry both strips of film, side by side. (Technicolor Corporation.)

movements are synchronized with one another, and the exposure of the action and matte is made simultaneously, frame by frame (Fig. 8.19).

At least four different processes have been used in conjunction with such a camera to produce traveling mattes. Each of these achieves its purpose by separating and recording light of distinctly different wavelengths, or bands of wavelengths, on each of the two strips of film. The wavelengths selected for this purpose differ in each case and provide the name by which the processes are known.

The infra-red process

The actor is posed in front of a black nylon velvet drape which has been treated with dye (sometimes backed up with sheet aluminum foil) so as to reflect a maximum amount of non-visible infra-red radiation. The velour drape is illuminated with ordinary incandescent lamps (which contain a substantial amount of infra-red radiation). Alternatively, a translucent screen may be employed, illuminated from behind by filtered lamps which radiate only infra-red wavelengths.

Fig. 8.17. Front view of the Technicolor camera, with the lens mount swung open. One of the Mitchell movements can be seen to the left of the beam-splitter, 90° to the optical axis. (Technicolor Corporation.)

The actor is also illuminated with incandescent lamps; however, the fresnel lenses of the lamps are coated with a dichroic filter medium which passes wavelengths in the visible spectrum, but sharply attenuates radiation in the infra-red region, 700–900 nanometers (Fig. 8.20).

The beam-splitting prism of the Technicolor camera is also coated with a dichroic filter medium which is identical to that used on lamp lenses. The effect of the coating is to pass only visible wavelengths of light to the action negative which is loaded into the intermittent movement behind the prism. Either black-and-white or color emulsions can be used for this record, all of them being virtually insensitive to infra-red radiation. The same dichroic filter coating *reflects* only infra-red radiation, 90° to one side, so as to strike the traveling-matte film which is loaded into the other intermittent movement (Fig. 8.21). An infra-red sensitive emulsion is employed here, which is sensitive not only to infra-red but also to blue light and ultraviolet radiation. However, the dichroic filter coating on the prism insures that this film will be exposed only by wavelengths in the range 700–900 nanometers.

The effect of such a system is to simultaneously produce an action negative and a traveling matte, each being recorded with different wavelengths of light. The action negative is exposed only by visible light

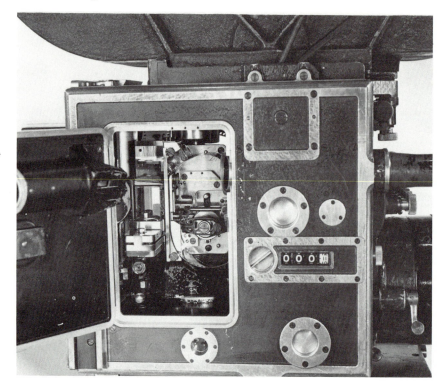

Fig. 8.18. Left side of the Technicolor camera, with loading door open. The second intermittent movement is located directly to the right of the beam-splitter, its film running perpendicular to the optical axis. (Technicolor Corporation.)

reflected from objects in the foreground. A color master struck from this negative will be black in the background area, and therefore self-matting (Fig. 8.22). The traveling matte, on the other hand, is exposed only by light reflected from the infra-red backing, and is therefore clear in the area of the actor's body and opaque in the surround. For purposes of composite printing, this strip of film is step-printed onto a high-contrast stock, producing a male traveling matte which is opaque in the area of the foreground action and clear in the surround (Fig. 8.22).

Since the matte is produced separately from the action negative, this system allows for the faithful reproduction of smoke, transparent objects and fine-mesh materials in the foreground, all of which are recorded on the self-matting action negative. Since only infra-red radiation is used for the production of the traveling matte, any visible color may be employed in the costumes, make-up or props, without fear of their becoming invisible in the final composite. Since the wavelengths used for the production of the traveling matte fall outside of the visible spectrum, these non-visible wavelengths may be subtracted from the actor's illumination without distorting the color rendition and balance which are recorded by the production negative. Finally, since the action negative is self-matting, a

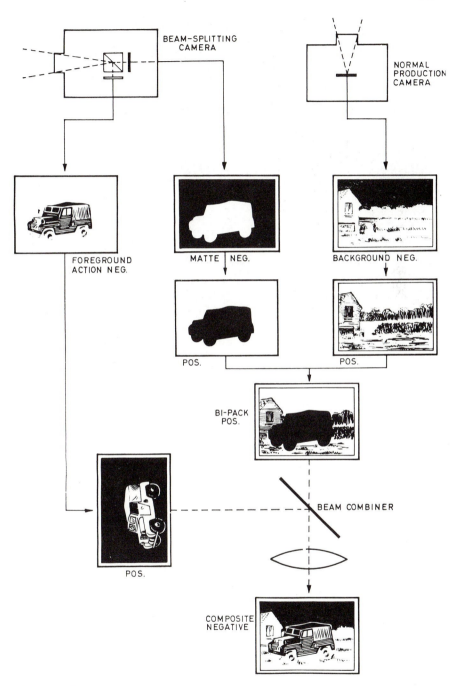

Fig. 8.19. The multi-film traveling-matte system, as used with any of the beam-splitting techniques described in the text. The diagram shows a beam-combiner or aerial-image type printer being used for final printing of the composite negative. Alternatively, this step can be conducted through successive printing steps on a conventional optical printer. (British Kinematography Society.)

Fig. 8.20. Sound-stage set-up for an infra-red traveling-matte shot. The Technicolor camera is positioned at center. Floor lamps provide minus-IR illumination for the actor. Overhead, and at the far sides, strip lights illuminate the black velvet screen behind the performer with infra-red light. (MPO-Videotronics, Inc.)

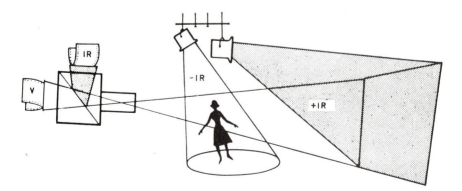

Fig. 8.21. The infra-red system runs a conventional color or black-and-white negative through the camera's rear movement, and an infra-red-sensitive stock through the right-angle movement. Mutually exclusive filtering systems separate the performer (lighted with minus-infra-red illumination) from the infra-red-illuminated backing, and record them on the separate pieces of film. (JSMPTE.)

Fig. 8.22, part 1. Positive print from the self-matting action negative, produced by means of the infra-red process.

Fig. 8.22, part 2. Positive print made from the infra-red-sensitive traveling matte. (MPO Videotronics.)

counter-matte need not be employed during final composite printing, thus minimizing registration error (Fig. 8.23).

In theory, once the action negative and traveling matte have been shot, all that remains to be done in the process is to strike a color master from the negative and to make the final composite through bi-pack optical printing. In actuality, however, additional steps are required to correct the size of the traveling matte's image so that it matches that of the action negative. This is necessary inasmuch as infra-red radiation does not focus in the same plane as visible light, thus producing a matte image which is larger than that of the action record. The correction of the traveling matte is made through reduction optical printing. It is sometimes also necessary to prepare and use a faint female 'cover matte' over the self-matting foreground image to prevent a mild fogging or veiling of background detail in the composite.

When properly executed, the infrared system produces excellent results. The process, as it is used in the United States, was invented and patented by Leonard Pickley, and was greatly improved and elaborated by MPO Videotronics Inc. of New York, from which organization licenses may be obtained.

In the Soviet Union, a variation of the process employs a multi-strip camera similar to the Technicolor camera, to photograph the actor in front of a black, infra-red-rich backing, as described above. The exposed color negative, which is self-matting, is held after the first exposure. The

Fig. 8.23. A composite shot produced for a TV commercial by means of the infra-red process. (MPO Videotronics.)

traveling-matte strip is processed, yielding a female matte which is clear in the area of the actor's body and opaque in the surround. A high-contrast dupe is printed from this, producing a male matte which is clear in the surround. During subsequent exposure, the male traveling matte is run in bi-pack in a production camera with the 'held' negative of the actor on the sound stage. The background image, such as an exterior scene, is then photographed directly onto the production color negative *through* the surround of the bi-packed male matte, producing a composite image.*

The ultraviolet process

The actor is posed in front of a clear, translucent screen which is illuminated from behind with ultraviolet light from fluorescent lamps.

The foreground action is illuminated with conventional incandescent lamps from which ultraviolet radiation is subtracted by Wratten 2B filters.

The Technicolor camera is employed in the same fashion as in the infrared process, except that the beam-splitting prism is coated with a Corning filter medium, and an ultraviolet-sensitive black-and-white stock is used to record the traveling matte.

The effect of this process and apparatus is to insure that only ultraviolet radiation will be *reflected* off the beam-splitter's surface to strike the traveling-matte stock. The same coating *absorbs* ultraviolet and *passes* only visible wavelengths to the action negative behind the prism.

* This process has been further developed by the addition of an electronic masking process which requires pre-processing of selected layers of a specially-prepared color film stock. This technique, which is quite complicated, is described by Joseph Alexander, 'An infrared traveling matte system with electronic masking', *JSMPTE*, June, 1979, p. 410.

As in the case of the infra-red system, the traveling matte which is produced with ultraviolet radiation is clear in the area of the actor's body and opaque in the surround. Through step-printing, a traveling matte is produced which is suitable for final composite printing – opaque in the area of the foreground action and clear in the surround. A color master which is struck from the action negative will be black in the surround and, therefore, self-matting.

The ultraviolet process offers substantially the same advantages as that of the infra-red, although transparent objects in the foreground are sometimes rendered undesirably dark or opaque because of their low ultraviolet transmission. This process also shares the same limitations of the infra-red system in that it produces a traveling-matte image which is not the same size as that of the action negative. In this case, the matte is smaller than the action record and must be enlarged appropriately through optical printing before the final composite can be made. As with the infra-red system, a faint female cover-matte may be required to prevent fogging of background detail in the composite.

The ultraviolet process is protected by patents which are owned and licensed by Warner Bros. Studios.

The sodium process

The best-regarded multi-film system to be employed in recent years for the production of traveling mattes is the 'sodium-vapor' process. It is almost identical in operation and results to the infra-red and ultraviolet systems, except that it produces a matte image which is identical in size to that of the action negative, thus eliminating the necessity for reduction or enlargement of the matte before final composite printing.

A brilliant-yellow screen is used for the backing, and is illuminated either from the front or the rear with ordinary sodium-vapor lamps which emit monochromatic yellow light with a wavelength of 589 nanometers. The foreground action is illuminated with incandescent lamps, operating at 3250 K, which are filtered with didymium-coated glass filters, which subtract monochromatic yellow from the actor's lighting (Fig. 8.24). A variation on this technique, developed by Petro Vlahos and used at the Disney Studios, employs an unusually sharp-cutting filter in the beam-splitting optics, thereby eliminating the need for didymium filters over the foreground lamps.

The sodium process is intended to be used with Eastman's negative color stock type 5247, which is relatively insensitive to monochromatic yellow. It also capitalizes upon the fact that very little monochromatic yellow is reflected by an actor's face; rather, the flesh tones as we perceive them are produced by a combination of wavelengths falling in the red and green portions of the spectrum. For this reason, monochromatic yellow can be subtracted from light reflected from the foreground action without noticeably changing the color balance or fidelity of the recorded image.

Again, the Technicolor or Rank camera is employed for original photography. A sharp-cutting interference-filter pellicle, which is incorporated into the camera's beam-splitter, transmits only monochromatic yellow light from the backing to the traveling-matte record. The same

Fig. 8.24. The sodium-vapor traveling-matte process in operation at Walt Disney Studios. Julie Andrews performs in front of a brilliant yellow backing for a scene in *Mary Poppins.* Later, background detail will be added behind her. (Technicolor Corporation.)

beam-splitter reflects all other wavelengths except that of 589 millimicrons to the action negative, which records the foreground scene. Additional filters are inserted into the apertures of the two intermittent movements – monochromatic yellow in front of the traveling-matte stock and didymium in front of the color record – thus ensuring that neither film will be contaminated by wavelengths intended for the other.

As with the infra-red and ultraviolet systems, either incandescent or arc lamps, or a combination of the two, may be used for foreground lighting, provided that the arcs are appropriately filtered to match the color temperature of the incandescent. Additional filtering is necessary when using the sodium process inasmuch as the didymium filters, which are employed for wavelength separation, lower the color temperature of light reaching the color negative. Accordingly, incandescents require a blue filter to raise the resulting color temperature to the recommended 3200 or 3250 K, while arc lamps require a yellow filter rather than the usual orange.

One disadvantage of the sodium process, which annoys some cameramen, is that higher light levels will ordinarily be required for any given relative aperture and for any given film stock, due to the fact that the camera's optical system absorbs quite a bit of light in the process of imaging the scene onto the two pieces of film. This lighting of the set to a higher light level may involve additional time and cost, depending upon the nature of the scene and the manner in which the traveling-matte footage will be cut into the preceding and following scenes. Conversely, the cinematographer may use a higher-speed film or a larger relative aperture, for any given light level, but these steps may produce footage which will not cut well into surrounding footage. In addition, considerable separation must be created between the performer and the background screen so that the performer's body will not be contaminated by the sodium-vapor radiation. Finally, the Technicolor camera's optical system is not well-suited for the use of either wide-angle or anamorphic lenses.

Over the years, the Walt Disney Studios Organization has been most active in the United States in developing the sodium process for studio production. Most recently, however, that organization has shelved the process in favor of the blue-screen system, which it feels offers equally fine quality, while being easier to work with.

Fig. 8.25, part 1. Storyboard sketch for a scene in Walt Disney's production of *Mary Poppins.* The storyboard, when approved, represents the director's conception of the finished shot, and is the point of departure for the art director, the cinematographer, and the special-effects supervisor. In this particular case, a fantasy sequence is planned in which animated penguins will perform with Dick Van Dyke in a dance routine.

'Garbage mattes'

Whatever the traveling-matte system used – single-film, multi-film, blue-screen, sodium, or other – the background screen or painted flat which is used need be no larger than necessary to provide an outline around the body of the performer or miniature. It is by means of that surround that subsequent separation will be achieved and a traveling matte produced. A considerable saving in time and cost can be gained, therefore, by using a background screen of minimum size. In the process, however, surrounding wall areas and miscellaneous bric-à-brac (century stands, floor lights, motion-control tracks, etc.) will probably be photographed onto the color negative, the images of which must be removed so that they will not

Fig. 8.25, part 2. The storyboard conception has now been realized in a sodium-vapor traveling-matte shot of Dick Van Dyke and Julie Andrews, who perform in front of the bright yellow backing.

Fig. 8.25, part 3. The final composite, with painted background and animated cartoon figures added. In one 1500 ft film sequence, more than 180 sodium shots were used. (All photos courtesy of Walt Disney Productions.)

appear in the color negative or the traveling matte. To this end, a 'garbage matte' is prepared which is configured to block out all unwanted detail outside of the background screen area. In practice, a color master of the action is rotoscoped onto a matte board, and a black matte is shaped which obscures the unwanted surrounding detail. This painted black matte is photographed on motion-picture film, producing a matte strip which is run in bi-pack with the original traveling matte at the time that the male counter-matte is prepared, thereby producing a finished male matte which is opaque out to the edges of the frame (Plates 3 and 4). A counter-matte made from the 'garbage' matte strip is run in bi-pack with the color master during subsequent printing operations, insuring that unwanted detail in the surround is excluded. In the case of a moving camera shot, it will be necesary to animate the garbage matte, frame by frame.

Photography of background action

Photography of the background 'plate' is relatively uncomplicated. Nonetheless, attention must be paid to the matching, between foreground and background images, of perspective lines, scale relationships, and camera motion. The precautions to be observed here are almost identical to those involved in background projection, and are described in Chapter 10.

Ordinarily, it will be found more convenient to photograph the background plate first, and then to stage the foreground action to match it. However, the sequence of operations is usually immaterial from a technical point of view, and should depend entirely upon the demands of the particular scene and the preferences of the production crew.

For both the background and foreground photography, medium-speed emulsions, normally exposed and processed, will ordinarily give the best quality. For the sake of convenience, the background negative is ordinarily shot with a full (silent) aperture plate in the camera. This allows for flipping of the color master in the projector head of the optical printer without obstruction of the image by the sound-track area of the Academy mask. It may also be found desirable to photograph the foreground action with a full-aperture plate, in which case both background and foreground images may be reduced to Academy aperture on the duplicating negative during final composite printing. Finally, super-formats such as 8-perforation-pull-down 35 mm Vistavision, 5-perforation-pull-down 70 mm, and 8-perforation-pull-down 70 mm Dynavision can be used for original photography with the blue-screen processes, for subsequent reduction to 35 mm composites.

Special techniques

Contact printing of traveling-matte composites

Ordinarily, the production of a traveling-matte composite is considered a function of optical printing. However, many of the effects which have been described may also be achieved through bi-pack contact printing. This technique is described in Chapter 6.

For best results, the contact-printing process is limited to composites in which the background scene either does not move (as with still photographs or paintings) or in cases where the background image is animated from frame to frame (as with wipes and hand-drawn action).

It *is* theoretically possible to combine color masters of both foreground and background action through *tri-pack* contact printing, inasmuch as the intermittent movements of most process cameras will register three strips of film simultaneously. Such a system would require the running of the

Fig. 8.26. The 'Quad', four-headed, Vistavision-format optical printer built at Industrial Light and Magic Company for use on Lucasfilm's production of *Return of the Jedi.* Bruce Nickelson, head of the optical department, stands next to the machine's electronic control panel. (Courtesy of Lucasfilm, Ltd.)

color master and the duplicating raw-stock emulsion-to-emulsion, with the traveling matte or counter matte running in front of both, its emulsion in contact with the base of the master positive. It also requires the use of a tri-pack magazine or the special spooling of short lengths of color master and traveling-matte strips on the same core. The result, in either case, will be a visible, out-of-focus matte line around the foreground image, due to the physical displacement of the traveling matte away from the emulsion of the raw stock.

The bi-pack process camera may also be used for conventional contact printing of color masters, duplicating negatives, and traveling-mattes inasmuch as it is inherently a high-quality (albeit slow-moving) step printer.

In-the-camera printing

For really low-budget operations, in which neither the purchase of a process camera nor the purchase of optical printing services can be afforded, traveling-matte composites *can* be made with conventional equipment. What is required is a production camera which is capable of accepting a four-chamber magazine and whose intermittent movement will register two strips of film in bi-pack.

Assuming that a self-matting record of foreground action, and its traveling matte, have been produced, then the first printing – that of the foreground scene – is conducted in exactly the same fashion as with a process camera. The self-matting color master of the foreground is loaded into the intermittent of the production camera, in contact with the duplicating negative raw stock. The production camera is then focused on an illuminated white card which provides light for the printing of the master onto the raw stock.

Once the first printing is accomplished, the dupe negative is rewound to start position, and the color master of the foreground is replaced with its traveling matte, which is opaque in the area of the actor's body and clear in the surround. The camera may now be used at an exterior location for the recording of the background scene, which is photographed directly onto the duplicating negative raw stock, *through* the traveling matte.

Obviously, this is a less convenient system than that of optical printing and one in which any error in the performance of the background action or in the balance of exposure, color temperature, and perspective will require the re-shooting of the entire composite. Some insurance against error can be had by printing a number of identical takes of the foreground action in the laboratory, and then photographing the background scene for an equal number of takes, with as many variations in exposure balance, perspective match, and performance as seem required. Presumably, out of the many composite takes, at least one will be found acceptable. cinematographers may also discover that the duplicating color negative raw stock, although suited for the printing of the foreground action, is not suited for direct photography of background detail. Obviously, a good deal of testing of this technique will be necessary before success is achieved.

For color composites, the use of a production camera in this manner requires that the color master of the foreground action be self-matting. If this is not so, then a counter-matte would have to be run in tri-pack with it, which would not be practical.

Still another technique requires that the traveling matte be produced in a beam-splitting camera. The traveling matte is processed following exposure and a high-contrast male matte is printed from it. However the self-matting foreground record is held for subsequent re-exposure. Later, on location, the male matte is loaded into the production camera in contact with the previously-exposed but undeveloped negative of the foreground, and the background action is photographed through the traveling matte, directly onto the original negative.

Obviously, with such techniques, the possibility of error in the matching of the two components is considerable, and a number of takes should be made as insurance against exposure miscalculations and accidents in performance. Also, at the time that the foreground action is filmed, extra test footage can be run off, subsequently re-exposed with a test-take of the background scene, and slop-processed on the spot. Examination of the test composite will reveal whether the match and balance of elements is as it should be before the final take is made.

Needless to say, *all* optical printing should be planned so as to allow for a maximum number of printing operations with as few duplications of the film stocks as possible. If, for example, a traveling-matte composite is to conclude with a dissolve or a skip-frame alteration, it is pointless to compromise image quality by conducting the different printing operations in separate stages. With a little extra effort, transitions and other optical manipulations can be incorporated into the footage at the same time that the composite is produced, thus eliminating a complete generation in the duplication process. As another example, changes in emulsion position and screen direction can be made during the optical printing of the original negative to a color master, following which the master can be used for further printing of composites and transitions.

Special problems

35 mm versus 16 mm

In conventional past practice, the traveling-matte process has been pretty much limited to 35 mm production, partly because of a lack of concern and equipment for the smaller gauge, and partly because of the peculiar technical problems involved.

In the first place, it is only within the last few years that really satisfactory traveling-matte techniques have been developed for 35 mm, let alone 16 mm. Secondly, whereas the registration accuracy of contemporary intermittent movements is sufficiently precise for multiple printing in 35 mm, the same tolerances become unacceptably gross when applied to a 16 mm image which has only one quarter as much area.

Inasmuch as the perforations and pilot pins employed in 35 mm work are much larger than in 16 mm, they are inherently capable of more exact registration. Also, the shape of the perforations on 35 mm duplicating negatives and color masters are specially designed for maximum registration accuracy.

Finally, considered relative to the size of perforations and images, any compromise of registration integrity which is due to a given amount of film shrinkage will understandably be far greater in 16 mm than in 35 mm, due simply to the difference in dimensions.

Had the 16 mm film remained an amateur medium, the need for certain types of professional special effects in this gauge would never have arisen. After the Second World War, however, the 16 mm film was embraced as a fully-profesional communication medium in industry, education and broadcast television, and with such enthusiasm and success as to create a demand for the same kind of technical versatility as formerly prevailed in 35 mm work. Subsequent improvements in 16 mm film stocks and equipment rendered such technological ambitions feasible.

Whether the state of the art in 16 mm production will ever reach the point where the more intricate traveling-matte techniques will be practical seems questionable. Already, however, many of the less-complicated effects are being regularly achieved, using different methods which are more appropriate to the smaller gauge.

For wipes and certain types of hand-drawn animated-matte effects, the whole problem of registration weave and jiggle can be minimized by using either bi-pack *contact* printing or aerial-image printing. Since relatively large drawings of the traveling matte are optically reduced in these processes, and used from frame to frame to vary the pattern of light passing through the color master, the registration accuracy which results is just as good as is achieved in 35 mm work with conventional traveling-matte strips.

As equipment and film stocks improve, it is even conceivable that conventional 35 mm traveling-matte methods may become practical for 16 mm. This author, for example, has used traveling mattes in 16 mm bi-pack optical printing in order to produce silhouette composites. The results were quite good.

Emulsion positions

For the best quality of bi-pack composite printing, it is essential that the emulsion of the traveling matte be run in contact with either the color master in the printer head, or the duplicating negative in the process camera. Inasmuch as both the projector head and the process camera are capable of bi-pack operation, the final printing of a traveling-matte composite can be conducted in a variety of different ways.

1. During *both* first and second runs, the color masters and their respective mattes are run through the projector head. Their images, in each case, are optically printed onto the duplicating negative.

2. During the first run, a self-matting color master of the forground can be *contact*-printed to the duplicating negative, within the process camera. During the second run, the counter-matte is also run in contact with the negative, but the background master is printed optically.

3. During the first run, the foreground color master is copied optically, while its matte is run in contact with the duplicating negative. During the second run, the counter-matte is run in contact with the negative, while the background scene is copied optically. (Alternatively, both sets of film can be reversed during each of the exposures.) This method is the least to be desired, since it requires an exact 1:1 printing ratio and exceptional accuracy in registration, both of which are easier to specify than to achieve.

Presumably, between the first two printing methods, one will be found appropriate for whatever emulsion positions are employed for matte, counter-matte, background, and foreground films. If necessary, however, emulsion positions can be changed through ordinary optical printing, preferably during preparation of color masters and counter-mattes.

Special-design optical printers

The precision of the traveling-matte process has always been compromised to some extent by the necessity for successive exposure of the duplicating negative. Despite the high standards of accuracy with which the strips of film are registered, each separate 'run' through the optical printer contributes its share of weave and jiggle to the finished composite.

In recent years, new types of optical printers have been developed with which both the foreground and background films, and their respective traveling mattes, can be printed simultaneously. These are the triple-headed printers manufactured by a variety of organizations, previously described and illustrated in Chapter 7.

Since each of the three printer heads is equipped for bi-pack operation, a total of six strips of film can be printed at one time. Traveling-matte shots of great complexity, which would otherwise require many successive duplications and printing passes, can be executed in a single run through the machine.

Color masters versus color separations

Throughout this chapter, for convenience sake, reference has been made principally to the use of color masters in the duplicating processes involved in the creation of a traveling-matte composite. Many workers prefer to make black-and-white color separations from the original color negative and to re-combine these separate strips, with appropriate color filtering, during the printing of the duplicating color negative. There is no question that the use of color separations lends itself to a wider range of color balance changes than does that of color masters. Whether one or the other method produces finer-grained and sharper images, however, is a matter of continuing controversy between equally competent workers. In the end, experimentation, experience, and the preferences of the individual worker or shop will determine the technique used.

Traveling mattes vs. background projection

Inevitably, comparisons arise between the traveling-matte and background projection processes. *Both* provide methods by which foreground action can be 'jigsawed' directly into a background scene. *Both* offer the following advantages:

1. Exterior scenes may be simulated on the sound stage, thus providing ideal acoustical conditions for the recording of dialogue, and maximum artistry and control in the lighting of foreground action.

2. By photographing foreground and background action separately, difficult or hazardous scenes may be produced with safety and convenience, e.g. scenes of interiors of moving vehicles or of an actor balancing on the edge of a precipice. By the same virtue, utterly impossible composites can be manufactured for fantasy effects – actors may play dual roles in the same shot, automobiles can be made to fly across the sky, and so forth.

3. Background scenes of foreign or inaccessible locales can either be photographed separately or pulled out of the stock-shot library and integrated with foreground action on the sound stage.

4. By combining foreground and background scenes which were originally photographed at different times, more attention can be paid to the direction of action in each component, and maximum precision can be gained in the timing of the two. This is of particular importance when large numbers of actors perform complicated actions in different parts of the picture.

3. Once the equipment for either background projection or traveling-matte work is set up, individual shots and re-takes can be photographed fairly rapidly – the more shots taken each time the equipment is assembled, the lower the 'per shot' cost.

In contrast to background projection, the traveling-matte process offers a number of unique advantages:

1. The original photography can be done on a relatively small stage.

2. Contrariwise, the size of the foreground set is limited only by the size of the traveling-matte backing, which, in turn, is limited only by the size of the stage. For this reason, the traveling-matte process is particularly well-suited to wide-angle shots and wide-screen formats.

3. Either the background or foreground action can be photographed first. Further, the foreground can be photographed long before the exact nature of the background has even been decided upon. Actors who may not be available during regular production schedules may be photographed separately and later matted into background action.

4. The quality of the composite is better than with background projection. There is no 'hot-spot' to contend with, and the grain, contrast, and color fidelity of the background image is superior. Most important, the foreground and background in a traveling-matte shot are equally sharp. It can be argued, of course, that the conventional photography of close-ups and medium-shots produces a soft background image. Nonetheless, most producers insist upon as sharp a background as possible when ordering effects work – particularly when wide-screen systems are being employed.

5. Individual set-ups on the sound stage are accomplished far more rapidly with the traveling-matte process, because only the foreground components need to be recorded at that time. Since the backing which is employed remains the same for each shot, there is no delay in the selection of plates, the focusing of a projector, the changing of arcs, or the rewinding of plates for re-takes. The problem of 'splash light' contaminating the background screen is far less a problem than in projection work, thus allowing for more intricate and artistic lighting of actors. There is no special noise problem arising out of projector operation. The camera can be tilted to whatever extent seems dramatically and compositionally appropriate on the sound stage; later, the background plate can be photographed so as to match its perspective. Finally, it is not necessary to tie up expensive crews and sound

stage space during the balancing of background and foreground light levels, contrasts, and color temperatures, inasmuch as these operations are conducted later.

6. Once the foreground action and matte have been produced, the background scene may be changed any number of times as may be desired during composite printing; errors can be corrected and experimentation pursued.

7. Since the composite of background and foreground action is produced from separate strips of film, the maximum amount of precision can be realized in the timing and manipulation of the two (or more) elements.

8. Since the background and foreground images are equally sharp, the process can be used to create extreme depth-of-field effects without optical distortion.

9. Since the final composite is not produced on the sound stage, the original photography for a traveling-matte shot can be conducted with a minimum of equipment. (In the case of the blue-backing technique, standard production cameras and conventional lighting may be employed throughout.) Once the original photography is completed, the film can be turned over to a special-effects laboratory for all subsequent printing operations.

10. The color balance between foreground and background can be corrected any number of times in the laboratory until it is perfect, whereas background projection requires a perfect balance at the time of photography – there is no opportunity for subsequent correction.

11. Traveling-matte foregrounds can be shot at a wide range of camera speeds and later composited with similarly-photographed backgrounds. Many background projectors, on the other hand, are incapable of running in interlock at speeds other than 24 frames per second.

Despite its many advantages, however, the traveling-matte process is, in certain respects, *inferior* to background projection:

1. Since the background and foreground scenes are photographed at different times, it is impossible for the director and cameraman to view the finished composite while the actors perform, and to be sure that the perspective and scale relationships of the two match. One solution to this problem has been achieved with sophisticated new electronic matting systems such as the 'Ultimatte', which provide an accurate preview of the finished composite. This is described in Chapter 13. Another solution – providing that the background has already been photographed – is to strike a 'thin' color master from the background negative and to insert a single frame of the positive into the optical system of the 'through-the-lens' viewfinder, thus allowing the director to see the foreground action superimposed over the background detail, while lining up the shot.

2. Without being able to view the background action during the performance, the actor is at an even greater disadvantage than the director. The problem becomes particularly acute when the actor is

expected to respond to particular events in the previously-photographed background, or when eye contact must be maintained between performers in both areas. One solution calls for the timing of already-recorded background events with a stop-watch and the cueing of performers with hand signals during the take. Some studios achieve the same results by running the background scene over closed-circuit video monitors which surround the actors, outside of camera range.

3. Although the traveling-matte camera may be set in any desired position for the photography of the foreground action, it may not be panned or tilted once the scene is underway unless identical camera movements occur during photography of the background. A reasonable amount of dollying towards and away from the actor can be tolerated, providing extreme long shots are used in the background. Electronic motion-control apparatus which allows for precisely-matched action of foreground and background scenes is described in Chapter 13.

4. Insofar as the more complicated traveling mattes are concerned, the original photography is currently confined to 35 mm film stocks and equipment – at least if superior quality is required. Background projection, on the other hand, may be used with any gauge of equipment.

5. For high-budget productions using large crews, the traveling-matte process offers maximum quality at the lowest cost per sound-stage hour. Nonetheless, the process is undeniably expensive, particularly when the more sophisticated techniques are employed, and when a relatively small number of shots per sound stage 'set-up' are involved.

For low-budget operations, for organizations in which small crews are allowed to work for a longer period of time on each shot, and for assignments in which the ultimate in composite quality is not demanded, background projection will be found adequate and less expensive, particularly when the organization owns its own equipment for the front projection of plates or the back projection of 'stereo' transparencies.

6. Depending upon the traveling-matte system employed, considerable trouble may be encountered in eliminating matte-line fringes, and in compositing foreground images in which transparent or blurred objects and certain colors are present. These problems do not arise with background projection.

7. Using background projection, the 'dailies' are returned within 24 hour after photography. Traveling-matte shots, on the other hand, may be tied up in the laboratory for weeks.

8. Present-day multi-film traveling-matte systems require exotic light sources and filtering media. However, it seems likely that the same kind of matte separations which are produced with these systems could also be achieved by lighting the foreground and background elements of the scene with differently-polarized illumination, and then separating the two by means of mutually-exclusive polarizing filters within the beam-splitting camera.

9

Aerial-image printing

Until fairly recently, many of the special cinematographic effects employed by 35 mm workers have not been available to the professional 16 mm producer. This has been particularly true of traveling-matte techniques which, for reasons already reviewed in Chapter 8, have not proved technically suitable or economically feasible for the smaller-gauge stock. It has been apparent for some time that other methods would have to be developed to provide a special-effects capability for the growing 16 mm field. One of these new techniques, now widely employed by 16 mm producers, is that of aerial-image printing.

Actually, this is not an entirely new technique, it having been used from time to time by optical effects and animation workers in the Hollywood industry since the 1930s. Its widespread use in the 16 mm field occurred much later, however.

Principles of the process

An aerial image is a real image which is cast into space, rather than on to a screen, ground glass, or piece of film. If, for example, we set up an 8 × 10 inch view camera, and focus a scene upon its ground glass, we have caused a real image to be produced at the plane of the viewing glass, where, suitably diffused, it becomes clearly visible. If, with the camera in the same position, we now remove the ground glass entirely, the real image becomes an aerial image. The focused image still exists in the same position, but since it exists only in space, it cannot be seen with the eye.

What is important from our point of view is that this invisible aerial image can be re-focused by a second optical system so as to produce a real image at another position. At the same time, any art-work which is placed into the plane of the aerial image will be picked up by the supplementary optics with equal clarity and definition. If the art-work is opaque in certain of its areas, then it will matte-out portions of the aerial image. If, at the same time, the art-work is transparent in other areas, it will pass certain portions of the aerial image to the supplementary optics. If the illumination of the self-matting art-work and the brightness of the aerial image are properly balanced, then both will appear of equal brightness when re-focused by another optical system. Finally, if the supplementary lens system is made to cast a real image onto a piece of film, then a permanent record of the composite of (1) the projected aerial image, and (2) the directly-photographed art-work will be made, both elements being equally sharp and of equal brightness.

Using such a technique as this, it is possible to execute many kinds of composite shots, in which painted or photographic art-work is combined with live-action motion-picture images, without having to resort to bi-pack contact printing or traveling-matte optical printing, both of which are more time-consuming and the latter of which is quite costly.

In-the-camera technique

Over the years, workers have occasionally used direct aerial-image photography, instead of glass shots, to combine live action and art-work. Commercialy, such a system appeared in France many years ago under the trade name, 'Simplifilm', and in the United States as the 'Vistascope' system. The Vistascope took the form of a box about 3½ feet long and 16 inches high, open at both ends (Fig. 9.1). The box was mounted on a

Fig. 9.1. The Vistascope equipment for direct composite photography of both live-action and art-work by means of aerial-image optics. Either painted art-work on glass sheets, or cut-out photographs, are inserted into grooves in the aperture at center. In this position, they are in the plane of an aerial im ge cast by lenses within the right-hand section of the box. A viewing port is provided at left; alternatively, the composite can be viewed through the camera's viewfinder. A cut-out photo of a hallway, approximately 5 × 7 in, is seen in its holder, at right.

small lathe bed and a motion-picture camera was mounted at one end, its lens pointing into the box's interior (Fig. 9.2). This whole assembly was aimed at whatever scene was to be altered. Optical elements within the box created an aerial image of the exterior scene in a plane set midway in the box's interior. An aperture was cut into the side of the box at the point at which the aerial image was formed. Into this aperture, painted art-work on glass sheets, or cut-out photo mattes, could be inserted in grooves.

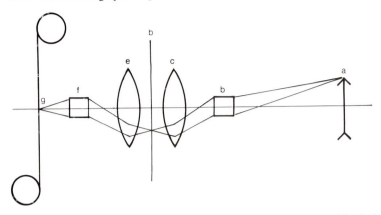

Fig. 9.2. Optics of the Vistascope system. An objective lens at the front of the device (b) collects light reflected from the subject at (a), which is passed through a field lens (c), forming an aerial image at (d). This aerial image continues on through the second field lens (e), is collected by the cameras' objective lens (f), and falls upon the film at (g). If art-work or a photo cut-out is placed in the plane of the aerial image at (d), it and the aerial image will be photographed simultaneously in equally sharp focus.

Fig. 9.3. The Vistascope shown mounted on a small lathe bed with a motion-picture camera. Assuming the use of a four-inch lens on a 35 mm camera, the effective focal length of the entire device becomes approximately 32 mm. The camera can be moved towards or away from the aerial image composite, either physically or by means of a vari-focal zoom lens.

Incandescent lighting units were positioned at each side of the box and their light was made to fall on the art-work within. The camera's lens was focused on the plane in which the art-work was positioned and into which the exterior, live-action image was caused to fall. The camera photographed both of them simultaneously – the art-work directly, and the aerially-imaged live-action component *through* the unpainted sections of the art-work or the cut-out areas of the photo. Properly executed, the composite was as convincing as a well-done glass shot, and had the advantage of producing equally sharp images of both components without concern for the depth of field which existed between the two.

A similar rig was developed by filmmakers at the Moody Institute of Science who were required to produce a shot of a bumble bee flying across a meadow, with both bee and background being kept in equally sharp focus! The filmmakers encased a live bee within a transparent plexiglass container, with one of its legs cemented to the inside surface so as to partially immobilize it. The bee in the container was positioned in the plane of focus of a set of aerial-image optical elements which were mounted, with a camera, on a small lathe bed. The whole contraption was aimed at a landscape background, and the camera simultaneously photographed both the bee and the meadow, as it panned across the latter. Since the aerial image was cast upside-down, the bee, too, had to be positioned upside-down. This did not amuse the bee, but it did place it in the proper position for photography. To add a final touch of realism, a small vibrator was attached to the plexiglass container. When operated at the appropriate moment of photographed 'flight', this roused the bee and caused it to move its wings.

Aerial-image printing

Aerial-image technique has, for many years, been used commonly for composite printing in the laboratory. In professional practice, two entirely different kinds of aerial-image technique and equipment have become commercially available within the last decade. The first of these utilizes a modified animation stand; the second, a modified optical printer. Both are suited for either black-and-white or color production, in either 16 mm or 35 mm gauge.

The animation stand system

Suitably adapted, a conventional animation stand can be used to conduct aerial-image printing. One such system (shown in Fig. 9.4) is manufactured by the Oxberry Corporation.

Using this system, as illustrated in Fig. 9.5, a fine-grain black-and-white or color master positive of a live-action scene is loaded into a projector which is positioned at floor level and to one side of the stand. An incandescent light source, ranging from 100 to 750 watts and suitably focused by achromatic condensers, illuminates the positive plate in the projector's intermittent movement. The image of the positive is projected by an $f/2.3$ objective to a front-silvered mirror located directly below the table of the stand. The mirror, which is set at a 45° angle, re-directs the projected beam upwards and through a pair of 9×13 inch condensers which produce a '10½ field' ($10½ \times 7½$ inch) aerial image at the top surface of the condensers. The optical system of the animation camera picks up the aerial image and re-focuses it on to raw stock where it is permanently recorded.

Interlocking drives

The motor drives of camera and projector are electrically interlocked so that synchronism is assured – as a new frame of raw stock is positioned in the camera's intermittent, so is a new frame of master positive registered in the projector (Fig. 9.6). If the camera and the projector are operated

Fig. 9.4. The Oxberry aerial-image animation stand. The projector at the base of the stand cast an aerial image into the same plane as the art-work, at the top of the table. Both the aerially-imaged color master and the art-work are then re-photographed simultaneously by the camera above.

without art-work in the plane of the aerial image, then the entire mechanism may be used as an optical printer. Also, since the pilot-pin movements of both the camera and projector will accept bi-pack loads, traveling mattes may be employed if desired.

If, however, art-work – such as a painted image on a transparent animation cel – is laid on to the animation cel board in the plane of the aerially-imaged master positive, then it will be photographed simultaneously with the live-action scene, both components being equally well-defined. Since the paints on the animation cel are opaque, the drawings are 'self-matting', obscuring those portions of the aerial image which would otherwise be picked up by the camera lens. Since the cel is transparent in all other areas, the aerial image passes through it and is recorded by the camera.

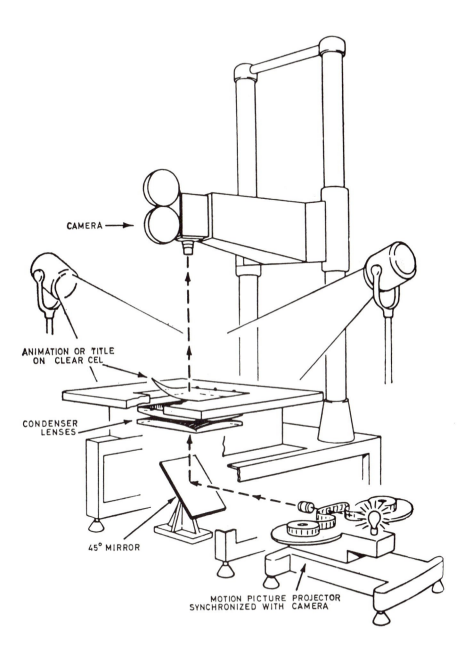

Fig. 9.5. A diagrammatic representation of the Oxberry aerial-image system.

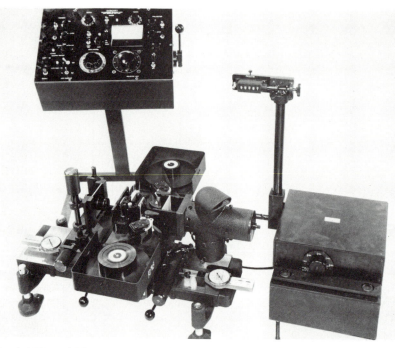

Fig. 9.6. The aerial-image projector and its electrical controls. Like the process camera, it incorporates a fixed pilot-pin movement for maximum registration accuracy.

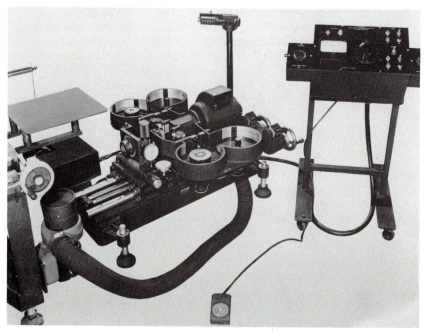

Fig. 9.7. Another model of the aerial-image projector, this one equipped for bi-pack operations.

Making the image visible

The aerial image which is cast into the plane of the animation cel board is, of course, invisible to the eye. When it becomes necessary for either the effects cameraman or an artist to see the projected live-action scene, a visible image can be produced by simply placing a sheet of tracing paper or ground glass on top of the animation table. The aerial image can also be seen with the camera's through-the-lens viewfinder.

With the aerial image cast on to a sheet of tracing paper which is registered by means of peg bars, the projection system may be used as a rotoscope, allowing the matte artist or animator to trace matte lines and to design his art-work with great precision. The horizontal animation-type table which is used in this system provides a convenient surface on which the artist can work.

Assuming that the animation stand and its associated equipment are properly designed, then the rigidity of the components, the pilot-pin movement of the projector, and the peg-bar registration system on the table-top will all combine to provide matte-line accuracy between live-action and art-work components. Since the aerial image and the art-work are photographed simultaneously, only one 'pass' through the animation camera is necessary for composite photography, thus reducing matte-line weave and jiggle to a minimum. The process can be used with either 16 mm or 35 mm stocks, or with a combination of the two.

Low light levels

Because of the optical efficiency of the aerial-image system, relatively low light levels are involved in projection of the master positive. Incandescent lamps ranging from 100 to 200 watts are generally used, although the lamp house will accept bulbs up to 750 watts, if necessary. Since such a relatively small amount of light is used for projection, there is little danger of 'burning' the live-action image through the paints and inks which are used on the animation cels. During exposure, the art-work can be lit with front lights at whatever illumination level is required. Since the aerial image exists only in space, rather than on a translucent screen, there is no danger of washing it out.

Using the animation-stand system, the only limitation to the aerial-image process is its inability to provide zooms in or out on the art-work and the projected image. The alignment of optics in aerial-image printing is fairly critical, and, in the case of the Oxberry unit, the size of the aerial image is fixed at $10\frac{1}{2} \times 7\frac{1}{2}$ inches. Once the components have been permanently aligned, the camera may not be moved towards or away from the animation cel board, or the aerial image will pass out of focus and disappear. Neither may the compound table or the camera be moved laterally, or optical misalignment will occur. By using the peg tracks and/or a floating peg assembly, however, art-work can be moved in conventional north–south, east–west, rotational or diagonal movements. Theoretically, using the animation-stand arrangement, it would be possible to build an assembly in which the projector, animation board, camera, condensers, and all of the optical components could be made to move continuously with respect to one another, thus keeping both the art-work and the projected image in focus during zoom movements. The engineering problems involved are formidable, however.

For the time being, should zoom effects be required which involve *both* the aerial image and the art-work, they must be produced by combining art-work, which is animated to give the effect of a zoom, with an aerially-imaged plate which was originally photographed with zoom or dolly movements. Zoom effects which involve *only* the aerial image may be produced by inserting a reticle-quality ground glass into the plane of the image, extinguishing the front lights and the room lights, and simply moving the animation camera towards or away from the ground-glass image, changing focus all the while. The quality of such work is not likely to be as fine as is ordinarily achieved through optical printing, however.

Applications and techniques

The aerial-image process combines most of the features of both optical and bi-pack printing; so it will produce virtually any effect obtainable with either system.

Optical printing

With the exception only of image-shift and image-size changes such as zooms and push-offs, all optical printing maneuvers are easily accomplished by simply re-photographing the aerial image with whatever space-time manipulations seem desirable; these include skip frame, hold-frame, multiple printing, reverse printing, dissolves, fades, wipes, superimpositions, split-screen, and rotating screen effects. The aerial-image assembly may also be used to enlarge 16 mm to 35 mm (or to reduce in contrary fashion) by simply exchanging the intermittent and film-feed movements in the camera and projector from one gauge to another. A variety of 'shadowboard' accessories provide for additional distortions of the image, including diffusion, fog, ripple, and fragmentation effects (Figs. 9.8 and 9.9).

Fig. 9.8. This shadowboard assembly mounts underneath the camera and provides a variety of optical effects, including wipes, optical flips, image fragmentations, optical diffusion and ripples.

Fig. 9.9. Close-up views of the shadowboard accessories. Top: a holder for the accessories. Middle: the wipe device. Bottom: the optical flip attachment.

Titles

Exceptionally-fine superimposed title effects can be easily and rapidly achieved with aerial-image techniques, and with results which are far superior in 16 mm to anything produced through the optical printing of traveling mattes.

The title and its drop-shadow are drawn or hot-press-printed on to two animation cels. These are registered and positioned on the animation table-top in the plane of the projected aerial image. In order to 'composite' the title and the live-action background, only one pass through the camera is necessary. The projected aerial image passes through the clear areas of the cel and is photographed directly. The opaque lettering of the title, being front-lit, reflects light which provides for its exposure while matting-out those portions of the aerial image which are positioned behind it. Dissolves between titles are easily accomplished by (1) fading out on both the first title cel and the aerial image, (2) replacing the first title cel with the second, (3) backing up the raw stock and the background plate to the beginning of the fade-out, and (4) fading in on the aerial-image plate and the second cel in the same number of frames as for the first part of the dissolve.

Since traveling mattes are not employed for such title effects, image weave and jiggle are avoided entirely. Equally important, the definition of the title is not compromised by the many steps of duplication which are necessary in traveling-matte work. Matte-line bleed is completely eliminated – fine lines and delicate pen strokes within the body or at the edges of the title letters can be rendered with perfect clarity.

If it is desired that the title letters should move, then they may, of course, be animated from frame to frame. Animation also allows for the combination of live-action and cartoon figures – a popular technique for television commercials. During the planning and animation stages, the live-action component is rotoscoped by means of the aerial-image projector on to translucent paper registered on top of the animation table. Taking the live-action image as a point of departure, the artist may develop whatever animated action he wishes to integrate into the scene by simply sketching his art-work directly on to the animation paper.

As the artist works on through the different stages of lay-out, pencil tests, in-between animation and cel painting, the effect of the composite can be seen and appraised at any time by means of the camera's viewfinding system. Working in this manner, the animator is able to integrate the live-action and animated components with great precision and with whatever complexity is required by the script – cartoon characters can 'enter' and move around the live-action scene, and can be made to respond to live-action events. The same technique can be used to add 'sparks', 'twinkles', 'flashes'. 'stars', 'ripples', and highlights to live-action scenes – all popular devices for achieving novelty or fantasy effects.

One recent television commercial employed animation and aerial-image techniques to suggest the 'cleaning' of a live-action scene by a hand which held a soapy sponge, sweeping back and forth across the scene. Such an effect can be achieved by printing the aerial image of the projected plate through an animation cel on to which a light neutral-density wash or tint has been laid. By alternately rotoscoping and photographing the plate, frame by frame, it is possible for the artist to detemine the position of the sponge and to wash off the neutral-density tint in synchronism with it. As an alternative method, the appropriate changes in density could be animated from frame to frame on separate cels.

Static matte shots

There is a wide variety of shots, similar in appearance to those described in Chapter 6, which can be easily and rapidly executed through aerial-image printing. Unlike bi-pack printing, only one pass through the camera is necessary, thus minimizing registration weave and jiggle, and reducing both the time and the expense required for the work.

A sheet of registered tracing paper is laid on to the animation table top and the live-action component is rotoscoped on to it with the projector. An artist traces the matte lines and transfers them to a clear acetate cel. Using the same techniques of perspective projection and draftsmanship which apply in bi-pack printing, the artist develops a new set of images to replace certain portions of the live-action scene, painting directly onto the cel with conventional animation paints and inks. Depending upon the demands of the film, the style can be either realistic or stylized.

Perhaps the greatest advantage of aerial-image technique for this work is the facility it provides for viewing the composite at any stage of preparation. With the art-work cel registered on the peg board, both the art-work and the live-action image which it partially obscures and replaces, can be seen in final register through the camera's viewfinder. Any corrections which are necessary in the matching of perspective, form, line, texture, color, or tone can be easily determined without having to run off test footage.

Unlike the bi-pack printing method, however, it is not possible to 'fuzz-off' or soften the edges of the matte line for blending purposes so long as the art-work and the aerial image are to be photographed simultaneously – the matte line will always remain fairly sharp. Because of this, many workers lay out the matte line so that it follows sharp edges in the live-action set: window sills, door jambs, moulding on the wall, and so forth. Should it be absolutely necessary that the matte line be softened then either it must be drawn so by the artist, or two runs through the camera will be necessary, using cut-out mattes and counter-mattes in each case which are positioned on a sheet of glass, slightly out of the plane of focus of the aerial image.

The applications to which image replacements of this sort can be put are practically limitless, the more obvious ones already having been described in Chapter 6.

As with bi-pack printing, the matte-shot painter must bring considerable talent, skill, and experience to this work if the effect is to be convincing. Often, however, equally good results can be realized at a fraction of the cost by using cut-out photo mattes similar to those described in Chapter 6.

Assume, for example, that a live-action scene is to be matted into the tube area of a television set. The TV set is photographed with a still camera and an 8 × 10 inch enlargement prepared. The image of the tube face is cut out of the enlargement with a razor blade or knife. The cut-out photograph is registered in proper position on top of the animation stand's table-top and the live-action insert is projected with the desired action appearing in the cut-out area of the enlargement. Both the live-action insert and the still-photo surround are combined simultaneously by the animation camera, the photo cut-out obscuring the aerial image in all parts of the picture except that of the TV tube face. If desired, a black-and-white plate may be used for the scene inserted into the tube area and a color photograph for the surrounding detail.

Split-screen matting

Aerial-image techniques also provide a method of combining different sections of two or more live-action plates, using techniques which are superficially similar to those employed in bi-pack contact printing. The plates are rotoscoped on to tracing paper laid on the animation stand's table-top. The matte lines are traced on to the paper and are then transferred to opaque cardboard sheets which are cut with scissors to conform to the shape of the lines. Two (or more) matching cardboard mattes and counter-mattes are prepared in this manner, all of them registered with peg-bar perforations to provide for proper registration. During subsequent aerial-image printing steps, the different live-action 'plates' are successively photographed by the animation camera until a complete composite image results.

As the cardboard masks are used here only to obscure certain areas of the aerial image, they are not front-lit. Should a soft matte line be desired between image components, it is necessary to position the cardboard cut-outs slightly out of the sharply focused plane of the aerial image.

The simpler kinds of split-screen shots can be rapidly and inexpensively executed with such techniques, particularly those shots which involve obvious matte-line separations between image components. Naturally, all split-screen composites will require as many passes through the camera as there are different plates to be combined.

Traveling mattes

As with the bi-pack optical or contact printing system, it is possible to provide traveling-matte effects with the aerial-image system. On the one hand, the whole assembly may be used as an optical printer, employing conventional traveling mattes which have been produced by methods described in Chapter 8. The mattes and counter-mattes may be run in bi-pack either in the projector with the plate, or in the camera against the raw stock. As with most traveling-matte work, two or more passes through the equipment will be necessary. Because the image of the master positive is alternately enlarged, reduced, re-imaged, and otherwise 'manhandled' by the aerial-image system, however, it cannot be reasonably expected that the resulting image quality or registration accuracy will be quite as fine as with conventional optical printing.

The aerial-image assembly may also be used to produce intricate hand-drawn traveling-matte effects of the sort described in Chapters 6 and

8. The animation work involved is no less laborious, but does allow for the composite of live action and animated art-work to be made in one pass through the camera and projector.

Three-dimensional art-work

Although the alignment of aerial-image optics is fairly critical, the depth of field which extends upwards from the plane of the image is sufficiently great at moderate relative apertures to allow for the combination of three-dimensional art-work with the live-action scene. For example, a packet of cigarettes can be placed directly on to the animation table-top and combined in one pass with the projected live-action background. Other, similar objects with dimensions which do not exceed an inch or so can be similarly used. Such three-dimensional objects may also be animated from frame to frame if desired. Such a technique offers considerable speed and economy in operation, together with maximum quality in composite reproduction – particularly when compared with traveling-matte methods.

Day-for-night effects

Aerial-image technique provides an effective means by which conven- tionally-photographed daytime exteriors can be converted into night shots. The aim, as in all day-for-night work, is to darken the sky tone, to create or emphasize practical incandescent lights within the scene, to increase the key-to-fill ratio, to decrease the overall brightness of the scene, and (for color emulsions) to employ different colors in separate parts of the scene in a dramatically conventionalized fashion.

To achieve these ends, the daylight plate is rotoscoped on to the animation table-top and matte lines are drawn so as to separate sky areas and to outline windows and artificial light sources. With the matte lines transferred to an animation cel(s), inks and paints are used to darken the sky areas and (for color emulsions) to impart a dark-blue tone.

Artificial lights in the scene, as well as selected windows in buildings, are painted with warm-yellow pigments to suggest their night-time operation. If desired, the overall color cast of the scene can be shifted somewhat towards the blue in conventionalized fashion by laying a light-blue gel over the art-work on the table-top or by inserting a light-blue filter into the optics of the aerial-image projecor. The overall brightness of the scene can be lowered either through underexposure of the composite or by printing-down during final preparation of the release prints.

Excessive fill light in shadow areas can be reduced by interposing registered cels in which these areas are darkened with transparent neutral-density media. Shadows which do not exist in the original scene can be drawn directly on the animation cels with opaque or barely transparent inks and paints.

Evening sky detail – moon, stars, and moonlit clouds – together with distant artificial street lighting effects, can also be added on animation cels. Should such shots remain on the screen for very long, it will be found best to animate some of the lighting detail in the background so that they flicker, move, blink, and otherwise show movement from frame to frame. It is even possible, should the budget permit, to add animated automobile headlights moving down distant streets.

Color distortions

All kinds of color change, distortion, and manipulation are possible through aerial image printing. Using the machine, first, as an optical printer, color scenes may be wholly or partially desaturated in the middle of sequences by dissolving back and forth between step-printed color and black-and-white master positives of the same shot.

Second, portions of a full-color, live-action scene can be replaced with black-and-white image components which have been painted on to an animation cel which is registered in the plane of the aerial image, color emulsions being used in both the projector and camera for such an effect. Conversely, colored art-work can be used to replace portions of a black-and-white, live-action scene. In such a case, a black-and-white plate is projected aerially into the plane of an animation cel which bears colored art-work, the composite being picked up on a color emulsion in the camera. For example, if there were any good reason for doing so, it would be possible, with this technique, to combine a vivid blue sky with an otherwise black-and-white landscape.

Third, using these same techniques, black-and-white animated figures or other action can be combined with a colored live-action background, and vice-versa. (A much more difficult shot is one in which black-and-white live-action is combined with a colored background – or vice-versa. Such a shot will require traveling mattes.)

Finally, by passing all or portions of the aerial image through colored filter gels, the live-action scene can be tinted and toned to whatever extent is desired. Either transparent filter media can be used and cut with scissors to different shapes, or a transparent wash can be painted on to a registered animation cel so that its shape matches that of objects and masses in the live-action scene.

Optical printer system

The effects which have been described so far in this chapter were produced by an optical system which produced an aerial image at the plane of the table-top of a modified animation stand.

It is possible, however, to achieve identical results by employing an entirely different system of aerial-image optics, in which the color master of the live action is photographed directly, and the art-work is imaged into the plane of the master positive. Such a system employs a modified optical printer from which the lamp house has been removed. The master positive is illuminated, instead, by modulated light transmitted through a translucent matte board panel which is positioned 10 or 15 ft away (Figs. 9.10 to 9.12).

Aerial-image printing with such a system requires two passes through the camera. Let us assume, for example, that a title (hot-press-printed or

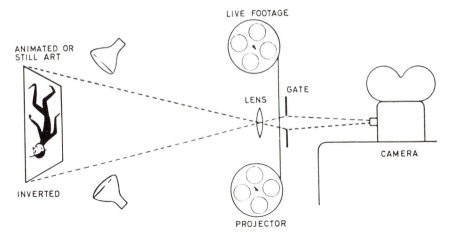

LIVE FOOTAGE

ANIMATED OR
STILL ART

GATE

LENS

CAMERA

INVERTED

PROJECTOR

Fig. 9.10. The horizontal aerial-image system. Art-work, painted on a transparent animation cel, is mounted upside down on the easel at left, and imaged into the plane of the color master at center. The process camera, right, re-photographs both in a two-step printing procedure.

Fig. 9.11. The horizontal aerial-image unit, as developed by Cinema Research Corporation. Animated cartoon figures, which are to be matted into a live-action background, are mounted, upside down, at left. During the first printing, the animated cels are illuminated from the front against a black background, and are photographed by the process camera at right. The aerial-image optical system is contained in the printer head, center.

Fig. 9.12. During second printing, the same animation cel is illuminated from the rear, providing the light with which to print the color master which runs through the Acme printer head (center). (For the purposes of this illustration, a piece of ground glass has been inserted into the printer head's intermittent movement.) The image of the color master, appropriately modulated by the silhouetted art-work, is finally cast into the focal plane of the process camera (right), where it is recorded on the duplicating negative.

painted on to a clear animation cel) is to be matted into a live-action background.

During the first run, the color master (or reversal-original in the case of 16 mm color) is threaded into the intermittent movement of the printer head. The animation cel which bears the opaque title letters is registered over the translucent glass panel of the matte-board. The front lights are extinguished and the title cel is illuminated from behind. Since the ink or paints used for the title are opaque, light cannot pass through these portions, but does pass through the transparent surround.

The light which passes through the cel is focused by an optical system as an aerial image in the plane of the color master, thus modulating the image of the color master with the shape and form of the title. The lens system of the process camera re-photographs the color master which is illuminated in all of its areas except those in which the title's letters appear.

After the first exposure, the raw stock in the process camera is rewound to start position and the color master in the printer head is removed. The back-lighting for the title cel is extinguished and the front lights are turned

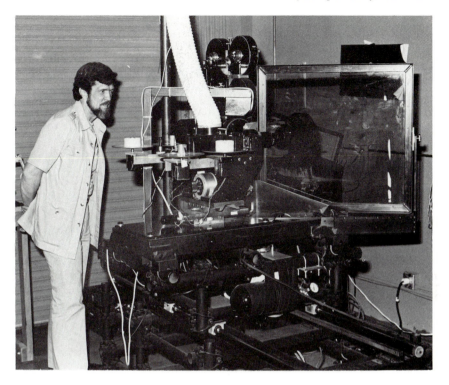

Fig. 9.13. An elegant and versatile piece of equipment which combines the functions of optical printing, front projection, rear projection, and aerial-image printing. The machine was developed by Industrial Light and Magic Company for Lucasfilm's production of *Return of the Jedi*. It consists of an 8-perforation-pull-down Vistavision-format projector, left, which projects the image of the film in its intermittent movement onto the surface of a two-way mirror, right. The image is reflected at 45°, out of the picture at the right. A modified 35 mm Bell & Howell 'Standard' camera (at center, rear) photographs the image cast by the projector *through* the two-way mirror, as reflected from a reflex screen, out-of-frame, right. Special-effects supervisor Richard Edlund examines the equipment.

on. A dead-black card is placed behind the transparent title cel so that light will be reflected only from the area of the lettering. Now, with the title cel registered in the same position as for the first exposure, and still sharply focused as an aerial image into the same plane it occupied during the first run, the raw stock in the process camera is again exposed, this time picking up the aerial image of the title, and jigsawing it into the live-action background.

All other types of previously described aerial-image effects may also be realized with such a design as this, although, of course, the operations are just the contrary of those employed in the animation stand system. For matte shots, for example, the color master of the live action is inserted into the intermittent movement of the printer head and is projected, rotoscope fashion, on to the matte-board panel where an artist draws the appropriate matte lines on registered animation paper. After the matte lines have been

Fig. 9.14. A view of the modified Bell & Howell 'Standard' camera at right, with bi-pack magazines and an anamorphic 'squeeze' lens mounted on it. (The white label on the lens indicates nodal point/entrance pupil positions on the lens for pan and tilt movements of the camera.) At left, the Vistavision-format projector. In center, the two-way mirror, seen from the edge of its frame.

transferred to a cel and the desired art-work painted, the cel is re-mounted on the matte-board panel. By printing in two passes, as just described, the new image components are jigsawed into the live-action scene.

Since this design is built around an optical printer, it is also suited for all effects which are conventionally produced with such apparatus, either with or without the aerial-image optics being involved: skip frame, multiple printing, split-screen work, hold-frame, traveling mattes, and so forth. Also, since the aerial-image components which are involved here are somewhat less complicated than in the animation-stand system, it is possible to design its optics to allow for image-size changes. Used in this fashion, the camera may be zoomed in or out on the color master with the art-work being imaged sharply and in proper size and scale in the plane of the live-action positive. The entire unit can also be used as a horizontal animation crane.

This kind of aerial-image printer was originally introduced to the professional 16 mm trade around 1953 by Cinema Research Corporation of Hollywood. For several years, the company operated a single machine of this sort, providing aerial-image effects for its West coast customers.

Fig. 9.15. A view of the apparatus, as seen from the other end of the room. The image from the Vistavision projector in the previous illustration, reflected off the two-way mirror, is cast onto a sheet of reflex screen mounted on an easel at center, and is re-photographed by the camera, which shoots *through* the mirror. In this configuration the entire machine operates like a clumsy, oversized optical printer. If, however, a painted matte is mounted on the easel, in front of the reflex screen, then the two elements – the projected Vistavision plate and the painted replacement images – can be photographed either simultaneously or in separate passes through the camera. At the other end of the room, seen in the foreground in this photo, a second Vistavision-format projector is located which can be used to provide a second projected image. Such an image either (a) can be cast upon a diffusion screen mounted on the easel, and picked up by the camera on the other side, or (b) can be re-transmitted by large field lenses mounted on the easel, in aerial-image fashion, again to be picked up by the camera on the other side. The camera and both of the projectors are capable of being run in synchronism, or independently of one another, in forward and reverse modes, and with all of the skip-framing and multiple framing capabilities of an optical printer.

The two systems compared

Both kinds of aerial-image printer described are capable of excellent work when properly built and operated. Both are suited for 16 mm or 35 mm work in either black-and-white or color. Each design has its peculiar advantages.

The animation-stand system provides maximum speed inasmuch as only one pass through the projection and camera movements is necessary. Since a modified animation stand is employed, it is available for all of the uses to which such a piece of apparatus is conventionally put. Such a system requires, however, that the live-action image be passed through a variety of enlarging, reducing, and collimating optics which tend to degrade the quality of the live-action component somewhat.

The optical-printer system, in comparison, provides for the photography of the color master directly, thus preserving the maximum amount of quality in the live-action image. Because of the somewhat simpler construction employed, it is possible to produce zooms and image-size changes which cannot be accomplished with the other system. Also, since the apparatus is essentially an optical printer, it can be used to produce all of the high-quality effects for which such a piece of equipment is conventionally employed. Nonetheless, two exposures through the process camera and printer head will always be required for aerial-image composites. This necessarily reduces the speed of operations. At the same time, it makes color corrections and manipulations of the art-work and live action quite convenient, since they can be conducted in separate steps.

Both designs are fairly expensive to manufacture. In either case, of course, the buyer also acquires either a complete animation stand or an optical printer, either of which can be used for numerous other assignments besides aerial-image printing.

10

Rear projection

Like the traveling-matte process, background projection provides a method by which the figure of an actor can be convincingly combined with a background scene photographed elsewhere. Simply stated, the actor performs in front of a large translucent screen onto which a positive photographic image of a background is projected (Figs. 10.1 and 10.2).

Fig. 10.1. A typical rear-projection shot. The camera, in foreground, photographs the actors, who perform in front of a high-diffusion screen, center, onto which an image of the background is projected by means of the projector at rear. A wind machine is operated at left to provide an appropriate amount of 'breeze', and a microphone on a boom picks up the actors' dialogue. The background projector being employed in this case is an elaborate triple-head machine developed by the Photo Process Department of the Rank Organization's Engineering Division.

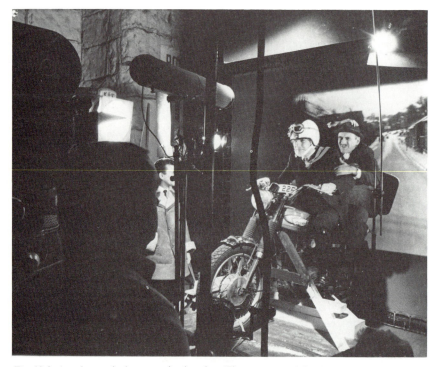

Fig. 10.2. Another typical rear-projection shot. The camera, at left, photographs the actors who perform in front of a background image produced on a high-diffusion screen, at right. The image shown here is 9 × 11 ft. Unseen, behind the screen, is the projector which produces the image. (Pinewood Studios. The Rank Organization.)

Either a still transparency (a 'stereo') or a motion-picture positive (a 'plate') may be employed for this purpose.* In either case, assuming that a great many technical requirements are met, a convincing composite of foreground action and background detail will result. In this chapter, conventional rear projection (sometimes called 'process photography' or the 'transparency process') is examined, while in Chapter 11 a variation of the technique – the 'front-projection system' – is described.

Significantly, in the literature of special-effects cinematography, the largest number of articles and reports have been devoted to background projection, reflecting the popularity which this technique has enjoyed during the last five decades. Quite possibly, too, more money has been spent over the years for the development of background projection than for any other composite process.

---

* These terms may confuse workers with a background in still photography in which field a 'plate' is a glass-base, photographic transparency – negative or positive. In motion-picture parlance, however, a 'plate' is simply a conventional positive motion-picture background scene for composite photography, black-and-white or color.

The term 'stereo', on the other hand, is used to refer to a *still* image (or the positive transparency from which it is produced) used in the background area of a composite motion-picture shot.

Fig. 10.3, part 1. An elaborate rear-projection shot for the production of *The Last Voyage of Henry Hudson* at the National Film Board of Canada. Full-scale deck section of a ship is positioned in front of the process screen (left), on which the projected background image can be seen.

Fig. 10.3, part 2. Photographic set-up for the above shot. The camera is mounted on a boom, at upper right. Wind machines are positioned next to the camera and behind the front sail. At far left, a key light is jibbed on a moveable support; during photography, its position is continuously shifted, producing the changing play of light and shadow of simulated moonlight. The process screen, mounted at the left of the set, is not visible in this photograph.

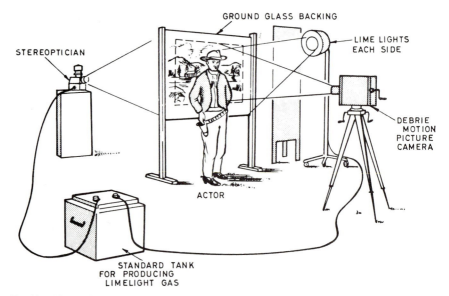

Fig. 10.4. No one knows who first employed rear-projection in film-production, but Norman Dawn used a set-up such as this as early as 1913 for two scenes in his production of *The Drifter*. The quality was so poor, at that time, that he abandoned the process.

The technique is certainly not new, having been used professionally at least as early as 1913 (Fig. 10.4). However, its widespread application to professional film production is generally dated from the late 1920s and early 1930s, at which time the introduction of sound rendered interior photography of simulated exterior scenes desirable. Today, after many years of development, background projection remains one of the most popular and most frequently used composite systems. Its advantages and disadvantages have already been detailed in the concluding pages of Chapter 8. Of its advantages, three are of particular importance and should be kept in mind whenever the technique's operations are considered.

1. The ability of the director and his crew to see the finished composite at the time that it is photographed.
2. The ability of the actor to see the background scene and to react appropriately to it.
3. The ability of the director to truck, dolly, pan and tilt his camera (within reason) while the actor performs in front of the projected background.

Equipment

The equipment employed for background projection may be as simple or as complicated as one desires, depending upon the type of composite involved, the scale of the set, the manner in which the foreground action is staged, and the amount of money available for the effect. Whatever the assignment, four kinds of equipment will be involved:

1. The camera.
2. The projector.
3. The screen.
4. (For moving background scenes) Interlocking controls for projector and camera.

The selection of equipment is determined, basically, by the type of background desired:

1. Still (static) images of background detail – no motion within the scene or by the camera (e.g. a landscape vista, without human figures or moving objects).
2. Fixed-frame, motion-picture images of moving background detail – an immobile camera, but with actors and other objects seen in motion within the frame (e.g. a city street, with moving automobiles and pedestrians).
3. Traveling shots of background action (e.g. a moving-camera shot of a busy city street, photographed from the front of an automobile as it heads down the street).

Still (static) backgrounds

The static background image, in which motion is not apparent, is nearly always produced by a still projector. The positive transparency or diapositive, and its image in the screen, is sometimes referred to as a 'stereo'.

For low-budget work, and the simplest of assignments, an inexpensive 35 mm slide projector can sometimes be used to produce satisfactory images. Because of the small size of the diapositive and the relatively low intensity of illumination employed, the scale of the 'set' is, of course, greatly restricted. A projected image which does not exceed 3 or 4 feet in width will usually be sufficiently sharp and bright for composite photography. The restricted size of such an image will ordinarily limit this kind of set-up to the photography of miniatures, in which it is desired to produce landscape or cityscape detail in the background areas.

Naturally, the better the design of the slide projector, the better the quality of the composite. As is the case with all background projection equipment, high-quality optics, which are capable of producing brilliant, flat-field and evenly-illuminated images, will give the best results.

For assignments in which actors must perform in front of fairly large screens, an entirely different and far more expensive kind of 'slide' projector must be used. In order to provide maximum sharpness in the greatly enlarged image, a larger diapositive is employed – usually $3\frac{1}{4} \times 4\frac{1}{4}$ or 4×5 inches in size. Because the diapositive is larger, a more expensive optical system will be required, capable of efficiently gathering light from the lamp house and projecting a sharp and evenly-illuminated image upon the screen, which may be from 50 to 150 ft distant. The projection lenses which are used should be available in a variety of focal lengths so as to satisfy the requirements of different set-ups.

Fig. 10.5. A composite of miniatures and a rear-projected background. (National Film Board of Canada.)

In order to produce a brilliant image over a fairly large area, a high-intensity light source will be needed in such a machine. For this purpose, high-intensity incandescent lamps up to 5000 watts, or carbon arcs with current requirements from 100 to 220 amperes, or quartz xenon lamps, are employed. The use of either quartz xenon or carbon arcs will, in turn, require the installation of a blower and an air-circulation system. This provides cooling of the diapositive while it is illuminated and prevents its buckling or outright destruction by the heat. Noxious or toxic gasses produced by carbon or xenon arcs may have to be piped out of the set area. Finally, because of the noise produced by the carbon arcs and the blowers, projectors must be silenced so that their noise will not be picked up by microphones on the set.

Obviously, the design and manufacture of such an instrument is considerably more involved than for a simple slide projector, and, as would be expected, its cost or rental fee is much higher. A typical 'stereo' projector is shown in Figs 10.6 and 10.7. The projector which is shown here employs a single diapositive, lamp house, and optical system (Fig. 10.8). Some other machines, however, have used two matched diapositives, with entirely separate optical systems and illuminants for each. The use of separate lamp houses allows for a considerable increase in image brilliance on the screen. One type of dual-head projector mounts the two diapositives and optical systems next to each other. Providing that a

Fig. 10.6. Rear view of a 'stereo' (static image) projector, with arc-lamp housing. (20th Century-Fox.)

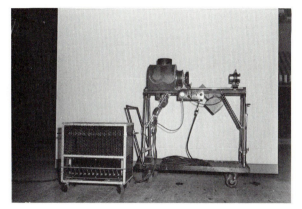

Fig. 10.7, part 1. Another type of 'stereo' (still-photo) projector, with its arc-lamp housing. The d.c. rectifier is positioned at lower left.

Fig. 10.7, part 2. Stereo diapositive mounted in a plate-holder of the above machine. During projection, this diapositive is positioned directly in front of the lamp house. Many plate-holders have adjustments for vertical, longitudinal, lateral and rotational movements. (20th Century-Fox.)

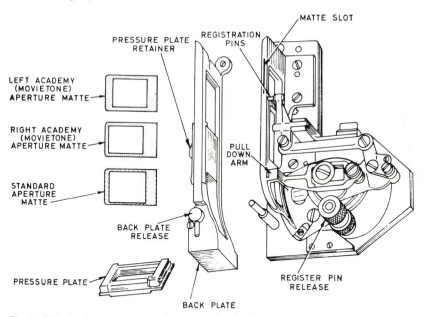

Fig. 10.8. Projection movement and apertures for the Mitchell background projector.

considerable distance separates the projector from the screen, the optical axes of the two projectors are virtually parallel and dissimilar keystone distortions are avoided. Another type of dual-head projector uses a set of mirrors which position the matched diapositives optically so as to virtually eliminate parallax differences. Both kinds of projector incorporate movable, calibrated lens and plate-holder assemblies which allow for the exact superimposition of the two images on the screen.

Moving (motion-picture) backgrounds

No matter how sophisticated the equipment, the projection of *still* images remains a relatively simple matter. When we set out to introduce motion into the background scene, however, we are led to a set of design and operational problems which are vastly more intricate in their solution.

In the first place, although the Maltese-cross movement of a conventional 35 mm projector is perfectly satisfactory for theatre projection, it is a very imprecise sort of intermittent movement for composite photography. Were such a projector to be used for process photography, the jiggling and weaving of the image would be immediately apparent on the screen when viewed against immobile, foreground set pieces. In the early days of background projection, many process shots were compromised by just such registration inaccuracies.

What is required for special-effects cinematography is a projection intermittent which is identical to that employed for the best-quality camera work – a pilot-pin movement of either the Bell & Howell or Mitchell design. Ideally, the movement will be capable of being removed and replaced with another with different pilot-pin positions. An intermittent movement which is designed for background projection work is shown in Fig. 10.8.

Second, because of the requirements for a brilliant screen image, unusually intense arc lamps are needed for illumination, especially when used with low-speed film stocks. Electrical current requirements can range from 150 to 225 amperes (Fig. 10.9). because of the intense illumination sometimes required, a blower and air-circulation system of high efficiency are needed to cool the machine and its intermittent movement while the film is traveling through it. Heat-absorbing filters of glass or water are sometimes employed to achieve the same effect.

Fig. 10.9. Right rear view of the Mitchell background projector, showing the arc-lamp housing.

Third, because of the considerable amount of noise caused by the intermittent movement, power drive, take-up reels, arc lamp and blower system, the projector must somehow be silenced so that the recording of sound-stage dialogue is not contaminated. Either the machine must be self-blimped or installed within a sound-proof projection room.

Fourth, because of the size to which the projected image must be enlarged, a high-quality, flat-field optical system must be used, it being essential that the projected image be equally sharp and evenly illuminated in all portions of the screen.

Also, a variety of focal lengths of projection lenses is required for different kinds of set-up on the stage. An $f/2$ relative aperture is typical for such work (Fig. 10.10).

Finally, the machine should be capable of being run in both forward and reverse directions.

All of these design requirements, together with others which will be mentioned later, render the manufacture of a background projector a

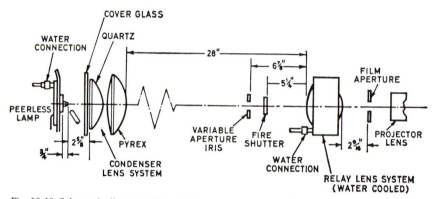

Fig. 10.10. Schematic diagram of the Mitchell projector's optical system.

Fig. 10.11. Mitchell background projector.

costly business, all the more so since the relatively small market dictates custom design and assembly. A typical design – the Mitchell – is shown in Fig. 10.11.

In past years, for the projection of motion-picture color positives onto unusually large screens, when color-film stocks were much slower than those employed today, some studios built projectors with three separate heads, each containing matched optical systems, intermittent movements, and lamp houses. Three identical plates were run simultaneously through the equipment and their images were superimposed optically upon the screen by a mirror assembly. Such machines were capable of delivering up to 125 000 lumens of light at the screen. The design of one instrument of this type is shown in Fig. 10.13, and another is illustrated in Fig. 10.14. fortunately, as finer-grained, higher-speed color emulsions have become available in recent years, the need for such exotic hardware has diminished.

Clearly, few low- or medium-budget producers will have the means for purchase or fabrication of even the simpler kinds of background projectors. Happily, as is the case with optical printing, background

Fig. 10.12. Forward section of the Mitchell background projector, with side door removed to reveal intermittent movement. The projector's motor is mounted directly below the film movement. A microphone-speaker (lower left) allows the operator to communicate with the camera crew on the other side of the screen. The entire head assembly, consisting of lens, movement and magazines, can be rotated around the optical center. Note the footage counter mounted next to the upper magazine. (Mitchell Camera Corporation.)

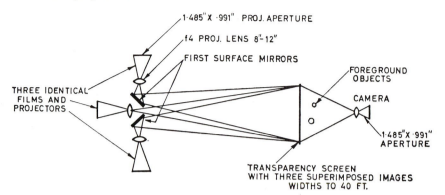

Fig. 10.13. Schematic diagram of the Vistavision-format, triple-head projector developed by Paramount Pictures Corporation. (JSMPTE.)

Fig. 10.14, part 1. An elaborate and costly triple-headed background motion-picture projector, designed and built by Pinewood Studio's Photo Process Department and the Rank Organization's Engineering Division. This apparatus consists of three identical projection machines employing either standard 35 mm single frame or 35 mm double frame, assembled on an electro-hydraulic base and involving virtually zero tolerances on print registration, image superimposition, and Selsyn-controlled optical objectives. Three identical 35 mm plates are run through the machines simultaneously. The middle projector (partially hidden) projects straight forward. The projected plates of the other two machines are superimposed upon the image of the first by means of mirror optics. Illumination is by high-intensity arc.

Fig. 10.14, part 2. Reverse angle of the previous illustration. The three plates in the separate machines have been superimposed precisely upon the high-diffusion background screen in the distance. The purpose of such a system is to produce much brighter and/or larger background images than otherwise could be produced with conventional equipment, and which are sometimes necessary for color cinematography in wide-screen formats.

projectors are available for rental, and a number of special-effects organizations throughout the world offer background-projection services to the impecunious producer.

These organizations maintain their own staff of skilled technicians and are capable, if required, of furnishing everything needed in the way of equipment and labor on either their own stages or those of the producer. Such an organization handles as much or as little of the special-effects operation as the producer desires – the photography of the background plates, the transportation of the portable projectors and screens to the producer's stage, the design of the set, the photography of the composite, and even the direction of the foreground action.

Considering the time, the experience, and the elaborate and expensive equipment which is involved, the cost of such service is sometimes surprisingly modest. Naturally, the greater the number of shots which are made once the equipment has been set up, the lower the 'per shot' cost.

Interlocking controls

With the introduction of movement into the background scene, the problem of synchronization of camera and projector arises. As each frame of positive film in the projector is registered and projected onto the screen, it is necessary that a new frame of negative raw stock be similarly registered in the camera. Furthermore, the shutters of the two machines must turn over at the same rate of speed so that the brightness of the projected and photographed background image will not vary from frame to frame.

As we have seen in Chapter 7, synchronism in optical printing is achieved by cable, gear, or chain drives between printer head and camera. Because of the distances involved between camera and projector in the background projection process, however, mechanical interlock is not practical. Instead, so-called 'Selsyn' interlock motors (220-volt, 3-phase) are used on the projector and the camera, both of which turn over at exactly the same rate of speed; as the shaft of the first turns through 10°, 20°, 30°, so does that of the second. Once both machines are 'up to speed', exact synchronism between both sets of shutters, pull-down claws and pilot pins is assured. Provision is usually made so that by rotating the stator winding of the projector's motor while the machine is running, it becomes possible to throw the motor in or out-of-phase with that of the camera.

The interlock system for the Mitchell background projector is shown schematically in Fig. 10.15.

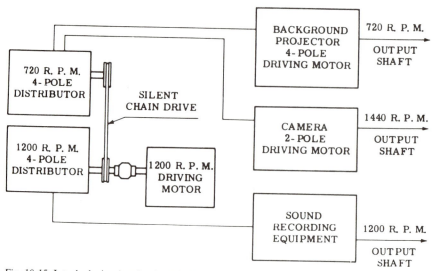

Fig. 10.15. Interlock circuitry for the Mitchell background projector.

Background-projection screens

Almost as much time and effort have been spent over the years on the perfection of background-projection screens as on background projectors. Historically, the problem has been to produce translucent media which offer (1) high-resolution images, (2) evenness of illumination, (3) high transmission, and (4) low flare. All four factors are affected by the size, shape, chemical composition and density of the diffusing and refracting elements used in the fabrication of the screen.

Virtually all screens used for background projection today have both diffused surfaces and internal diffusion, and are manufactured of ethyl cellulose or cellulose acetate. (Some experimental work has been done with fresnel and lenticular screens, but these are not yet sufficiently perfected in large sizes for professional work.)

Inevitably, some compromise is necessary in the design of a really satisfactory screen. On the one hand, it is desirble to provide as high a transmission factor as possible, so as to produce a brilliant image on the screen. The greater the brilliance, the greater the illumination which can be used on the foreground set. With increased set illumination, slower, finer-grained stocks can be employed for the photography, smaller relative apertures can be used to provide increased depth of field, and greater contrast through lighting can be gained.

Such an increase in transmission is ordinarily achieved by decreasing the amount of internal diffusion in the screen. However, a certain minimum amount of diffusion is necesary to produce an evenly-illuminated image and to minimize illumination 'fall-off' at the edges of the screen, the effect of the diffusion being to re-direct the rays of light from the projector back towards the lens of the camera. The screen image becomes a secondary light source of light which is viewable and photographable from angles not otherwise possible. If the illumination fall-off is sufficiently great, a vignette effect results which destroys the whole illusion of the composite.

The internal and external diffusion of the screen also minimizes the 'hot-spot' (sometimes called 'hot center'), an obnoxious burst of light in the center of the screen. The hot-spot is an inherent characteristic of rear-projected images. The pin-point light source of the intensely bright arc is naturally brighter at the center of the screen than is the surrounding image which is cast by the projector's lens. Image-forming light from the projector's lens has to travel farther to the edges of the screen than to the center; hence, a certain amount of fall-off at the edges is inevitable. Although this kind of hot-spot is inherent in rear projection, it can be reduced to the point where it is not noticeable. More than any other factor, the use of screens with sufficient external and internal diffusion reduced the hot-spot effect. Beyond a certain point, however, increased diffusion will led to a loss in transmission which, if sufficiently great, will render the image too dim for practical photography.

The term used to refer to the brightness of a rear-projected screen, relative to its ability to diffuse the light striking it and to produce an evenly-illuminated image, is called the 'luminance power' of the screen, or, more commonly, the 'gain' of the screen. A theoretical screen, providing maximum diffusion, so that rays of light of equal intensity were transmitted in all directions, would have a gain of unity, or 1. Such a screen would be least likely to suffer from 'hot spot', but its image would be very dim indeed, and so not suitable for background projection. As the external and internal diffusion of a screen is reduced, the transmission of the light through the screen becomes more directional; the screen becomes brighter along the central axis of the projector beam in relation to other parts of the screen. Such a screen might be found to have a gain of 2, or 5, or 10 – or whatever.* As gain increases, the image on the screen becomes more brilliant, allowing for more convenient photography from the point of view of exposure. On the other hand, a point is soon reached, with increased gain, at which the image begins to vignette, and the camera photographs a hot spot in the center of the screen.

The amount of hot-spot and fall-off which results in background projection is affected not only by the design and composition of the screen, but also by what engineers term the 'bend angles' of projector and camera. The total, limiting angle of a particular set-up is the sum of the angles formed by the camera and projector lenses at the center and a corner of the projected image, for a given film-aperture size, and assuming that the optical axes of the camera and projector are coincident (Fig. 10.16). All other things being equal, the greater the total bend angle the greater the amount of fall-off, and the more brilliant the hot-spot. If the total bend angle which is involved in a process shot can be decreased, a considerable reduction in illumination fall-off, and in hot-spot, will be achieved. This, as we shall see later, can be accomplished by varying the distance of projector and camera from the screen, together with the focal length of lenses employed.

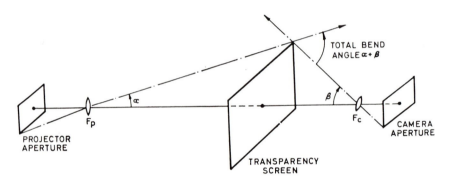

Fig. 10.16. Bend angles for rear projection.

Illumination fall-off is also affected by the 'pick-up' angle at which the screen image is photographed; which is to say, the angle formed by the axis of the lens with the surface of the screen.

The greater the pick-up angle, the greater the likelihood that the screen image will be recorded as being darker on the far side than on the near. Vignetting effects, as well as the absorption of particular wavelengths of light by the screen material, are also likely to be accentuated as the pick-up angle is increased.

To some extent, a certain amount of compromise is always necessary in the design of conventional background screens, so as to provide a nice balance of transmission and diffusion values. In recent years, however,

* The notion of luminance power, or 'gain', is a complicated one, and lies outside the ambit of this book's explanations. a useful description of both theoretical and practical engineering considerations in the design and use of such screens will be found in Armin J. Hill, 'Analysis of background process screens', *JSMPTE*, Vol. 66, July, 1957, pp. 393–400.

Fig. 10.17. Left: 720 rpm projector motor (four-pole stator and rotor winding). Ordinarily, this is used as a three-phase Selsyn motor; however, it can also be operated as a straight induction or 'wild' motor. During conventional background projection, this motor is interlocked with the 1200 rpm distributor. Right: the camera crew's microphone-speaker. (Mitchell Camera Corporation.)

research and development in process photography has led to the production of diffusion-type translucent screens of improved characteristics, capable of providing increased transmission without an increase in hot-spot and fall-off effects. Screens such as those developed for the industry by Stewart Film Screen Corporation offer transmission factors as high as 80 per cent without objectionable fall-off, providing that reasonable bend and pick-up angles are involved in the photography.

Conventional diffusion-type screens are available in seamless sizes up to 46 ft high and 88 ft wide. The screens are ordinarily bound and grommeted for tension mounting upon wooden or metal frames, with shock cords. The frames are equipped with casters and jacks which allow for convenient set-up and re-positioning of the screen for different kinds of shots. Screens can also be hung from the ceiling, catwalk or grid by means of cords. Most screens are washable and fire-resistant; properly treated and stored, they will last for many years.

Photography of background plates and transparencies

For all the effort that has gone into the design of equipment for background projection, the entire illusion of the composite will be compromised unless the same sort of care is used in the photography and preparation of background plates and 'stereo' transparencies.

For both stereos and plates, the largest possible film size is used for original photography so as to provide maximum resolution and minimum grain in the projected image. The photography of transparencies is oftentimes done with a 3¼ × 4¼ or 4 × 5 inch view or press-type camera, using cut (sheet) film. For color photography, either negative or reversal stocks can be used as the original recording material, the point being to end up with a positive transparency suitable for projection.

Alternatively, an 8 × 10 inch negative can be used for original photography and reduced to a 4 × 5 inch transparency. The camera may be tripod-mounted or hand-held. In either case, the shutter speed must be sufficiently high to overcome vibration of the camera and to produce images which will retain their sharpness when enlarged from 100 to 1000 times on a process screen, especially in those cases in which only a portion of that enlarged image is re-photographed by the camera on the other side of the screen. At the same time, small apertures are necessary to provide a depth of field which extends throughout the entire scene, from the nearest objects to infinity. Any noticeable out-of-focus softness, especially in foreground areas, destroys the illusion of the composite when the transparency is combined with sound-stage action.

For the recording of moving images on a motion-picture plate, pilot-pin registration is essential. A full (silent) aperture is used in the camera so as to provide the largest possible image. (For wide-screen format production in the theatrical film industry, Vistavision cameras, with an 8-perforation pull-down, are sometimes used to provide double-frame plates for background projection onto large process screens.)

In those cases in which the camera which photographs the plates does not move, absolute stability of the camera is essential, lest weave and jiggle of the projected image destroy the reality of the composite. Whatever the support may be – tripod, dolly, or boom – the camera and its accessories must be rigidly secured and protected from vibration due to wind, camera operation or ground movements.

On the other hand, in the case of moving-camera shots, a certain amount of vibration and jiggle can be tolerated. In either case, as with transparency photography, the selection of focal lengths and apertures must provide a depth of field which extends throughout the entire scene.

Perspective and depth

For the most convincing effects, it is important that perspective lines, vanishing points, and scale relationships which are begun in the foreground set be carried backward properly into the projected image (Fig. 10.18,

Fig. 10.18, part 1. This close-up was the final camera position after the camera had panned across a cityscape, across a canal, and across a building, and had come to rest on an actor standing at an open window. The necessary steps are shown in the following illustrations.

Fig. 10.18, part 2. The first step was to build a full-scale window, with living quarters beyond, and to photograph the actors in their performance. A photographic enlargement was made from the background plate at the start position of the dolly-in (lower left). This was turned over to the art director who sketched around it a rough perspective drawing of the complete cityscape.

Fig. 10.18, part 3. The art director's sketch was given to a matte painter, who prepared an 8½ × 6½ ft painting of the city on glass. The entire sheet of glass was painted with the exception of the window opening in the lower left-hand corner.

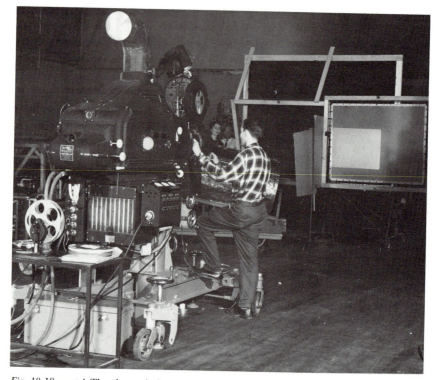

Fig. 10.18, part 4. The glass painting was set up on the sound stage with a process screen and background projector positioned behind the transparent window area. The previously-photographed plate of the live-action was projected onto the screen so that it fitted properly into the window aperture. The screen was located 1½ ft behind the painting, sufficient distance to allow for lighting of the painting without washing out the projected image.

part 2). The most difficult composites to achieve are those in which a given set begins in the sound-stage foreground and extends directly back into the projected image, with actors moving and performing in both foreground and background areas (e.g. a busy hospital corridor). Conversely, the simplest kind of composite to stage is one in which an isolated actor appears in a medium shot against a distant landscape, or in which background detail is seen through a window.

The depth of the foreground set is ordinarily kept fairly shallow for process photography so as to minimize optical depth-of-field problems. When using such a shallow set, it may be necessary to distort the shape and to mix the scale of different set pieces and props which stand between the actor and the projection screen, reducing their size and progressively changing their configuration as they approach the screen, so that a proper continuity of scale relationships occurs at the blend-line of foreground and background. Perspective and scale relationships between the foreground set and the background image can also be manipulated by photographing the background plate with shorter or longer focal-length lenses, thus expanding or compressing the shot as may be required.

Fig. 10.18, part 5. During final photography, the camera was trucked past different sections of the glass painting until it reached the projected live-action area. At this point, it dollied towards the process screen until the projected image filled the frame. Movement of the dolly was timed so that the camera reached the process screen at the right moment to re-photograph dramatically appropriate action in the projected plate. (All photos, National Film Board of Canada.)

Often, the foreground set is designed by the art director so as to match an already-photographed background plate. The technique by which this is accomplished is called 'perspective projection' and involves the linear projection, onto paper, of vanishing points, vertical and horizontal set lines, and particular intersecting points from the already-photographed scene. By means of a variety of triangulating techniques, the art director is able to produce floor and elevation-plan drawings of the background scene of the plate. He is aided in his task by information which is provided by the photographer of the plate: the distance from the camera to certain objects in the background, the camera's elevation and its angles of tilt and cant, the focal length of lens employed, and the dimensions of certain background objects. On the basis of this and other, inferred, information about the nature of the background scene, the art director is able to design a foreground set which exactly matches the background image's perspective lines and scale. Typical projections are shown in Fig. 10.19.*

* For a description of the drafting techniques employed, see John Gow, 'Problems of perspective – back projection and perspective', *British Kinematography*, April, 1948, pp. 130–6; and Wally Gentleman, 'Elementary motion-picture design perspective', *JSMPTE*, August 1963, pp. 609–13.

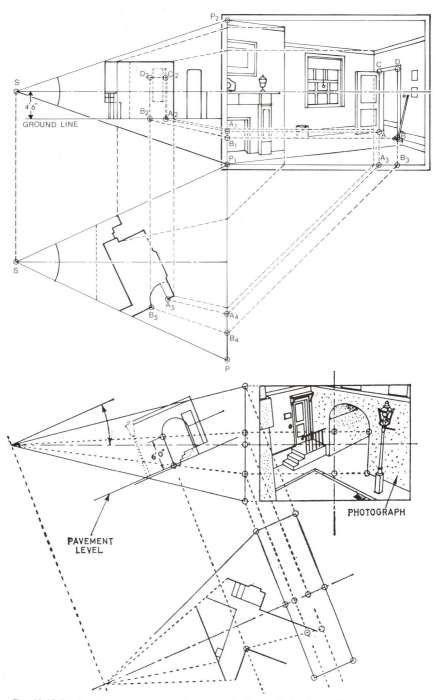

Fig. 10.19. It often becomes necessary in rear-projection work for the art director to prepare perspective 'projections' from which full-scale set pieces are built and integrated with previously-photographed background plates or art-work. Two examples of such 'projections' are shown here. (JSMPTE.)

Matching background and foreground

Cameramen who are sent out to photograph stereos and background plates should be instructed carefully as to the anticipated demands of the composite, with respect to foreground and background action, camera placement and movement, pictorial mood, and dramatic intent. They should also be cautioned against tricky or 'arty' compositions which will attract attention away from the actors and which will be difficult to match and work with on the sound stage.

Ordinarily, the background camera – whether still or motion-picture – will be set to photograph the background scene more or less 'head on'; that is, with the camera's optical axis parallel to the ground line and perpendicular to any verticals appearing in the scene. Excessive tilting of the camera, either up or down, produces converging verticals in the finished picture which may be difficult or impossible to correct during projection on the sound stage.

Although the background camera should be set to photograph its scene 'head on', the question arises as to whether to favor the ground or sky areas in placing the horizon line across the screen. Most process cameramen seem to favor a placement of the horizon line which provides $3/5$ ground area and $2/5$ sky. If the budget allows, the meticulous worker will make three shots of each background: the horizon dead center; horizon $2/5$ the distance from the top of the frame; horizon $2/5$ of the distance from the bottom of the frame. If the budget does not permit, however, and if there is any doubt in the cameraman's mind as to the intentions of the director during subsequent stages of process photography, then the horizon ought to be left dead center. Later, on the sound stage, the image can be enlarged or reduced, or shifted upwards or downwards by altering the position and optical system of the projector.

The height at which the background camera is operated depends entirely upon the viewpoint which is required for the composite. If an actor is to be posed on the sound stage in a full- or $3/4$-shot at ground level, then a normal camera height may be employed for photography of the background. If, on the other hand, the actor is to pose in front of an office window, through which we are to see the city beyond, then the background camera will have to be operated from the fifth, tenth, or twentieth floor of a building, depending upon the requirements of the scene.

For ground-level shots, the plate cameraman will find it useful to employ 'stand-ins' in front of the background scene, in poses which are similar to those which will be assumed later by the principal actors in front of the process screen. Once the proper camera height, angles, and movements have been thus rehearsed, the stand-ins are removed and the background plate is photographed.

Great care must be taken to prevent human figures or moving objects in the background plate from approaching too close to the camera, lest they later achieve a size on the projection screen which is noticeably larger in scale than the foreground actors and set. Should be be necessary for extras to enter the background scene during its photography (as in a trucking shot down a street), they must be made to enter the frame from its sides and at a reasonable distance from the camera. Should they enter too soon, and from a position directly next to the camera, they will appear as giants when projected onto the process screen behind actors on the sound stage. If necessary, shorter focal-length lenses can be employed.

When budget and time permit, it is best to take two or three shots of each background scene at different distances – either from different positions with the same lens, or from the same position with different focal lengths of lenses. Later, by being able to select just the right background plate or stereo, the director of photography will be able to exactly fill the background screen on the sound stage with the full-aperture image of the projected plate. Without such a selection at hand, it may otherwise be necessary to enlarge a portion of the background plate by pulling the projector back or changing the focal length of its lens, either of which will increase the grain structure and reduce the resolution of the projected image.

Moderately short focal-length lenses are often used for the photography of background plates. However, unless it is intended to really force perspective, extremely short focal-length lenses should be avoided. Not only will exaggerated perspective effects be produced on the screen which are difficult to match on the sound stage, but excessively short-focus lenses also have a tendency to produce vignetted images on the original negative and subsequent positives. In any such system such as background projection, where illumination fall-off is always a problem, additional vignetting in the plate or transparency will appear particularly pronounced when projected. Excessively long focal lengths should also be avoided for plate photography because of their tendency to compress different planes of action, slow down the speed of moving objects in the background, and generally destroy all sense of depth. Seen on a projection screen, and combined with normal foreground sets, such long-focus background images may seem unreal and ludicrous.

Duplicating background shots

Sometimes it becomes necessary to intercut shots from an exterior live-action sequence with re-staged background projection shots. This can happen when re-takes or additional scenes are necessary for dramatic purposes, and when, for one reason or another, the original location is no longer available or does not appear as it did when the location sequence was first photographed. At times such as these, it is essential that a set of either still transparencies or motion-picture plates of the original background be available, and that they were photographed under the same lighting and 'set dressing' circumstances which prevailed during production photography. The position of the sun at different times of the day, the direction of shadows across the set, climatic conditions such as wind, fog, mist, the color and saturation of sky tone, the presence, nature, size and movement of clouds, the exact location of set pieces, props, and greenery – these and numerous other variables must be the same in the background plate as they were in the original footage. Obviously, it is important that the special-effects cameraman be allowed to photograph his background plates or stereos as soon as possible after an exterior production take has been made, and with set conditions as nearly identical to those of the 'circled' takes as possible.

PROCESS PLATE LOG SHEET
COURTESY OF BILL HANSARD
(213) 780-2156

Production: _____ Director: _____ Date: _____

Location: _____ Cameraman: _____ Can #: _____

PLATE #:	FOR SCENE:	DAY	NITE	EXT.	INT.

Type of Film: _____ Camera: _____ Aperture: _____

Camera Height: _____ Lens: _____ F. P. S. : _____

'f' Stop: _____ Distance to Nearest Object: _____

Filter Used: _____ Camera Car Speed: _____

Degrees of Tilt: _____ Condition of Light: _____

Footage: _____ Test: _____

Laboratory Instructions: _____

Scene Description: _____

Sun Direction | Camera Angle

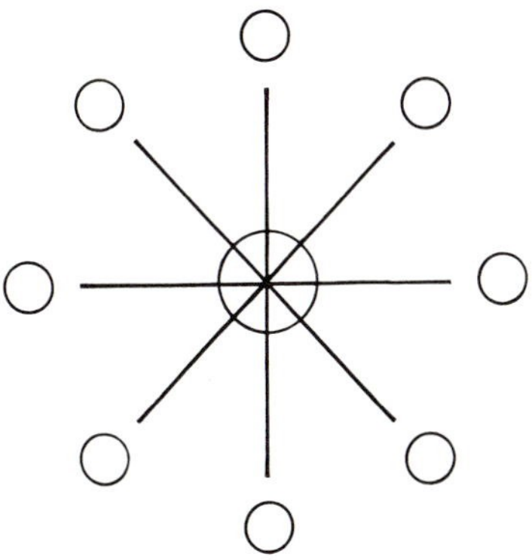

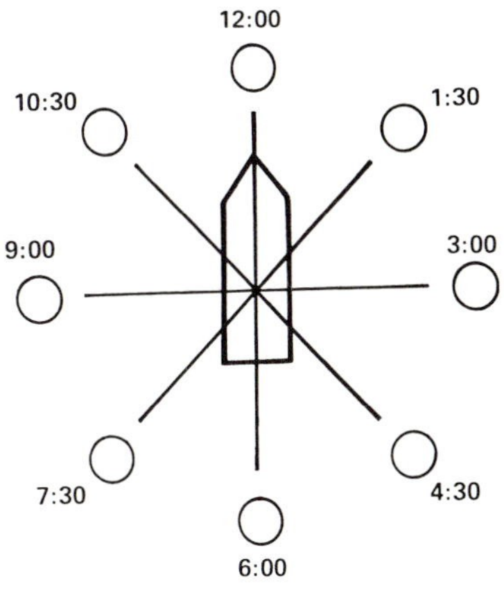

Fig. 10.20. A process photo log sheet designed by process-projection specialist Bill Hansard. It provides a permanent record of most of the pertinent conditions which obtained during photography which are likely to be of concern to the sound-stage crew at the time that they make the final background-projection shot.

Every background plate should be 'slated', and the circumstances of its photography recorded on an exposure sheet: the production title, the name of the cameraman, the run of scene numbers with which this background is associated in the production footage, the angle and character of the sunlight, and the time of day; also, the make of plate camera employed and its registration-pin position, the make, focal length, and relative aperture of lens, the raw stock, the elevation of the camera in feet, and the nature of any diffusion, contrast, or color-correction filters employed while photographing the plate (Fig. 10.20).

Film and exposure

Fine-grain, medium-speed emulsions such as Eastman's black-and-white XT Pan Negative and Plus-X, and color negative type 5247, are used whenever possible for the photography of background plates. Since most backgrounds are photographed with sunlight, the speed of such stocks is usually sufficient for the job. For photography during evening hours – particularly for moving-camera shots of traffic and street scenes – higher-speed stocks can be employed if necessary, the effect of grain in such shots being less noticeable because of the preponderance of shadow areas. Since the higher-speed emulsions have greater latitude, they are less likely, too, to produce halation from neon and uncovered street lamps. Extremely high-speed stocks should not be used unless absolutely necessary; otherwise, special attention may have to be paid to their processing so as to artificially increase their inherently lower contrast.

Exposure of the background negative should ordinarily be somewhat on the full side, producing reasonably dense negatives which can be printed down so as to produce rich, black shadows. Thin negatives tend to produce positives which show muddy, low-contrast shadow areas when projected. Thin negatives also tend to emphasize any scratching and abrasion.

Processing

Special attention must be given to the processing of the negatives and the positive plates. Some of the theatrical film studios of the past even went to the trouble of setting up special black-and-white laboratories devoted solely to the processing of such footage. Great care must be taken to avoid scratches, pin holes, pit marks, stains, and other blemishes, both during processing and subsequent handling stages. Magnified several hundred times on a process screen, these imperfections assume gigantic proportions when only a portion of the projected background is re-photographed.

The determination of proper contrast remains one of the most critical factors in the production of the plate, inasmuch as the illusion of the final composite depends upon the matching of contrast between the foreground action and the screen image. The gamma to which black-and-white negatives and fine-grain positives should be developed can only be determined experimentally, since the contrast of the projected image will depend upon many factors – the negative and print stocks used for the plate; whether contact or optical printing is used to produce the positive; whether color separations or duplicating color negative stocks are used to make the plate; the type of screen and the kind of projection optics employed; the key-to-fill ratio used for foreground lighting; and the production emulsion used on stage for final photography. For color cinematography, the cameraman must always bear in mind that the foreground action on stage will be photographed directly, in 'first generation', onto the negative color stock in the camera, whereas the background detail will be at least one generation removed. A good deal of experience and a certain amount of continuing experimentation will be necessary before consistent and satisfactory results are achieved in color background-projection photography.

These same variables also determine the proper density of the positive plate. For convenience, many cameramen order three 'bracketed' prints of each plate – the first printed with whatever printer light seems appropriate to the scene; the other two printed a couple of lights above and below the norm. Later, on the sound stage, one of the three prints will be found to be appropriate during composite photography.

For shots in which the background camera is immobile, it is desirable that the prints be made on either a step-contact or step-optical printer so that registration accuracy be preserved. As in optical printing, it is desirable, too, that pilot-pin positions be maintained consistently throughout the duplication process – either above or below the aperture. Should pin positions change anywhere along the line, they can be corrected through optical printing.

Automobile interiors

One of the most common uses to which background projection is put is the simulation of automobile interior scenes, the actors being seated within a real or break-away automobile chassis, with a moving-camera scene of traffic being projected onto the screen behind them (Figs. 10.21 and 10.22). For the photography of such background plates, the camera is mounted on an automobile, pointed in whatever direction is required for the scene, and set running while the vehicle moves through traffic. For best results, a specially-designed camera-car is employed which has running-board extensions and mounting pedestals on all four sides, and which is specially sprung with shock absorbers so as to reduce the amount of vibration transmitted to the camera.

The requirements for registration accuracy and camera steadiness are much less severe for this work than for static-camera shots, inasmuch as a certain amount of jiggle is expected in a moving background. For this reason, it is not absolutely essential that a pilot-pin movement be used.

Before the background plates are shot, the cameraman will need a considerable amount of information about the scene in which they will be used: the kind and size of automobile in which the actors will be seated, the sort of route which they are expected to take, the climatic conditions and the time of day or evening which is involved, the speed at which the car is supposed to travel, and any special behaviour which it is expected to display – stops and starts, turns, accelerations and decelerations.

Fig. 10.21. Studios which provide rear-projection services sometimes stock a collection of cut-away automobile frames which allow for convenient positioning of camera and lights.

Naturally, the greater the extent to which the actors' dialogue and 'business' are cued to the scene projected behind them, the more difficult and intricate a job it is to photograph the background plate. If the scene is complicated enough, it may be necessary for the director or his assistant to accompany the background cameraman and to supervise the timing and staging of the plate.

Shooting from various angles

The background scene is usually taken from a variety of angles, so as to allow the sound-stage cameraman to photograph the actors from any angle the director wishes. The most common angles used are straight-back, 45° back on either side, and 90° to either side. Occasionally, too, the need arises for shots taken straight forward and 45° forward on either side.

These differently-angled plates can either be shot with a single camera on successive trips, or with multiple cameras operating simultaneously on a single run. The latter arrangement is usually employed when some peculiarly recognizable action takes place in the background which must be synchronized with sound-stage dialogue at the time that the projection composite is photographed. It is also necessary when the dialogue or 'business' of the actors within the car calls the attention of the audience to particular events transpiring in the background plate. The use of such synchronized plates allows the director and editor to cut from close-up to

Fig. 10.22. If a cut-away frame is not available, a real vehicle can be used. For the production of *Calvary*, an ambulance was brought into the sound-stage, a process screen positioned beyond the far window, and a traveling shot photographed with rear-projected street detail. The projector is located in a sound-proof booth located above the 'Silence' sign. (Unusual Films, Bob Jones University.)

over-shoulder shot, to medium two-shot, and so forth, without having to worry about jump cuts in the background action.

In most cases, however, so long as the traffic background scene remains substantially similar from one foot of film to the next, it is usually possible, from shot to shot, to 'cheat' the editorial relationship between matched-action coverage of the actors in the foreground and the different background images which are produced behind them. The assumption in such cases is that the audience is too preoccupied with the dramatic situation developing within the automobile to pay much attention to the background scene.

Ideally, whether using one or several cameras for the photography of a traveling-background plate, each of the separate angles will be recorded on a different piece of film. Sometimes, however, either for lack of time or money, only one side of the street will be photographed for the 45° or 90° shots. Later, on the sound stage, the same background plate can be used for shots in either direction by simply flipping the film in the projector. This economy works so long as recognizable signs do not appear in the background which will, of course, be reversed. It also reverses the position of traffic, so that it appears to be on the wrong side of the road; this may or may not be apparent, depending upon the width of the street, the angle of the shot, and the speed of the camera-car.

Speed of camera-car

Attention must be paid to the speed at which the camera-car is driven while the plates are photographed. Ordinarily, shots taken straight back or straight forward may be photographed with the camera-car travelling at whatever speed the scene calls for. When shooting at a 45° or 90° angle to one side, however, some reduction in speed will be found necessary so as to minimize blurring of the image and to avoid the resulting optical illusion that the car is moving faster than it actually is. The same effect could be achieved by photographing side-angle plates at a higher camera speed, of course, but this would slow down the actions of pedestrians who are seen in the background; for this reason, it is best to reduce the speed of the camera-car. Typical recommended variations in automobile speed for different angles are indicated in Fig. 10.23.

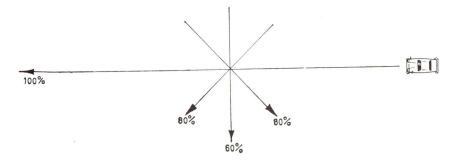

Fig. 10.23. Because moving background plates which are shot from side angles appear to move much faster than those photographed head-on, it is necessary to reduce the camera-car speed at side angles to give a realistic appearance. This diagram suggests the amount of reduction necessary. For example, if the car is driven at 70 mile/hour for straight-ahead shots, it should be driven 42 mile/hour for 90° shots, and 56 mile/hour for three-quarter shots, fore-and-aft. (Courtesy of *American Cinematographer.*)

Lenses and viewpoint

Ordinarily, moderately short focal-length lenses (e.g. 40 mm or 35 mm on a 35 mm camera) are used for the photography of background plates, thus providing a perspective and an angle of view which appears most normal when projected behind the actors. The additional angle of view provided by such lenses is particularly needed when the back window of the automobile is fairly large, or when actors are posed inside an open convertible. If, on the contrary, only a portion of the background traffic is viewed through a small back window, then a normal 50 mm lens can be employed. For side-angle shots, at 45° and 90° the shorter focal lengths are quite essential to produce a realistically-appearing wide angle of view and to reduce the high-speed, blurred effect which results from shooting from such positions.

It is important that the elevation of the background camera, with respect to the highway, be appropriate to the scene in which the plate will be used, the height of the camera being determined by the kind and size of automobile in which the actors will perform on the sound stage. On the camera-car, the elevation of the camera is adjusted so as to duplicate a point of view which would be gained by putting the same camera within the sound-stage automobile mock-up and photographing the actors at shoulder-level. Naturally, the elevation of the background plate camera above the pavement will be different for a sports car than for a full-size automobile. For the same reason, background plates which are to be projected behind the windows of a bus or outside the cab of a truck must be photographed from a high elevation. In all cases, the background camera must be set to photograph its scene with the axis of the lens approximately parallel to the highway; there should be no noticeable tilting up or down. It may be found desirable, however, to position the horizon line so as to favor the pavement slightly. This provides an angle which is appropriate for the sound-stage camera which operates at the eye-level of the actors within the cut-away automobile.

When passing over certain types of terrain – as when moving up, down, or over a hill – the horizon position will naturally vary upwards and downward. Ordinarily, this kind of route will be avoided by the cameraman; in any case, such radical changes in horizon position should not be corrected by adjusting the background plate camera, since they are appropriate to the terrain which is being photographed.

Depending upon the context of the background scene, additional realism can be added by creating moving shadows, on stage, to fall upon the faces of the actors in the automobile, thereby duplicating the way in which trees or buildings cast such shadows in real life. For night effects, moving beams or splashes of light, differently colored, can be played across the faces of the actors in the car to simulate the effect of street lights and neon lights in nearly buildings. Similarly, when an automobile in the background plate with bright headlights is seen to pass the sound-stage automobile, additional realism will be achieved by playing a moving beam of light across the actors' faces at the appropriate moment, just prior to the passing of the vehicle.

Sound-stage operations

It is the nature of conventional background projection to require a fairly large stage for its proper execution – at least, if large screens and images are to be involved. Naturally, the length of projector 'throw', the distance of the camera from the screen, and the focal length of lenses on both machines can vary with each shot and set-up.

Bend-angles

The most crucial factor arising out of these variables is the bend-angle which results between projector and camera, relative to the corners of the screen. Typical bend-angles which are produced by different focal-length combinations of projector and camera lenses are shown in Fig. 10.24. For quality reproduction, in which fall-off and hot-spot are to be minimized, most cameramen and engineers recommend that the limiting bend-angle should not exceed 17°. It will be noted, by examining these figures, that a reduction of the bend-angle is more easily accomplished by increasing the focal length of the camera lens than that of the projector. The choice of a

TYPICAL BEND-ANGLES

Camera Lens	Projection-lens focal lengths				
	5 in	6 in	7 in	8 in	9 in
30 mm	28.1	27.2	26.5	26.0	25.6
50 mm	19.6	18.7	18.0	17.5	17.1
75 mm	15.0	14.1	13.4	12.9	12.5
100 mm	12.7	11.8	11.1	10.6	10.2

Fig. 10.24. The figures indicate limiting bend-angles in degrees for standard Movietone (1.33:1) apertures (0.980 in × 0.715 in) in camera and projector.

75 mm lens for the camera and a 6 inch lens for the projector is a popular one; longer focal lengths on the camera will reduce the bend-angle substantially but may produce an unacceptably shallow depth of field for sound-stage operation. Bend-angles are also determined by the size and aspect ratio of the film format employed and the distances at which the camera and projector are placed away from the screen. These distances, in turn, depend upon the size of the image which is required for a particular set-up.

In practice, the projector is usually positioned at a distance from the screen about twice that of the camera. The total distances which result between the camera and projector may range anywhere from 150 to 300 ft. As a practical rule-of-thumb, the following formula will be found useful in determining the projector 'throw' distance for a given screen width and projection focal-length lens in order to fill the screen with the picture area of the plate.

$$\text{Throw (in feet)} = \frac{\text{Focal length (in mm)} \times \text{width of screen (in feet)}}{X}$$

Here, 'X' is the width of the stereo or plate format (35 mm Movietone, 35 mm Vistavision, 4 × 5 stereo, or whatever), in millimeters.

Such guides to equipment placement are quite approximate and vary with the format and aspect ratio of film used in both the projector and camera. They also vary in those cases in which only a portion of the background plate is used to fill the entire screen, in which case either the projector will have to be pulled farther away from the screen or a lens of shorter focal length will have to be employed (Fig. 10.25).

BACKGROUND PROJECTION CHART

CAMERA LENS		PICTURE WIDTH	MOVIETONE APERTURE THROW			FULL APERTURE THROW			STEREOPTICAN	
2"	3"		5" Lens	6"	7"	5" Lens	6"	7"	4x5" Slide	3¼x4" Slide
2	3½	1	5½	7	8	5	6	7½	3½	4
9	13½	4	23	27½	32	21	25	29	13½	16½
13½	20½	6	34½	41½	48	31	37½	45½	20	25
16	24	7	40	48½	56	36½	43½	51	23½	29
18	27	8	46	55½	64½	41½	50	58½	26½	34
20½	30½	9	51½	62	72½	47	56	65½	30	37½
22½	34	10	57½	69	80½	52	62½	73	33½	41½
25	37½	11	63	76	88½	57	68½	80	36½	46
27	41	12	69	83	96½	62½	75	87½	40	50
29½	44	13	74½	90	104½	67½	81	94½	43½	54
31½	47½	14	80½	96½	112½	73	87½	102	46½	58½
34	51	15	86	103½	120½	78	93½	109½	50	62½
36	54½	16	92	110½	128½	83½	100	116½	53½	67
38½	57½	17	97½	117½	136½	88½	106	124	56½	71
41	61	18	103½	124½	144½	93½	112½	131	60	75
43	64½	19	109	131½	152½	99	118½	138½	63	79
45½	68	20	115	138½	161	104	125	146	66½	83½
50	75	22	126½	152	177	114½	137½	160½	73½	92
54½	81½	24	138	166	193	125	150	175	80	100

Add 10 Ft. For Projector & Working Space   16" Lens

Fig. 10.25. A background projection chart, suitable for either front- or rear-projection computations, which relates the distance of camera and projector from the screen to (a) aperture format (Movietone or full); (b) picture width, and (c) focal lengths of camera and projector lenses. Projection distances for 'stereo' diapositives are also shown. (Courtesy Bill Hansard.)

A straight projection throw is always to be desired, providing that the sound stage is sufficiently large to allow it. Sometimes, however, when large-screen images must be produced on a small stage, one or more mirrors can be used to 'fold' the beam of the projector; these allow the cameraman to position the projector closer to the screen without having to change the focal length of the lens and thereby increase the bend-angle. Depending upon the number of mirrors employed, the plate may end up by being reversed; this can be corrected by simply flipping the plate in the projection intermittent. In any case, the best quality of mirror must be used – preferably front-silvered – if double reflections and optical distortions are to be avoided. The alignment of such a mirror system is fairly critical and the length of time required for its installation should not be underestimated.

The re-positioning of the projector, using 'folded' optics, will bring the projector much closer to the screen than is usual in background projection. Special care must be taken under such circumstances to 'blimp' the projector so that the sound of its operation is not picked up by the microphone on the other side of the screen.

Permanent installations

The more permanent a background-projection installation can be made, the more economical it will become over a period of time. In the theatrical film industry, some organizations have set aside a complete stage for the exclusive use of the process department. Given such a facility, the projector can be permanently mounted and aligned at one end of the stage – within a sound-proof room or on an elevated platform, if desired. Turntables, treadmills and false floors can be more-or-less permanently installed, proper sound recording or isolation equipment can be provided, exhaust tubes for the evacuation of smoke and gasses from the arcs or xenon lamps can be permanently attached to the projector, supports for special kinds of lighting can be rigged on catwalks, grids or light bridges, and all sorts of accessory equipment can be positioned close at hand for day-to-day work. Assuming that the production organization expects to undertake a considerable amount of process photography, the cost of tying up such a stage will be more than repaid through the savings in time and labor which are achieved during actual production. Many of the same economies are made possible for the low-budget producer when he uses the services and permanent stage facilities of a professional process organization.

Aligning projector, screen and camera

The positions of the background projector, screen and camera upon the sound-stage floor will depend upon the nature of the foreground set and the action with which it is to be integrated. A certain amount of planning is necessary to ensure that ample room is left on both sides of the projector-camera axis for set pieces, props and lighting and sound equipment.

For convenience sake, a straight line can be chalked, painted or taped onto the stage floor, along which the positions of the three process components can be established. For conventional work, it is necessary that the optical axis of the projector lens be normal (perpendicular) to the surface of the screen. Any marked vertical or horizontal displacement of these two components, relative to one another, produces a keystone distortion of the image and illumination fall-off on the side of the screen farthest from the projector. In these respects, the alignment of projector and screen is far more critical than for the camera and the screen. Even using modern screens, the projector's optical axis should not be off the normal more than 5°.

Ordinarily, the pick-up angle of the camera will be more-or-less 'head-on' to the screen in which case the optical axes of the two machines will be coincident, mutually normal to the surface of the screen and parallel to the floor of the stage. Naturally, this coincidence of axes will not prevail if the camera is tilted or panned during the shot. Using a modern screen, the camera can be pivoted in this fashion through as much as 25–30° with good results. Pick-up angles in excess of 35° or 40° are not useful, partly because of fall-off, partly because of distortion.

Occasionally, either because of the peculiarities of the foreground set or because the production camera is required to shoot upward or downward at an acute angle, it becomes necessary to angle the screen and to elevate or lower the properly-tilted projector so as to keep its optical axis perpendicular to the screen. Some of the larger studios have constructed heavy-duty hoists or elevators on which their projection equipment can be mounted and raised or lowered to whatever height is required. Equipment such as this saves considerable time and money during production, but is expensive to design and fabricate.

When working with a permanently-mounted projector, it is necessary to vary the distances of screen and camera to conform to the projector's fixed position. When all three components are portable, however, considerable latitude in placement is afforded. Portable background projectors are mounted on movable platforms which can be rolled on castors to whatever position is desired. Jacks on the platform provide a means of anchoring the machine securely in its final position. Once positioned, the head of most projectors can be rotated through a 180° arc, and tilted up or down through 10° to 20°.

Projection equipment

The projectionist will require a variety of accessories for his work, not the least of which is a work bench and a set of high-speed rewinds. Racks for film storage and equipment for splicing of leaders, and for cleaning of the positive plates and stereos, will also be needed.

An intercom system is oftentimes provided between the projector and the camera position – some background projectors provide this as a built-in feature (Figs. 10.12 and 10.17). By means of the intercom, the director of photography can quickly and quietly communicate whatever instructions are necessary during both set-up and final photography. To reduce noise on the set still further, some studios have installed a 'cue-light' console which allows for instructions to be given silently to the projectionist during the making of a shot.

A full (silent) aperture should be used in the projector whenever possible, assuming, of course, that the plate has been similarly photographed. The somewhat larger image size produces a sharper and finer-grained picture for a given screen size. (On the other hand, the larger format produces larger bend angles than does the smaller.) Some background projectors also provide an oversized aperture by means of which the perforations of the plate can be projected onto the screen. Magnified several hundred times, the perforations provide a reference point for the measurement of projection – intermittent accuracy. A yard stick or other straight-edge can be mounted on a Century-stand and placed next to the vertical or horizontal edges of the projected perforations. Any jiggle or weave which is caused by inaccurate projection registration will be immediately apparent. If, on the other hand, the perforations appear steady and the image jiggles, then it is obvious that registration has been compromised either during original photography or during duplication of the plate.

The screen may be hung from the ceiling or catwalk by means of cords, or may be strung up on a movable rack. In either case, sufficient tension, evenly applied, must be used to ensure a wrinkle-free surface.

Because of the thickness of the screen, an entirely different focus may be produced on one side than on the other. An image which is in focus on the projectionist's side may be noticeably out of focus as it is photographed by the camera. Since the projectionist cannot see the other side of the screen during operations, he can never be entirely sure that the picture is sharp. For this reason, focusing is often done on the camera side by remote control. A small stepper or servo motor is connected with the focusing apparatus of the projector's lens, and a long control line is run out to the camera position, where the cameraman or one of his assistants focuses the picture visually upon the camera side of the screen.

Eliminating hot-spot and fall-off ·

Ordinarily, some difference in brightness between the center and edges of the screen can be tolerated before this brightness difference is perceived and photographed as a 'hot-spot'. Photographically, the extent to which such a brightness difference will become noticeable in the finished, composite positive print depends in part upon the inherent latitude and contrast of the negative stock used in the camera. One's awareness of this difference is further influenced by the nature of the background image and whether it is immobile or in motion. Some background pictures, by their compositional nature, do not produce as severe a hot-spot as others. Also, the moving image of a plate is more likely to reveal the presence of a hot-spot than the immobile image of a stereo, since the hot-spot always remains in the same, fixed position.

Should a hot-spot be apparent, any one of a number of steps can be employed to reduce it to a minimum.

Graded screens

In past years, many of the translucent screens employed were 'graded'; which is to say, their surfaces were fabricated in such a way that the center of the screen was thicker than the edges, thus absorbing a considerable amount of projected light at that point and evening out the brightness of the image. These screens were never really successful. They were difficult and expensive to make and they compromised the sharpness of the projected image. They also required 'head-on' pick-up angles and immobilization of the camera – any other kind of alignment would shift the position of the denser, central portion of the screen out of the hot-spot area.

Modern diffusion screens

In modern times, 'graded' screens have been replaced by diffusion types which offer both a minimum amount of illumination fall-off and a maximum amount of transmission.

Many types of screens with varying amounts of diffusion are available, each of which is suited to a particular kind of job. For conventional motion-picture photography, screens with relatively high transmission are used. Because of the lesser amount of internal diffusion built into the screen, these require moderately long throw distances so as to avoid fall-off caused by excessive bend angles.

Reduction of bend-angles

A noticeable reduction in hot-spot and fall-off can be achieved by simply reducing the bend-angles formed by projector and camera lenses with the screen. Such a reduction may be achieved by increasing the focal length of lenses used on the camera and/or projector, and increasing the distance of the projector and camera from the screen.

Assuming that the bend-angles which are used are sufficiently small to provide a satisfactory reduction or elimination of the hot-spot, there is nothing to be gained by pulling the camera and projector still farther away from the screen and mounting even longer focal-length lenses. Excessively long focal-length lenses on the camera produce a depth of field too shallow to hold foreground action in front of the screen.

Reduction of pick-up angles

Ordinarily, a modest amount of panning and tilting of the camera can be done during process photography so as to follow action in the foreground area. As the pick-up angle is increased, however, a fall-off of illumination on the far side of the screen will be recorded on the film. Pick-up angles in excess of 40° should be avoided, not merely because of fall-off but also because of the optical distortion which results. This distortion effect is the same as is perceived by members of the motion-picture audience who are seated close to the screen and far to one side or the other. It is particularly noticeable in process photography since it occurs only in the projected image and not in the foreground acting area.

Misalignment of camera and projector optical axes

Although extreme pick-up angles should be avoided, a certain amount of mis-alignment of camera and projector optics can serve a useful purpose. For 'head-on' shots, many cameramen purposely tilt the camera up or down so that its optical axis is 3–4° off that of the projector's. The reduction of hot-spot which results is sometimes quite marked.

Manipulation of projection optics

Many modern background projectors acept specially-designed condensers which deliver more light to the peripheral areas of the plate than to the center. This can be achieved either by altering the optical formula of the condensers, or by adding into the condensing system a graduated neutral-density filter which is darker in its center than at its edges. The alteration of condenser optics in this fashion modifies the light *before* it reaches the plate.

It is also possible to reduce hot-spot by altering the *projected* beam of light. To this end, small metal discs are inserted into the projection optics which block light passing through the central portion of the lens, thereby reducing the brilliance of the projected plate in its center. The same effect can be achieved by either mounting a sheet of optical glass a couple of feet in front of the projector's lens and spraying the center of the sheet with a neutral-density medium, or by attaching a piece of neutral-density filter to a long, thin wire and suspending it in the center of the projection beam.

None of these techniques is really satisfactory, however. In the first place, all require a fairly critical and time-consuming alignment of components if they are to achieve their purpose. Secondly, all of these techniques reduce the sharpness of the projected image. When opaque discs are used *within* the projection optics, the effect is to reduce the sharpness of the *entire* screen image. Since the discs block out the axial rays of light the image on the screen is produced almost entirely by the rays of light which pass through the periphery of the lens. These peripheral rays of light are most likely to suffer from the various types of spherical and chromatic aberration which afflict all lenses, and the resulting overall screen image suffers accordingly. When neutral-density filters are used outside the projection optics, the effect is to reduce the sharpness of the *center* of the picture.

Finally, the reduction of hot-spot which is offered by this technique is obtained only if the camera is permanently aligned and immobilized, 'head-on' in front of the screen. Any change in camera position or pick-up angle during the shot causes the hot-spot to reappear.

Manipulation of plate density

By altering the density of the positive plate (or stereo) in its center, it is possible to produce the same diminution of hot-spot as is produced optically with discs, but without the attending reduction in image sharpness.

The aim is to produce a stereo or plate diapositive which is substantially more dense in its center than in the normally-printed image at its edges. This may be accomplished in a variety of ways. For the preparation of 4 × 5 inch stereos, the center of the diapositive may be 'burned in' by means of conventional darkroom practice. The technique is so well known that it does not require amplification here.

For alteration of positive motion-picture plates, either optical printing or bi-pack contact printing can be employed. For optical printing, while a straight 1:1 positive print is made from the original negative, a graduated neutral-density filter – appropriately darkened at its edges and clear in the center – is interposed between the process camera and the printer head. Alternatively, if the design of the optical printer allows, the same sort of graduated filter could be inserted into the condensing system of the printer head.

In the case of bi-pack contact printing, the original negative and a color master positive stock are threaded into the intermittent movement and the camera is focused upon a matte-board on which the peripheral areas have been darkened with charcoal or pastels and the central section left white. By adjusting the lens of the camera slightly out of focus, the texture of the rendering can be obscured and a nice gradation of light values is produced.

Although these techniques for manipulating plate density produce screen images of greater sharpness than are obtained by modifying the projection optics, it is still necessary that the camera be aligned and immobilized 'head-on' in front of the screen. Should the camera move, or its pick-up angle change during the shot, the hot-spot will reappear.

'Hiding' the hot-spot

If all other techniques fail, it may still be possible to eliminate the hot-spot by simply hiding it behind a set piece, prop, or figure in the foreground. Fortunately, this happens as a matter of course when the actor is photographed in medium-shot, directly in front of the camera.

Placement of actors, sets and props

A certain amount of compromise is ordinarily necessary in setting up a scene for process photography. On the one hand, the long focal-length lenses which are used to reduce bend-angles, together with the rather large apertures employed for this work (e.g. $f/2.5$ to $f/5.6$) produce a shallow depth of field in the foreground area in front of the screen. Because of the shallow depth of field, actors must be placed as close as convenient to the projected image; otherwise, one or the other will be rendered out of focus.

On the other hand, the closer the actors stand to the screen, the more difficult it is to light them attractively without splashing light onto the face of the screen, thereby causing flare and washing out the contrast of the projected image.

The problem is further complicated by the introduction of set pieces and props into the shot. Properly scaled and 'cheated' for perspective match, these will enhance the realism of the composite. At the same time, the presence of these pieces may force the actors to work farther away from the screen. Compromise, then, always enters into the staging of a process shot. The particular distances of actors and set pieces, focal length of lenses, relative apertures, sizes of screen image, illumination levels, and speed of production emulsions are all intimately related.

Peculiar problems arise when, following completion of a medium-shot in process photography, the actor and camera must be brought closer together for a close-up. In such cases, it is ordinarily necessary to move *both* the camera and actor closer to the screen so as to overcome the decreasing depth of field which results. When this is done, it is desirable that the plate or stereo be changed to another shot of the same background which offers a somewhat *greater* angle of view. If this is not done – particularly in the case of long-shot backgrounds – then a curious effect may result. In conventional photography, the field of view of the background does not change noticeably as we move the camera in a few feet toward the actor. In process photography, however, the same move by the camera greatly decreases the field of view which is captured of the background vista. This happens because the background image, being artificial, is permanently fixed in its perspective, field of view, and scale. The effect is even more marked when the camera is dollied towards or away from the screen. Particularly in those cases in which deep foreground sets are integrated with a projected background, any dollying movement produces appropriate perspective changes in the foreground sets, but none in the background plate.

Also, as the camera is brought in closer to the screen, the hot-spot may become apparent due to increasing bend-angles, and the grain structure of the plate or stereo may become noticeable.

One other kind of problem may arise if the camera is trucked laterally, parallel to the screen – the effect of motion parallax which is apparent in the foreground set will not be duplicated in the background image. This, again, is most noticeable if an elaborate foreground set is employed.

Lighting and exposure

Despite the considerable amounts of research which have gone into process photography, the last stages of execution – lighting and exposure – remain pretty much an empirical matter, dependent upon the individual experience and skill of the cameraman. For such assignments, no amount of instruction or theoretical knowledge can prepare even the most competent cameraman who has not had the opportunity for trial-and-error experimentation.

Avoiding splash light

The lighting of the foreground action must be conducted so as to provide a satisfactory illumination level and attractive modelling of the actors, but without splashing light onto the front or back surfaces of the screen. Splash light, if sufficiently bright, causes flare at the surface of the screen and decreases the contrast of the background image – sometimes washing it out entirely. Happily, modern screens can tolerate far more splash light than older types.

Cross-lights are used whenever possible to key the actors and to light the set, the barndoors of the lamps being adjusted to keep the back edge of the beam from striking the screen. So long as the actors remain a good distance from the screen, conventional 45° lighting may be used for their illumination. As the actors move closer to the projected background, however, it becomes increasingly necessary to light them from the sides. An actor who is positioned directly in front of the screen is virtually impossible to light except with 90° side-lighting, back-lighting, or top-lighting.

Since the background image can be contaminated by frontal lights, fill-lights at the camera position cannot be as powerful as in conventional practice. Alternatively, frontal fill-light is provided from above and slightly to one side of the actor. For convenience sake, a light bridge is sometimes built around the foreground set, onto which both key and fill-lights can be hung. Occasionally, too, fill-lights can be set on the floor and angled upwards; this may or may not create peculiar modelling effects, depending upon the nature, angle, and strength of the key lights with which they are combined.

Back-light, top-light, and kickers can be used as in conventional practice, although care must be taken to avoid contaminating the *back* side of the screen in doing so. Accent lights such as these can often be used to overcome inadequacies which may result in the frontal lighting of a process shot.

All lights which operate from in front of the screen should be carefully controlled – fill-lights with flags and spot-lights with barndoors – so as to illuminate only the foreground area. Lamps should be examined to see that they are not leaking light through their air vents, seams, or lamphouse doors. A certain amount of flare may also result from light which is reflected off the floor and back onto the surface of the screen. Assuming that the floor does not show in the shot, it may be found helpful to paint it black or to spread a tarpaulin over its surface. Finally, during the production take, extraneous stage and house-lights should be extinguished so as to reduce the ambient, non-production light level to a minimum.

Matching background lighting

The lighting problem is further complicated by the requirement that shadows and key-light directions be produced in the foreground area which will match those in the plate or stereo. Also, the key-to-fill ratio used for the actors must be appropriate for that shown in the background picture. The closer the match, the more convincing the composite.

Obviously, the sound-stage cameraman is limited by the character of the plate or stereo that has been provided him, and if the plate photographer has not thought out his work carefully, the sound-stage cameraman may spend long periods of time trying to duplicate it.

The process cameraman and his crew must plan their days' work on the sound stage so that as few lighting set-ups as possible will serve for a particular selection of plates. For example, given a number of process shots which are designed to simulate exterior scenes occurring during the passing of a day's time, efficient planning will provide for the photography of all the 'morning' shots at one time, with foreground shadows falling in the right direction and with key lights set at approximately the proper elevation to match that of the sun in the background picture. Later, photography with the 'afternoon' or 'mid-day' plates will require entirely different lighting set-ups on the stage to match the changing positions of the sun.

When foliage appears in both the live-action foreground and the projected background, the foreground vegetation must be lit so that it photographs with the same color, brightness, hue and saturation as that appearing in the background. Sometimes, it will be found necessary to over- or under-light the foreground foliage, relative to the actor's lighting, or even to spray these pieces with dye, so as to achieve a proper match.

The role of experience and experimentation

At no point in the rear-projection process is trial-and-error experience so necessary as in balancing the brightness of the projected background with the illumination of the live-action foreground. The problem is less acute when 'stereo' projection is used, since the background image is continuously projected. For plate photography, however, neither the inexperienced eye nor the exposure meter will indicate the kind of composite which will be photographed by the motion-picture camera.

On the one hand, the projected motion-picture is interrupted by the shutter of the background projector, whereas the foreground set is lighted continuously. The image on the screen, therefore, is inclined to appear dimmer to the eye than the foreground actors and set pieces. In addition, inasmuch as a camera-type shutter is often employed in the projector, considerable flicker results which is irritating and deceiving when viewed by technicians on the set. This flicker is not recorded on the film, of course, since the camera's shutter is properly synchronized with that of the projector.

Secondly, certain types of film, both black-and-white and color, are more sensitive to the bluish-white light of the projector's arc than to the warmer incandescent or quartz-arc lamps which illuminate the foreground. For this reason, an arc-illuminated background image which appears somewhat dim to the eye may photograph nicely, on such stocks, when combined with a more warmly-lit foreground. For process work in color cinematography, a different kind of carbon arc is used which produces illumination of a lower color temperature which matches that of incandescent or quartz-arc lamps. Alternatively, the light from the projector can be filtered down to a warmer hue, or the color masters used for plates can be printed to a warmer balance.

Many cameramen find that a deep green or blue viewing filter provides a psychological aid in estimating the balance of foreground and background brilliances. Obviously, a great deal depends upon the density, contrast, and character of the plate or stereo which is employed. Some cameramen have learned to employ either conventional reflecting exposure meters or narrow-angle spot photometers to measure the brilliance of the screen image. The readings which are gained from plate images require considerable interpretation, however, since the meter is as easily fooled as the eye by the interrupting shutter of the projector. Using a narrow-angle spot photometer at camera position, one recommendation calls for any part of the projected background which is supposed to reproduce dead white (measured in foot-lamberts) to be three-quarters of the illumination level of the foreground illumination (measured in foot candles). Thus, if a reading of 75 foot-lamberts is gained from a bald-white sky or a performer's white shirt in the projected background, an appropriate illumination level for the live-action foreground might be 100 foot-candles.

Such formulae provide only approximate guides and points-of-departure for the serious worker. Cameramen who expect to do process photography must demand and expect to take time for pre-production tests. Because of the many variables which operate between plate and stereo photography, and sound-stage set-ups, only experimentation can provide the individual worker with the experience necessary for consistently competent work. For best results, if time and budget allow, a short test strip of film can be photographed in the sound-stage camera, then quickly developed and examined before the final production take is made. Still cameras, of either conventional or Polaroid types, cannot be used for this purpose, unless their shutters can be electronically synchronized with that of the background projector. Video-tap set-ups for viewing and taping of the rehearsal and final takes, must also be designed to take the intermittent nature of the background image into consideration, inasmuch as (in the USA) the video camera samples at the rate of 30 frames per second, whereas the background-image and motion-picture camera operate at 24 frames per second.

A photographic balance between foreground and background can be achieved by varying the brilliance either of the projected image or of the foreground lights. Projection brilliance can be altered by (a) inserting neutral-density filters into the condensing optics, (b) changing the relative aperture of the projection lens, (c) changing the aperture of the iris diaphragm which is sometimes built into the condensing optics, or (d) varying the amperage of the projector's arc.

Sometimes, an ordinary contact-printed print is used for lining-up and lighting purposes, the step-printed positive being saved for final photography. Similarly, for color work with 'stereo' projectors, a black-and-white positive can be used for lining-up, and the color positive for final photography, thus minimizing any fading of the color dyes.

Special problems and techniques

Smaller-than-normal screens

Sometimes, it is desirable to produce a screen image in which full-scale actors or props are reduced to smaller-than-normal scale. Historically speaking, one of the first applications of this technique is to be found in the 1933 version of *King Kong*, in which plates of actors were projected onto very small rear-projection screens which were integrated into miniaturized sets in which the miniature figure of 'Kong' was animated. Another historical example which comes to mind is that of the 1940 film, *Dr Cyclops*, in which full-sized actors were photographed on plates which were then projected onto small screens set into a full-scale set in which the actor Albert Dekker performed. In the finished composite, the full-scale actors appeared to have been shrunk into a fraction of their original size.

Still other, more common, applications of small-screen background projection occur in scenes in which television or computer monitors are required to operate and to show either computer data or graphics or television images. It will not work to photograph a CRT (cathode ray tube) directly, for the electronic system samples its images (in the USA) at a rate of 30 images per second, while the sound motion-picture samples at the rate of 24 images per second. As a consequence, the two systems operate out of phase when a CRT is photographed with a motion-picture camera, causing black 'bars' to roll through the picture. Provided that actors are not obliged to walk in front of these electronic images, it is possible to matte-in the desired graphics or television images by means of either in-the-camera matte shots, bi-pack printed matte shots, or optical printing. If the actor must pass in front of the tube, however, it will be necessary to use either background projection or a traveling matte of the actor. Several recent science-fiction films, which show numerous computer CRT monitors being operated in the control rooms of spaceships, produced the computer read-out data and graphics seen on these screens by means of 16 mm rear projection, the shutters of the various 16 mm projectors being synchronized with that of the sound-stage camera.

Background projection combined with matte paintings

Elsewhere in this book, descriptions are provided of methods for combining live-action detail with painted-scene components, either through in-the-camera matte shots, glass shots, bi-pack printing, or optical printing. It is also possible to create quite attractive and convincing composites by combining background projection and painting (Fig. 10.18). The principal advantage of such a system is the same as for conventional, full-scale background projection – it is possible to see the composite at the time of its photography, and to gauge more accurately the character of the final product. For such work, one way or another, the small background screen is 'built into' the support onto which the paints are laid. In many cases, the screen is mounted directly behind, and on the projector side, of a sheet of glass. The painting is laid onto the camera side of this sheet. A typical frame of the live-action component is projected onto the screen, and the artist works around this component, painting a surround which fits perfectly with regard to perspective lines, image detail, textures, colors and brightnesses. The principal problem involved here is to photograph both the background and painted images in such a manner that the painted picture is properly exposed, but that the background image is not washed out. Oftentimes, the two components will be shot in separate, repeated passes of the film through the camera.

For the first exposure, the projector is turned off, and the painting is illuminated. A jet-black card is placed between the screen and the back surface of the glass to insure that no exposure occurs in the area of the screen. The painting is photographed in a first exposure, and the film in the camera is rewound to start position. During second exposure, the lights which illuminated the painting are extinguished, and the screen image is photographed alone. If motion-control equipment is available, it is possible to pan, tilt, or truck off the original framing of screen and painting, making two passes of the film through the camera, as described above, with identical camera movements being made in each case.

Smaller-than-normal background projection screens can also be combined with foreground miniatures (as, for example, the upper section of a miniature ship combined with scenes of full-scale vessels moving behind it in the background). In this case, composite photographs of both foreground miniature and background image can be made a frame at a time, in double-exposure, a black card being inserted behind the miniature and in front of the process screen for the first exposure of a particular frame, then a second exposure being made on the same frame with the card removed, the lighting on the foreground miniature extinguished, and the background image being turned on. This procedure is repeated, frame by frame, for the entire shot – a tedious but effective technique.

Multiple and oversized screens

Should the cost be warranted, it is possible to multiply the number of rear-projection screens so as to produce a background scene of unusual length across the back of the set. In such cases, two or more projectors can be used, and the junction between screens hidden by set components.

Matching plates or stereos can be combined in this manner into an apparently continuous vista. This is a quite complicated and expensive undertaking, however, especially in color cinematography. Background plates or stereos which are to be produced on separate screens with separate projectors must be staged and photographed with the greatest care so as to insure a sound-stage match in perspective, scale, subject matter, continuity of movement, brightness and color balance.

Several years ago, a different approach to wide-screen rear projection was developed at MGM Studios, employing three different projectors. Each of the projectors covered a different section of the screen. The first of the three plates provided the right-hand component, the second the left-hand, and the third the central section of the screen image. (There was some overlapping of detail in adjoining plates.) Gobo-like devices were interposed between each of the projectors and the screen to allow for alignment and mergings of the three images, so that the blending between plates would not be apparent. This was a complicated and costly process, however, and is not likely to be of immediate interest to the low- or medium-budget producer.

11

Front projection

As is probably apparent from the previous chapter, conventional rear-projection techniques, although admirably suited for well-financed productions, may not be suitable for modest ones. The equipment involved is costly, large stages with long 'throw' distances must be employed, and considerable skill and experience must be acquired by the technique's practitioners before consistently satisfactory results can be expected.

Happily, many of the same effects and advantages of rear-projection technique are available to the lower-budget producer through the use of the so-called 'front-projection' system.

Principles of the technique

The front-projection system – also known, variously, as the 'Scotchlite Process', and the 'Alekan-Gerard Process'* – uses a reflecting screen behind the actor rather than a diffusing translucent screen, with the background image being projected from in front of the screen, rather than from the rear.

---

* Late in 1949, shortly after the commercial introduction of 'Scotchlite' sheeting, research and development of the 'front-projection' technique began under the auspices of the Motion Picture Research Council in Hollywood, in association with the Stanford Research Institute and Minnesota Mining and Manufacturing Co. The first known report on this work was published in January of 1950, and was followed during the next eighteen months by additional MPRC Bulletins which described the process and which were distributed throughout the Hollywood motion-picture industry.

Subsequently, in March 1952, an independent inventor, Will F. Jenkins of Virginia, filed for two US patents on such a process, both of which were granted on December 20, 1955 (No. 2 727 427 and No. 2 727 429).

During this same period, substantially the same process was developed in Europe by two Frenchmen, Alekan and Gerard. This process was patented by Alekan in Great Britain on February 13, 1957 (No. 768 394) and the patents were acquired by the J. Arthur Rank organization.

Depending upon the particular part of the world in which this process is employed, it may be found desirable to operate under patent license. In the United States, because of the prior development and publication of the process by the Motion Picture Research Council, the validity of the Jenkins patent, and of foreign patents on the same process, is not clear.

The projector – whether plate or stereo – is positioned at one side of the camera, with its optical axis at 90° to that of the camera. Its projected image is reflected onto the screen by a beam-splitter placed in front of the camera at a 45° angle to both the camera's and projector's optical axes (Fig. 11.1). The camera photographs both the image on the screen and the actor standing in front of it by shooting *through* the beam-splitter.

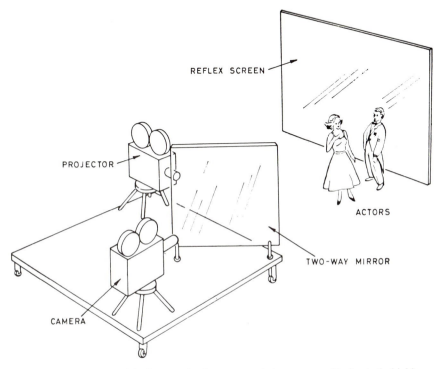

Fig. 11.1. Components of the front-projection process. Actors are posed in front of a highly reflective reflex screen. The background image is cast by a still or motion-picture projector, the beam of which is reflected off a two-way mirror or pellicle over the figures of the actors and onto the reflex screen. A camera photographs the actors and the reflected image behind them simultaneously. (US Patent illustration No. 2,727,427.)

The process operates upon the principle that if the reflected background image is projected directly along the optical axis of the camera's lens, then the shadow of the actor which is cast upon the screen will be masked exactly by the body of the actor, and will therefore not be visible.

The process has achieved great popularity in recent years, having been used extensively in such major feature films as *2001: A Space Odyssey, Earthquake, Towering Inferno, King Kong (1976), The Battle of Britain, Black Sunday, Close Encounters of the Third Kind, Star Wars, Superman,* and numerous others. it has also been used widely, with good success, by low-budget film producers. The size of screens employed have ranged from three or four feet wide up to the 80-foot wide screen used in the production of *Superman.*

Equipment

The Screen

The key to such a system lies in the nature of the reflecting screen employed. Conventional theater screens are designed to provide considerable diffusion of the projected image, so that a uniformly brilliant image will be seen by all the members of the audience. In order for the front-projection system to be feasible, however, an entirely different kind of screen has to be employed – a so-called 'reflex' or self-collimating screen – which has the effect of returning virtually all of the light from the projector *directly back* towards the source of illumination. Without such a high reflectance, the brilliance of the plate or stereo will not be sufficiently bright for practical photography. Also, unless the difference between the

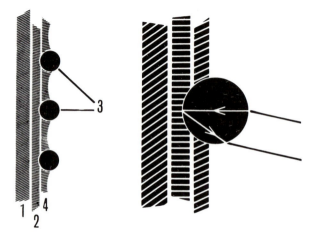

Fig. 11.2. Schematic diagram of one type of reflex screen. Left, a cross-section of the screen, greatly magnified. Layer No. 1 is the support upon which the screen is mounted. Layer No. 2 is a transparent, synthetic resin, containing reflective particles, and into which are imbedded the glass beads (3). Layer No. 4 is another resin which contains a black pigment which supports the beads further and which also hides the layer No. 2 so that it is not visible between the beads. The only portion of Layer No. 2 which is optically functional is that which lies directly behind each of the beads, and which reflects light forward. Each square inch of the screen contains approximately 250 000 beads. At right, a hypothetical beam of light enters a single bead, is bent, reflected from the inner surface, and emerges out of the bead in a line parallel to that on which it entered. Because of the very small diameter of each bead (0.005 in), the emerging beam of light is virtually coincident with the entering beam. (Courtesy of *American Cinematographer*.)

amount of light reflected from the screen and that reflected from the actor's face and costume are considerable, the projected image will be seen on the actor's body.

A variety of beaded reflex screens have been used for many years, of course, to solve certain kinds of projection problems. Such screens are coated with a colorless adhesive into the surface of which are embedded hundreds of thousands of small spherical beads of crown glass, each of which has a refractive index of up to 1.5. A beaded reflex screen offers a much narrower angle of reflection than a flat-white or 'aluminized' screen, and returns far more of the light directly back towards the projector. For this reason, such screens are usually employed in long, narrow theaters, plus providing more brilliant images for a given illumination level in the projector's lamp house.

Despite the relatively high reflectance of conventional beaded screens, however, it has never been high enough to allow for the kind of front-projection technique described here. It was not until the late 1940s that a suitable screen for such purposes was introduced by the Minnesota Mining and Manufacturing Corporation under the trade name of 'Scotchlite' – a high-reflectance sheeting with a very narrow angle of reflection. The product immediately found wide application in industry, particularly as a reflecting element in traffic signs and advertising billboards. A few years later, a similar type of material, designed expressly for front-projection photography, was introduced by the Rank Studios of England – the Alekan-Gerard ('Transflex') screen.

Reflex (or 'retro-reflective') screens, such as the Scotchlite and Alekan-Gerard type, employ literally millions of spherical, glass-bead lenses, compounded of flint glass and rare earth elements, with indices of refraction up to 1.9. Each tiny bead, approximately 0.002 inches in diameter, reflects incoming light straight back to its source.

Scotchlite sheeting is available in a variety of surfaces for front-projection work, of which the most highly reflective at the present time is type # 7610 (high-gain) sheeting, estimated by its manufacturer to be 1600 times brighter than a perfect diffusing white surface, at $0°$ divergence angle. This surface has proved a popular choice for the fabrication of large background screens suitable for motion-picture production. For smaller screens, in which it may be desired to bring the front lights close to the optical axis of the lens, 3M corporation also provides types # 7615 and 7620 (so-called 'high-contrast') sheeting, estimated to be at least 600 times as bright as a conventional white screen, at $0°$ divergence angle.

Front-projection screens can be purchased, ready-made, from suppliers. On the other hand, the fabrication of a small or medium-size Scotchlite screen is not that difficult a process, and can be undertaken by anyone who is reasonably handy. The sheeting is available in maximum widths of 2 feet, and in lengths up to 50 yards. Types 7610 and 7615 surfaces can be made into screens which can be rolled up. Surface type 7620, however, can be used only on rigid or semi-rigid surfaces.

Scotchlite may be had in a number of colors. For front-projection work, however, a 'colorless' (silver) surface should be used. Any tint in the screen distorts the color values of the projected image when photographed with color film. Should more than a 50-yard roll of sheeting be required for the making of a large screen, arrangements can be made with the manufacturer to obtain multiple rolls which are matched, with fair precision, for any residual color tint and for brightness.

The surface upon which the screen is laid must be uniformly flat and free from warp. Any substantial irregularities in the surface will be noticeable in the projected background image. According to the manufacturer, successful mountings have been made on the following substrate materials:

Flexible	*Rigid*
Background papers	Acrylic sheets
Non-stretchable fabrics	Painted walls, plywood, hardboard
Quality window shade materials	and plasterboard, if non-chalking paint

This author has also successfully mounted Scotchlite screens on sheets of glass.

Scotchlite sheeting is backed by a pressure-sensitive self-adhesive which is made ready for mounting by stripping off a top-surface liner. 3M Corporation recommends that the sheeting be applied horizontally, the separate two-foot lengths being overlapped a generous 1–2 inches (Fig. 11.3). (Butted seams or separations between strips cause dark lines in the

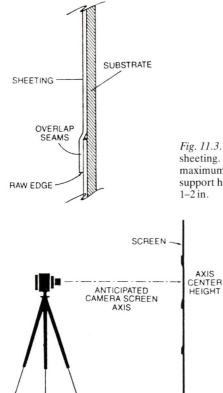

Fig. 11.3. Recommended overlap pattern of Scotchlite sheeting. The material is available in 2 ft widths and in maximum lengths of 50 feet. It is mounted onto the support horizontally, with the edges overlapped by 1–2 in.

Fig. 11.4. Relative to the height of the camera, the horizontal strips of Scotchlite sheeting should be mounted so that the exposed raw edge of each overlap faces away from the camera.

subsequent background image.) Relative to the average height of the camera, the sheets should be mounted so that the exposed edge of an overlap faces away from the camera (Fig. 11.4).

Cotton gloves should be worn while working with this material to prevent fingermarks and other blemishes. Complete instructions for mounting the material are available from the manufacturer, Minnesota Mining and Manufacturing Co., General Offices, 3M Center, PO Box 33681, St Paul, MN 55133.

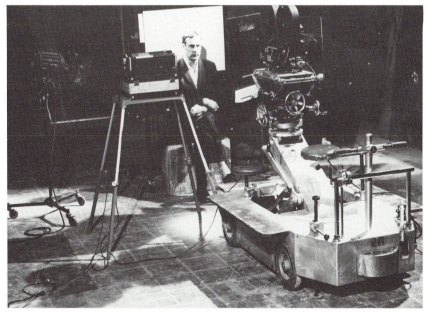

Fig. 11.5, part 1. Operational set-up for a simple front-projection shot. The screen shown here is quite small and suitable only for close-ups. A 35 mm slide projector, left of the camera, provides the background image for this shot. (UCLA.)

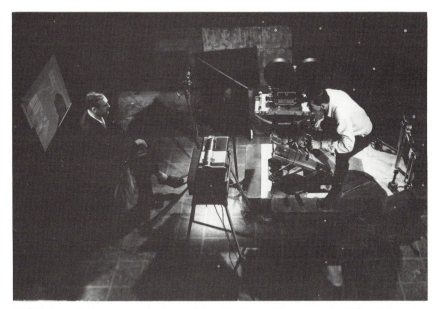

Fig. 11.5, part 2. A two-way mirror is positioned in front of the camera at a 45° angle to both the camera's and the projector's optical axes. The slide projector's beam is reflected off the front surface of the mirror and onto the reflex screen, while the camera photographs the composite of actor and background *through* the mirror. A black flag is positioned on the far side of the mirror to absorb that portion of the background image which passes through the mirror.

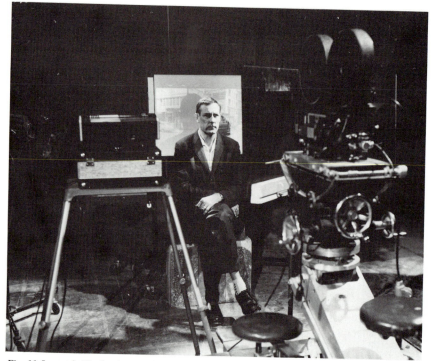

Fig. 11.5, part 3. The background image appears quite faint unless the eye or camera is positioned directly along the system's optical axis. In this photograph, the actor's shadow can be seen on the reflex screen behind him. Assuming (1) that the focal length of projection and photographing optics are properly matched, and (2) that the optical axes of the camera and projector are coincident, then this shadow will be masked exactly by the actor's body.

Fig. 11.5, part 4. The front-projection composite, enlarged from a 16 mm frame.

Scotchlite is a fairly forgiving material. However, the surface of the finished screen should be protected against abrasion and soil, as well as undue handling and chemical contact. Minor fingermarks tend to be more noticeable to the eye than they are through the camera, and can ordinarily be ignored. Overcleaning should be avoided. It is desirable, however, to keep especially clean any overlapped edges of Scotchlite which face upward. It is upon these edges that dust will accumulate in time, and will become apparent as streaks or lines in the projected background image. When necessary, cleaning of the screen can be undertaken with a dry, lint-free cloth. If absolutely necessary, the screen can be cleaned with a mild detergent and water. Soap should never be used on its surface, nor should solvents or abrasives.

The beam-splitter

Essential to front-projection is the beam-splitter (or 'beam-combiner', if you will), with which the projected image is re-directed along the optical axis of the camera's lens. This may take the form of a two-way mirror, an optical flat, or a pellicle.

Two-way mirrors both transmit and reflect light; in conventional practice, the reflecting surface faces the projector and the transmitting side faces the camera (Fig. 11.8). They are available from most plate glass dealers in a variety of grades. The cheapest quality may be had in a size of 3×4 feet for perhaps $50.00 and will give fairly good results. Understandably, the best-quality work requires more expensive mirrors.

The reflectance of a two-way mirror ranges anywhere from 20 to 40 per cent. Unfortunately, this kind of mirror absorbs a great deal of the light which is reflected back from the actor and the reflex screen and which passes through the mirror on its way back to the camera's lens. For convenience sake, an ideal two-way mirror might offer equal reflectance and transmission. On the other hand, a mirror which favors the foreground, with greater transmission than reflectance, will allow for a smaller f/stop and greater depth of field, all other things being equal.

The beam-splitter used at Pinewood Studios in England, which is treated with a thin coating of titanium, provides approximately 50 per cent transmission. Beam-splitting mirrors, treated with chromium alloy coatings in a wide variety of transmission/reflectance ratios, are available from several companies, one of which is the Liberty Mirror Company of Brackenbridge, Pennsylvania, a Division of Libbey-Owens Ford Company. One of the most popular of these provides 70 per cent transmission and 30 per cent reflectance.

This problem of light absorption can be almost entirely avoided by using a very thin, high-quality optical flat, instead of two-way, mirror. Since the reflectance of such a surface is relatively low, however, it will be necessary to use a higher level of illumination in the projector's lamp house than would be required for a two-way mirror. Also, unless the sheet of glass is quite thin, the projected image may be reflected off both the front and inside rear surfaces of the glass, producing a second, out-of-register 'ghost' image on the screen.

Fig. 11.6, part 1. Sound stage set-up for a front-projection shot. The reflex screen has been erected at left, the projector/camera rig at right, set pieces and microphone boom at center. For the purposes of illustration, the reflex screen is being lit here by a 5 kilowatt lamp at the position of the still camera with which this photograph was taken – hence, the reflex screen appears brilliant.

Fig. 11.6, part 2. Sound stage set-up from camera position. The camera is pointing straight towards the reflex screen which appears dark since the projector which carries the background plate is not operating.

Fig. 11.6, part 3. Final composite. Note that the bodies of the performers exactly mask their shadows on the reflex screen. (Pinewood Studios.)

Fig. 11.7, part 1. A compact, mobile, front-projection system designed by Bill Hansard in collaboration with Sherman Fairchild. A refinement of the system which Hansard used on Paramount's production of *Catch 22*, this unit weighs approximately 1600 lb, as compared with the 4000 lb of equipment involved in conventional process projection. The entire rig is soundproofed and stands 54 in high by 36 in wide by 69 in long. The background image is projected vertically upwards and is reflected off the beam splitter, above, and from there to the reflex screen. The camera photographs the reflex screen image and the actors in front of it by shooting through the beam-splitter.

Such 'ghost' images can, however, be avoided by using a third type of beam-splitter called a 'pellicle', which is a very thin sheet of clear plastic film about 0.0003 inches thick. Because the reflecting surface is so thin, double reflections are avoided. Also, because of their thinness, pellicles are much lighter than glass optical flats.

One manufacturer provides a variety of pellicles with the following typical reflectance-to-transmission values: 16%:64%; 33%:33%; 15%:85%; 33%:67%. This variation in reflection-transmission ratios depends upon the type and thickness of the neutral reflective coating which is applied during manufacture through vacuum-evaporation techniques.

Pellicles are available in sizes up to about 5 × 7 inches. They are not affected by climatic conditions or mechanical shock, but must be carefully protected from dust, scratches, spray, and moisture. Also, they are inflammable at high temperatures. If desired, some manufacturers will supply pellicles properly mounted on rectangular frames machined from Dural tube or flat stock.

Fig. 11.7, part 2. Interior of the projector in the Hansard-Fairchild unit. The film passes from the feed spool, below, to the intermittent movement, above, and then back to the take-up spool, below. A mirror, at center, reflects light from the lamphouse upwards through the film and through a lens system, at top, to the beam splitter outside and above this unit. Illumination is provided by a 2000 watt lamp, and power requirements are 30 ampere, 220 volt, 3-phase a.c., 50 or 60 cycles. Note the Mitchell-type, pilot-pin intermittent movement. (Front Projection Company/Sherman Fairchild Enterprises.)

The mirror mount

Whatever type of beam-splitter is employed, a suitable mount will have to be fashioned for it. The mirror or pellicle should be firmly secured within a wooden or metal frame. The frame, in turn, should be mounted so that its position can be varied vertically, laterally, or longitudinally with respect to the camera. Ideally, it will also be gimbal-mounted so that the 'yaw', 'pitch', and 'roll' of the mirror can also be changed.

The camera and mirror can either be mounted together on a small lathe bed or separately mounted on individual supports. In either case, the mirror mount must be capable of being quickly and accurately adjusted to different positions. In addition, provision ought to be made so that the camera and/or projector can be moved towards and away from the mirror. Once a final adjustment has been made, the mirror mount must be absolutely rigid, and the surface of the mirror free from vibration. Assuming that a good deal of front-projection work is to be undertaken, much time and effort can be saved by constructing a permanent mount for the entire assembly.

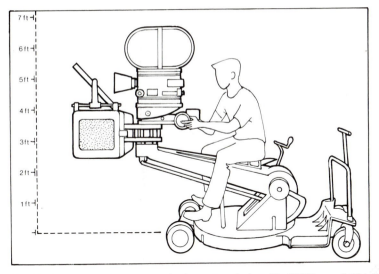

Fig. 11.7, part 3. Another front-projection system designed by Bill Hansard. This light-weight unit is 18 in high by 18 in wide by 23 in long, and weighs only 200 lb. The unit attaches to the front of the camera dolly or crane, with its two-way mirror extending upwards in front of the camera. Power requirements are 30 amperes 100/125 volt a.c. current, of either 50 or 60 cycles. The mount allows for nodal-point positioning of the camera. The projector incorporates a Mitchell-type, pin-registered movement, capable of being operated from 1 to 48 frames per second in crystal-controlled synchronism with the camera.

Operating procedures

For satisfactory results, a number of conditions must be met in assembling and aligning the components of a front-projection system.

The screen must be set as nearly perpendicular to the axis of the camera's lens as possible. This is easily achieved by extending a tape measure from the lens of the camera, successively, to each of the four corners of the screen, and adjusting the screen's position until all four measurements are equal.

The distance at which the screen is set from the camera depends, of course, on the size of the background image and the copy ratio desired, and the perspective problems involved in matching foreground and background.

Alignment

Assuming, ideally, that the gauge of the plate is identical to that of the camera's raw stock (e.g. 35 mm), the camera and projector should be situated with the front nodal points of their lenses at identical distances from the beam-splitter, and on coincident optical axes.* In the event that dissimilar format sizes are involved, then it will be found useful to have a variety of focal length lenses on hand for the projector so that the distance

---

* The use of anamorphic lenses on camera and/or projector presents special problems, one of which is that there are dual sets of front and rear nodal points involved. These matters are discussed in Petro Vlahos, 'The Front Projection Process of Composite Photography', *JSMPTE*, September 1971, p. 685.

Fig. 11.8, part 1. Front-projection rig used at Pinewood Studios for the production of *On Her Majesty's Secret Service*. The unit incorporates a 35 mm Mitchell background projector and a 35 mm Panavision reflex camera. This assembly was designed and built by Charles Staffell, Rank Organization engineer, for which he received an Academy Award.

Fig. 11.8, part 2. Close-up of the beam splitter and camera mount assembly shown in the previous illustration. The camera is mounted with horizontal vernier adjustments, fore and aft vernier adjustments, and camera nodal point tilt device. By adjusting the position of the beam splitter, the optical axes of the projector and camera lenses are rendered coincident.

of the projector's lens from the beam-splitter and the size of the projected image can be varied, if necessary.

Assuming that plate and raw stock gauges are identical, then matching focal-length lenses may be used on both the projector and camera. Under these circumstances, a 1:1 copy ratio will result, and the camera will photograph exactly the projected image. For convenience, a somewhat shorter focal-length lens may be used on the projector, thus providing a slightly larger image than can be photographed by the camera. For composites in which only a portion of the background will be used (e.g. a cityscape seen through a window) for purposeful distortions of perspective, or for pan and tilt movements, shorter or longer focal-length lenses may be employed on either the camera or projector, as the need arises.

If possible, it is desirable to isolate the camera, projector and beam-splitter from any nearby reflective surfaces. Since the beam-splitter is only partially reflective, a certain amount of the projected image passes through it and continues along the optical axis of the *projector*. Should this beam of light strike a bright surface, the image of the plate will be reflected back off the camera side of the beam-splitter, and will be added, out-of-register, to the composite image. If necessary, a dead-black 'flag' or curtain can be positioned to the side of the camera to intercept and absorb this unwanted image. Care must also be taken to keep splash light off the projection (reflecting) side of the beam-splitter, lest flare be produced which will contaminate the projected image.

Alignment of the camera, projector and beam-splitter is fairly critical. a major misalignment is immediately apparent as a distinct shadow of the actor upon the screen. A slight misalignment, as seen with the camera's through-the lens viewfinder, gives the impression of a matte line or fringe around one side of the actor's body, similar to that of a badly executed traveling-matte shot. The closer the actor is positioned to the screen, the less the change of this fringing or 'halo' effect; conversely, the farther the actor from the screen, the more likely a fringe around the body. The fringe or halo also increases as the camera is brought close to the actor, whatever his position relative to the screen. The problem is complicated by the fact that a theoretically perfect masking of the actor's shadow by his body will occur only when the apertures of the camera and projector are stopped down to pinpoint size. Under ordinary circumstances, the fringe or halo effect will not be noticeable when the camera and projector lenses are opened up. However, a combination of large apertures, proximity of the camera to the actor, and distance of the actor from the screen, can produce substantial fringing problems. In such circumstances, it is often possible to shift the fringe to one side of the body and then to frame in such a manner as to throw the fringe out of the picture.

If actors are required to move within the shot, these movements must be rehearsed while the equipment is being adjusted. Often a misaligned system will produce a perfect composite with the actor in one position, and a matte line or shadow as he moves into another.

Ordinarily, alignment can be easily determined by sighting through the camera's optical system. As an additional alignment aid, some workers employ a probe which is constructed of a small, flat panel onto which a piece of the reflex screen material has been mounted. The board is attached to a long, thin rod and is inserted into the approximate position of the actor in front of the screen, with the projector operating but without a plate in the intermittent. If the alignment of the components is correct, then, as the probe is viewed through the camera, it will merge into the screen without showing a shadow or matte-line fringe. If, on the other hand, an all-round fringe appears, then either the camera is mounted too far *back* or the projector is mounted too *near* the beam-splitter. Should the camera be mounted too close to the beam splitter, relative to the projector's position, a shadow may appear behind the probe along the edge which is closest to the optical axis of the camera. Since misalignment of the system is most noticeable when actors and objects are located close to the camera and distant from the screen, this is the position in which the Scotchlite-covered probe should be placed during testing.

This system of alignment is most useful, and the presence of the shadow is most apparent to the human eye, when the reflectance of the Scotchlite-covered probe is identical to that of the screen behind it. Positioning the probe in the projection beam, away from the screen and towards the camera, will naturally cause it to seem brighter than the screen behind it. This brightness can be reduced by tipping the probe towards the horizontal, until its brilliance matches that of the screen, as seen with the camera's through-the-lens viewfinder. Finally, the projector lens should be stopped down to its smallest aperture while this test is being carried out. If fringing follows the opening-up of the projector's aperture, the optical condenser should be examined. At wide projector apertures, off-center condenser optics may produce fringing around one side of the target.

Since misalignment is so immediately apparent, cameramen will ordinarily have little trouble in mastering the technique and in producing consistently satisfactory composites. The procedures for alignment which have been outlined here are those recommended for the best possible results, using large screens and for shots in which actors are required to change positions. However, good results have been achieved by many workers with very modest equipment and mismatched components, in cases where the demands of the shot were not too great.

Unlike rear-projection techniques, once the projector, camera, beam-splitter and screen have been finally set, none of these components can be moved or altered easily during the shot. On the other hand, changes in camera position from shot to shot (as from medium to close-up) may be executed, providing that (1) the front-projection assembly is re-positioned closer to the actor, (2) the optics are re-aligned, and (3) a new plate or stereo of the same background, but with a different field of view, is projected so as to match perspective, size and space relationships from shot to shot.

Pan-and-tilt movements of the camera are possible if a nodal-point is used, and if the front nodal points of the camera and projector are situated in the same position relative to the beam-splitter.

Lighting

Just as in rear-projection work, the effect of key and fill lights upon the background plate may be determined easily by viewing the projected image through the camera's viewfinder and turning the separate lights on and off. Because of the nature of the reflex screen, the system is much more tolerant of splash light on the screen than is rear projection, providing that such light originates outside an arc of 30° on either side of the camera's optical axis (Fig. 11.9). Obviously, if degradation of the plate is apparent when a light is turned on, then the lamp's position should be shifted further to one side, away from the optical axis. Most certainly, if the cinematographer can see with the eye any kind of flare or of shadow cast upon the screen, then it surely will be photographed by the camera.

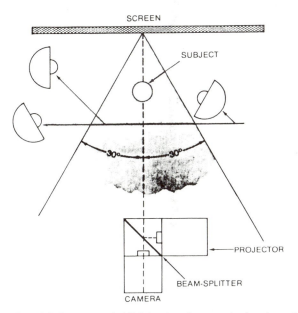

Fig. 11.9. Recommended lighting for a front-projection shot using Scotchlite #7610 high-grain sheeting. Lighting may be directed as desired, but is preferably placed outside the shaded area. Lights directed toward the subject from within the shaded area may reduce background color contrast.

The beam-splitter assembly, and other optical characteristics of the front-projection equipment render the system especially sensitive to flare produced by back-lights. For this reason, rim lighting should be avoided, minimized or, if absolutely necessary, carefully flagged off. On the other hand, should it be artistically desirable, a controlled amount of flare – whether white or colored – can be introduced into the beam-splitter system in order to create a glow at the horizon line or along the top of the frame.

Happily, there is virtually no hot-spot problem in front-projection photography, inasmuch as the background image is being reflected from the screen rather than being diffused and refracted through it. Should any slight fall-off occur around the periphery of the image or in the corners, this is usually a sign that the projection optics are faulty or that vignetting has occurred in the preparation of the plate or stereo. Should vignetting be a problem, it can usually be solved by pulling the front-projection assembly

Fig. 11.10, part 1. Another front-projection composite, this time using a Vistavision-type format. The background image is a static diapositive, produced by a 'stereo' projector, at right. (Pinewood Studios.)

Fig. 11.10, part 2. The 'stereo' projector used to produce the composite shown in the previous illustration. At left, the unit is seen in its lowest position, with the camera at normal studio height. The camera tilt positions which are possible are shown in double-exposure. At right, the rig is shown in an upward tilt attitude.

away from the screen a short distance, thus enlarging the background image a little, and/or changing to a slightly longer focal-length lens on the camera. Also, if absolutely necessary, any of the previously described techniques for the correction of hot-spot and fall-off in rear projection can be used.

One of the advantages of the front-projection system is the relatively low light level used in the projector's lamp house (e.g. 500–1000 watts for 16 mm projection and 200 watts for a 35 mm slide projector). Even after taking into account the loss of light in the beam splitter, it is estimated that only one footcandle of light on the screen is required to balance a foreground light level of 200 footcandles. This 200:1 ratio illustrates why

Fig. 11.11. Another example of a front-projection composite. (The Rank Organization.)

the projected image, even if cast upon the white shirt of an actor, will not be photographed by the camera. Nonetheless, bulletins of the Motion Picture Research Council recommend that very low light levels be avoided, as well as plates or stereos in which large, dark masses predominate. The nature of the reflex screen is such that excessively low light levels may produce granularity and a decrease in resolution of the background image. In some cases, this characteristic may render the system inappropriate for day-for-night composites. Granularity in the background plate can be reduced somewhat by de-focusing the background image slightly, thus approximately the reduced depth-of-field produced when photographing conventional scenes with relatively large apertures. All other things being equal, the smaller the relative aperture the better. It tends to reduce flare in the system, and it provides the maximum amount of precision in the masking by the actor's body of his shadow.

Grain in the background image is accentuated by the nature of both rear and front projection, in that both the foreground action *and* the background images are photographed simultaneously by the color negative stock in the camera. Not only has the background image gone through a generation of duping, but it ought properly to be copied with a fine-grained color duping stock. Instead, it is copied by the production color negative in the camera, which has a much larger grain structure. In effect, one creates an unfavorable 'split-screen' test of color emulsions, and the quality of the background image necessarily suffers in comparison with that of the foreground, live-action scene.

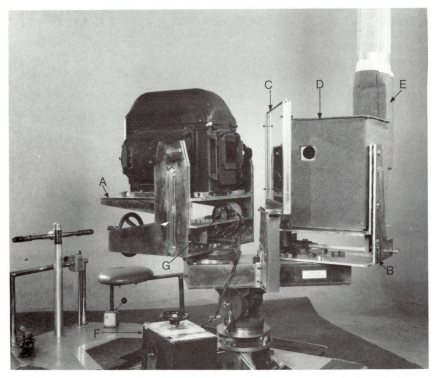

Fig. 11.12, part 1. A one-of-a-kind front-projection rig built at Bob Jones University. This particular equipment incorporates a Kodak Carousel projector to produce static 'stereo' images on the screen. Shown in this photograph are (a) nodal point panning and tilting head for the Mitchell 16 mm camera, (b) nodal point panning and tilting head for the projector, (c) the adjustable mount for the beam-splitting two-way mirror, (d) a sound-absorbent blimp for the Carousel projector, (e) a chimney which vents heated air from the projector and which dissipates the noise of the projector upwards out of the range of the microphone. This chimney extends upwards 12 ft, (f) a Selsyn transmitter motor for remote follow focus of the camera, and (g) a Selsyn repeater motor, linked by a transmission belt to the follow-focus system.

Fig. 11.12, part 2. Reverse angle shot of equipment shown in the previous illustration.

Fig. 11.12, part 3. Crew members set final adjustments before making a shot with the Bob Jones front-projection rig. The projector blimp is open, revealing the Carousel projector within.

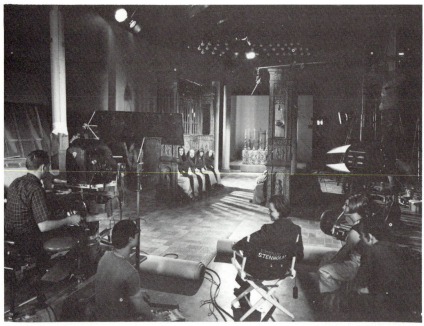

Fig. 11.13, part 1. A set-up on the sound stage for a front-projection shot in the Bob Jones University production of *Flame in the Wind*. The reflex screen at the back of the simulated church set is blank, inasmuch as the projector is not yet turned on. Notice the black 'flags' which are positioned around the beam splitter to prevent undesirable reflections.

Fig. 11.13, part 2. The final front-projection composite. The ornate carved wall behind the altar is being projected by the 35 mm Carousel projector. Notice that the candelabra on the altar exactly mask their shadows on the screen.

Fig. 11.14. A 16 mm front-projection system manufactured in Japan by the Seiki Company. The projector has a maximum film capacity of 400 ft and features a registration pin intermittent movement which operates at a fixed 24 frames per second. Camera and projector can be operated either separately or in interlock. The light source is 2000 watts.

All of the other problems involved in matching the live-action foreground to the two-dimensional projected background which apply to rear projection are identical in front-projection work. Among these are the matching of key-light direction, key-to-fill ratio, overall contrast, color balance, perspective lines, scale, angle of view, and relative movements.

Projection, registration and synchronism

For front-projection work, image resolution and registration integrity are not quite as severe the problems they are with rear-screen processes. Indeed, for low-budget work, fairly good results can be had by employing either a 35 mm slide projector or an audio-visual 16 mm projector, providing that the projection equipment is of good design and in good repair, and that the copy ratio which exists between camera and projector is 1:1 or greater. If, on the other hand, the copy ratio is changed so that the camera re-photographs only a portion of the stereo or plate, then, of course, an increase in grain and decrease in sharpness will occur.

Despite the fact that 16 mm projectors are not presently available with pilot-pin movements, their intermittent movements are oftentimes steady enough for front-projection work. Whereas the conventional 35 mm background projector employs a camera-type, single-bladed shutter, a 16 mm projector uses a two-or-three-bladed shutter, producing a 48-fields-per-second or 72-fields-per-second image on the screen. It is, therefore, impossible for the camera to fail to record some sort of background image from frame to frame, even though the brightness of the image may vary as the projector and camera go in and out of phase with each other.

Ideally, as in rear-projection work, synchronous, interlock motors should be used on both the camera and projector. This assures, first, that both remain in phase throughout the take, and second, that the operators can adjust the two motors so that the maximum amount of light is delivered by the projector onto the screen for each frame of the plate.

At second best, synchronous, non-interlock motors can be used on both camera and projector. This assures that whatever the particular brightness of the background image may be, it will not vary throughout the take. Some cameras allow the operator to change the relationship of the camera's shutter to that of the projector, once both machines have been set in motion.

Finally, it is sometimes possible to use non-synchronous, non-interlock motors on the projector and/or camera and still get satisfactory results. The effect which must be prevented in such cases is a gradual change in the brightness of the projected image. Whether this change becomes apparent to the viewer depends on a number of factors. First, if the 'wild' motors on the projector and camera are fairly constant in their speeds, then they will go out of phase so gradually that variations in plate brilliance will not be too noticeable. Second, if a raw stock emulsion with a reasonable amount of latitude is used in the camera, this will partially compensate for any changes in the brightness of the background. Thirdly, if a projector with a three-bladed shutter is employed, a greater number of 'flashes' of each frame ('fields') of the plate will be produced upon the screen, and brightness differences due to in-and-out-of-phase shifts will become still less apparent. Finally, if each front-projection shot is kept to a minimum length, the viewer will not have the time and opportunity to become aware of gradual changes in background brightness.

Noise

Unfortunately, the proximity of the projector to the actors' microphone does raise a noise problem. If this process is used for sync-sound production, some sort of projector blimp and/or highly directional microphone will have to be employed.

Exposure

Proper exposure for front-projection photography can only be determined experimentally by each worker. The variables which are involved include the illumination level of the projector, the illumination level of the foreground action, the reflectance and absorption of the beam-splitter, the size of the projected image, the reflectance of the screen, and the sensitivity of the raw stock. Assuming the use of a medium-speed emulsion, and depending upon the nature of other variables, exposures can range anywhere from $f/2.3$ to $f/8$. If available, the use of a 235° degree camera shutter, as is found in the 16 mm Maurer camera, will help to compensate for light losses due to inexpensive and inefficient beam-splitters.

Fig. 11.15, part 1. An unusual and highly portable front-projection system developed by David Samuelson in England. The Samcine Front Projection System employs a rebuilt Mitchell BNC 35 mm camera, at left, which has been converted into a 35 mm projector, thereby utilizing an otherwise obsolete camera which offers silent operation and a highly-accurate registration movement. The BNC has been modified to allow for illumination of the film from behind, and a lamphouse with a 250 watt tungsten halogen projector lamp has been fitted to the side of the BNC to provide illumination. The projector mount will also accept a Vistavision-format projector, as well as a 35 mm Carousel slide projector. A number of different makes of camera can be fitted to the assembly, synchronous drive between camera and projector being achieved by electronic slaving. Virtually any fixed-focal-length or zoom lens in excess of 25 mm can be used on the camera and/or projector.

Fig. 11.15, part 2. Side view of the Samcine front-projection rig. Flag at right prevents reflection of light off the back side of the mirror into the camera's lens.

Most cameramen find that only a short period of experimentation is necessary before they acquire the experience and data necessary for production work with their own particular equipment. If necessary, however, both exposure and lighting balance can be checked during production through 'slop-test' processing of short lengths of test footage before the final takes are made. It is also possible to use a Polaroid film magazine on a 4 × 5 view camera or 35 mm camera for such purposes. This is a time-consuming business, however, inasmuch as the motion-picture camera must be removed from the assembly and replaced by the still camera. The still camera must then be aligned so that it records reflected light from the foreground and from the screen in exactly the same fashion as the motion-picture camera. Finally, the complete composite can be viewed directly by means of a video tap in the camera's optics which re-directs a fraction of the incoming image to a television pick-up tube, the electronic image of which can be viewed either in a video viewfinder or on a full-sized video monitor.

Special techniques

Masking techniques

Because of the nature of the front-projection system, it lends itself to a most curious and useful kind of composite manipulation. Under certain circumstances, it is possible to set up a front-projection shot in such a manner that the actor is allowed to pass *into* the plate and to walk *behind* objects which are part of the already-photographed background scene. In this respect, it has some of the same versatility as the traveling-matte process.

Let us assume, for example, that the background picture is that of a store or business establishment photographed head-on. A standing mail box is included in the shot, located near the edge of the sidewalk. Should it be desired that the actor on the sound stage appears to pass *behind* the mail box, then a large cardboard cut-out is prepared which exactly matches the shape of the projected image of the mail box, and which is located a suitable distance away from the reflex screen. The cut-out is now covered with Scotchlite sheeting, which is trimmed to match the shape of the cut-out.

Now, during photography of the composite, the actor may freely pass behind the cut-out, which reflects the image of the mail box – he may even pause behind it and pretend to deposit a letter into the mail slot. On the screen, the illusion is perfectly convincing. The same technique can be used to allow the actor to climb the steps of a porch or stairway which are part of the background picture. The requirement in every case is that the objects in the plate, behind which the actor must pass or on which he must walk, be duplicated with cut-outs or wooden forms which are positioned properly on the sound-stage floor, matched in size to that of the projected image, and covered with Scotchlite sheeting.

Inasmuch as there is a limit to the depth of field of the projected image, so there is a limit to the distance from the screen at which such objects can be placed. If this distance exceeds the projector's depth of field, then the reflected image of the 'foreground' objects will be thrown out-of-focus. Understandably, this technique works best when fairly large background images are produced, and when deep-focus optics are employed. One will also find that the cut-out Scotchlite screen is considerably brighter than the rest of the image on the screen behind, depending upon how far forward this cut-out flat is positioned. This additional gain must be reduced, either by using one of the less-reflective Scotchlite surfaces (such as type # 7615), or by introducing into the optics of the beam-splitter an appropriately-cut piece of neutral density gel which conforms to the shape of the Scotchlite-covered flat.

The same effect – that of actors passing behind objects in the plate – may also be achieved by modifying the beam-splitter assembly so that non-reflected light which passes through the beam-splitter along the axis of the projector is transmitted through a supplementary lens and allowed to fall upon a small reflex screen. Assuming that these components are aligned with great care, then both reflected images – from the large screen and the small one – will match exactly. Assuming further, that complementary mattes and/or various types of art-work are introduced into the optical system of the beam-splitter, which correspond in position to the placement of set components in the background plate (e.g. a door leading into the set area), then the actor can again be made to appear to be moving into the plate detail and behind objects in the background image. A nice example of this technique is found in the television mini-series, *Inside the Third Reich*, in which the actor portraying Adolf Hitler is permitted to walk into authentic surviving still photos of the interior of the German Chancellory, as if it were either the original or a full-size reconstructed set of it. This technique is fairly complicated, and requires considerable modification of the front-projection beam-splitting assembly. Among other things, much higher light levels will be found necessary in the projectors employed, owing to the greater absorption of light by the multiple beam-splitters and other optics involved. This and many other variations on the front-projection process are described in the professional and patents literature. Variations include the use of multiple screens, multiple projectors, and multiple beam-splitters. In recent years, a front-projection system called Introvision has become available to film producers which offers such modifications of the basic front-projection system.

Zoom effects

If absolutely necessary, a zoom lens may be used on the camera during a front-projection shot to simulate a dolly shot, in or out. However, the problems which result may make this kind of lens more trouble than it's worth.

First, as the focal length of the lens changes, the front nodal point will shift its position. Ideally, the camera will also be simultaneously and synchronously moved an appropriate distance to compensate for that change, so as to keep the nodal points of camera and projector continuously coincident. Failing this, the whole system may go out of adjustment, and a fringe or shadow may begin to appear around or to one side of the actor.

Also, as the focal length of a vari-focus lens is increased, the effective aperture increases, and, as has been noted, the likelihood of fringing increases with larger apertures on the projector and/or camera. In addition, as the focal length increases, so will the graininess of the background image. Whether this is noticeable or not depends upon a number of factors, the most important of which is the copy ratio between camera and projector. Should the original ratio be greater than 1:1 (as with the production of a reduced background image on the screen as seen through a window), then the increase in grain as the copy ratio drops to 1:1 may not be apparent. Should the ratio begin at 1:1 and diminish, however, the camera will begin copying a smaller and smaller portion of the background plate and grain will increase dramatically. Whatever the copy ratio, the experience which different workers have had with this process suggests a maximum increase in focal length of 50 per cent before an increase in grain becomes apparent.

Finally, as the focal length of a zoom lens is increased, the perspective and scale relationships between the foreground and background images may become inappropriate. Unlike a conventional dolly shot, a zoom-in, in either front or rear projection, will cause distant objects in the projected background to advance towards the camera, together with the foreground objects – a phenomenon which does not occur with a true dolly shot. This undesired change in background scale can be avoided by dollying the *entire* front-projection rig – camera, projector and beam-splitter – towards the screen, thereby maintaining a constant size of background image in the resulting composite. Such a move is easier to prescribe than to achieve, however. Apart from the problems involved in maintaining optical alignment, one must also compensate for the increasing brilliance of the projected image. For example, it is estimated that a short dolly movement of five feet, from 50 to 45 feet from the screen, will cause an increase in screen brilliance of approximately 20 per cent.

As early as 1969, the Motion Picture Research Council had suggested the use of zoom lenses on *both* the camera and the projector, so that as the focal length of the camera's lens was increased, that of the projector's lens was decreased, thereby maintaining a constant size of background image. Such a system requires interlocked stepper or servo motors on both lenses. It also requires a motorized supplemental iris on the projector lens which will open and close in appropriate amounts as the projector's focal length is made shorter or longer. In the middle 1970s, such a system was introduced to the trade under the ZOPTIC trade name, originally in association with the Neilson-Hordell Company of England. This system allows for realistic, simulated dolly movements towards and away from the performer while maintaining a constant size of background image (Fig. 11.16). Depending upon the manner in which the scene is staged, the camera may appear to be dollying towards a stationary performer, or the performer may appear to be moving towards a stationary camera – or a little bit of each. This equipment was used to good advantage in the filming of flying sequences in both *Superman I* and *II*. It is, however, an expensive piece of apparatus to build, and a difficult one to operate, and is not likely to be of immediate interest to the low-budget producer.

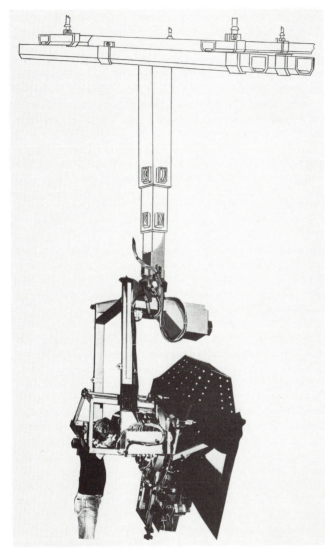

Fig. 11.16. Another unusual and quite complicated front-projection rig, called the ZOPTIC system, originally introduced in association with the Neilson-Hordell Company of England. This system uses synchronously operated, matched zoom lenses on both the camera and the projector. The system allows for dollying movements towards or away from performers while maintaining a constant size of background image. The camera and projector, which are located at the bottom of this photograph, are suspended from overhead rails on which the entire rig may be moved across the stage, pushed and guided by the camera operator. (Courier Films Ltd.)

Panoramic screens

One of the most interesting applications to which the front-projection system can be put is the simulation of walking or running shots in front of a projected background. The Scotchlite screen which is built in this case is completely circular, with the front-projection rig situated at the center of the circle, capable of rotating through 360° as the performer walks or runs in front of the screen. Onto the screen in projected a suitable plate which was photographed by a trucking camera. This arrangement allows for convincing movements of the performer and looks more realistic than does a truncated shot of an actor running 'in place', or running on a treadmill or on the edge of a turntable. It also allows the performer to walk or run past other performers, and foreground set pieces, in a realistic fashion. Finally, it provides a quiet environment for sound recording, which is difficult to achieve with the noise produced by most treadmills and turntables. To be effective, however, such a Scotchlite screen will have to be fairly large and will tie up the better part of a good-sized sound stage.

Front-projection matte shots

As is the case with rear projection, front-projection technique can be used to produce live-action images which are composited with matte paintings. The painting is laid onto glass, a section of which is left clear for the live-action component. The front-projection screen is mounted directly behind the sheet of glass. Theoretically, it ought to be possible to photograph both components simultaneously, but in practice, the shot is ordinarily made in two passes, the screen area being rendered opaque with a black card inserted into the area directly behind the sheet of glass and in front of the screen during the first exposure; the card being removed and the lighting of the painting extinguished during the second pass. This technique has been used with good results on such recent productions as *Dragonslayer, The Spy Who Loved Me*, and *Raiders of the Lost Ark*. The technique allows for considerable speed in operation. As with all through-the-lens-type composites, a good idea of the finished composite can be gotten at the time the shot is made, rather than having to wait for the results to come back from the laboratory. Also, test shots can be made, processed, and gotten back for examination more quickly than would be otherwise possible with optical printing. Assuming that nodal-point mountings are employed on the camera and projector, and that an automatically compensating iris is used on the projector, then pans, tilts, and dolly/zoom movements can be made over the combination of projected image and painting.

All of the problems, cited elsewhere, which obtain in the making of a painted matte shot are involved here. Among other things, the painted backround or surround is photographed at first-hand, while the live-action component will have already gone through a generation of duping at the time of final photography. If one wishes, a conventional-production color negative, such as type 5247, can be used in the camera for final photography. This will favor the quality of the painting at the expense of the live-action, inasmuch as the production negative stock is not really suited for color duplication. On the other hand, duplicating color stock can be used in the camera, which will theoretically favor the live action, while producing somewhat unpredictable results in copying the painting. Alternatively, color-separation positives can be used in the projector and multiple passes made to create the finished composite. Obviously, a good deal of experimentation will be found necessary here before consistently good results can be expected.

Scotchlite in costumes and sets.

Unusual effects can be achieved by inserting pieces of Scotchlite into costumes or set pieces and then projecting images or scintillating light patterns onto them during photography of the live-action scene. Such was the case with a transformation scene occurring in *Altered States*, in which the flesh and costume of actress Blair Brown was covered with small pieces of Scotchlite material onto which were projected images of molten lava, the final effect being one of volcanic eruptions from within and out of the body.

Scotchlite sheeting has also been inserted into the area of the tube of a television set to allow for front-projection insertion of simulated television images in a scene.

Creation of blue-screen backgrounds by front projection

The cobalt-blue background required for traveling-matte work can be produced on a Scotchlite screen through front projection, rather than by a rear-illuminated translucent screen or a front-illuminated backing. The projector is turned on without a plate in its intermittent, and an appropriate blue filter is inserted into its optics. This technique was used for photography of a tank-shot simulation of a thermonuclear mushroom cloud which appeared in the film-for-television feature, *The Day After*. The foreground was photographed with high-speed cameras, and the light level of the blue background which was required was higher than could be conveniently produced with a conventional neon-back-lit bluescreen. Instead, an intensely bright cobalt blue background was produced through front projection. This technique had the additional advantage of avoiding the blue-spill of light which sometimes afflicts rear-illuminated bluescreen shots.

Needless to say, the projected blue background which is produced for such purposes must be uniformly bright and meticulously clean. If any lines or blemishes from either the projector or the Scotchlite screen appear in the background, they will be carried onward into the traveling-matte composite which is made during final optical printing. To avoid such blemishes and lines, it may be found useful to de-focus the projector's optics somewhat, and to focus the camera's lens so that the screen falls outside the far limit of the lens' depth of field, and is, therefore, blurred.

Front-projection vs. rear projection

At this point, the respective advantages and disadvantages of the front- and rear-projection processes are probably apparent to the reader. The summary which follows should also be considered in relationship to the distinctions previously made between background projection and traveling-matte techniques at the conclusion of Chapter 8.

The front-projection system offers the following advantages:

1. It is, in its simplest form, a relatively inexpensive system, the screen, two-way mirror and mirror-mount costing little to acquire and assemble.

2. Although the best quality of projection equipment – with 4 × 5 inch stereos and 35 mm plates – will, of course, produce the best possible quality in the background image, quite satisfactory results can be had, in shooting simple set-ups, with conventional, inexpensive audio-visual projection equipment. Relatively low-wattage incandescent lamps may be used in the projectors, rather than arcs.

3. The system can be used on small stages, inasmuch as the projector and camera are located on the same side of the screen.

4. There is no hot-spot problem.

5. Flare caused by splash light striking the screen is much less likely to occur than in rear projection.

6. Much larger screens are feasible than is the case with rear projection.

7. For 16 mm practice, in which plate projection is involved, expensive interlocked servo motors need not necessarily be employed. Under certain conditions, satisfactory composites may even be made using 'wild' motors on the camera and projector.

8. Under ideal circumstances, the quality of the background image is equal or superior to that of rear-projection, since the resolution and contrast are not compromised by the diffusion and transmission of the picture *through* the screen.

9. By covering portions of the foreground set with reflex-screen material, or by inserting a secondary Scotchlite screen into the modified optics of the beam-splitter, a performer can be made to appear to walk *into* the background scene and *behind* objects which appear in the plate or stereo.

10. Apart from its obvious usefulness to the low-budget producer, the front-projection process also is widely used for high-budget productions, using superbly engineered projection/camera ensembles. For such productions, screens as large as 40 × 100 feet have been used.

By contrast, the front-projection system displays the following disadvantages:

1. For the very best work, with moving image plates, a first-class, professional front-projection system will have to be fabricated, the cost of which is fully as great as a rear projection system.

2. Once the camera, projector and beam-splitter have been aligned, no trucking or dollying of the rig is possible, except with great difficulty. Pans, tilts and modest zooms are possible if nodal mounts are used for camera and projector.

3. Depending upon the size of the background image, and the alignment of the optics, there may be limits to the distance towards and away from the camera through which actors can move without producing a fringe or shadow on the screen.

4. Because of its proximity to the actors' microphones, the projector must be silenced for sync-sound production.

5. For best results, underlit, dark masses should be avoided in the background plate or stereo, in order to avoid granularity in the image. In some cases, this may render the system unsuitable for low-key or day-for-night composites.

6. One of the principal complaints in dealing with the front-projection system is that under certain circumstances, it may produce a grainy background image – particularly when the background plate or stereo must be enlarged optically, with a copy ratio of less than 1:1; that is, when the camera lens photographs less than the full frame of the projected image, assuming that both camera and projector employ the same gauge and format of film. This kind of graininess can be reduced by using as large a format as possible in the projector. An 8-perforation (Vistavision) format is sometimes used for such work. For Stanley Kubrick's production of *2001: A Space Odyssey*, 8×10 inch glass diapositives were used in the stereo projector.

7. As is the case with rear projection, a certain amount of degradation of the background image must be expected, since the plate or stereo has already gone through a generation of duping at the time of photography, and is also being photographed by a production color negative in the camera which is unsuited for the duping of color film.

8. It is virtually impossible for actors in a front-projection shot to see the image on the screen behind them. For this reason, if they are to respond to action occurring in the plate, they must be cued by crew members off-camera when particular actions are required. Alternatively, it is possible to use a camera with a video tap in the optics which will deliver a composite image to an off-camera video monitor which the actors can glimpse out of the corner of their eyes.

Miniatures

From time to time, the need arises for the photography of elaborate or unusual sets, whose cost of construction in full scale cannot be fitted within the budget, or whose operation and photography cannot be safely conducted.

For example, it may be desired that views of sixteenth-century London be presented, either complete in themselves or as background detail in a live-action sequence. Obviously, since sixteenth-century London no longer exists, its representation must somehow be re-created, and at a minimum of expense.

As another example, a story may be laid on board a large, ocean-going vessel. Extensive long-shot footage of the ship at sea may be required, in which the vessel executes a variety of maneuvers in both calm and stormy weather. The ship may even be required to founder and sink. Clearly, the chartering of a large ship would be very costly. Any attempts which are made to capture clear and attractive shots of the ship in a high sea or storm will generally be found impracticable, as many a newsreel or combat cameraman has discovered. Finally, even the most liberal budget cannot accommodate the scuttling of a full-sized vessel. An economically similar problem arises when a real building, city street or complete town must be destroyed by fire, flood, earthquake or other disaster to satisfy the imagination of the script-writer.

As a final example, a typical war-drama may call for the crash of an airplane on a battle-field, in the midst of which a number of soldiers are seen, huddled in their fox-holes and trenches. Such a scene, if filmed in full-scale, would be extremely expensive, while injuries among both the actors and technicians would far exceed what they and their insurance companies consider appropriate for these occupations.

These situations and many others call for the use of miniatures – which is to say, representational models which are built, operated and photographed so as to appear to be genuine in character and full-scale in size.

Miniatures can be photographed: (a) complete in themselves, (b) as background detail viewed through windows or doors (a 'set miniature') or (c) as image-replacement components of a composite. In all three applications, miniatures are more versatile and believable than painted backgrounds or matte shots. Miniatures offer a three-dimensional quality which the finest artist can only approximate in a two-dimensional representation. Miniatures can be lighted from a variety of angles and the lighting can be changed from shot to shot, whereas a matte painting must have its highlights, its shadows and its perspective permanently fixed at the time of its rendering. Finally, certain types of miniature may be operated in motion, thus enhancing the illusion of their reality.

Miniatures can be classified as being either static or mobile. The first class usually takes the form of buildings, landscapes and set pieces which are viewed as if in long shot. The latter class of miniature provides representations of ships at sea, automobiles, human figures, airplanes, railway trains, explosions, avalanches and so forth. Some complex miniature sets include both static and mobile components.

For cinematographic purposes, the introduction of any kind of motion into a miniature set renders it a mobile miniature. Such motion, when properly controlled, can increase the realism of the miniature immensely. However, because of the peculiar relationships which exist between the size and speed of real and miniature objects, the operation of a mobile miniature is vastly more complicated than that of a static one. The nature of these relationships should be fully understood by the effects cameraman before he attempts this kind of photography.

Time-scale relationships

It is a characteristic of 'real-life' events on this planet that objects of a particular size and mass which operate in a given kind of environment will accelerate, move, decelerate and fall at certain rates of speed, traveling through particular increments of distance in predictable increments of time.

An automobile passes through a period of acceleration as it pulls away from a stop, its motor gradually overcoming the forces of gravity, friction and other factors which would otherwise render it immobile. Should the same automobile be driven off a cliff, it will fall through space at a gradually-increasing rate of speed until it strikes the earth below. At this point, depending upon the height of the cliff and the angle at which the car strikes the earth, the shape and structure of the car will be altered in a generally predictable fashion – much of its body will be telescoped together, while other portions will be twisted and torn away. If the surface which it strikes is canted, the car will turn and tumble as it continues to fall downward, gradually disintegrating through impact.

A large, ocean-going vessel moves in an equally predictable fashion. The height at which it rides in the water, the speed at which it moves, the size of the bow wave and stern wake which it produces, the extent to which it 'heels' during a turn and the speed with which it executes the turn are all functions of its size, mass and displacement, operating in a particular kind of sea. Similarly, the rate of speed with which a human being ambulates, with which an airplane maneuvers in an ocean of air, or with which a volcano erupts and spews lava are all characteristic of each object's size and mass, and of such environmental forces which act against them.

The environmental factors include the force of gravity, which is (for all intents and purposes) a constant factor at any place on the earth's surface, the angle of incline along which earth-bound objects move, the buoyancy of objects in air and water, the velocity and direction of air and ocean currents, and friction. Assuming that all of these many variables can be determined and specified, then the behavior, rate of travel and direction of moving objects in nature can be predicted with considerable accuracy. Scientists do so every day, working from formulae which have been developed during several centuries of investigation.

Behavior patterns of moving objects

Very few of us who work in the field of motion-picture production are intimately familiar with these formulae. Quite possibly, many of the people in our audience may not even be aware that they exist. Nonetheless, all human beings 'see' the world around them in a way which psychologically embraces the scientist's mathematical expression of natural laws. We all do this naturally, without bothering to think very much about it. It would be unnerving, indeed, to see an automobile shoot off at 50 miles an hour from a dead stop, without passing through a period of accelleration. It would be an equally eerie experience to see the same car hit a brick building at high speed, and to bounce off, undamaged. Even the most technologically innocent individual would be startled to see a fixed-wing airplane make a right-angle turn in the sky, or to watch a 20000 ton passenger ship pivot abruptly at a point amidships and twist left or right through 90° while under way in a body of water. Experience and common sense lead us to expect that familiar objects in motion will behave in a certain kind of way, depending upon their size, their mass and the environmental factors which act upon them. Any noticeable deviation from this behaviour leads us to suspect that our eyes are not functioning properly, that we are psychologically disturbed or that we are being deceived.

The effects cameraman who sets out to photograph a mobile miniature nearly always works to deceive his audience. To succeed, he must duplicate, with reduced-scale models, the already-mentioned characteristics of real-life objects, *but relative to the reduced scale of the miniature set.* To this end, he works partly from mathematical formula, partly from insight, partly from experience, and partly from trial-and-error experiment.

For convenience, the specialist in miniature photography works with as large a model as is feasible. As the scale of the miniature decreases, the problems involved in operating and photographing it realistically increase proportionately, due to the increasing disparity between the speeds at which the full-size original and the model replica move.

If we drive a real automobile over a cliff and watch it fall through space until it strikes the earth below, the period of time which passes before impact will be naturally determined by the force of gravity acting upon the free-falling object. Now let us assume that we build miniatures of the cliff and of the automobile which are 1/12 scale in size, or one inch to the foot. If the real automobile is 12 ft long, the model will be 1 ft in length. If the real cliff extends 120 ft above the earth below, our sound-stage replica will stand 10 ft high.

So long as nothing moves in this miniature set, and assuming that it is properly lit and 'mounted', a very convincing illusion of reality can be achieved by photographing it in conventional fashion with a motion-picture camera. The moment we push our miniature automobile over the edge, however, the illusion is instantly shattered. The miniature automobile falls much too rapidly with respect to the scale of the miniature. It falls through space at the same acceleration rate as a real, 3000 lb automobile, but it has only a fraction of the distance to travel.

The miniature car reaches the bottom of the 10 ft cliff in about four-fifths of a second, whereas a full-size car would take about 2.7 seconds to fall 120 ft from a real cliff.*

Also, unless the miniature car has been specially built, rigged and weakened, it will bounce of the bottom of the miniature set, virtually undamaged – the mass of the miniature and its velocity at impact are simply too low to cause the kind of damage and disintegration which we associate with the real-life event. The total effect upon the screen is, therefore, ludicrous, and the otherwise convincing illusion of the miniature scene is ruined.

Mathematical formulae

If a 'gravity-drop' miniature is to appear realistic on the screen, the speed of its moving components must be slowed down an amount which is proportionate to their reduction in scale. The way in which this is done is to increase the rate of speed with which the film passes through the motion-picture camera, thus expanding real time upon the screen and restoring the proper time-scale relationship to the moving miniature.

We discover that wherever gravity effect occurs – as with falling objects, toppling buildings, explosions, wave action and the like – all linear dimensions appear to be magnified as the square of the magnification time. That is, the miniature scale is equal to the square of the time scale.

Knowing this, we can arrive at a formula which provides the proper factor by which to increase the camera speed for any given scale:

$$\sqrt{\frac{D}{d}} = f$$

where D is the distance in feet for the real object, d is the distance in feet for the miniature (this fraction being simply the reciprocal of the scale of the model), and f is the factor by which the camera's operating speed is increased.†

In the example of the plummeting car which was previously given, the scale of the miniature was 1/12; that is, the distance through which the

---

* The formula which is used here is $s = 16t^2$, where s is the distance in feet and t is time.

† For a detailed mathematical analysis of the relationships involved here, see J. A. Ball, 'Theory of mechanical miniatures in cinematography', *Trans. SMPE*, May 1924, p. 119, and G. F. Hutchins, 'Dimensional analysis as an aid to miniature cinematography', *Journal SMPE*, April 1930, p. 377.

falling 1 ft model passed was 10 ft, as compared with a 120 ft drop for a real 12 ft car. Substituting these values in our formula, we have:

$$\sqrt{\frac{120}{10}} = f$$

$$\sqrt{12} = 3.5$$

Therefore, in order to photograph our miniature set of the falling car correctly, we must increase the camera's normal operating speed of 24 frames per second by a factor of 3.5, or to approximately 84 frames per second. Additional computations for typical miniature scales are given below:

Camera speed adjustments for miniature photography

Miniature scale	Camera-speed increase factor	Adjusted operating speed for camera
1/2	1.4	33×/second
1/4	2	48×/second
1/8	2.8	67×/second
1/10	3.2	77×/second
1/12	3.5	84×/second
1/16	4	96×/second
1/20	4.5	108×/second
1/24	4.9	117×/second
1/36	6	144×/second
1/48	7	168×/second
1/64	8	192×/second
1/100	10	240×/second

Insofar as conventional motion-picture cameras are involved, it is not feasible to work with a scale much smaller than 1/64, because of the difficulty encountered in operating intermittent movements at speeds higher than 200 frames per second. Indeed, it is generally recommended that any miniature, whether static or mobile, should not be built much smaller than 1/24 scale (½ inch to the foot). Not only does a further reduction in scale require high-speed camera drives and movements, but it involves exceptionally fine, difficult and time-consuming work in the construction of the miniature so as to preserve detail.

Mathematical rules of the road such as these provide a point of departure for the cameraman and miniature builder. In the end, however, only experience will provide just the right solution for a particular scheme. In all cases, we are striving for a particular dramatic effect, and on many occasions we may have to violate the mathematically proper values in order to achieve this end. Excessive overcranking of the camera can destroy a miniature's appearance just as much as undercranking, particularly in scenes of explosions or water splashes. If the camera is overcranked too much, particles of debris or water will appear to float in mid-air for prolonged periods. Special problems may also arise in the operation of complex miniature sets in which the scales of the different mobile components are mixed and therefore call for different camera speeds, or in which different miniature components move in entirely different media, such as air and water. Assuming that we blow up a miniature ship in a tank-shot, for example, the camera speed which is selected to properly render the falling of debris may not be appropriate for the wave action in the tank.

When complicated mobile miniatures are employed, many workers will wish to shoot test footage at a variety of speeds before the final take is made. In those cases where a miniature is destroyed, prudence dictates the simultaneous coverage by several cameras, operating over a range of speeds. As a last resort, miniature footage which has been photographed at the wrong camera speed can be corrected through skip-frame or multiple frame optical printing.

Miniature construction and operation

Strictly speaking, it is not the purpose of this text to deal with either mechanical effects or construction techniques. However, inasmuch as the operation and photography of miniatures is so closely associated with their design and fabrication, it seems appropriate to discuss these matters in passing.

Fig. 12.1. Some idea of the scale of a working miniature can be gained by comparing the size of the special-effects technician in the photograph with the science-fiction ship at his feet. (EMI Studios, Elstree.)

Far more than with any other type of special-effects technique, successful miniature work requires long and careful pre-planning. In the theatrical film industry, miniatures are the most expensive kind of special effect, and there is little room for error in their basic design. Some of the industry's more complicated miniature sets have cost very large amounts to construct.

Fig. 12.2. A selection of miniature ships and aircraft, in mixed scales, at EMI Studios at Elstree, England.

Even in the non-theatrical film industry, where costs are much lower, a substantial amount of time and energy may go into a miniature sequence, for although a simple miniature can be fabricated in a couple of days and photographed in a few hours, a complicated set may be weeks in preparation and several days in photography. In all cases, extensive pre-planning will be necessary to reduce costs and to avoid delays.

Ideally, the services of an art director will be available throughout the planning and construction stages. In a large organization, the special-effects department often has its own art director who is a specialist in this kind of work. In a smaller unit, these services can be provided by the supervising art director of the particular production in which the miniature is to appear.

The art director, in conference with the director, producer and photographic personnel, provides a number of alternative visualizations

Fig. 12.3. Academy-Award-winning special-effects worker Danny Lee positions a miniature space ship for the filming of *The Black Hole*. (Courtesy Walt Disney Productions.)

for the finished scene. Ordinarily, these take the form of rough sketches which are appraised by different members of the production team for dramatic suitability, technical feasibility, and cost.

Once the basic idea of the scene is decided upon, finished drawings are prepared which serve as a point of departure for the work ahead. If the miniature is a complex one, or if it must be integrated into a live-action composite, then problems of linear perspective and scale will immediately arise. Accordingly, the art director may prepare perspective 'projections' and complete blueprints for the construction of the set.*

During the planning stages, a variety of questions will arise which supervisory members of the production team will be called upon to answer.

Function of the miniature

Will the miniature be photographed 'as is', or as background detail seen through a window, or as a replacement component in a composite shot? If, for a composite shot, miniature and live-action components are to be combined in the laboratory or through on-stage techniques, which component will be photographed first?

Photographers of miniatures must always remember that they are working against the disbelief of the audience, and that of all special-effects techniques, the miniature shot is the most difficult to execute realistically. The very purposes to which a miniature is commonly put, as with destruction scenes or the simulation of expensive and exotic sets, leads the audience to suspect that they are looking at a replica rather than the real thing. Only the finest, large-scale miniatures can survive close scrutiny on a

---

* For a description of the design techniques employed, see Wally Gentleman, 'Elementary motion-picture design perspective', *Journal SPMTE*, August 1963, p. 609.

motion-picture screen for prolonged periods of time. For this reason, miniature sets which are photographed 'as is' are usually cut fairly short by the editor.

Miniatures which are combined with live action, on the other hand, gain immensely in believability, particularly when there is nothing unusual in the scene or its direction to lead the audience to suspect that effects techniques are operating. When a miniature set is seen through a window behind the actors, or when the miniature component is composited with live-action in the laboratory, the attention of the audience is naturally directed to the live-action component and the miniature serves as pictorial embellishment to the shot's overall design. Accordingly, these combination shots can be left on the screen for much longer periods of time.

When miniature and live-action components are to be composited in the laboratory or through on-stage techniques, it will usually be found more convenient to build the miniature first and to design the live-action scene around the photographed miniature footage.

Static or mobile?

If the miniature is to be mobile, what is the nature, speed, direction and duration of its movements? How much flexibility must be built into the miniature so as to allow for last-minute changes in these movements? Will the mobile components be gravity-fed, cable-driven, self-propelled or animated?

Whenever possible, the force of gravity is used to provide motive power for miniature components. The movement which results is the smoothest and most natural that can be achieved. A gravity-drop can be used whenever mobile components fall through space (as with an explosion, a collapsing structure or wave action in a tank-shot) or when they pass downward along an incline (as with an automobile, an avalanche or a flowing stream).

When gravity effect does not operate in a miniature set, the components are usually pulled with cable, cord or piano wire, the type and size of these materials depending upon their visibility and the size of the moving miniature. In those cases where the pull-cord is visible, piano wire or transparent monofilament fish line can be used effectively. These kinds of wire are very thin, extremely strong, and virtually invisible. Piano wire is quite brittle, however, and may require gradual changes in tension; if it is jerked, it may snap. Piano wire can be rendered still less visible by rubbing it with plumber's putty so as to reduce reflections. Some workers also speckle the wire with dots of black paint so as to produce a broken pattern which will blend into the background detail.

In order to smooth out the movements of a 'cable-driven' component, and to achieve greater realism when impact action is involved, the miniature is sometimes pulled at a greater speed than its scale would ordinarily call for. If, for example, a miniature automobile must be seen crashing into a building, the effect is greatly enhanced if the automobile's speed is sufficiently increased so as to compensate, at the moment of impact, for its relatively low mass. Such an increase in relative speed must

Fig. 12.4, part 1. A miniature set of the city of Las Vegas is assembled in table-top fashion for the production of *One From the Heart* (Zoetrope Studios).

Fig. 12.4, part 2. For this view of the miniaturized Las Vegas, ¼ in scale automobiles are added, each of which is controlled manually with wires. The 'chicken-coop' lighting units have been positioned above the miniature to provide overall fill light. Key lighting and accent lighting is provided by 2 kW incandescent lights mounted on stands at the edge of the miniature set.

be photographically compensated for by an increase in camera speed which is additional to that already determined on the basis of the set's scale.

Sometimes, mobile miniatures such as automobiles and railway locomotives can be self-powered, although this is not considered a really satisfactory technique owing to the difficulties encountered in smoothing out their motion.

Finally, components can be 'stop-frame' animated, a single frame of film being taken of each position of the moving miniature. This is the least satisfactory method that can be employed. The direction, speed and behaviour of the miniature must be planned just as carefully as for an animated cartoon; expensive and time-consuming experimentation is nearly always necessary and mistakes are easy to make. Also, the effect is nearly always jerky. Unlike conventional cinematography of a moving object, in which the image of the object is slightly blurred from frame to frame, each photograph of an animated miniature is sharply focused. The effect which results is frequently 'cartoonish': the object jerks along in an unnatural manner and the illusion of true motion is lost. Operators of mobile miniatures must also bear in mind that, with the exception of gravity-drop set-ups, all moving miniatures must be artificially accelerated and decelerated as they start and stop, so as to conform to the behaviour of full-scale objects in motion. If motion-control equipment is used to move the miniatures, the computer can be programmed to produce a convincing blur to the individual images of moving objects. (See Chapter 13.)

Fig. 12.5. A close-up of a snorkel camera tube, with its movable mirror located at the end of the tube. Here, the equipment is being used to photograph miniature office buildings for a television commercial (see pages 375–376).

The most difficult kind of miniature to move is that of a human figure. For this reason, it is rarely attempted and is used only with figures which appear in the far distance and which are involved in some sort of cyclic action, such as the rowing of a boat (see Fig. 12.23 part 3).

What is the scale?

As a general rule, miniatures are built to as large a scale as the budget permits. Some of the 'miniatures' employed in the theatrical film industry are gigantic. The miniature tanker built for the James Bond thriller, *The Spy Who Loved Me*, was 63 feet long! The miniature ships used for *Plymouth Adventure*, *Mutiny on the Bounty*, and *Tora, Tora, Tora* were of similar size – large enough to allow crew members to rise within the ships without being seen. Some of the miniature buildings which appear in the fire sequence of *In Old Chicago* were built over 8 feet high (Fig. 12.6), while buildings built for the Hollywood Boulevard sequence in *1941* were 25 feet high!

Fig. 12.6, part 1. Burning, exploding miniatures from the Twentieth Century-Fox production in *In Old Chicago*. These are fairly large miniatures, some of them standing 8 ft high.

Fig. 12.6, part 2. The miniature warehouse explodes and begins collapsing, the structure having been selectively pre-weakened to allow for a particular collapse pattern.

Fig. 12.6, part 3. The entire building collapses. As the last roof timber hits the ground, mechanical fire effects in the foreground are increased and a wall of fire sweeps upward from the canal to obscure the frame. (All photographs Kenneth MacGowan Collection.)

Where the budget permits, the scale will usually range from 1:4 (3 in/ft) to 1:12 (1 in/ft). Surprisingly, it is often less expensive to build a large miniature than a small one. The cost of large materials for a large miniature is relatively slight compared to the labor which goes into the detail work on a small one. It is far easier to cut and mount architectural 'gingerbread' for a 6 ft miniature building than for one which is 1 ft high. Smaller scales for mobile miniatures will also require extremely high-speed camera drives and movements, which are expensive to obtain and troublesome to operate. For these reasons, it is generally recommended that mobile miniatures should be built to a scale no smaller than 1:24 (½ in/ft) (Fig. 12.7).

Fig. 12.7. A miniature built to 1:24 scale. Construction is of pine strips and corrugated cardboard. (UCLA.)

Single-scale or mixed-scale?

If the miniature is sufficiently large, it can be built entirely in one scale. A 'single-scale' miniature takes its own perspective and can be photographed from a variety of angles and positions. If, on the other hand, the miniature must be built to a relatively small scale, it may be necessary to 'force' perspective by mixing the scale of the different components and distorting the shape of those pieces which are nearest to the camera, thus artificially increasing the illusion of depth (Fig. 12.10). Such 'mixed-scale' miniatures can be photographed only from a relatively few camera positions, however. Indeed, in some cases, where a great deal of distortion has been built into the set, it can be photographed from only *one* position. Such a pre-determination of camera position naturally reduces the flexibility of the miniature and requires the ultimate amount of care and thought in pre-planning.

Fig. 12.8, part 1. Sometimes a so-called 'miniature' is built to quite a large scale. Here, construction is under way on the miniature of the dirigible with the title role in Universal Pictures production of *The Hindenburg*. The frame of the miniature has been completed and is being examined by director Robert Wise.

Fig. 12.8, part 2. The finished miniature – 25 feet in length (1/32 full size). When 'flown' across the stage, it will be suspended by four very thin wires. The miniature is wired for internal lighting and for the operation of its motors.

Fig. 12.8, part 3. Close-up detail of the forward section of the miniature dirigible, showing some of the internal lights.

Fig. 12.8, part 4. A technician makes last-minute adjustments prior to photography. The miniature airship is flown in front of a set of the ice-bound polar region through which the doomed ship passes on its last trip to the United States.

Fig. 12.8, part 5. Photography of the miniature in a sequence in which the airship crosses the polar regions. An appropriate set has been created, below, of sea-borne ice and snow, and a painted sky cyclorama has been mounted at the rear.

Fig. 12.8, part 6. Another view of the miniature during final photography. As it is moved past the painted sky cyclorama, artificial fog is made to settle across the lower part of the frame to simulate low-hanging clouds. In this view of the miniature, the four wires by which it is 'flown' can be seen. (All photographs courtesy Universal Pictures.)

Fig. 12.9. Mixed-scale set of a graveyard from the UCLA production of *Heels of Silver*. The entire miniature is only about 2 × 3 ft. To compensate for its small size, perspective is greatly forced by building the foreground pieces much larger than the rear. Relative aperture is *f*/6.3, with single-source incandescent lighting.

How is the miniature built?

Ideally, a miniature set will be designed and constructed from the ground up, each part being separately and specially fabricated. Under these conditions, the scale of the various components, together with their perspective and spacial relationships, can be best matched to one another (Fig. 12.10).

The most difficult and expensive components to construct are mobile pieces which represent familiar objects – trains, automobiles, trucks, ships, airplanes, carts, wagons, tractors and so forth. If the budget permits, these will be individually crafted, their size being pre-determined by the scale selected for the surrounding miniature set. For low-budget production, however, many workers purchase models (pre-finished or in kit form) from hobby shops or mail-order manufacturers. A wide variety of miniature automobiles, planes, ships, and similar items are available from these sources. The quality of reproduction, in most cases, is extremely fine, and the cost is not very great. Moreover, many items – such as railroad trains and airplanes – are available in a variety of scales and so lend themselves to use in a mixed-scale set (Fig. 12.11).

Whenever components are purchased, however, the entire miniature set must be built to conform to the component's scale; also, if a variety of

Fig. 12.10, part 1. For the UCLA production of *Heels of Silver*, construction of a mountain-village miniature begins with this framework. Wood ribs conform, roughly, to the shape of the mountain peaks and valley floor, and are attached to a ramp which is elevated at the rear.

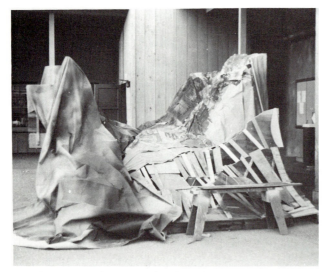

Fig. 12.10, part 2. The topography of the miniature is developed further. Strips of wood connect the rib supports and are, in turn, covered with canvas.

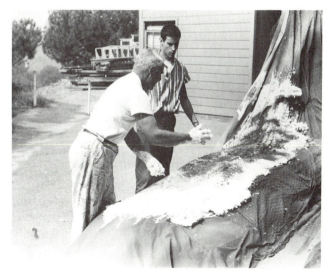

Fig. 12.10, part 3. The canvas is covered with wire netting, to which a mixture of plaster and dirt is added.

Fig. 12.10, part 4. The main body of the miniature is now strong enough to support the weight of technicians who begin positioning scale-model buildings.

Fig. 12.10, part 5. Some of the miniature components are permanently attached to the main support; others are positioned loosely to allow for last-minute changes in arrangement.

Fig. 12.10, part 6. Components are individually painted and aged, following which a fine cover of pumice, Fuller's earth or rottenstone is sprinkled over the entire miniature.

Fig. 12.10, part 7. Preliminary lighting of the set begins. Depending upon the complexity and size of the miniature, this may take hours or even days. Overall illumination for this miniature is about 1000 footcandles.

Fig. 12.10, part 8. Lighting completed, the crew prepares for final photography. The camera is mounted on a dolly for a slow move into the miniature from a long shot of the 15 × 20 ft set to a medium close-up of one of the buildings.

Fig. 12.10, part 9. The final shot. By intention, the lighting is somewhat 'theatrical'.
Back-lighting predominates, but cross lights have been added to accentuate texture and form.
A glow light has been added at the horizon to separate background detail from the black sky.
Photographed in 16 mm with a 20 mm lens, relative aperture was $f/6.3$, with focus secured on
the middle foreground.

purchased items are employed in the same shot, their individual scales
must match or complement one another. Unfortunately, most commercially manufactured models are built to a very small scale. In the case of
model railroad pieces, for example, the range of scales run from about
1/120 to 1/48.

Such small-scale models require high-speed camera drives to compensate for gravity-drop motion in the set, together with great care in the
construction of the surrounding set pieces.

Standard model-railway scales

Gauge	Measurement	Proportion
O	1/4 in/ft	1:48 scale
S	3/16 in/ft	1:64 scale
OO	4 mm/ft	1:75 scale
HO	3.5 mm/ft	1:86 scale
TT	1/10 in/ft	1:120 scale

Fig. 12.11, part 1. For the production of *Red Runs the River*, at Bob Jones University, it was required that a railroad trestle be blown up at the moment that a period railroad train passed over it. First step was the construction of a 25 ft length of track and surrounding countryside over which the train passes as it approaches the trestle. The camera, which can be seen at the foot of the miniature, was trucked along its own dolly track. The trucking movement of the camera pulled the train along at the same time, the two being connected by means of a steel rod attached to a pipe extension rigged to the camera dolly.

Many otherwise-excellent manufactured models (or model kits) display one or more glaring inaccuracies in their design. Model railroad cars, for example – particularly in O gauge – are often built with wheels which are far thicker, relative to their circumference, than those of full-size stock. Seen on the screen, such discrepancies can destroy the whole illusion of the set.

To satisfy the demands of hobbyists, model manufacturers build a tremendous amount of detail into their products, each rivet, bolt, plank and brace being finely outlined. For motion-picture purposes, however, many of these models are *too* finely detailed. So long as these pieces are used in a miniature set which takes its own perspective, they photograph nicely. Should they be placed in a small, mixed-scale set, however, in which perspective is forced through frequent and drastic changes of scale, some of the pieces may appear excessively detailed for particular positions in the set. In real life, full-size objects which are located at progressively greater and greater distances from the viewer are perceived as being less and less finely detailed, this decrease in perceived detail being a function of out eyes' limitations.

Fig. 12.11, part 2. The miniature locomotive was re-worked from a commercially-available Super-O-gauge toy model. Its electric motor was removed and replaced with a specially-built smoke-maker. The others cars were either re-modelled or completely rebuilt of balsa wood, then aged and painted with appropriate designs and lettering. Extra 'grain-of-wheat' lamps were added to the interior of the locomotive and the cars to provide adequate 'practical' lights for the scene. Power for the smoke-maker and interior lights was delivered by electric wires which ran underneath the cars and through expanding coils of wire between each car, thus allowing for separation of the cars during their fall through space. The wires were trailed out of the last car to an off-set power supply.

Should the miniature builder find it necessary to compress vast distances by mixing scales, he must not only force linear perspective but detail perspective as well. When mixed-scale components are separated by only a foot or so, they will be recorded by the camera with virtually identical sharpness, whereas the illusion of the set may call for a decrease in detail which would be appropriate for a quarter-mile separation. Accordingly, the detail which is built into background pieces must diminish in proportion to their reduction in scale.

The operation of miniature ships in water involves a variety of special problems, many of which are discussed in a later section. Whenever possible, these ships will be custom-built from wood, in fairly large sizes. Most manufactured ship models are built to such small scales as to defy their realistic operation and photography in a tank. If manufactured models (or model kits) must be used, the largest available scale should be selected. Obviously, the model must be watertight and buoyant, and must

Fig. 12.11, part 3. The trucking shot of the miniature train before it reaches the trestle. The scene is backed up by a dimly-lit cyclorama. This part of the sequence was photographed at 48 frames per second.

Fig. 12.11, part 4. Constructed of pine, the bridge was built to 1/48 scale (¼ in to the foot) and measured 9 ft in length. Many of the pine 'timbers' were pre-weakened to provide for an appropriate collapse pattern during the bridge's destruction. The surrounding terrain is made of hardware cloth, covered with plaster, dirt and rocks. Small juniper branches are used to simulate trees. The 16 mm Mitchell camera is positioned between the technicians in the center of the photograph, protected by a sheet of safety glass.

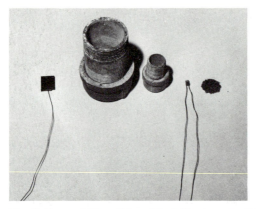

Fig. 12.11, part 5. Demolition of the bridge is accomplished by electrically-operated powder charges (so-called 'bullet hits') strategically located near pre-weakened sections of the miniature. Two sizes of 'bullet hits' are shown here, made of 2 in and 3 in pipe. A 2 gram measure of black powder was used for each charge, fired by the electrical squibs shown above.

Fig. 12.11, part 6. One of the 'bullet hit' charges is installed near the base of the trestle. Note the saw cuts which have been made half-way through the bridge supports, just above the technician's hand, to help ensure an appropriate collapse pattern.

Fig. 12.11, part 7. Establishing shot of the bridge, As the train passes onto the trestle, the powder charges are detonated. The train is pulled by means of a thread, attached to the front of the locomotive by means of an 'S' hook, which is designed to disengage when the train falls downward into the gap. The entire sequence was photographed at 128 frames per second so as to slow down the action to conform to the reduced scale of the set. Relative aperture was $f4$, with an overall illumination level of 2000 foot-candles.

Fig. 12.11, part 8. Charges are set off, destroying the central section of the trestle according to plan. Additionally, a 2×3 in container of black powder, covered with loose dirt, vermiculite and dry plaster at the base of the bridge is set off for visual effect.

348

Fig. 12.11, part 9. The train hits the gap in the trestle left by the explosion.

Fig. 12.11, part 10. Timbers from the exploding bridge hit the miniature trees on the right side of the frame.

Fig. 12.11, part 11. The train drops into the gap.

Fig. 12.11, part 12. The locomotive hits the bottom of the gorge, followed by the rest of the cars.

Fig. 12.11, part 13. Artificial steam is introduced at the bottom of the set by a fog-machine to suggest the explosion of the train's boiler.

Fig. 12.11, part 14. Additional steam is produced as the train settles to the bottom. Dust and debris are beginning to settle. Destruction of the miniature set is now complete. (Bob Jones University.)

Fig. 12.12, part 1. Miniature buildings created for Universal Pictures' production of *Earthquake*. The buildings are positioned on the back-lot hillside of Universal Studios so as to blend perfectly with real buildings in downtown Hollywood, below. The miniatures were built and arranged so that a simulated view from the 25th story of any single building would not show traffic moving below.

Fig. 12.12, part 2. Close-up detail of individual buildings.

Fig. 12.12, part 3. Components of the miniature set are readied for photography of the partial destruction of the miniatures during the simulated earthquake.

Fig. 12.12, part 4. The miniature buildings are systematically destroyed for particular takes during and following the first earthquake shock.

Fig. 12.12, part 5. Close-up details of the partially destroyed miniature buildings. Note that the interiors of the miniatures are fully dressed so as to appear realistic when the outer shell collapses. (All photographs courtesy Universal Pictures.)

float in the water at a height which is appropriate to its apparent displacement. Wooden models, if available, are generally to be preferred to plastic ones; they are sturdier, heavier, more realistic in appearance and easier to modify.

Is water to be used?

The use of real water in a miniature set must be planned for during design stages. Those sections of the set over which water will pass must be waterproofed or built of materials which will not leak or deteriorate when brought into contact with fluids. Waterproof paints may have to be used, while materials such as gravel and sand may have to be mixed with glue and permanently fixed to the set, rather than be allowed to lie loose.

If the water must be seen flowing, as down a river or bursting through a dam, then provision must be made for the piping of a proper volume of the liquid to the outlets and for control of the rate of flow. The run-off of water must be collected, and, if the flow of water is to be continuous, some provision must be made for recirculation.

Fig. 12.13, part 1. The climactic special-effects scene of Universal Pictures' production of *Earthquake* is the bursting of the Hollywood Hills dam – a scene which is supposed to occur in the very early morning. Here, special-effects workers make last-minute preparations before the dam is blown and thousands of gallons of water are released. The scale of the miniature dam, at left rear, can be judged from the size of the man standing on it.

Fig. 12.13, part 2. A reservoir, built behind the face of the miniature dam, holds 53 000 gallons of water, held back by hydraulic gates.

Fig. 12.13, part 3. A section of the fully-dressed miniature hillside below the dam. The scale of the miniature is apparent from the size of the effects worker in the photograph.

Fig. 12.13, part 4. Few types of miniatures are so difficult to photograph realistically as are water shots. For this sequence, eleven different cameras were positioned strategically around the miniature set, most of them turning over at four to five times normal speed – 96 to 120 frames per second! The actual time of day is late afternoon–early dusk. The sequence is shot in 'day-for-night' fashion, which gives the proper effect to simulate a very early morning event.

Fig. 12.13, part 5. The cameras are manned and are turning. The explosive charges set into the face of the miniature dam have been detonated and the hydraulic gates behind the dam have been opened to release the water. And nothing happens! It is a nervous minute for the filmmakers, as the film races through the high-speed cameras, before the dam finally fractures and collapses as planned.

Fig. 12.13, part 6. The wall of the miniature dam breaks and thousands of gallons of water begin rushing downward over the miniature buildings on the hillside below.

Fig. 12.13, part 7. The full force of the water is now felt as the miniature set below is destroyed.

Fig. 12.13, part 8. Watery devastation of the miniature set is now nearly complete, as the water approaches the miniature freeway below. The 'fan tail' of water in center is caused by a waterproofed camera over which the water is pouring. Of the eleven cameras, two were placed to end up in, or under, the water – one stationery and one floating. The footage from those 'subjective' camera positions was good, but limited. (All photos courtesy of Universal Pictures.)

Because of the difficulty in working with real water and in photographing it realistically, substitutes are sometimes employed. For waterfall effects, marble dust, mixed with flour, can be used instead of water: it is easier to handle and control and it looks just as natural as the real thing. For small-scale sets, where the action of running water must be slowed down, heavier, more viscous fluids are sometimes substituted. Far-distant scenes of pools, lakes or ponds are often simulated by laying hundreds of thin strips of Cellophane horizontally across an inclined board. The strips are overlapped slightly and are loosely attached so that each strip is free to move a fraction of an inch. If a fan or wind machine is directed towards the loosely mounted strips, they will flutter slightly, giving a shimmering effect. An appropriate amount of back-lighting will provide the reflective glare which we associate with a large body of water.*

Is there any destruction?

Will any impact action be involved in which components of the miniature will be expected to be destroyed, crushed or altered in shape?

Just as the rate of camera speed must be altered in order to photograph mobile miniatures realistically, so must the *construction* of miniatures which are involved in impact action be suitably modified. Such components must be built of weaker materials than those which would be employed in the real structure, or must be pre-weakened so that they break or disintegrate in an appropriate manner. The rule in such cases is to reduce the strength of the construction materials in exact proportion to the reduction in scale. If a miniature set, built to 1:10 scale, shows a boulder crashing down upon a building, then the wood employed to construct the model building must be 1/10 the strength of that normally used in such a structure (woods such as balsa or sandalwood might be appropriate). Alternatively, if stronger woods are used, selected pieces must be deeply scored from within so that the pieces will fracture easily when struck by miniaturized objects (Fig. 12.13).

Any explosion or burning?

Exploding or collapsing buildings must be rigged and pre-weakened so that they distintegrate in a natural and dramatically suitable manner. The work which goes into their construction is considerable, for each brick or plank which separates from the rest of the structure upon demolition must be painted and aged separately, before the miniature is assembled. Also, the interiors of exploding or collapsing buildings must be fairly well finished off, sometimes even to the extent of filling them with miniature furniture.

The determination of stress points and the setting of demolition charges is a kind of work which requires much experience and experimentation; even the specialists of the theatrical film industry make frequent mistakes. If the charges are too weak, the miniature is destroyed without producing a pictorially satisfying effect. If it is too large, the miniature may simply

* For a description of the technique, see the *Motion Picture Research Council Bulletin* No. 58.545, Feb. 23, 1951.

vaporize, together with a good deal of the nearby photographic apparatus. In some states of the USA and in many other countries, the services of a licensed pyrotechnics specialist, or 'powder man', are legally required, together with an appropriate license to purchase and detonate explosive materials.

Often a relatively small amount of explosive can be used to produce the proper visual effect, and the main body of the pre-weakened miniature can be collapsed mechanically. The whole structure can be built like a 'house of cards', with the main beams loosely mounted on supports which are released electrically. Also, sections of wall can be pulled out of position with piano wires.

When miniatures are burned, the type of fire which is desired will determine the construction employed. For complete destruction, the entire set is built of soft pine; for selective conflagration, those sections which are supposed to burn are built of pine, those which must remain out of plaster. A mixture of kerosene and gasoline can be sprayed over selected portions of the set to guide the fire. Gasoline by itself burns too quickly. Kerosene should be blended with it to slow down the conflagration; kerosene also adheres nicely to the set components. To simulate an oily, gasoline-tank fire, add strips of paving or roofing tar to the inside walls of the miniature pieces.

For safety and convenience, miniature fires are started on cue with electrical detonators or spark gaps. In all cases, an exploding or burning miniature requires appropriate precautions for fire-control, lest the make-believe conflagration becomes a real one. Volatile liquids which are used on the sound stage to start or 'shape' the fire must be used judiciously and in as small a quantity as is necessary, from shot to shot. Surplus or reserve supplies of these liquids should be stored away from the set area. Appropriate fire-fighting equipment should be placed at hand, and the crew trained in its use ahead of time. When large miniatures are burned, the nearest professional fire department should be alerted and its personnel called in for consultation, despite whatever inconvenience this may entail – it is far less expensive to conform to local fire regulations than to rebuild a sound stage.

If an indoor set is used, high light levels have to be maintained, lest the brilliance of the fire exceed that of the overall illumination, in an unnatural fashion. As with water, fire is always difficult to miniaturize; for this reason, miniatures which are meant to be burned are built to as large a scale as is feasible (Fig. 12.6). In some cases, when small-scale sets are used, it will be found necessary to burn the fires some distance *behind* set components so that the scale of the flames will match that of the miniature. It is also possible and sometimes desirable to add flames through optical or matte printing.

What is the camera position?

Will the camera be static? If so, what will be its exact position and height with respect to the miniature? If the camera will move, what kind of movements, positions and elevations can be expected – lateral and longitudinal dolly shots, boom shots, traveling shots over the miniature?

Generally, the camera will be positioned so as to provide a head-on shot of the miniature which approximates the eye-level view which a scaled-down person would have if he were part of the scene. In some cases, still better results follow from an angle which is just slightly below eye-level. High angles should usually be avoided since they nearly always emphasize the miniaturization of the set and diminish its realism.

If a large, single-scale miniature is involved, the camera can be positioned at a variety of angles and can even be moved over it on a boom. Mixed-scale sets, on the other hand, require particular camera positions for their best rendering and do not always allow movements towards or away from the set. Pans and tilts may nearly always be made, although a nodal-point mount should be used for the camera so as to avoid improper parallax motion between different components of the set: this is particularly important when working with mixed-scale miniatures. Whatever kinds of camera movement are involved, they must be exceedingly smooth and slow in execution. The cinematographer must realize that as the scale of the miniature is reduced, so must the speed with which the camera is panned, tilted or moved. Unevenness or excessive speed will pretty well destroy the illusion of the shot.

Where will the set be photographed?

Will the miniature be built and photographed on the sound stage or on the 'back lot'? If it is to be built outside the stage, what provisions will be necessary to protect it from the elements?

For convenience, many miniature sets are built out-of-doors and are illuminated by sunlight. For daytime scenes, the combination of sunlight and skylight provides the most realistic kind of lighting, together with high light levels. It also provides sharp, single-source shadows which are otherwise difficult to duplicate with artificial lights.

What other effects are needed?

What kinds of lighting will ultimately be employed – daylight, incandescent or arc? High, medium or low-key? Will any portion of the miniature be self-illuminated (as with the windows of a building, the portholes of a ship, the headlights of a car, or street lamps)? Will any of the lights be expected to move, flicker or be turned on and off? What are the total power requirements for the lighting and operation of the set?

Will wind effects be required in the scene?

How will far-distant sky and cloud effects be incorporated into the finished scene – painted sky backings, background projection, glass-shots, bi-pack printing or optical printing?

Construction techniques

A variety of materials can be used for miniature construction. Plasters and moulded plastics are sometimes employed where complicated compound surfaces must be produced, and metal is used when great strength is required for bracing and support. In most cases, however, wood and wood products are used for model building. Wood is inexpensive, it is universally available, it can be easily cut and shaped, and it can be easily aged. Nothing looks so much like wood in a miniature as wood itself, and, for fire scenes, it burns realistically.

Mounting the set

Miniature sets are nearly always mounted upon elevated platforms, the construction of which is often of the open-joist benchwork type (Fig. 12.16). This kind of construction is economical in the use of materials and provides convenient access to interior sections of the set for the installation, operation and repair of power leads, mechanical devices and pipes. Its elevation off the ground or stage floor also allows the

Fig. 12.14, part 1. One way to make a moon. A cut-out photograph of the moon is hung in front of a cobalt blue backing for insertion into a star field by means of a glass shot.

Fig. 12.14, part 2. Another way to make a moon. A rear-illuminated photographic transparency of the moon is photographed through a tank of water into which pigments are introduced so as to create artificial clouds. Additional clouds are produced in the foreground by means of dry-ice fog machines. (From the production of *One From the Heart*. Zoetrope Studios.)

Fig. 12.15. For the simulation of flickering stars in the sky, a perforated sheet of opaque board is lit from behind. Long strips of clear 35 mm motion-picture stock are suspended in the path of the light. The breeze from a small fan is directed against the strips, causing them to move and thus intermittently interrupt the rear illumination in different sections of the backing. (National Film Board of Canada.)

photographic personnel to mount their cameras at convenient working positions when shooting 'eye-level' shots, and to mount lights below the level of the set, if desired. The platform is positioned so as to leave ample space on all sides for changes in camera position, and for such lighting equipment, wind and fog machines, Century stands, water pumping equipment, and other devices as may be involved. A space of 6 to 10 ft should also be provided *behind* the set to allow for the mounting of a sky backing or cyclorama.

For landscape scenes which show valleys, rolling hills, mountains and the like, a basic frame of wood supports is first built which corresponds roughly to the shape of the terrain. Over these wood supports either burlap or ¼ in contractor's wire screening is stretched and tacked. The mesh material is then stiffened so as to fix its shape and to give it supportive strength. Burlap is stiffened by painting it with a 'sizing' compound; wire mesh is stiffened by covering it with a plaster mix. The stiffened cloth or metal fabric provides a foundation which now approximates the outlines of a landscape scene and which is strong enough to support miniature objects on its surface. Properly built, it is even strong enough to be walked upon (see Fig. 12.10).

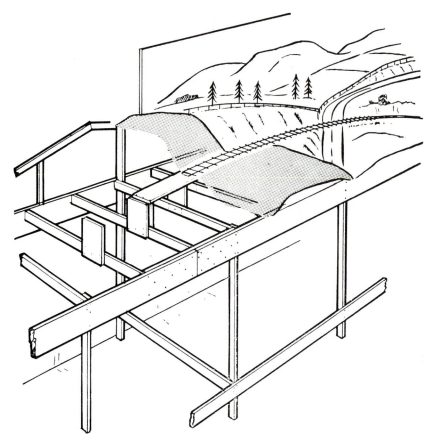

Fig. 12.16. Open-joist construction. (Kalmbach Publishing Company.)

This foundation can be painted an appropriate color and a variety of materials can be sprinkled on it to produce a particular kind of scene. Finely-sifted dirt provides the basic earth-cover, while sand will pass for gravel. In most cases, these materials can be allowed to lie loose upon the surface of the foundation. In a few cases, however, particularly when rain must fall, when wind machines are used or when strong vibrations are present in the set's operation, it may be necessary to mix these materials with glue and to attach them permanently to the foundation. Dirt which is used for those sections of the set which are closest to the camera must be sifted particularly fine, lest each clump of particles appear as a boulder on the screen. When unusually fine particles are required, pumice, Fuller's earth or rotten-stone can be sifted over the dirt.

Choosing the material

A variety of other materials provide satisfactory substitutes for everyday, full-scale objects, the proper choice depending upon the character and size of the miniature and its distance from the camera. Sawdust, dyed green, can pass for grass, while weeds, fragments of sponge and certain types of

Fig. 12.17. For the ABC Television documentary space adventure, *Infinite Horizons*, a technician leans out from the camera crane's arm to sprinkle granulated salt over the miniature set below, putting the finishing touches on a dusty, unpaved country road. (Filmeffects of Hollywood.)

blossoms will pass for shrubbery. Full-size trees can be simulated with large, flowering weeds, or with twigs and branches of trees. for color cinematography, all of these materials can be painted or sprayed with appropriate pigments. Great restraint must be used in selecting colors, however, or the final result will appear garish and false; low-saturation colors, suitably greyed-out, are always best. Bodies of water can be simulated with Cellophane strips, as described earlier in this chapter.

Roads and cityscapes

Concrete highways are represented by strips of wood painted medium grey, on which the appropriate kind of lane divider is painted white. Streaks of dark paint can be applied to the centre of each lane to suggest the tar streaks and overall discoloration which occur with age; painted-on cracks in the pavement complete the illusion. If the perspective of the set is to be forced, these wooden highway strips can be cut in tapering shape and their lane lines gradually narrowed so as to artificially suggest the converging of perspective lines which occurs in real life with increasing distance. The same kind of distortion can be produced in a city miniature by progressively narrowing the width of the streets as they pass away from the camera.

Miniature houses and buildings may, or may not, be constructed in complete form, depending upon the requirements of the scene. If the set is to be photographed from a variety of positions, then the individual components must be nicely finished off. Sharply focused pieces which are located close to the camera must be meticulously 'dressed' so as to match the familiar, real-life object: shades and curtains must be provided for windows, doors should have latches or doorknobs, tombstones must have inscriptions, automobiles must have license plates, and so forth. If on the other hand, these pieces are located some distance from the camera, much less care need be put into their finishing; indeed, perspective effects *require* a much grosser kind of finishing for far-off objects, in a mixed-scale set. Distant views of mountains or cityscapes, for example, can often be represented with simple cardboard cut-outs, rather than three-dimensional models.

In those rare cases in which the cinematographer and art director can confidently plan the final lighting, a great deal of effort can be saved by constructing those areas of the set which will fall into heavy shadow in rough form, and finishing off only the well-lighted portions.

Infinity backgrounds

Should it become necessary for the camera to truck, laterally, across the face (width) of a miniature set, problems of motion parallax may arise which, if not solved, will ruin the believability of the scene. In real life, as we drive along a highway, and look out through the window, 90° to the direction of travel, the nearest objects whiz by so fast as to be blurred, both to the eye and to the motion-picture camera. Objects in the middle distance move more slowly and remain within our view long enough for us to see some of their details. The farther away objects are located, the slower they appear to move. Finally, objects many miles away – a range of mountains, a distant cityscape, a moonlit sky filled with stars – appear to be either fixed in space or moving hardly at all.

If these peculiarities of motion parallax which exist in nature are not duplicated in our miniature set, then all of our work will be compromised by background components which move much too fast, relative to the scale of the miniature. For this reason, it is necessary to create a so-called 'infinity background' for any shot in which the camera trucks laterally past the miniature. This is a largish painted backdrop (or photograph), incorporating whatever detail goes with the foreground miniature. The infinity background is suspended on rails and is made to move along with, and parallel to, the camera, either at exactly the same speed or just slightly lower than the camera's trucking movement. In the finished film, the background will appear fixed in its position, or will move ever so slightly from moment to moment. In this fashion, the illusion of a distant vista behind the foreground miniature details will be greatly enhanced. Needless to say, the background painting or photograph must be created in the proper scale to match the foreground detail, and must display lighting which matches that of the foreground.

For the Francis Coppola production of *One From the Heart*, a traveling-camera shot was required of actors talking in an open automobile, driving through the desert suburbs of Las Vegas, with a variety of more-or-less realistic hotels, trees, industrial buildings, streets, and such in the backround. For stylistic reasons, it was decided to create the background which was seen behind the actors with miniatures rather than real-life detail. For this series of shots, a quite long miniature set was created in ¼ inch scale, running 90 feet in length, from one corner of the effects stage to the other (Fig. 12.18 parts 1–7). Since several different auto-travel shots were required at different times of the day, a variety of infinity backgrounds were painted to show sunrise, noon, late afternoon and sunset lighting. Both the camera and the painted background were mounted on precision rails, and both were pulled along, in synchronism, by a motor-driven cable, past the miniature buildings in the foreground, the painted background moving just a bit slower than the camera (Fig. 12.18 part 6). The effect on the screen was quite attractive, but, as so often happens during the editing process, nearly all of the anticipated auto scenes were eliminated, and only a few seconds of the miniature desert scene appeared in the finished film.

Finding the model-builder

Film producers must bear in mind that the construction of miniatures is always an expensive and time-consuming business – the effeceiveness of this kind of effect and its role in solving difficult production problems must always be balanced against its cost. Happily, because of lower labor costs, miniature work is considerably less expensive in the non-theatrical film

Fig. 12.18, part 1. Beginning construction of a 90 ft-long miniature of the streets, buildings, hotels and casinos of Las Vegas for the Francis Coppola production of *One From the Heart*. The miniature set is intended to be incorporated as background detail behind performers in moving automobile shots. The camera which will photograph this miniature set will be driven along precision rails, seen here extending the length of the stage.

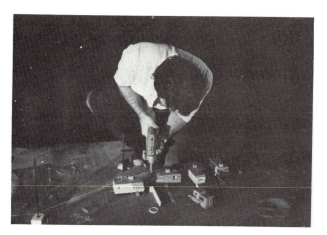

Fig. 12.18, part 2. A model maker installs hidden electrical wiring for a cluster of miniature buildings. The entire miniature set is built to a quarter-inch scale.

Fig. 12.18, part 3. Another model maker puts finishing touches on an elaborate miniature neon sign for the Hacienda Hotel and Casino. This simulation of neon signs required hundreds of tiny 'grain of wheat' bulbs, each individually controlled so as to allow for the complicated cycles of neon light movements typical of the full-scale Las Vagas signs.

Fig. 12.18, part 4. Electronic equipment designed expressly for operation of the hundreds of individual bulbs in the various simulated neon signs in the set.

Fig. 12.18, part 5. A view of the high-intensity lighting provided for photography of the miniature. A row of 2 kilowatt incandescent spotlights are hung above and at the front of the 90 ft-long miniature, each lamp angled off at 45°. These provide key-light simulation of sunlight. Directly overhead, through the entire length of the miniature, hang 'chicken-coop' frames, each containing nine photoflood-type lamps which provide fill light for the set. High intensity lighting is required to allow for small f-stops and reasonably deep depth of field. On the other hand, the set lighting can not be allowed to wash out the relatively feeble 'grain-of-wheat' bulbs used in the simulated neon signs.

Fig. 12.18, part 6. Photography of the finished miniature set. Note the 'infinity background' behind the miniatures which travels on rails of its own as the camera moves along, past the set.

Fig. 12.18, part 7. Visual effects supervisor Wally Gentleman checks composition and focus for another shot of the miniature. This time it is lit for an evening effect. The camera is positioned at a simulated height of about 4½ feet above the pavement.

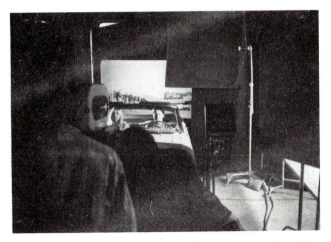

Fig. 12.18, part 8. The final composite of foreground actors in a full-scale, open automobile, and a rear-projected plate of the miniature streets and buildings of Las Vegas, behind them. Camera is in foreground, at left.

industry than in the theatrical field. In many cases, a small production organization will have an art director, a cameraman, a set-construction worker or others who have a natural aptitude for this kind of work, while in-plant industrial film units can often draw upon the talents of model-builders who are assigned to their own company's design and engineering sections. Lacking such personnel, producers who operate in major metropolitan areas can contract much of this work to professional model-making firms which service architects and contractors. Finally, there are talented amateur model builders in almost every community, many of whom are delighted to work on motion-picture projects at very reasonable fees – some of the finest miniatures which this author has ever seen were built for a Los Angeles film producer by a 14-year-old boy! Amateurs such as these can usually be located through the stores and firms which sell model-making supplies or through advertisements placed in the leading hobby magazines.

In this section, only the superficialities of model-building practice have been suggested; the techniques and materials employed are infinitely varied, and, in their complexity, fall outside the scope of this book.

The photography of miniatures

Despite all the work which has gone into the construction of a miniature set, its appearance on the screen will be compromised if it is not properly photographed.

It is essential, first, that the optical depth of field for a miniature shot extend throughout the entire set. This calls for relatively short focal-length lenses and/or fairly small apertures, particularly in the case of mixed-scale sets in which the foreground components are placed close to the camera. Short-focus lenses provide the maximum depth of field, while forcing the perspective of the set. Even with relatively deep-focus lenses, however, the apertures required may range from $f/5.6$ to $f/16$. For medium-speed emulsions, the use of such apertures demands fairly intense illumination. Sunlight is ideal for such assignments.

Lighting

When daylight scenes are simulated on the stage with artificial lights, it is essential that double shadows be eliminated. Ideally, arcs will be used for this kind of work. Their intense brilliance allows for coverage of large areas, and they produce the crisp shadows which one associates with sunlight. If incandescent lamps are employed, their beams must be carefully overlapped, and spill light contained with barndoors and gobos so that individual components of the set will not throw shadows from multiple sources. The fill-lights which are used to simulate skylight must be properly diffused so that they, too, do not add unnatural shadows. In some cases, it is possible to use bounce light for this purpose, the beams of selected lamps being reflected off large sheets of diffuse reflector-board.

Many cinematographers also diffuse their key lights, it being felt that an overall soft illumination will enhance the realism of the miniature. The choice of harsh or diffuse key lighting is an artistic one, and depends upon the nature of the miniature and the particular effect desired. Sometimes, diffuse light can be used for the subordinate sections of the set and harsher lighting for those few areas which are dramatically or pictorially important.

If desired, a semi-transparent cookalourus, or 'cookie', can be interposed between the key lights and the set to throw a mottled pattern of light upon the miniature which approximates the shadow patterns caused by overhead clouds. If the scene is left on the screen for a prolonged period of time, the 'cookies' can be moved very slowly to suggest the passage of off-screen clouds across the sky. When raw sunlight is used for the lighting, strips of scrim cloth or muslin can be stretched over the set to achieve the same effect. Also, large sections of scrim cloth can be suspended over an outdoor, sunlit set to provide overall diffusion.

For both daylight and evening scenes, front light should be avoided, since it flattens out the scene and destroys much of the depth and detail values that have been built into the set. A 45–90° key light, on the other hand, emphasizes the three-dimensionality of the miniature.

Night and evening lighting

Night scenes in miniature, particularly those of cityscapes, buildings, factories and the like, offer considerable latitude in their lighting, inasmuch as the light sources come from so many angles. Accent highlights can be added with 'kickers' and backlights. Continuous tones in the set (such as on building walls) can be broken up into attractive shadow patterns with 'cookies'. Depth effects and detail-work on the buildings can be accentuated through crosslighting. Practical lights can be operated within components to add greater realism, and different planes of the set can be contrasted and separated artistically with alternating areas of light and shadow.

The lighting of an evening miniature scene must be meticulously planned and executed, for it requires far more finesse than for a full-scale set. Interior lights, in particular must be subdued so that they will not appear over-bright – a small, low-wattage lamp within a miniature house will give the same appearance as a 2000 watt 'Junior' inside a full-scale building. If convenient, interior lights should be operated through variable rheostats so as to allow quick and convenient changes in their brilliance to match the overall illumination of the set. In some cases, interior lights can be simulated by using reflective materials on the *outside* of the components to reflect light from the stage lamps – small pieces of Scotchlite sheeting or aluminium foil can be pasted over windows, thumb-tacks can be mounted along the edge of a miniature ship to represent portholes, and so forth.

Quite often, the cinematographer will wish to add a dim 'glow light' to the horizon by directing a low-wattage spotlight or floodlight against the lower edge of the sky backing, behind the set. This light separates the buildings from the dark sky and approximates the effect gained when evening city scenes are shot at dusk. Without such an horizon glow, many of the miniature buildings will simply fade into blackness, and their production values will be lost.

Special problems may arise if the 'practical' lights operated on or from within miniature buildings are too dim for satisfactory exposure. It is the nature of miniature photography that maximum depth-of-field is required to hold all of the miniature detail in sharp focus, thereby contributing to the illusion of reality. In some cases, the brilliance of these practical lights can be increased by simply boosting the voltage or using higher-wattage lamps. In other cases, however, as with the operation of very tiny lights in simulated neon signs, the brilliance of the individual lights cannot be increased beyond their normal operating level. By themselves they may not be photographable unless large f/stops are employed. On the other hand, large f/stops produce shallow depth of field which throws part of the miniature out of focus. One solution, described in Chapter 13, is to use an intervalvometer and/or motion-control equipment, which allows for per-frame exposures far in excess of normal cinematography. Also, higher-speed color negative stocks are now available from manufacturers which provide both high sensitivity and good image quality. These allow for photography at small f/stops with moderate light levels.

Landscapes at night

An entirely different set of photographic problems is involved in the lighting of a night scene of a miniature landscape. In real life, a landscape is illuminated at night by moonlight. This illumination is virtually identical to that of sunlight, except that it is of much lower intensity and is not supplemented by the skylight which fills shadows. Indeed, many time-exposure still photographs which have been made of moonlit landscapes are virtually indistinguishable from sunlit shots.

Accordingly, the cinematographer must decide whether his lighting of an evening landscape miniature will be naturalistic or theatrical in style. If naturalistic, then one key light (or a set of key lights operating from the same position) will be used to illuminate the whole area of the set. Fill-lights will not be used, inasmuch as the cinematographer will wish to produce the deep rich shadows which are typical of evening. These shadows can be accentuated by keying the set with a 90° cross-light or even a backlight. A black or dark-grey sky backing will be used behind the miniature to duplicate the dark sky of night, although a low-level glow-light can be added to the backing along the horizon to separate the mountains, trees and hills from the sky areas.

Stars can be added to the evening sky by positioning thumbtacks over the area of the sky backing to reflect pinpoints of light from a small floodlamp. Alternatively, small holes can be punched into the sky backing and illuminated from behind. A twinkling effect can be added by suspending long strips of clear motion-picture film between the holes punched into the backing and the rear illumination (Fig. 12.15). A fan is directed towards the strips, causing them to move gently, thus interfering intermittently with the light source and creating a twinkling effect when viewed from the set side of the backing.

The same technique can be used with mural backgrounds or cardboard cut-outs which are used with cityscape miniatures, to suggest the turning on and off of lights in distant buildings. Finally, the shot will be slightly underexposed (or underprinted in the laboratory) to suggest the overall darkness of evening.

The cinematographer may, on the other hand, wish to light the scene more theatrically, in which case kicker and back lights will be used in addition to the key lights so as to highlight different features of the landscape (Fig. 12.10). This kind of accent lighting is unmotivated and non-naturalistic, but is something of an artistic convention. Providing that it is not overdone, audiences will accept it, just as they accept the very theatrical kinds of lighting which are commonly employed in full-scale, interior sets. In the end, the style of lighting for the miniature will depend upon the nature of the set, the dramatic style of the film's direction and the lighting conventions which have been established for the entire production.

Diffusion techniques

Sometimes, the reality of a miniature set can be enhanced by purposely 'degrading' the image, first so as to simulate certain types of aerial and detail perspective which occur in real life, and second, so as to deceive the audience sufficiently so that it suspends disbelief and accepts the miniature set as a real scene. This kind of degradation can be accomplished in a variety of ways, one of which is to photograph the scene with diffusion or fog filters over the lens. The amount of diffusion can range from light to heavy, depending upon the size and character of the miniature and the style of the film. Properly executed, diffusion softens the edges and details of the components and makes them appear larger and more lifelike. (Unfortunately for special-effects workers, the general style of cinematography has tended away from diffusion during the last decade and towards needle-sharp, deep-focus images. Should an over-diffused miniature shot be cut into a sharply photographed film, it will, of course, appear false.)

Alternatively, if the scene and story allow, a fog machine can be operated to lay down a haze or fog over the entire set. Additionally, large sheets of scrim cloth can be mounted in front of the more distant sections of the set, thus decreasing the detail and contrast of the background components. If the set is fairly large, a number of such scrims can be used, one in front of the other. Those components which are supposed to be situated at progressively greater and greater distances from the camera will accordingly lose more and more of their detail and their contrast or color saturation. This technique is particularly useful with mixed-scale sets, where vast changes in distance have to be simulated with components which are separated by only a few feet.

A light mist or fog effect can also be produced over the entire image by means of a glass shot set-up. A sheet of glass is angled off 45° to the optical axis of the lens, and an illuminated white card (or a light box with a sheet of opal glass) is positioned at 90° to one side of the camera. The camera photographs the miniature *through* the glass, but also picks up the overall, low-level, white light from the illuminated card, which is reflected off the surface of the glass. This has the effect of increasing the light level in the shadow areas, decreasing contrast, and producing an overall effect of mist or fog. If desired, of course, the reflected light can be given an appropriate color for a subtle tinted effect.

One of the most useful lighting tools for miniature photography is the Polaroid camera, with which test photographs can be made and appraised as the lighting proceeds. Film for this camera, whether black-and-white or color, should be selected to match the production emulsion as closely as possible.

The production emulsion itself should be chosen to match that of the bracketing sequences between which the miniature shots are inserted. Ordinarily, medium-speed stocks will be selected for this purpose, although departures from conventional emulsions will sometimes seem more appropriate. For the black-and-white photography of *Sink the Bismarck*, for example, Tri-X was selected since its coarse grain matched that of the production and newsreel footage which was employed throughout the film.

When high-speed camera drives are used for the photography of mobile miniatures, the aperture and pressure plates of the camera must be kept meticulously clean. Any piece of grit or emulsion deposit will scratch the film beyond salvage and will pile up emulsion scrapings at a frighteningly fast rate, sometimes to the extent of damaging the intermittent assembly through pressure. The film must be loaded through both the movement and the sprocket drives with great care, and the camera *must* be equipped with buckle-trip switches – at 164 frames per second, an uncontrolled film jam can cause extensive damage.

One final admonition for the photographer of miniatures which are operated out-of-doors – take care that flying insects and birds do not pass unnoticed through the field of view. Their presence in a reduced-scale set lends a novel but inevitably compromising effect to the completed scene.

Periscopes and snorkel systems

In the photography of miniatures, it is often desirable to place the camera lens *within* the miniature set, with the optical axis of the lens positioned an inch or two above the surface. If the face of the miniature is open, and if the camera does not have to move, it may be possible to position the camera directly in front of the set and to get the shots which are desired. Alternatively, an inclining prism, such as that manufactured by the Samuelson Group, can be used to lower the effective lens position of the camera.

If, on the other hand, it is necessary that the camera actually moves *through* the miniature, with its lens very close to the surface, then a different photographic set-up will be required. For such purposes, a periscope lens extension may do the job. The camera is positioned on a boom or crane so that it faces downward towards the miniature set. An optical periscope device with a right-angle mirror is inserted between the turret of the camera and the lens. The periscope effectively lowers the position of the lens to the surface of the miniature (Fig. 12.19). If the shot

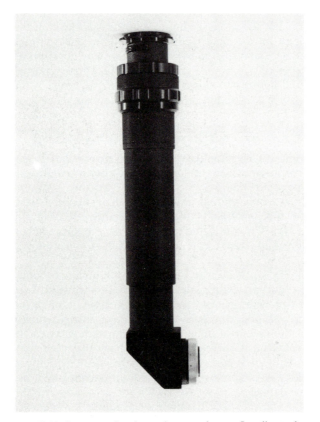

Fig. 12.19. One type of periscope lens attachment. It redirects the optical axis of the camera, horizontally by 90°, so that it is parallel to the miniature set and is located only a couple inches above the surface of the set. (Century Precision Optics.)

Fig. 12.20. Another type of periscope lens attachment called a 'pitching lens', seen here photographing the miniature space ship, *Cygnus*, from the production of *The Black Hole*. It can tilt up or down through several degrees of arc, as well as rotate through a full 360°. (Courtesy Walt Disney Productions.)

Fig. 12.21. A very versatile piece of equipment for the photography of miniatures – the Kenworthy 'snorkel camera' system. It allows the camera to move in and out, through and around components of a miniature set as if the production camera were itself miniaturized and were located 1–2 inches above the surface of the set. The camera, at right, is mounted face down, its lens replaced with an extension-tube 'snorkel' optical system containing relay lenses. A movable mirror at the bottom of the tube re-orients the optical axis of the lens system. The mirror can tilt up and down through several degrees of arc, and can rotate through 360°, making both kinds of moves on a point, with a zero turning radius. The image which results is picked up by a video tape within the optical system and is imaged on a video monitor, left, while the shot is being photographed on the film in the camera.

Fig. 12.22. Another view of the Kenworthy snorkel camera being moved across stage – over, through and around a large miniature set used in the feature film production of *Logan's Run*.

is not too demanding, this tactic works well. For more complicated shots, a so-called pitching lens can be used, which allows for the rotation and tilting of the entire tube assembly. Still more flexible is the optical system employed in the Kenworthy Snorkel System, which incorporates a movable mirror at the base of the tube which can be tilted both up and down, and through a 360° turn, with a zero-pan and tilt radius. This is an elaborate piece of equipment incorporating, among other things, a video tap which allows for remote viewing of the scene and operation of the mirror assembly (Figs. 12.5, 12.20 and 12.21).

Both simple periscopes and more complicated snorkel systems incorporate relay lenses which inevitably absorb a certain amount of the light which passes through them. For this reason, higher-than-normal light levels are usually necessary for miniature photography using this kind of equipment.

A few special-effects organizations have also constructed cameras whose lens boards can be tilted, as on a view camera. This allows for an artificially expanded depth of field when the camera is brought close to miniatures. Accessories such as this are ordinarily used in association with motion-control equipment.

Tank-shots

One of the most common uses to which miniatures are put is the representation of ships at sea. For MGM Studios' production of *Plymouth Adventure*, for example, over 25 per cent of the entire picture footage was comprised of miniature-ship shots, photographed in tanks.

Fig. 12.23, part 1. An interior 65 × 40 ft tank built at Bob Jones University. The walls of the tank are plywood, attached to a welded steel frame. The walls are coated with tar on their surfaces and joints to prevent leakage, then covered with layers of sisal craft paper and painted. The cyclorama at the back end of the tank was painted to simulate a cloudy sky.

Fig. 12.23, part 2. Photography of a tank shot for the production of *Wine of the Morning*. Waves are created by manual operation of empty 55 gallon oil drums, at left. A four-bladed airplane propellor, powered by a 5 horse power motor, provides wind effects and whips up spray. Rain is produced by six shower heads, fed by a fire hose. The camera, operating at 96 frames per second, is located at lower left, about 6 in above the surface of the water.

Fig. 12.23, part 3. A miniature ship (scale 1:12) carries a battery-powered motor which propels the oars. Human figures are moulded from rubber.

Fig. 12.23, part 4. Final miniature tank shot. Both incandescent and arc lamps were used for the lighting of the scene, supplemented by four banks of flashbulbs for lightning effects. The flashbulbs were fired in rapid succession so that their flashes would last long enough to appear realistic on film. (Bob Jones University.)

Despite their great usefulness, however, these are among the most difficult kinds of shot to pull off realistically, due to the dissimilarity in behavior between a full-size ship and a reduced-scale replica, under way in a body of water. The problem is that the scale of the ship can be reduced, but the scale of the water cannot. As workers in the field have discovered, you cannot make 'small water'. Whatever the size of the ship, the body of water in which it floats behaves substantially the same – the height of the waves, the distance between waves, and the ebb and flow of its current occurring in a natural fashion. If a very small miniature ship is placed in a tank and a wave machine set operating, the model will bob around in a manner which is completely unrealistic. For this reason, ship miniatures are built to as large a scale as the budget and size of the tank will allow.

Fig. 12.24, part 1. Construction of an outdoor tank for miniature shots at the National Film Board of Canada.

Fig. 12.24, part 2. A metal support is erected at the back end of the tank for mounting the sky cyclorama. Note that the back wall is slightly lower than the other sides, allowing for a horizon spillway. A trough along the back edge collects the overflow for re-circulation.

Fig. 12.24, part 3. The outdoor tank in use. A wind machine has been positioned alongside for use in a storm sequence.

Fig. 12.24, part 4. Lining up a tank shot for the Film Board's production of *The Last Voyage of Henry Hudson*.

Size and viewpoint

Typical scales employed in the theatrical film industry for tank shots range from 1:24 to 1:4. Thus, at 1:16 scale, a 26 000-ton passenger vessel with an overall length of 640 ft would be represented by a miniature which is 40 ft long. An 80 ft yacht, miniaturized to the same scale, would be five feet long. Clearly, these are fairly large miniatures, as are the tanks which are required to hold them. The tank used at Pinewood Studios, England, for the production of *Sink the Bismarck* was 240 ft wide at its rear, tapering to 110 ft in the foreground, with a back-to-front distance of 200 ft. The depth of tank was 3½ ft, and the miniature replica of the *Bismarck* which was floated in it was 30 ft long! For the MGM production of *Gorgo*, for which a section of the Thames and central London was duplicated at 1:30 scale, a tank 300 ft wide was employed. For the MGM production of *Plymouth Adventure*, a 3 ft deep, 300 × 300 ft tank was used.

Many such tanks are provided with wells in their centers, from 12 to 30 ft deep, to provide additional depth for the sinking of a ship. Tanks are also provided with a back-wall spillway, built slightly lower than the other three sides. Over this spillway, a continuous stream of water is made to flow. This edge of water blends nicely against the sky backing and provides a very convincing artificial horizon which appears many miles distant.

At least one very large tank, on the Isle of Gibraltar, was also built so as to take advantage of sight lines along the surface of the water which allow for the optical blending of the water in the tank with that of the ocean in the distance. More commonly, shots of real water, whether in the ocean or in a lake, are matted in and blended with the water in the miniatures tank. This requires a nice match in the hue and saturation of the water color, as well as the size, direction, and activity of the two sets of waves.

Nearly always, these tanks are built out-of-doors, where sunlight can be used for the overall illumination. As with landscape miniatures, soft, diffuse lighting of high intensity is much to be desired. Raw sunlight can be diffused by passing it through large sheets of scrim cloth which are suspended over the tank. Often, the appearance of the shot can be further enhanced by laying down a fog or light haze with fog machines. If the scale of the ships and the size of the tank is sufficiently large, artificial fog can also be used to simulate clouds against the sky backing. Alternatively, clouds can be painted on to the sky backing, added with glass-shots at the time of photography, or added in the laboratory through optical or bi-pack printing.

One of the most difficult photographic problems in this kind of work is the securing of sharp focus over the entire set. Nothing compromises a tank-shot so much as out-of-focus foreground water. Since the camera is usually located fairly close to the surface of the water, and inasmuch as the expanse of water which is photographed extends from the artificial horizon to the lower edge of the frame, depth of field becomes a real problem. High illumination levels, fairly fast film stocks, small apertures and/or somewhat shorter than normal focal-length lenses are nearly always required.

For the sake of proper perspective rendering, and a realistic viewpoint, the camera is usually mounted with its lens anywhere from one to four feet above the surface of the water. The exact height will depend upon the scale of the miniature ships. The larger the scale, the higher the camera position and the less the depth-of-field problem. Sometimes, the camera is positioned outside of the tank; in other cases, it is floated within the tank on a raft. Differences of opinion prevail as to whether the camera should be rocked. Some cinematographers feel that if the camera is allowed to pitch and roll, it simulates the view which would be had from a nearby ship; others feel that it only irritates the audience (Fig. 12.25).

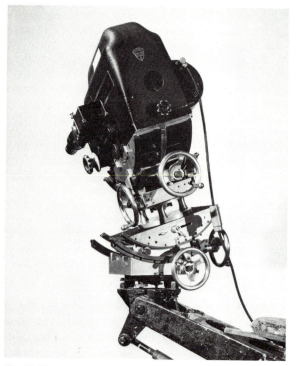

Fig. 12.25. To simulate the rocking of a ship at sea, this camera has been mounted on a dual set of geared heads, providing both fore-and-aft and side-to-side movements. (National Film Board of Canada.)

Moving the miniature

Miniature ships are pulled across the tank with underwater lines. They should not be run along tracks, since a track-guided drive restricts the pitching and rolling movements which one associates with a vessel under way. When to or more miniature ships are operated in the tank, the background vessels will often be built to a smaller scale than the foreground ones. This mixing of scale allows for the ships to be floated within a few feet of one another, but to appear to be separated by several hundred yards.

No matter how large the scale of a miniature ship, however, its speed and mass will rarely be sufficient to produce a natural-looking bow wave, or to cause it to heel over properly during a turn. Acordingly, these characteristics must be artificially created. Supplementary lines attached to the rear side of the miniature vessel can be operated during a turn to produce an appropriate amount of 'heel'. Because a ship turns from its stern, rather than from its bow, the movement of a miniature ships' stern must be accelerated at a faster rate than that of its bow when changing direction. Attention should also be paid to the direction in which flags are flown. On power-driven craft, pennants ordinarily stream towards the stern; on a sailboat, towards the bow.

Wave and water

For distant ships, a fairly realistic bow wave can be painted on to the hull. For nearby ships, and for the most realistic effect, compressed air is released through vents in the bow. Compressed air, in small, controlled amounts, can also be used to simulate the wake of oars in a rowboat. A stern wake is simulated by releasing compressed air at the stern, sometimes together with white paint. Alternatively, dry ice can be inserted into a container below the water line at the stern to provide the same effect. torpedo wakes can be created mechanically with compressed air, or the wake can be superimposed in the laboratory through optical printing.

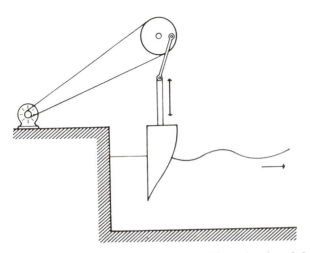

Fig. 12.26. A motor-driven wave generator. The wedge-shaped plunger rises and falls rhythmically in the water, producing waves which travel outward across the tank. (courtesy of *American Cinematographer.*)

Although one cannot make 'small water', surface tension can be reduced by adding chemical wetting agents. This renders the surface of the water more manageable, and the behavior of the model ships more believable. The water in the tank is usually muddied or dyed so as to reduce its transparency and to prevent the camera from picking up the far side or bottom of the tank. As an additional precaution, the bottom and sides are usually painted a deep blue or black.

A small amount of detergent or white paint can be added to the water to produce a naturalistic foam effect – too much detergent, however, will form bubbles.

Waves of varying sizes and velocity can be created with wave-forming machinery set alongside the inside edge of the tank walls. Empty, sealed oil drums can be used for this purpose, being mounted on brackets and periodically submerged and raised (Fig. 12.23 part 2). In other cases, special wave-making forms are used, one example of which is shown in Fig. 12.26. For storm sequences, as well as for sailboat shots in which full, undulating sails must be shown, wind machines are operated alongside the tank (Fig. 12.24). If these machines do not whip up sufficient spray by themselves, streams of water can be directed by pipe, downward in front of the fan blades, with care being taken to protect the camera, hot lamps and electrical circuitry on the set from moisture.

Fig. 12.27. The outdoor tank for floating miniatures at the Pinewood Studios of the Rank Organization, England. Its width is 230 ft in the back narrowing to 110 ft in front, and its length is 196 ft. The backing is 240 ft wide by 60 ft high. The tank holds 800 000 gallons of water and takes five days to fill. Some idea of the size can be gained from the figures of the two workman standing just in front of the backing at center. (The Rank Organization.)

Miniatures underwater

Simulated underwater shots are sometimes required, as when a submarine is seen maneuvering 20 or 30 ft under the ocean's surface. These miniature vessels are pulled along piano-wire or mono-filament guide lines. Since the propellers are seen in these shots, the miniature must be rigged with an internal, battery-driven motor to drive the screws. The water is muddied or dyed to produce a realistically obscure view, which also serves to hide the guide and pull wires. If the submarine is supposed to be operating in fairly shallow water, attractive and realistic reflections can be added to the underside of its hull by slowly moving a tray at the bottom of the tank, into which broken pieces of mirror have been scattered. Overhead lights which shine down into the water will be reflected back in a broken pattern, as if from a sandy bottom. 'Cookies' can be operated in front of overhead lamps to break up the lighting pattern on the sides and top of the hull. Occasionally, underwater shots are photographed 'dry'. The submarine is suspended on wires in mid-air against a dark background. At the same time, ripple filters are moved slowly in front of the camera lens while

Fig. 12.28, part 1. A hanging miniature is a partially-constructed model which is interposed between a full-scale set and the camera. It is used as a kind of three-dimensional glass shot to add missing details or to replace image components. Here, an elaborate vaulted ceiling, built in miniature, is being added to a set on the production of *Monte Cristo*.

Fig. 12.28, part 2. The finished composite. Note the false perspective which is produced by continuously varying the scale of the hanging miniature.

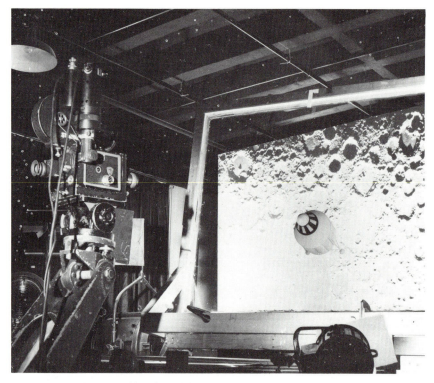

Fig. 12.29. Another type of hanging miniature. The three-dimensional space vehicle is attached to a sheet of glass and photographed against a photo-mural of the moon's surface. (National Film Board of Canada.)

underwater reflections and shadow patterns are added with 'cookies' and mirrors. Alternatively, underwater effects can be added through optical printing.

To finish off the illusion, the underwater set must be properly 'dressed' with rocks, sea flora and a sandy bottom if the vessel is to be shown operating near the ocean floor.

Hanging miniatures

Occasionally, a small miniature is positioned between the camera and the full-scale set during photography, so as to appear part of the background detail. This is called a 'hanging miniature' and serves the same function as a glass-shot. 'Hanging miniatures' are superior to glass-shot paintings in that they offer a three-dimensional quality and can be lit from several angles. However, their design and construction is quite complicated, since their scale and perspective lines must match those of the real set exactly.

Hanging miniatures are most commonly used to add ceiling detail (Fig. 12.27).

Electronic and computer systems

For more than 30 years, overly enthusiastic promoters have predicted the imminent replacement of photographic imaging systems by electronic ones. Today, seen in retrospect, their enthusiasms seem both technologically premature and economically unrealistic.

For the moment, film remains the favored recording medium wherever high image quality and the ability to spin off copies on a variety of formats is required, and it seems likely to remain so for several more years to come.

Be this as it may, a variety of marriages have *already* taken place between photographic, electronic, and computer technologies. Some of these are ill-advised matings, the long-term prospects for which do not seem bright. Other, more agreeable, marriages appear destined for a long and prosperous future. Some of the latter of these appear well suited for special-effects cinematography, and it is these which we will examine in this chapter.

Blue-screen preview systems

One of the most difficult problems which workers encounter in dealing with traveling-matte systems is that of envisaging and predicting what the final composite of foreground and background elements will look like. Directors, in particular, are reluctant to place artistic control in the hands of the special-effects supervisor, the latter of whom can only describe, with words, or storyboard sketches, the expected results. As for the effects supervisors themselves, it takes a great deal of experience before they can estimate and predict, with precision, the likely balance of perspective, brightnesses, lighting, motion parallax, color, hue and saturation, and other elements which exist between the different image elements.

In recent years, some special-effects workers have minimized this problem by using 'electronic preview systems' which produce a composite color image upon a video monitor in which the separate image elements are matted together. In some cases, the familiar 'chroma key' system, which is used commonly by local television stations, is employed for this purpose. A video camera (or video tap on a motion-picture camera) produces the image of the performer in front of a blue screen. A second camera (or a film chain) provides the background element, and the chroma-key system composites them, instantly, upon the video screen. Such a system was employed on the production of *Superman* to allow for preview of the numerous and complicated traveling-matte 'flying' shots which appear throughout the film.

A somewhat more elegant system was created for Francis Coppola's work at Zoetrope Studios in the early 1980s. It employs a system called the Ultimatte Electronic Compositor, invented by film and video engineer Petro Vlahos, and produces an extremely high-quality composite, in which the familiar matte line, typical of chroma key, is absent (Figs. 13.1–13.2, Plate 7).

Fig. 13.1. Director Francis Coppola (left) and engineer/inventor Petro Vlahos (right) stand in front of a rack-mounted Ultimatte compositor system used at Zoetrope Studios in Los Angeles. The Ultimatte allows for visualization of a finished traveling-matte composite prior to final photography. Trial runs of foreground and background elements can be viewed by the director and his associates on the video monitor, left rear, until just the right combination of image components, lighting color balance, and timing is found.

Of course, even the Ultimatte system is not good enough for the final motion-picture photography. Systems such as this are used solely for preview purposes. They convey, instantly, to both special-effects workers and the director, the appearance of the finished shot. Perspective, scale, brightness, hue, saturation, and motion-parallax relationships which exist between the different image elements can be appraised and changed instantly. Expensive errors are avoided and the best possible combination of elements can be made with confidence. Most important of all, directors are able to retain artistic control over the special-effects process.

Fig. 13.2. A performer is composited into a shot of a Las Vegas casino's neon sign, forty feet above the street. Engineer Clark Higgins adjusts controls on the Ultimatte compositor.

Assuming the continued, successful use of such preview systems, the next step in their development will be to relate their electronic 'pointer readings' for the various image elements, to the wedge tests made by the optical printing department. Quite possibly, the entire business of preparing wedge tests, and the processing and appraisal of those tests, can be eliminated. Should this be so, the speed with which both test and finished composites are made should be increased greatly, reducing the wait for rushes from the effects department, and minimizing the costs involved in such work.

The electronic storyboard

Conventional storyboards have been used for years in the production of both feature and non-theatrical motion pictures (Fig. 13.3). Numerous sketches, ranging in size from 3 × 5 to 8 × 10 inches, are prepared of each of the major set-ups in a sequence. These are assembled in order and pinned up onto cork boards where the director, art director, cinematographer and special-effects supervisor can view them. The order in which the sequences, scenes and shots appear can be changed by simply removing particular sets of sketches and moving them elsewhere. Complete sequences, or sections of sequences, can be removed altogether, or replaced with new sketches representing additional action. Storyboards are especially useful to special-effects workers in estimating the likely look of a sequence so that everybody on the production can see and agree upon the visual design, action, screen direction, and other variables involved.

At Francis Coppola's Zoetrope Studios, a unique electronic storyboard was created in 1981, for use by him on a number of productions, including *One From the Heart, Rumblefish, The Outsiders*, and *Cotton Club*. The electronic storyboard takes the form of a console at which both video and audio inputs can be mixed, arranged, re-arranged, removed, and inserted, just as with a conventional television mixer.

Fig. 13.3. Conventional storyboards have been part of motion picture planning practice for decades. These storyboard sketches outline an opening special-effects sequence from *One From the Heart.*

As in ordinary practice, hundreds of storyboard sketches are prepared, pinned up on to cork boards, and arranged in preliminary fashion to the satisfaction of the director and other creative supervisors on the production (Fig. 13.4). Once a fairly substantial number of sketches has been hung and approved, they are then numbered sequentially and removed. One by one, the individual sketches are then photographed with a video camera, and their individual images are recorded on digital frame-store disks.

Fig. 13.4. Production planning room at Zoetrope Studios, the walls of which are covered with elaborately detailed storyboard sketches for the production of *One From the Heart.*

The computer-controlled storage system of the electronic storyboard is capable of producing, at the push of a button, one single sketch from among several hundred, depending upon the wishes of the director. Once the sketches are placed into the computer's memory, all kinds of arrangements with regard to their appearance, disappearance, storage, and chronological order can be made. Finally, once a particular sequence of sketches has been determined, it is rendered fixed in the memory of the computer by another push of the button.

Fig. 13.5. The electronic storyboard machine at Zoetrope Studios. Engineers make the daily systems check of the components. At far left, the video camera which picks up and transmits images of storyboard sketches, art-work, and still photos to a digital frame store system housed in the console.

Other types of image material, such as polaroid shots and test footage from the special-effects laboratory machine, can be inserted into the tape-storage memory of the storyboard machine, and these materials can also be arranged in chronological order, being called forth automatically at the appropriate moment as the chronologically ordered sketches are produced.

All of the various image elements are displayed visually upon a color video monitor set into the face of the console (Figs. 13.5, 13.6 and 13.7). In addition, a rough audio-track which contains the script dialogue and proposed sound effects and music can be synchronized with the storyboard images, so that the sketches and test footage are produced upon the video screen in synchronism with the dialogue 'scratch track', from instant to instant.

By building into the electronic storyboard a blue-screen preview device such as the Ultimatte, described above, it is also possible to preview, at leisure, the various options available for the combining of image elements in a particular traveling-matte shot. Finally, it is possible for each of the various creative workers who use the machine to record into memory their own particular proposals regarding chronology, image design, photography, and such, for subsequent review and judgement by the director.

Fig. 13.6. A bank of ¾ in videocassette playback machines. Test footage made either with a conventional video camera, or with a video tap on the motion picture camera, is fed from these playback units into the electronic storyboard as needed.

Fig. 13.7. Director Coppola (left) and an associate discuss a sequence which they have just run on the electronic storyboard.

Taken as a whole, the electronic storyboard provides the ultimate machine for previewing the likely 'look' of the finished film. It assists the director in staging the various scenes and in selecting or rejecting particular scenes which are proposed in the script, depending upon their likely dramatic effectiveness in the finished film. It assists the art director, costumer and prop builders in the planning and execution of their work. In particular, it helps the special-effects supervisor – first, to design the effects shots, and second, to communicate to the director, in the most vivid and concrete kind of way, the supervisor's proposals, options, and intentions.

Motion-control systems

In previous chapters on fixed mattes and traveling mattes, we have referred to the occasional shot in which it is desirable to be able to move the camera, either in a pan, a tilt, or a dolly movement, over all components of the matte shot's composite image. Obviously, such a shot would require equipment which allows for precise, *repeatable* camera moves during each step of photography. In recent years, an ingenious

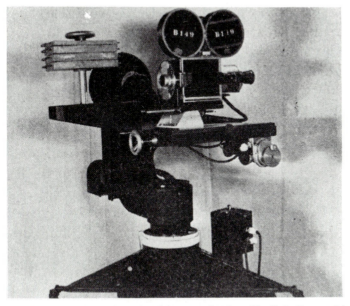

Fig. 13.8. An early motion-repeating system developed by O. L. Dupy at Metro-Goldwyn-Mayer Studios in 1949 for moving-camera matte-shots. Pan and tilt movements of the Bell & Howell camera generated electronic pulses which were recorded on an acetate recording disk. When the acetate was played back later, during photography of the matte painting, the laboratory camera made pan and tilt movements which were identical to those of the original live-action photography. (JSMPTE.)

technology, called 'motion control', has emerged and become available for just such moving-camera matte shots. Both complicated and expensive, 'motion control' systems have extended greatly the flexibility and versatility of conventional and traveling-matte systems.

In principle, there is nothing new about the motion-control of cameras. As early as 1949, O. L. Dupy of MGM Studios had constructed a motion-control system (sometimes called a 'repeater head') which allowed for pans and tilts over the different elements of painted matte composites.* The original camera moves over the live-action component were made with a camera mounted on a differentially-geared head. Camera movements were sensed by electrical motors attached to the head, changes in the position of the geared head producing voltage variations which were processed and transmitted to an acetate disk recorder. The recorder, powered by a common-drive system identical to that on the geared camera head, recorded signals which indicated camera tilt and pan changes during the original photography of the live-action component. Subsequently, during photography of the matte painting, the acetate disk was played back and the signals caused the camera head to make pan and tilt movements which were identical to those of the first exposure (Figs. 13.8 and 13.9).

Fig. 13.9. Acetate recording and reproducing apparatus for the 1949 MGM system, together with power supply, controls, amplifiers, and other electronic equipment in a portable cabinet. (JSMPTE.)

The maximum real-time rate of pan-and-tilt movements was 25° per second, which was more than ample for most kinds of shots. The system worked quite well for its time, although it was limited by the relatively unsophisticated kinds of electronic components then available in 1949, as well as the absence of mini and micro computers for control purposes, all of which precluded the kind of sophisticated motion-control photography which has become commonplace within the last decade.

* O. L. Dupy, 'A motion repeating system for special-effects photography', *JSMPTE*, March 1950, p. 290.

Some motion-control systems are quite modest, and allow only for pans and tilts over painted matte composites. Other, more complicated rigs, permit movements of the camera over the entire sound stage – longitudinally, laterally, and vertically. Typically, stepper motors are attached to all rotating shafts on the camera, on the camera's gear head, and on the dolly or crane on which the camera is supported. Stepper motors take their instructions from electrical pulses which are delivered, as needed, by a computer.* With each pulse, the stepper motor moves one or more increments, through whatever degrees of arc are desired in the motors' 360° revolution. The increments through which the rotor of each stepper motor can turn can be quite small – a fraction of a degree – in which case the movements of the camera's gear head and the camera crane will also be minute. Stepper motors also control the intermittent movement of the camera, allowing for synchronism between individual exposures and the movements of the camera and crane. Most important, once the total array of movements of the camera and the crane have been entered into the computer's memory, these movements can be repeated, over and over, with great precision. Some of these rigs are capable of repeating predetermined movements and positions to within 1/1000th of an inch, at any point in time, and in synchronism with the exposure of any particular frame of film.

Motion-control systems are used almost exclusively for the photography of inanimate art work and miniatures. If the miniatures are meant to move, turn, twist, cant, display lighting effects, or be animated in their structural features, then they, too, will be motion-controlled. They will be attached to a support which is capable of moving them in whatever manner is desired, and which carries electrical cables for any internal operations of the miniature. All of these motions can be made to repeat, in synchronism with particular moves of the camera, and the exposure of the film, frame by frame.

In no sense do the movements of the motion-control equipment occur in real time. On the contrary, most such equipment is *incapable* of operating in real time. The progress of a motion-control shot is painfully slow. A movement of the camera on its crane, across the sound-stage floor, photographing a shot which will last for five seconds on the screen, may take half a day's time to photograph.

The uses to which the equipment is put are varied. It is used, first, for multiple exposures of miniatures and their mattes. For example, on a first pass, the camera might photograph the miniature against a black backing, producing a self-matting color negative shot of the miniature. The motion-control system takes the camera back to start position, and the same run is made again, this time with a medium or high-contrast black-and-white stock in the camera, photographing the same miniature, in the same positions, relative to the same frame numbers, but this time with the miniature silhouetted against either a blue screen or a white screen. Still additional passes can be made, if required, for the photography of 'cover mattes'. Each time, the computer-directed apparatus returns the

* See, for example, Jerry Faughn *et al.*, 'Interfacing a stepper motor to your apple', *Cider*, October 1983, p. 122; and Joseph Long, 'Control your lab with a stepper motor', *Microsystems*, May 1984, p. 80.

camera to precisely the same place on the stage relative to the position of the miniature and in synchronism with the same frame number as occurred during previous exposures. The computer can be programmed so as to produce accelerations and decelerations of both camera and miniature components. The focus adjustment of the camera's lens is controlled by a separate stepper motor, and, if the camera features a swinging lens board to provide extra depth of field when passing close to a miniature, this, too, will be operated automatically upon instructions from the computer. A nodal point mount is used for the camera, and all pan-and-tilt moves are computer-controlled.

The image components and mattes which are produced in this manner can be later composited in the optical printer, as previously described. Alternatively, 'in-the-camera' composites of high precision are possible with such equipment, the fitting of the various image components together being made by the camera on successive passes, with appropriate lighting and/or silhouetting of the various image components and backgrounds occurring from one pass to the next. The number of elements and passes which have sometimes been photographed and composited using such equipment is staggering – scores of different elements being fitted together, piece by piece, exposure by exposure.

Motion-control equipment is also used for the greater-than-normal exposures which are necessary for deep-focus photography. In conventional, 'real-time' operation, the camera's 170° shutter provides an exposure time of about 1/50 second at 24 frames/second. By contrast, motion-control equipment is capable of opening the camera's shutter for far longer periods of time, as may be necessary for exposures using very small relative apertures and medium-speed color stocks. The motion-control computer functions as an intervalometer, instructing the motor driving the camera's shutter to stay open for whatever length of time is necessary. Conventionally, the f/stop is kept consistent throughout all of the various passes which the camera makes in photographing the various components of the matte shot. Changes in f/stop produce slight increases or decreases in image magnification which may be great enough to ruin the subsequent fitting together of the various mattes and image components.

Some motion-control units allow the camera operator to move the camera personally during the set-up run, either with conventional gear cranks or with joysticks, and to frame the shot through the viewfinder as the camera assembly moves very slowly across the stage towards the miniatures. The moves made by the human operator are recorded into the computer's memory and are played back for the operation of the equipment during photography. Other systems require that instructions for camera, crane, lens, shutter, and miniatures movements be given to the computer by means of a typewriter keyboard. Still other systems combine these capabilities, allowing the camera operator to make the first run, and to frame the shot in conventional fashion, then instructing the computer to 'even out' and 'sophisticate' all of the operator's camera moves, and to produce plotted motion curves, accelerations, and decelerations which are mathematically perfect.

Motion-control systems can also be used for the photography of moving, three-dimensional miniature vehicles and characters. By causing the object to move during part of the period when the shutter of the camera is open, an appropriate amount of blur can be introduced into the image, just as occurs during conventional, full-scale photography. The result is a quite convincing kind of movement on the screen which contrasts sharply with the stroboscopic, 'stuttering' effect which is produced by ordinary stop-frame photography. This kind of work is sometimes referred to as 'Go-Motion' photography.

Typical of the finest quality of motion-control equipment which is available today is that found at the Walt Disney Studios, where an entire stage has been set aside for their so-called 'ACES' system (Automatic Camera Effects System).*

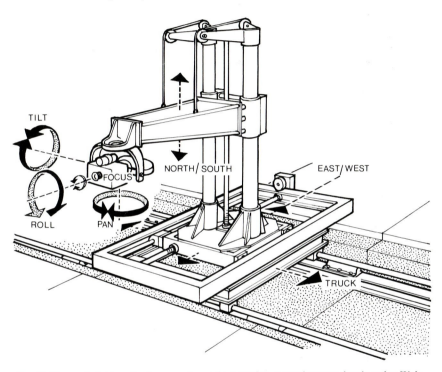

Fig. 13.10, part 1. Schematic diagram of a modern motion-control system developed at Walt Disney Studios. Designated as 'ACES' (Automatic Camera Effects System), the apparatus is capable of making repeatable moves 68 feet across the stage, as well as providing lateral and vertical movements of the crane, and pan, tilt, and roll movements of the camera.

The system consists, first, of a motion-picture camera mounted on a crane which can be made to move across the stage floor on precision rails (Figs. 13.10, parts 1 and 2). The camera can tilt and pan through 360°, and roll through 720° on each of these axes. The camera can also move vertically (North/South) a distance of four feet, laterally (East/West) a distance of four feet, and longitudinally, in a trucking motion across the

* The ACES system was conceived and designed for Art Cruickshank, Peter Ellenshaw and Eustace Lycett by Don Iwerks, Bob Otto, David Inglish, David Snyder and Steven Crane.

Fig. 13.10, part 2. The ACES system on stage undergoing alignment tests. Note computer monitors and keyboard controls at desk in foreground. A video tap in the camera allows operators to see the image as it is being photographed on film in the camera.

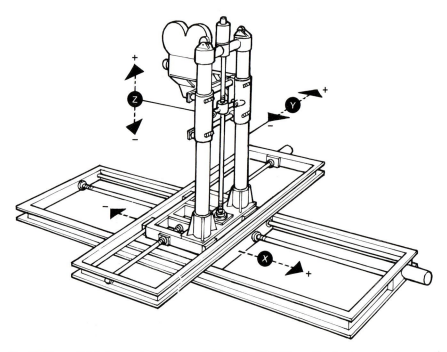

Fig. 13.10, part 3. Motion control is also available at the Walt Disney Studios for painted matte photography. The Matte-Scan camera crane, seen here in a schematic drawing, makes computer-programmed longitudinal, vertical and lateral moves relative to the matte board.

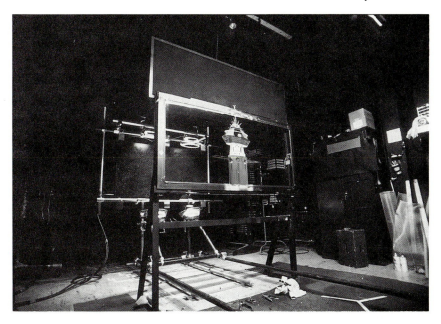

Fig. 13.10, part 4. Matte board assembly set up in multiplane fashion, for matte-shot photography with the Matte-Scan camera system. Front glass painting, right, obscures part of the star field painted on the back easel. The equipment is set for a painted matte shot for *The Black Hole*. (All photos Walt Disney Production.)

stage, a distance of 68 feet. The system also includes a second crane which carries the miniature(s) being photographed. The miniature(s) attached to it can be moved in yaw, pitch or roll fashion, and can be moved across the stage on a 30-foot set of rails (Fig. 13.10, part 4).

A video tap in the optical system of the camera allows the operator of the system to see the image being photographed on a video monitor. All movements of the camera crane and the miniatures crane are controlled by a minicomputer, as are adjustments of the camera's focus and film movement. The computer calculates all in-between increments of position and movement involved as the camera and the miniature pass through key positions on the stage floor, relative to each other. The computer makes such calculations for all of the axes of movement of all of the mechanical components. Sensors and limit switches prevent the camera crane from accidentally smashing into the miniature or other set pieces.

Unlike many other systems, a real-time rehearsal of a shot is possible, the composition and field of view of the shot being viewed on a video monitor by the system's operators during the continuous movement of the camera through its designated journey. The image on the video monitor may be recorded on videodisc or videotape, from moment to moment or from frame to frame, for subsequent replay and detailed study. Following video rehearsal of the shot, the camera can be returned to its start position, changes in the programming of the system can be made, and an instant replay of the camera moves can be executed, with precise repeatability of moves from frame to frame. This repeatability of positions and movements can be achieved with mechanical tolerances of the order of 1/100th of an inch.

Real-time photography of the shot is also possible. However, as is the case with much motion-control work, photography typically extends over a period of hours or longer. Some shots have lasted several days, the equipment being turned off overnight, the film left in the camera, and the system started up again the following morning without the loss of a single frame of film, and with the camera moving forward to the next increment of movement, position and photography from precisely the point at which it had been shut down the previous day.

Two blue screen backings are available for photography with the ACES system: a portable 16 × 25 foot screen, the lamps for which are operated with high-frequency a.c. current, and a 38 × 72 foot screen, movable on a 200-ft track, whose lamps are powered by d.c. current. For rear-projection photography, a process projector has been designed especially for the system. It provides for either 4 or 8-perforation pull-down formats, and is equipped with a 1600-watt Xenon lamp.

The moves of the various pieces of equipment through different positions on the stage can be designated 'by the number', the various positions, incremental moves and destinations being punched into the computer by means of a keyboard (Fig. 13.10, part 2). Fundamentally, the operator specifies to the computer a series of key camera positions, and the computer then calculates all in-between points automatically. Alternatively, the camera can be moved by jogging controls to whatever positions produce attractive and appropriate photographic compositions on the video monitor, and the computer can be instructed to automatically read into memory the position coordinates of the camera and the sequence of those coordinates which were involved.

The 35 mm camera employs a Richardson intermittent movement which is capable of either 4- or 8-perforation pull-down formats. The magazine capacity is 400 feet. The camera accepts either Leitz or Mitchell BNCR lenses, as well as a pitching (periscope) lens. Follow-focus for all lenses is automatically set and changed by the computer during photography. The camera is equipped with two shutters, the first a mechanical variable shutter (0–180°), and the second, an electronic shutter. Capping of the optical system by the electronic shutter is automatic during rewinding of the film.

Performance specifications for the system are as follows:

The camera mount

Axis	Travel	Positioning accuracy	Slew-rate
Pan	360°	0.01 degrees	36 degrees/second
Tilt	360°	0.01 degrees	36 degrees/second
Roll	720°	0.01 degrees	36 degrees/second

The camera carriage and crane

Axis	Travel	Positioning accuracy	Slew-rate
North-South	48''	0.01 inches	6 in/second
East-West	48''	0.01 inches	6 in/second
Truck	68'	0.01 inches	3 ft/second

The miniatures support and crane

Axis	Travel	Positioning accuracy	Slew-rate
Model truck	30'	0.01 inches	3 ft/second
Model pitch	90°	0.01 degrees	36 degrees/second
Model roll	90°	0.01 degrees	36 degrees/second
Model yaw	360°	0.01 degrees	36 degrees/second

The ACES camera system, which operates on-stage, is complemented and supported in the painted matte department by still another sophisticated motion-control rig, called the 'Matte-Scan System'.* This is comprised of a stop-motion camera mounted on a crane which photographs matte paintings which are mounted on a matte-board support. The camera crane is capable of making a variety of moves, depending upon the instructions it receives from a computer. The camera can be moved towards and away from the matte painting, and laterally (East/West) or vertically (North/South) across the painting's face (Fig. 13.10, parts 3 and 4). The apparatus includes a pin-registered rear-projection process projector. The system may be operated in multiplane fashion, with several layers of art-work 'stacked', one in front of the other. All moves by the camera are repeatable under computer control, the positioning of the mechanical components being achieved with tolerances in the order of 1/1000th of an inch. Instructions to the computer are made by means of either a teletype keyboard or by punched paper tape.

The Matte-Scan camera is a modified 35 mm Bell & Howell which provides either 4- or 8-perforation pull-down formats. It is powered by a stepper motor which can make exposures which range from infinitely long, in stop-motion fashion, to one-quarter second exposure per frame. Follow-focus and the stop-motion movement of the film are also computer-controlled.

Performance specifications for the system are as follows:

Axis	Length of moves	Positioning accuracy	Slew rate
X (truck)	71''	.001 inches	6 in/second
Y (East-West)	50''	.001 inches	6 in/second
Z (North-South)	26''	.001 inches	6 in/second

* The Matte-Scan system was conceived and designed for Harrison Ellenshaw by Don Iwerks, Bob Otto, and David Snyder.

Other fine motion-control systems have been created by the ILM group at Lucasfilm Ltd, by Apogee Inc., by Bo Ghering Productions, by Dream Quest, Elicon and other organizations (Fig. 13.12).

Today, many animation stands and optical printers also incorporate motion-control equipment which allows for complicated line-ups, printing operations, and camera moves to be executed under computer control in a fraction of the time previously required for manual operations.

Fig. 13.11. A very sophisticated motion-control camera system built at Industrial Light and Magic for use on Lucasfilm's productions of *The Empire Strikes Back*, and *Return of the Jedi*. The camera employs a 35 mm Vistavision format. Visual-effects supervisor Richard Edlund holds the system's remote control unit in his hand. (Courtesy Lucasfilm, Ltd.)

Despite the great flexibility which motion-control equipment brings to special-effects work, however, this is an expensive technology to buy or build, and the more complicated and versatile systems are simply not affordable for low or medium-budget production.

Electronic rotoscoping

The creation of a static, rotoscoped, matte edge is a relatively simple exercise, assuming that the two or more elements which are to be jig-sawed together do not move relative to one another. When they do move, however, a substantial amount of hard-drawn matte-work may be necessary to produce the scores, or even hundreds, of individual drawings which are required. This kind of work is not creative, but it does require precision, consistency, and a fair amount of expertise. It is time-consuming, and it is expensive.

Recently, the first of what might be called 'electronic rotoscoping' systems have been introduced to the trade. One of the most interesting of these is called STAR (Scene Tracking Auto Registration), developed by Bo Gehring Associates in California. The system allows for virtually automatic creation of moving matte-line edges which result from camera movements during original photography, and for the live-action component to be composited with computer graphics, or conventionally-painted elements. In practice, the live-action film is projected, one frame at a time, onto a digitizing tablet. The tablet, which is 30 × 40 inches in size, is claimed to be accurate to 1/1000 inch, and to produce an effective resolution of 30 000 by 40 000 points. Operation of the equipment requires establishment of four reference points within the scene, each of which lies in a different plane. Once these have been established, the computer automatically tracks movements made by the live action camera and relates them properly to positions of the complementary painted or computer-graphic art-work, and the matched, moving matte-line edges (Fig. 13.12).

Electronic-image compositors

Without doubt, of all the marriages between conventional cinematographic and electronic-imaging systems, the one which has been looked forward to most enthusiastically by the film-making community is that which would produce an 'electronic-image compositor'. This would be the electronic equivalent of the optical printer, using film as both the input and output recording medium, but performing all of the conventional optical printing manipulations electronically. Some designs envision a 'film-in/film-out' system, which would not require the intermediary storage of digitized data. Other designs assume the intermediary storage of data on magnetic tape or disc. Whatever the ultimate design, such an electronic optical printer would offer speed, convenience, and a preview capability far greater than that provided by contemporary optical printers. Hopefully, it would also offer lower costs to the motion-picture producer.

Over the last decade, a variety of different designs have been developed, and prototypes either built or attempted. Historically, some of the more important of these have been the Electronic Composite Photography and Image Modification System conceived by Petro Vlahos and Wilton R. Holm of the Research Center of the Association of Motion Picture and Television Producers, in association with Image Transform, Inc. Subsequent development of such a system was undertaken by Vlahos at the Vlahos-Gottschalk Corporation, and, so far, has surfaced in the form of the excellent Ultimatte analog video compositing system described elsewhere in this chapter.

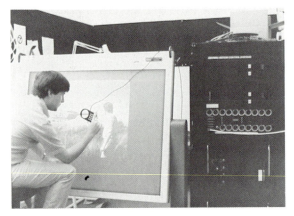

Fig. 13.12, part 1. A form of electronic rotoscoping developed at Bo Gehring Associates. The live-action scene, which is to be combined with either computer graphics or a painting, is rear-projected onto a high-resolution digitizing tablet.

Fig. 13.12, part 2. A special-effects worker establishes for computer-monitored reference points for objects lying in different planes within the live-action scene.

Fig. 13.12, part 3. Computer graphics are generated for compositing with the live-action component. (Courtesy Bo Gehring Associates.)

Another system was developed in prototype form by special-effects workers Frank Van Der Veer and Barry Nolan, and was used to create a half-dozen two-element composite images in the film production of *Flash Gordon*. The Van Der Veer compositor is a 'film-in/film-out system, employing both analog and digital image-processing techniques. The analog version of each frame of image is modified by digitized data generated from the image. The resulting modifications are presented on a 3300-line CRT tube where they are re-photographed onto film. The system is said to provide a high speed of operation, reportedly requiring a nine seconds processing time per frame.

Still another system has been developed at Pacific Electric Pictures Corporation and has been used in the production of composites for filmed television commercials. This system is one which stores digitized data taken from motion-picture images onto magnetic tape – as much as five miles of tape for one 30-second sequence!

Other well-known people at work on such a system include John Whitney, Jr, and Gary Demos at Digital Productions, and Ed Catmul, Alvy Ray Smith, David DeFrancesco and their associates at the Computer Development Division of Lucasfilm, Ltd. The Lucas system has been described in general terms as one which reads the input motion-picture images with a laser beam, converts the images into digital data which is manipulated electronically in a variety of artistically useful ways, and then laser-prints the resulting modified and composited images back onto motion-picture film.

So far as is known, all of the prototype systems currently in existence scan and reproduce their images with a resolution far greater than the 525-line system employed in American broadcast television. A discussion of scanning systems and video resolution is beyond the ambit of this book's text.* However, it is commonly held that a scanning resolution in excess of 1200 lines must be employed to avoid the detection of those lines when the final film image is projected onto a large theater screen. Eastman Kodak's type 5247 color negative has been said to have an equivalent resolution of about 1400 lines. However, a discussion of only resolution does not take into account numerous other peculiarities of photographic image formation. Most engineers, both electronic and photographic, agree that a great deal of pioneering work will have to be done before electronic imaging can compete realistically with that of contemporary photographic systems, both with regard to image quality and to the per-frame processing time required to turn out footage. Workers in the field disagree over the likely efficiency of these proposed systems, but at least one special-effects veteran, Linwood Dunn, has estimated that if an electronic compositor could turn out one frame of finished film per minute, it could compete realistically with photographic optical printers.

There is no question that the introduction and perfection of an electronic optical printer could theoretically revolutionize the process of composite cinematography and optical printing. In addition to all of the capabilities of

---

* For an extended discussion of the issues involved, see Chuck Champlin, Jr., 'The electronic optical printer', *American Cinematographer*, April 1983, p. 76.

a modern optical printer, such a system would be able to enhance photographic images, minimize grain, add color to black-and-white images or alter colors radically, multiply image elements to whatever extent desired, correct over- and under-exposure, and remove scratches or wires from within the picture area. It is even theoretically possible that such a device could separate designated foreground details out of the background without the need for blue-screen backings, and that computer software could be designed to accomplish this, more-or-less automatically, with a minimum of human instruction. 'With such a system, the images of expensive miniatures, set pieces, props, crowds, water and sky scenes, and the like might be 'stockpiled' and retrieved at will for use in new films! In theory, at least, all things are possible with such a system.

Whether such a piece of equipment is technologically feasible, and, if so, whether it will prove to be both practical and competitive, in quality and in cost, when compared with contemporary optical printing, remains to be seen.

Bibliography

The bibliography which follows is designed to supplement and amplify the material presented in the text. It covers a period of 75 years, from 1909 to 1984, and cites approximately 600 periodical articles (of which some are duplicated in more than one category), 19 books, 40 book articles, 16 unpublished research papers and two monographs.

Insofar as possible, items have been categorized according to subject matter. However, many articles review processes other than those indicated by the subject heading under which they are listed. Annotation has been limited to those items whose content could not be inferred easily from the titles.

The bibliography is a selective one from which 10 types of articles are excluded: mechanical effects; set construction techniques other than for miniatures; time-lapse cinematography; live television effects; amateur cinematography unless quite advanced; cinephotomicrography; animated cartoon production; high-speed cinematographic effects; routine production lighting effects; and foreign-language periodical literature.

Books

Agel, Jerome, *The Making of Kubrick's 2001.* New York: New American Library, 1970

Bessy, Maurice, *Les Truquages au Cinéma.* Paris: Les Editions Prisma, 1951

Bessy, Maurice and Lo Duca, Giuseppe, *Georges Méliès, Mage.* Paris: Les Editions Prisma, 1945

Brodbeck, Emil, *Movie and Videotape Special Effects.* New York: Amphoto, 1968

Brosnan, John, *Movie Magic.* New York: St. Martin's Press, 1974

Bulleid, Henry A. V., *Special Effects in Cinematography.* London: Fountain Press, 1954

Bulleid, Henry A. V., *Trick Effects with the Cine Camera.* London: Link House Publications, 1936

Caunter, Julien, *How to Make Movie Magic.* London: Focal Press, 1971

Clark, Frank P., *Special Effects in Motion Pictures.* New York: SMPTE, 1966

Dunn, Linwood G., and Turner, George E. (Ed.), *The ASC Treasury of Visual Effects.* Hollywood: American Society of Cinematographers, 1983

Finch, Christopher, *Special Effects: Creating Movie Magic.* New York: Abbeville Press, 1984

Hotschewar, M. V., *Filmtricks und Trickfilme.* Dusseldorf: Knapp, 1954

Monier, Pierre, *Des Effets Spéciaux.* Paris: Publications Photo-Cinéma Paul Montel, 1968

Perisic, Zoran, *Special Optical Effects in Film.* London: Focal Press, 1980

Schechter, Harold and Everitt, David, *Film Tricks: Special Effects in the Movies*. New York: Harlin Quist, 1980

Seeber, Guido, *Der Trickfilm in Seinen Grundsatzlichen Moglichkeiten*. Berlin: Lichtbild-buhne, 1927

Stuler, Alexander, *Filmtricks und Trickfilme*. Knapp, Halle, 1937

Whitfield, Stephen E. and Roddenberry, Gene, *The Making of Star Trek*. New York: Ballantine, 1968

Wilkie, Bernard, *Creating Special Effects for TV and Films*. London: Focal Press, 1977

Wilkie, Bernard, *The Technique of Special Effects in Television*. London: Focal Press, 1971

Unpublished research papers

Azarmi, Mehrdad, 'Optical effects cinematography – its development, methods and techniques'. Unpublished Doctoral Dissertation, University of Southern California, 1973

Baker, Larry Nile, 'A history of special effects cinematography in the United States, 1895–1914'. Unpublished Master's Thesis, West Virginia University, 1969

Christophersen, Sverre Haakon, 'A study of current methods and techniques used in the creation of matte shots for films'. Unpublished Master's Thesis, University of Southern California, 1952

Clark, Frank, 'Special effects in motion pictures: A study of some methods of producing mechanical special effects'. Unpublished Master's Thesis, University of Southern California, 1963

Elgabri, Ali Z., 'A bibliography of special effects patents'. Unpublished research paper, Dept of Theater Arts, University of California, Los Angeles, 1963

Hilfinger, Harrison Penrod, 'A study of the life and writings of Lewis W. Physioc as they relate to the cinema'. Unpublished research paper, Dept of Cinema, University of Southern California, 1940

Hilfinger, Harrison Penrod, 'A study of the significance and application of special effects to the cinema'. Unpublished Master's Thesis, University of Southern California, 1942

Hilfinger, Harrison Penrod, 'A survey of contemporary methods for the production of special effects'. Unpublished research report, Dept of Cinema, University of Southern California, 1941

Kelley, David, 'Front-screen projection as a film production technique'. Unpublished Master's Thesis, Michigan State University, 1971

Lehman, Michael F., 'The microdensity of image boundaries fabricated by the color-difference blue-screen traveling-matte process'. Unpublished Bachelor of Arts thesis, Rochester Institute of Technology, 1981

Lunette, Ernestine, 'Méliès, magician of the movies'. Unpublished Master's Thesis, American University, 1967

Mauk, William, 'In-the-camera matte techniques'. Unpublished Master's Thesis, University of Kansas, 1969

Mercer, John, 'Optical effects and film literacy'. Unpublished Doctoral Dissertation, University of Nebraska at Lincoln, 1953

Poe, Robert, 'History and survey of optical special effects printing in theatrical films'. Unpublished Master's Thesis, University of Southern California, 1964

Rahman, Badia, 'An inexpensive optical printer'. Unpublished research report, Dept of Speech and Dramatic Art, University of Iowa, 1965

Rahman, Badia, 'An investigation of the Schüfftan system for low budget film production'. Unpublished Master's Thesis, University of California, Los Angeles, 1965

Monographs

Barry, Iris, *Georges Méliès, Magician and Film Pioneer*. New York: The Museum of Modern Art Library Publication, 1939

Elgabri, Ali, *A Bibliography of Special Effects Patents*. Columbus: The Department of Photography and Cinema, Ohio State University (1969)

Articles in books

Alton, John, 'Special illumination', *Painting with Light*. New York: The Macmillan Co., 1949, pp. 57–59. Treats rear projection briefly

Anderson, Howard A. Jr., 'Miniatures', *The ASC Treasury of Visual Effects*. Hollywood: American Society of Cinematographers, 1983, pp. 183–192

Anonymous, 'Background process', *American Cinematographer Manual*. Hollywood: American Society of Cinematographers, 1960, pp. 305–320

Anonymous, 'Day for night cinematography', *American Cinematographer Manual*. Hollywood: American Society of Cinematographers, 1960, pp. 384–387

Anonymous, 'Traveling matte systems', *American Cinematographer Manual*. Hollywood: American Society of Cinematographers, 1960, pp. 365–369

Bennett, Colin Noel, 'Trick kinematography', *The Handbook of Kinematography*. London: Kinematograph Weekly, 1911, pp. 85–98

Bennett, Colin Noel, 'Trick subjects', *The Guide to Kinematography*. London: E. T. Heron & Co., 1917, pp. 59–65

Cameron, James R. and Dubray, Joseph A., 'Trick photography', *Cinematography and Talkies*. Woodmont, Conn.: Cameron Publishing Co., n.d., pp. 129–139

Carrick, Edward (Edward Craig), 'Backings and trick shots', *Designing for Films*. London: Studio Publications, 1949, pp. 96–104

Chambers, Gordon A., 'Process photography', *Cinematic Annual II*. Hollywood: American Society of Cinematographers, 1931, pp. 223–227

Clarke, Charles, 'Putting clouds into exterior scenes', *The Technique of Motion Picture Production*. New York: Interscience Publishers, Inc., 1944, pp. 20–23

Clarke, Charles, 'Special photographic effects', *Professional Cinematography*. Hollywood: American Society of Cinematographers, 1964, pp. 152–167

Croy, Homer, 'How trick pictures are made' and 'The things that mystify audiences', *How Motion Pictures are Made*. New York: Harper & Bros., 1918, pp. 153–211

Cruickshank, Art, 'Combining Animation with live action', *The ASC Treasury of Visual Effects*. Hollywood: American Society of Cinematographers, 1983, pp. 241–246

Dunn, Linwood G., 'Cinemagic of the optical printer', *American Cinematographer Manual*. Hollywood: American Society of Cinematographers, 1960, pp. 360–364

Edlund, Richard (Don Shay, Ed), 'The Empire Strikes Back', *The ASC Treasury of Visual Effects*. Hollywood: American Society of Cinematographers, 1983, pp. 265–262

Edouart, Faricot, 'The Paramount transparency process projection equipment', *The Technique of Motion Picture Production*. New York: Interscience Publishers, Inc., 1944, pp. 104–109

Gregory, Carl Louis, 'Trick work and double-exposure', *Motion Picture Photography*. New York: New York Institute of Photgraphy, 1920, pp. 267–287

Henney, Keith and Dudley, Beverly, 'Motion picture photography – process photography', *Handbook of Photography*. New York: Whittlesey House, 1939, pp. 702–707

Hulfish, David S., 'Trick pictures', *Motion Picture Work*. Chicago: American School of Correspondence, 1913, Part II, pp. 155–162

Ives, C. E., Muehler, L. E. and Crabtree, J. J., 'Making a fade-out by after-treatment', *Cinematographic Annual II*. Hollywood: American Society of Cinematographers, 1931, pp. 35–45

Jones, Bernard E., 'Making trick films', *The Cinematograph Book*. London: Cassell & Co., 1915, pp. 186–193

Knechtel, Lloyd, 'Optical printing', *Cinematographic Annual II*. Hollywood: American Society of Cinematographers, 1931, pp. 267–270

Lescarboura, Austin C., 'Tricks of the screen', *Behind the Motion Picture Screen*. New York: Scientific American Publishing Co., 1921, pp. 184–202

Levitan, Eli L., 'The optical printer', 'The bipack', *Animation Techniques and Commercial Film Production*. New York: Reinhold Publishing Corp, 1962, pp. 73–95

Lutz, E. G., 'Trick cinematography' and 'The unusual in camera work', *The Motion Picture Cameraman*. New York: Charles Scribner's Sons, 1927, pp. 99–141

McKay, Herbert, 'Trick work', *The Handbook of Motion Picture Photography*. New York: Falk Publishing Co., 1927, pp. 211–217

McKay, Herbert, 'Trick work', *Motion Picture Photography for the Amateur*. New York: Falk Publishing Co., 1924, pp. 184–197

Madsen, Roy, 'Multiple exposure techniques', *Animated Film*. New York: Interland Publishing Co., 1969, pp. 159–170

Monier, Pierre, 'Special tricks and effects', *The Complete Technique of Making Films*. London: Focal Press, 1959, pp. 178–209

Sersen, Fred, 'Making matte shots', *Cinematographic Annual II*. Hollywood: American Society of Cinematographers, 1931, pp. 87–92

Sersen, Fred, 'Special photographic effects', *The Technique of Motion Picture Production*. New York: Interscience Publishers, Inc., 1944, pp. 37–42

Spencer, D. A. and Waley, H. D. 'Cartoons and trickwork', *The Cinema Today*. London: Oxford University Press, 1939, pp. 126–142

Stull, William, 'Process cinematography', *The Encyclopedia of Photography*, VIII. New York: National Educational Alliance, 1943, pp. 2994–3005

Talbot, Frederick A., 'Trick pictures and how they are produced', *Motion Pictures – How They are Made and worked*. Philadelphia: Lippincott Co., 1912, pp. 197–263

Van der Veer, Frank, 'Matte painting techniques', *The ASC Treasury of Visual Effects*. Hollywood: American Society of Cinematographers, 1983, pp. 167–174

Wade, Robert J., 'Special scenic effects', *Designing for TV*. New York: Pellegrini and Cudahy, 1952, pp. 113–125

Wellman, Harold, 'Composite process photography', *The ASC Treasury of Visual Effects*. Hollywood: American Society of Cinematographers, 1983, pp. 211–220

Westheimer, Joseph, 'Optical effects', *The ASC Treasury of Visual Effects*. Hollywood: American Society of Cinematographers, 1983, pp. 229–236

Wheeler, Leslie, 'Trick photography', *Principles of Cinematography*. London: The Fountain Press, 1953, pp. 435–440

Articles in journals

Equipment

Gentleman, Wally, 'Motor drive pan, tilt and rotation devices for a motion-picture camera', *Journal SMPTE*, April 1965, Part I, p. 332

Kennedy, Sanford, 'Special equipment for filming *Star Trek – the Motion Picture*', *American Cinematographer*, Feb. 1980, p. 156

Kenworthy, N. Paul Jr., 'The Kenworthy Snorkel camera system today', *American Cinematographer*, August 1973, p. 1002

Kenworthy, N. Paul Jr., 'The new Kenworthy Snorkel-B camera system', *American Cinematographer*, March 1976, p. 332

Kiel, John P., 'A 35 mm Process Camera', *Journal SMPTE*, 55:551–8, May 1951. See also Kiel, 'The Acme process camera', *American Cinematographer*, Oct. 1951, p. 401.

Nettmann, Ernst (Bob), 'Pitching lens – A unique and versatile optical relay system', *American Cinematographer*, Jan. 1980, p. 82

Palen, Vern, 'Integrated design of animated film equipment', *Journal SMPTE*, April 1957, p. 197. See also Palen, 'The new Oxberry combination 35 mm/16 mm process camera', *American Cinematographer*, May 1956, p. 302

Reichard, Edward, 'Progress report: special effects', *Journal SMPTE*, May 1971, p. 348; and May 1972, p. 347

Ryan, Roderick T., 'Progress report: motion pictures', *Journal SMPTE*, May 1981, p. 370

Samuelson, David W., 'Introducing the Louma Crane', *American Cinematographer*, Dec. 1979, p. 1226

Scobey, Fred J., 'Progress report: special effects', *Journal SMPTE*, May 1978, p. 281

Winkle, Ed, 'Applied rod lens telescope cinematography (or 'How to out-Snorkel the Snorkel')', *American Cinematographer*, August 1977, p. 828

Registration procedures for special-effects cinematography

Ji-Zong, Wu, Norman, Richard N. and Carson, John F., 'A simple instrument for measuring image steadiness in 16 mm motion-picture cameras', *Journal SMPTE*, July 1982, p. 644

Kiel, John P., 'Film registration systems used in process photography', *Journal SMPTE*, July 1962, p. 493

Robertson, A. C., 'Pin registration', *Journal SMPTE*, Feb. 1963, p. 75

Shea, Robert P., 'Procedures of registration in process photography', *Journal SMPTE*, Oct. 1955, p. 559
Zavada, Roland J., 'Challenges to the concept of cancellation', *Journal SMPTE*, Dec. 1981, p. 1173

Fundamentals of special-effects cinematography

Abbott, L. B., 'The cameraman and special photographic effects', *American Cinematographer*, Oct. 1975, p. 1150
Anonymous, 'What you can produce on an animation stand', *International Photographer*, Dec. 1959, p. 18
Bellman, Kenneth and Wilson, Donald, 'Independent frame film production', *British Kinematography*, Nov. 1949, p. 141
Brockway, William W., 'Television and motion picture processes', *Hollywood Quarterly*, Oct. 1945, p. 85–94
Chamber, Gordon A., 'Process photography', *Journal SMPTE*, June 1932, p. 782
Claudy, C. H., 'Motion picture magic', *Scientific American*, May 15, 1915, p. 454. See also Claudy, 'Motion picture magic', *Scientific American Supplement*, Sept. 18, 1915, p. 184
Dunn, Linwood, 'Getting the most out of special effects', *The Cinemeditor*, Spring 1964, p. 9, and Summer 1964, p. 9
Gentleman, Wally, 'Elementary motion-picture design perspective', *Journal SMPTE*, August 1963, p. 609
Gentleman, Wally, 'Special photographic effects as an aid to low-budget production', *Journal SMPTE*, July 1962, p. 487
Gordon, Bert, 'Perspective makes the difference in special effects', *American Cinematographer*, Sept. 1965, p. 570
Gregory, Carl Louis, 'Trick photography', *Transactions, SMPTE*, No. 25, Sept. 1926, p. 99
Gregory, Carl Louis, 'Trick photography methods summarized', *American Cinematographer*, June 1926, p. 9
Harvey, Herk, and Lacey, Charles, 'Systematic control for special effects in 16 mm production', *American Cinematographer*, March 1956, p. 162
Howard, T. W. and Junge, Alfred, 'The rational application of special processes to film production', *British Kinematography*, Sept. 1951, p. 69
Jackman, F. W., 'The evolution of special-effects cinematography from an engineering viewpoint', *Journal SMPTE*, Sept. 1937, p. 293
Jackman, F. W., 'The special effects cinematographer', *American Cinematographer*, Oct. 1932, p. 12
Kellogg, Ray and Abbott, L. B., 'Some special photographic effects used in motion picture production', *Journal SMPTE*, Feb. 1955, p. 57. Reprinted in *American Cinematographer*, Oct. 1957, p. 662
Loring, Charles, 'The cinema workshop – special effects', *American Cinematographer*, June 1947, p. 208. Elementary techniques
Moultrie, F. C., 'Special effects for the amateur', *American Cinematographer*, Nov. 1945, p. 388. A review of in-the-camera effects available to the advanced amateur or the small commercial film producer.
Norling, J. A., 'Trick and process cinematography', *Journal SMPE*, Feb. 1937, p. 136
Patel, Dayabhai, 'Special photographic effects', *American Cinematographer*, June 1957, p. 379. Special-effects work in India
Rowan, Arthur, 'The function of special effects in today's movies', *American Cinematographer*, August 1953, p. 380
Sersen, Fred M., 'Special photographic effects', *Journal SMPE*, June 1943, p. 374
Spooner, A. M., 'Special effects for television and electronic films', *British Kinematography*, Feb. 1956, p. 41
Theisen, Earl, 'In the realm of tricks and illusions', *International Photographer*, June 1934, p. 8. A history of special-effects cinematography which enumerates several patents in the field
Walker, Vern, 'Special process technic', *Journal SMPE*, May 1932, p. 662
Waller, Fred, 'Illusions in cinematography', *Transactions, SMPTE*, No. 29, July 1927, p. 61
Waller, Fred, 'The needs of a trick photographer', *Transactions SMPTE*, No. 32, Sept. 1927, p. 663
Westheimer, Joseph, 'Principles of special photographic effects', *Journal SMPTE*, Dec. 1954, p. 217

Glass and mirror-shots

Clarke, Charles G., 'Cinematography in the Hollywood studios (1942): putting clouds into exterior scenes', *Journal SMPE,* August 1942, p. 92

Clarke, Charles G., 'Clouds made to order', *American Cinematographer,* July 1941, p. 315. See also Clarke, *American Cinematographer,* Oct. 1959, p. 611

Harmer, Paul R., 'Glass miniature and projection combined', *International Photographer,* Nov. 1934, p. 12

Henry, Joseph, 'Magic without mattes', *American Cinematographer,* Dec. 1961, p. 730

Horn, R. C., 'It's done with mirrors', *American Cinematographer,* Dec. 1956, p. 728

Static matte shots: 'in the camera and bi-pack printing

Anonymous, 'Disney's new matte scan system', *American Cinematographer,* Jan. 1980, p. 68

Anonymous, 'Ray Mamme's inventions', *International Photographer,* June 1933, p. 17. Description of the Mamme 'reversible matte process' and 'composite reduction process'

Anonymous, 'Special effects at RKO', *International Photographer,* Dec. 1940, p. 4. The use of matte shots at RKO

Bartholowsky, J. H., 'Plastic matte shots', *International Photographer,* Oct. 1940, p. 7

Bowie, Les (interview), 'Mattes and composites for *Superman, American Cinematographer,* Jan. 1979, p. 52

Campbell, Arthur J., 'Making matte shots', *American Cinematographer,* Dec. 1934, p. 347

Cline, Richard, 'Bi-pack effects with a bolex', *American Cinematographer,* March 1964, p. 140

Day, W. Percy, 'The origin and development of the matte shot process', *British Kinematography,* Sept. 1948, p. 74

Dupy, O. L., 'A motion repeating system for special effect photography', *Journal SMPTE,* March 1950, p. 290. A motion repeating system which permits changes in camera position while photographing the components of a static matte shot

Ellenshaw, Harrison, 'Creating the matte paintings for *The Empire Strikes Back',* American Cinematographer,* June 1980, p. 582

Ellenshaw, Harrison (interview), 'Making the unreal real with matte paintings', *American Cinematographer,* Jan. 1980, p. 70

Ellenshaw, Peter (interview), 'Designing a deep space world for *The Black Hole',* American Cinematographer,* Jan. 1980, p. 28

Fisher, Bob, 'Magical matte paintings for *The Wiz',* American Cinematographer,* Nov. 1978, p. 1078

Foster, Frederick, 'Mattes, miniatures and meticulous cinematography', *American Cinematographer,* March 1950, p. 82

Hague, E., 'Painted matte shots', *British Kinematography,* Dec. 1951, p. 166

Kaskin, Byron, 'Making modern matte shots', *American Cinematographer,* Nov. 1939, p. 493 and Jan 1940, p. 29

Hoke, Ira B., 'The cinema art service', *International Photographer,* April 1929, p. 12. Descriptions of the painted matte work of Lewis W. Physioc at Tec-Art Studios

Maxwell, Dennis D., and Swaim, Don L., 'Camera becomes printer and titler', *American Cinematographer,* June 1956, p. 378. Freeze-frame effects achieved with a production camera

Sersen, Fred, 'Making matte shots', *American Cinematographer,* July 1929, p. 31

Sullivan, Tom, 'Matte work for *The Blue and the Gray',* American Cinematographer,* March, 1983, p. 40

Whitlock, Albert, 'Reincarnating an 800-foot giant superstar', American Cinematographer, Jan. 1976, p. 38

Whitlock, Albert, 'Special photographic effects', *American Cinematographer,* Nov. 1974, p. 1330

Optical printing

Anonymous, 'The Acme-Dunn optical printer', *International Photographer,* March 1944, p. 18

Anonymous, 'Unique mini optical printer for super 8 and 16 mm', *American Cinematographer,* May 1975, p. 552

Anonymous, 'Printer speeds film editing', *Project Engineering*, July 1957, p. 161. Description of the Oxberry optical printer

Billings, Jack T., 'An improved method for critical focus of motion picture optical printers', *Journal SMPTE*, August, 1971, p. 624

Blair, Iain, 'Optical "illusions"', *On Location*, Oct. 1983, p. 76. A review of current optical printing work in Los Angeles and New York

Browning, Irving, 'Optical effects with any camera', *American Cinematographer*, June 1950, p. 198

Brunel, Christopher, 'Is there a doctor in the optical house', *American Cinematographer*, Sept. 1978, p. 888

Carter, William D., 'Wetprinting, the state of the art', *Journal SMPTE*, Sept. 1979, p. 600

Champlin, Chuck Jr., 'The electronic optical printer', *American Cinematographer*, April 1983, p. 78

Cowling, Herford Tynes, 'For trick work, Mr. Fred A. Barber announces the perfection of a wonderful new optical printer', *American Cinematographer*, March 1928, p. 7

Craik, Bert, 'Optical Printing – Its Uses', *Cine Technician*, Feb. 1936, p. 94

DeBurgh, Paul, 'Optical Printing', *Cine Technician*, May–June 1952, p. 66

Draper, William, 'Factory methods come to pictures', *International Photographer*, April 1940, p. 11. Description, by the author, of his design for an optical printer

Dunn, Linwood, 'Historic facts about the Acme-Dunn optical printer', *American Cinematographer*, May 1981, p. 479

Dunn, Linwood, 'The new Acme-Dunn optical printer', *American Cinematographer*, Jan. 1944, p. 11. See also Dunn, 'The new Acme-Dunn printer', *Journal SMPE*, April 1944, p. 204

Dunn, Linwood, 'Optical printer Handy Andy', *International Photographer*, June 1938, p. 14

Dunn, Linwood, 'Optical printing and technic', *Journal SMPE*, Jan. 1936, p. 54

Dunn, Linwood, 'Optical printing and technique', *American Cinematographer*, March 1934, p. 444

Dunn, Linwood, 'Tricks by optical printing', *American Cinematographer*, April 1934, p. 487

Gerstle, Ralph, 'Optical effects', *Films in Review*, April 1954, p. 171

Gordon, James, 'Contact printer for special effects', *American Cinematographer*, Nov. 1948, p. 375

Gregory, Carl Louis, 'An optical printer for trick work', *Journal SMPE*, April 1928, p. 419. See also Gregory, 'Optical printer for trick work', *Motion Picture Projectionist*, Jan. 1929, p. 7

Hartline, Kack, 'A new 16 mm optical printer', *American Cinematographer*, July 1944, p. 232. Description of a 16 mm optical printer developed by Dyatt Productions

Hitchins, A. B., 'Duplex optical printers', *Transactions of the SMPE*, Vol. 11, No. 32, 1927, p. 771

Hrastnik, Walter, 'Wet printing of motion-picture films with liquid application on a variable speed step-optical printer', *Journal SMPTE*, July 1977, p. 473

Knechtel, Lloyd, 'Optical printing', *International Photographer*, July 1930, p. 12

Landsman, Joseph K., 'The new Oxberry Model 5117 optical printer', *American Cinematographer*, June 1969, p. 566

Levy, Maurice, 'Optical effects for TV films and commercials', *American Cinematographer*, June 1960, p. 366

Lewell, John, 'Optical compositing and additional effects for *Jaws 3-D*', *American Cinematographer*, July 1983, p. 69

Lewis, John H., 'Additive exposures in process photography', *Journal SMPE*, June 1962, p. 449

Ott, Howard F., 'Liquid gate for optical printing', *Journal SMPTE*, April 1970, p. 333

Otwell, Harold M., 'A method for producing 16 mm location opticals', *Journal UFPA*, June 1949, p. 8

Palen, Vern, 'A newly designed optical printer', *Journal SMPTE*, Feb. 1958, p. 98. Description of the Oxberry 16 mm–35 mm optical printer

Palen, Vern, 'Saving scenes with opticals', *American Cinematographer*, Feb. 1964, p. 92

Reichard, Edward H., 'Progress report: motion pictures', *Journal SMPTE*, May 1, 1971, p. 348. Description of the Acme and Research Products optical printers etc.

Reichard, Edward H., 'Progress report: motion pictures', *Journal SMPTE*, May 1972, p. 346. Description of the Producers Service Co. optical printer and the Consolidated Industries wet-gate blow-up optical printer

Ryan, Roderick T., 'Progress report: motion pictures', *Journal SMPTE,* May 1981, p. 370. Description of the Oxberry multihead optical printer

Scobey, Fred J., 'Progress report: motion pictures', *Journal SMPTE,* May 1978, p. 281. A description of various new examples of visual-effects equipment, especially as used on particular recent productions

Scheib, Harold, A., 'A new concept of optical printer construction', *Journal SMPTE,* July 1965, p. 597

Sherwood, Larry, 'Editing and photographic embelishments as applied to 16 mm industrial and educational motion pictures', *Journal SMPE,* Dec. 1943, p. 476

Skittrell, Alfred C., 'Optical printing and optical printers', *Cine Technician,* Dec.–Jan. 1937–1938, p. 175

Sobel, Nat, 'The new visual idiom', *Journal SMPTE,* June 1951, p. 642, Review of optical effects available to motion-picture and television producers

Stockert, Henry A., 'Getting the most out of optical effects', *American Cinematographer,* Dec. 1965, p. 790

Van Trees, James Jr., 'Optical printing', *International Photographer,* June 1942, p. 18

Wade, Louise, 'Optical effects for *Return of the Jedi*', *American Cinematographer,* June 1983, p. 95

Walker, Vernon, 'Rhythmic optical effects for musical pictures', *American Cinematographer,* Dec. 1936, p. 504

Westheimer, Joseph, 'Optical magic for *The Muppet Movie*', *American Cinematographer,* July 1979, p. 706

Zavada, Roland J., 'Challenges to the concept of cancellation', *Journal SMPTE,* Dec. 1981, p. 1173

Zech, Harry, 'Making wipes in the printer', *American Cinematographer,* Dec. 1941, p. 574

Traveling mattes

Alexander, Joseph, 'An infrared traveling matte system with electronic masking', *Journal SMPTE,* June 1979, p. 410

Anonymous, 'Bag of tricks is emptied for *Mary Poppins*', *The Cinemeditor,* Summer 1964, p. 12

Anonymous, 'The dancing shoes', *American Cinematographer,* Sept. 1949, p. 318. Reprinted in *International Projectionist,* Nov. 1949, p. 20. A description of the 'dancing shoes' traveling matte sequence in the production', *Barkleys of Broadway*

Anonymous, 'Traveling matte systems', *American Cinematographer,* Sept. 1962, p. 538

Bartlerr, Dennis, 'Lighting and photographing traveling matte scenes', *American Cinematographer,* June 1981, p. 592

Beyer, Walter, 'Traveling matte photography and the blue screen system', *American Cinematographer,* Oct. 1963, p. 590; Jan. 1964, p. 34; April 1964, p. 208; May 1964, p. 266; Sept. 1964, p. 502; and Oct. 1964, p. 564

Beyer, Walter, 'Traveling matte photography and the blue screen system', *Journal SMPTE,* March 1965, p. 217

Blalack, Robert, 'Composite optical and photographic effects for *Star Wars*', *American Cinematographer,* July 1977, p. 706

Broggie, Michael, 'From gridiron to traveling matte', *The Cinemeditor,* Summer 1968, p. 14

Cruickshank, Art. 'In the land of magical effects', *IATSE Official Bulletin,* Spring 1969, p. 32

Dunning, C. Dodge, 'Composite photography', *Transactions SMPE,* No. 36, Sept. 1928, p. 975. See also Dunning 'Composite photography', *American Cinematographer,* Feb. 1929, p. 14. Description of all widely-used composite processes including the 1927 Dunning composite process

Dunning, Carroll H., 'Dunning process and process backgrounds', *Journal SMPE,* Nov. 1931, p. 743

Dykstra, John, Dorney, R., McCune, G., Sullivan, J., Beck, M. and Trumbull, D., 'Special effects for *Firefox*', *American Cinematographer,* Sept. 1982, p. 912

Erland, Jonathan, 'Reverse or negative bluescreen traveling matte process', *Journal SMPTE,* March, 1983, p. 268

Field, Roy (interview), 'The ultimate in optical illusions', *American Cinematographer,* Jan. 1979, p. 56

Field, Roy and Tony Iles, 'Modern techniques of optical trick cinematography', *American Cinematographer*, Sept. 1979, p. 892

Henderson, Scott, 'How special effects brought Elliot to life on screen', *American Cinematographer*, Oct. 1977, p. 1036

Hirschfeld, Gerald, 'Spectrumatte: new tool for TV', *Business Screen*, 20, No. 5, 1959, p. 35

Holm, Wilton R., 'The new electronic composite photography and image modification system (ECP & IM)', *American Cinematographer*, April 1975, p. 424

Hoult, Robert L., 'A black-and-white traveling matte process', *American Cinematographer*, Oct. 1959, p. 612 and Dec. 1959, p. 751

Hoult, Robert L., 'A travelling matte process for monochrome photography', *Proceedings of the International Conference of the Royal Photographic Society*, Sept. 1953

Hoult, Robert L., 'Traveling mattes in color', *American Cinematographer*, Nov. 1959, p. 676. Reprinted in *British Kinematography*, Jan. 1960, p. 12

Howard, Tom, 'Tom Howard on the travelling matte', *Cine Technician*, July–August 1941, p. 78

Langley, Brian, 'The travelling matte process', *Cine Technician*, March–April 1952, p. 46

Lerpee, Paul, 'Traveling matte tricks with 16mm negative', *American Cinematographer*, August 1935, p. 352

Levenson, G. I. P. and Wells, N. 'A method of making travelling mattes using a single-film camera', *British Kinematography*, Nov. 1951, p. 139

Lycett, Eustace, 'The sodium light travelling matte process', *IATSE Official Bulletin*, Summer 1969, p. 35

MacCulloch, Campbell, 'A new composite movie process', *Scientific American*, July 1931, p. 57. Explanation of the Dunning composite multi-film process.

Margutti, Victor L., 'Some practical travelling matte processes', *British Kinematography*, May 1960, p. 131

Martinelli, Anzo A., 'Photographing *The Invisible Man*', *American Cinematographer*, July 1975, p. 774

Matza, Joe, 'Magicam', *American Cinematographer*, Jan. 1975, p. 34

Matza, Joseph L. and Gale, John C., 'Magicam – The process and production techniques', *Journal SMPTE*, Oct. 1977, p. 728

Nicholson, Bruce, 'Composite optical photography for *The Empire Strikes Back*', *American Cinematographer*, June 1980, p. 562

Patterson, Richard, 'Making *The Invisible Woman*', *American Cinematographer*, April 1983, p. 42

Patterson, Richard, 'Ultimatte', *American Cinematographer*, Oct. 1982, p. 1041

Van Der Veer, Frank, 'Composite scenes for *King Kong* using the blue-screen technique', *American Cinematographer*, Jan. 1977, p. 56

Vidor, Zoli, 'An infra-red self-matting process', *Journal SMPTE*, June 1960, p. 425

Vlahos, Petro, 'A description of traveling-matte systems', *MPRC Bulletin* No. 58.428, May 25, 1959

Wells, Richard, 'Dreaming to scale', *American Cinematographer*, Oct. 1980, p. 1048. Magicam traveling-matte work with miniatures on the production of *Cosmos*

Westheimer, Joseph, 'Black-and-white applications of the blue-screen technique', *Journal SMPTE*, Nov. 1964, p. 949

Westheimer, Joseph, 'Optical magic for *The Muppet Movie*', *American Cinematographer*, July 1979, p. 706

Williams, Frank D., 'Inventor describes new process', *International Photographer*, Sept. 1932, p. 10. Description of an improved Williams double-matting, traveling-matte system

Williams, Frank D., 'Trick photography', *Journal SMPE*, April 1928, p. 537

Aerial-image printing and photography

Anonymous, 'Aerial-image techniques', *Industrial Photography*, Nov. 1959, p. 16. An interview with Maurice Levy of Eastern Effects, Inc.

Calhoun, John M. (Chairman), 'Progress report: special effects', *Journal SMPTE*, May 1962, p. 323. Description of the Eastern Effects Inc., optical and aerial-image printer

Lee, Francis and Palen, Vern, 'Special effects without mattes', *American Cinematographer*, Nov. 1960, p. 668

Palen, Vern W., 'Aerial image and animation', *American Cinematographer,* July 1959, p. 430

Palen, Vern W., 'Aerial image projector', *International Photographer,* August 1959, pp. 19–20

Palen, Vern W., 'Aerial image techniques', *American Cinematographer,* September 1963, p. 524

Russell, W. Dale, 'Aerial image cinematography', *American Cinematographer,* May 1967, p. 346

Ryder, Loren L., 'The Vistascope – new tool for motion picture production', *American Cinematographer,* August 1952, p. 338

Tressel, George and Andrews, Stanley, 'An aerial-image unit for industrial animation', *Journal SMPTE,* Nov. 1964, p. 956

Rear projection

Alton, John, 'Improvement for process department', *International Photographer,* Dec. 1946, p. 7. Proposed innovations in background projection technique

Alton, John, 'Postwar improvements', *International Photographer,* Sept. 1946, p. 8. Description of a turntable set mounting designed to facilitate fast, economical rear-projection cinematography

Anderson, Charles L., 'Background projection photography', *American Cinematographer,* August 1952, p. 342

Anonymous, 'A new type of background projector', *International Photographer,* June 1936, p. 10. Equipment and service offered commercially by George Teague

Anonymous, 'Availability of process screens and materials', MPRC Report No. 58.334-C, April 18, 1951

Anonymous, 'First rear projection specifications', *International Photographer,* March 1939, p. 21 and May 1939, p. 19. A report on rear-projection specifications prepared by the Research Council of the Academy of Motion Picture Arts and Sciences

Anonymous, 'Improved mount for process projector', *American Cinematographer,* June 1934, p. 70. A process projector mount designed by George Teague

Anonymous, 'Mitchell background projector', *American Cinematographer,* Nov. 1947, p. 391

Anonymous, 'Process for stills', *International Photographer,* Oct. 1937, p. 28. The Teague stereopticon slide rear projector

Anonymous, 'Process projection specifications: A report by the Research Council, Academy of Motion Picture Arts and Sciences', *International Projectionist,* May 1939, p. 17; July 1939, p. 18; and August 1939, p. 16

Anonymous, 'Rear projection big advance', *International Photographer,* April 1938, p. 30. Description of the new Mitchell rear projector

Anonymous, 'Recommendations on process projection equipment', *Journal SMPTE,* June 1939, p. 589. A report from the Research Council, Academy of Motion Picture Arts and Sciences

Anonymous, 'Wanger pic important for process work', *International Photographer,* Jan. 1939, p. 16

Ash, Jerome H., 'Using a process background in 16 mm pictures', *American Cinematographer,* August 1934, p. 176

Behrend, Jack, 'Rear projection', *Technical Photography,* Feb. 1982, p. 13

Berger, Frances B., 'Characteristics of motion picture and television screens', *Journal SMPTE,* August 1950, p. 131

Blanchard, Walter, 'Production economies with process photography', *American Cinematographer,* July 1934, p. 110

Campbell, Arthur, 'A fireproof process screen', *American Cinematographer,* Feb. 1934, p. 406

Carroll, Lee, 'Problems in rear projection', *International Photographer,* August, 1939, p. 5

Cobb, Norman E. and Glickman, Richard B., 'A rear-projection system for television composites using low-powered projection apparatus', *Journal SMPTE,* Sept. 1972, p. 672

Daily, C. R., 'High efficiency rear-projection screens', *Journal SMPTE,* Sept. 1956, p. 470

De Mille, Cecil, 'A director looks at process shots', *American Cinematographer,* Nov. 1936, p. 458

Dickinson, Desmond, 'Desmond Dickinson talks on back projection', *Cine Technician,* April–May 1937, p. 4

Dreyer, John F., 'Operational characteristics of rear projection', *Journal SMPTE,* August 1959, p. 521

Edouart, Faricot, 'The evolution of transparency process photography', *American Cinematographer,* Oct. 1943, p. 359

Edouart, Faricot, 'High efficiency steropticon projector for color background shots', *Journal SMPE,* August 1944, p. 97. Reprinted in *American Cinematographer,* October 1944, p. 332

Edouart, Faricot, 'The Paramount transparency process projection equipment', *Journal SMPE,* June 1943, p. 368. Reprinted in *International Projectionist,* August 1944, p. 7

Edouart, Faricot, 'Paramount triple-headed transparency process projector', *Journal SMPE,* August 1939, p. 171

Edouart, Faricot, 'Special laboratory for transparencies', *American Cinematographer,* Sept. 1934, p. 205. Description of the special processing given footage for rear projection at Paramount Studios

Edouart, Faricot, 'The transparency projection process', *American Cinematographer,* July 1932, p. 15

Edouart, Faricot, 'Using projection in photography', *Motion Picture Projectionist,* August 1932, p. 21 and Sept. 1932, p. 22

Edouart, Faricot, 'The work of the Process Projection Equipment Committee of the Research Council, Academy of Motion Picture Arts and Sciences, A. Faricot Edouart, Chairman', *Journal SMPE,* Sept. 1939, p. 248

Fear, Ralph G., 'Projected background anematography', *American Cinematographer,* Jan. 1932, p. 11

Foster, Frederick, 'The photography of background plates', *American Cinematographer,* Feb. 1962, p. 98

Gillespie, Arnold A., 'Laced process – A new system of rear projection process', *Journal SMPTE,* Nov. 1964, p. 949

Good, Frank B., 'A super-portable background projector', *American Cinematographer,* August 1933, p. 134

Gow, John, 'Back projection and perspective: problems of perspective', *Cine Technician,* May–June 1948, p. 96

Griffin, Herbert, 'Background process projector', *International Projectionist,* July 1936, p. 13

Griffin, Herbert, 'New background projector for process cinematography', *Journal SMPTE,* July 1936, p. 96

Harmer, Paul R., 'Glass, miniature and projection combined', *International Photographer,* Nov. 1934, p. 12

Harrison, Hartley, 'Problems of background projection', *American Cinematographer,* Jan. 1934, p. 353

Haskin, Byron, 'The development and practical application of the triple-head background projector', *Journal SMPE,* March 1940, p. 252

Henderson, R. W., 'Developments in time-saving process projection equipment', *Journal SMPE,* Oct. 1942, p. 245

Henry, Joe, 'The science of process photography', *American Cinematographer,* Jan. 1958, p. 36

Hill, Armin J., 'Analysis of background process screens', *Journal SMPTE,* July 1957, p. 393

Hill, George, 'Back projection', *Cine Technician,* Jan.–Feb. 1948, p. 29

Hill, George, Davis, Alfred and Gow, John, 'Back projection and perspective', *British Kinematography,* April 1948, p. 127

Hoult, R. L. and Harper, M. E., 'Process projection in colour', *British Kinematogrphy,* August 1953, p. 33

Jackman, Fred W., '"Process shot" economies made *Captain Blood* possible', *American Cinematographer,* Feb. 1936, 48

Joy, D. B., Lozier, W. W. and Null, M. R., 'Carbons for transparency process projection in motion picture studios', *Journal SMPE,* Oct. 1939, p. 353

Knott, Charles E., 'Some observations on the back-projection process', *Cine Technician.* Feb. 1936, p. 109

Levi, Leo, 'On contrast in rear-projection screens', *Journal SMPTE,* Dec. 1967, p. 1193

Lightman, Herb A., 'MGM's "Laced-process" rear-projection system', *American Cinematographer,* August 1964, p. 456

Lynn, R. A. and Bertero, E. P., 'Process projection of film for TV', *International Projectionist,* Sept. 1950, p. 16, and Oct. 1950, p. 8

Meyer, Herbert, 'Color slides for background projection process', MPRC Bulletin No. 58.464-A, Oct. 20, 1950

Meyer, Herbert, 'Elimination of static from process screens – Tenlo 10', MPRC Bulletin No. 58.619-A, June 25, 1952

Meyer, Herbert, 'Heat filters for process projectors', MPRC Bulletin No. 58.354-B, Oct. 12, 1950

Meyer, Herbert, 'Progress report for project 66-1: transparency screens and process photography', MPRC Bulletin No. 58.334-A, Jan. 20, 1950

Meyer, Herbert, 'Sensitometric aspects of background process photography, *Journal SMPTE,* March 1950, p. 275

Meyer, Herbert, 'Transparency screens and process photography', MPRC Bulletin No. 58.334-B, June 30, 1950

Miller, Harold and Manderfeld, E. C., '35 mm process projector', *Journal SMPE,* Oct. 1948, p. 373

Morgan, Earle K., 'Duplication of Kodachrome transparencies for background projection', Journal SMPE, August 1944, p. 93

Popovici, G. G., 'Background projection for process photography', *Journal SMPE,* Feb. 1935, p. 102. Reprinted in *International Projectionist,* April 1935, p. 17

Popovici, G. G., 'Recent developments in background projection', *Journal SMPE,* May 1938, p. 535

Ross, Hugh, 'High diffusion screens for process projection', *British Kinematography,* June 1950, p. 189

Ross, Hugh, 'A new still process projector', *British Kinematography,* Nov. 1950, p. 159

Rupkalvis, John A., 'Background projection equipment', *Technical Photography,* Nov. 1977, p. 48

Ryu, Keiichiro, 'Lumiscope lens-screen system for color television', *Journal SMPTE,* Sept. 1972, p. 668

Stull, William, 'The Paramount transparency air-turbine developing machine', *American Cinematographer,* June 1936, p. 236. Description of the special processing equipment devoted to footage for background projection at Paramount Studios

Stull, William, 'Process shots aided by triple projector', *American Cinematographer,* August 1939, p. 363

Tasker, Homer, 'Improved motor drive for self-phasing of process projection equipment', *Journal SMPE,* August 1941, p. 187

Taylor, Jack, 'Dynamic realism', *International Photographer,* Sept. 1948, p. 6. Description of background projection techniques used during the production of *Crisscross*

Teague, George, 'Ingenious accessories simplify making of special effects shots', *American Cinematographer,* Oct. 1938, p. 408

Tiffany, E. J., 'The new Mitchell background projector', *American Cinematographer,* Oct. 1943, p. 363

Vlahos, Petro, 'Infrared heat deflector for process projectors', MPRC Bulletin No. 58.354-A, May 25, 1950

Vlahos, Petro, 'Noise level of Mitchell process projector', MPRC Report No. 58.97-A, Sept. 23, 1948

Vlahos, Petro, 'Selection and specification of rear-projection screens', *Journal SMPTE,* Feb. 1961, p. 89

Walker, Vernon, 'Saunders cellulose screen reduces "hot spot"', *American Cinematographer,* Oct. 1932, p. 11

Walker, Vernon, 'Use of miniatures in process backgrounds', *American Cinematographer,* August 1934, p. 154

Worrall, G. H., 'New background projector for process cinematography', *Journal SMPE,* April, 1939, p. 442

Worrall, G. H., 'New background process projector', *International Projectionist,* March 1939, p. 20.

Front projection

Anonymous, 'Developing a unique new front-projection system', *American Cinematographer,* Sept. 1981, p. 872. Description of the Samcine Front Projection System

Anonymous, 'Front projection for *2001: A Space Odyssey*', *American Cinematographer,* June 1968, p. 420

Anonymous, 'Front projection – you might like it!', *The Aperture,* March 1973, p. 5

Anonymous, 'Grain caused by zoom and dolly shots in reflex projection composite photography', *American Cinematographer,* July 1969, p. 693

Anonymous, 'Neilson-Hordell dual screen front matte projector', *American Cinematographer,* Dec. 1976, p. 1362

Anonymous, 'Patent situation relative to the front projection technique of background process photography', AMPTP Research Bulletin No. B-014/01, July 22, 1968

Anonymous, 'Production with front-screen', *The Aperture,* Sept. 1972, p. 3

Anonymous, 'Zoptic takes off in a big way', *Screen International,* March 8, 1980

Canavor, Natalie, 'This year at the Calvin film workshop', *Industrial Photography,* March 1975, p. 12

Coop, Denys (interview), 'Of flying and front projection', *American Cinematographer,* Jan. 1979, p. 44. Description of front-projection work on the production of *Superman*

Ferderber, Skip, 'Introvision: "the grand illusion"', *Millimeter,* Sept. 1982, p. 105

Fielding, Raymond, 'The Scotchlite process', *American Cinematographer,* April 1962, p. 228

Hansard, Bill, 'Creating front projection effects for *Black Sunday', American Cinematographer,* August 1977, p. 832

Holm, Wilton R., '"Scotchlite" reflex reflecting material', AMPTP Bulletin No. B-001/03, May 1, 1970. Reprinted by National Film Board of Canada Technical and Production Services Branch, Montreal, 1974

Howard, Tom, Young, Freddie and Maoletti, Gianfranco, 'Front projection: Europe', *American Cinematographer,* Nov. 1968, p. 864

Lightman, Herb A., 'On the European film production scene – London', *American Cinematographer,* Nov. 1968, p. 842

Meyer, Herbert, 'Front projection process photography with Scotchlite', MPRC Report No. 58.334-D, August 6, 1951

Overton, Dewey K., 'Front process projection', *IATSE Official Bulletin,* Spring 1969, p. 35

Palmquist, Philip V., 'More facts about front projection', *American Cinematographer,* July 1969, p. 688

Palmquist, Philip V., 'More facts about front projection', *IATSE Official Bulletin,* Autumn 1969, p. 7

Perisic, Zoran, 'Flying with Superman', *American Cinematographer,* Sept. 1979, p. 882. Description of the Zoptic front-projection system

Perisic, Zoran, 'Zoptic special effects', *BKSTS Journal,* December 1980, p. 622

Perisic, Zoran, 'Zoptic special effects device', *American Cinematographer,* Sept. 1977, p. 926

Rider, L. F., 'The Alekan-Gerard process of composite photography', *American Cinematographer,* July 1962, p. 428. Reprinted from an article appearing in *British Kinematography*, March 1962

Rupkalvis, John A., 'Background projection equipment', *Technical Photography,* Nov. 1977, p. 48

Schwartz, Milton J., 'Technical advances stir new interest in beam splitters', *Industrial Photography,* August 1962, pp. 32–33

Vlahos, Petro, 'An alignment procedure for front projection', AMPTP Bulletin No. B-044/01, March 6, 1970. Reprinted by National Film Board of Canada Technical and Production Services Branch, Montreal, 1974

Vlahos, Petro, 'Front projection Mirrors', AMPTP Bulletin No. B-026/01, Feb 5, 1969. Reprinted by National Film Board of Canada Technical and Production Services Branch, Montreal, 1974

Vlahos, Petro, 'The front-projection process of composite photography', *Journal SMPTE,* Sept. 1971, p. 685

Vlahos, Petro, 'Grain caused by zoom and dolly shots in reflex projection composite photography', AMPTP Bulletin No. B-030/02, April 14, 1969. Reprinted by National Film Board of Canada Technical and Production Services Branch, Montreal, 1974; and in *IATSE Official Bulletin,* Autumn 1969, p. 10

Vlahos, Petro, 'The problem of grain in the reflex projection system for composite photography (front projection)', AMPTP Research Center Bulletin No. B-030/01, March 31, 1969. Reprinted by National Film Board of Canada Technical and Production Services Branch, Montreal, 1974; in *IATSE Official Bulletin,* Autumn 1969, p. 7; and (co-authored with Wilton Holm), in *American Cinematographer,* July 1969, p. 690

Whitehall, Richard, 'A step forward for the film technology of the Seventies', *American Cinematographer,* March 1970, p. 242. Description of a portable front-projection system designed by William Hansard in association with Sherman Fairchild

Miniatures

Anonymous, 'Jap targets in miniature', *International Photographer*, Nov. 1945, p. 5

Anonymous, 'Miniatures', *International Photographer*, July 1937, p. 23

Anonymous, 'Panning and tilting off and on miniatures', *International Photographer*, July 1933, p. 42

Anonymous, 'Super miniature astounds', *International Photographer*, August, 1933, p. 25

Anonymous, 'Wizard of miniatures', *International Photographer*, March 1940, p. 16. Biographical sketch of Frank William Young, special-effects miniatures expert at Hal Roach Studios

Ball, J. A., 'Theory of mechanical miniatures in cinematography', *Transactions SMPE*, No. 18, May 1924, p. 119

Blanchard, Walter, 'Destroying Pompeii – in miniature', *American Cinematographer*, Dec. 1935, p. 519. An interview with Edwin G. Linden

Boyars, Albert, 'Dolly shots in miniature', *American Cinematographer*, Jan. 1957, p. 24

Bryan, John, 'Design and use of the miniature in motion picture production', *British Kinematography*, Nov. 1948, p. 145

Challis, C. and Kelly, G. W. 'The photographic problems encountered in filming the feature *Sink the Bismark*', *British Kinematography*, June 1961, p. 167

Cruickshank, Art, 'Photographing miniatures on a massive scale', *American Cinematographer*, Jan. 1980, p. 48

Dow, James, 'The Magicam miniatures constructed for *Star Trek – The Motion Picture*', *American Cinematographer*, Feb. 1980, p. 153

Dreier, Hans, 'Motion picture sets', *Journal SMPE*, Nov. 1931, p. 789

Dykstra, John, 'Miniature and mechanical special effects for *Star Wars*', *American Cinematographer*, July 1977, p. 702

Fiebiger, Daniel, 'Disney's miniature effects rig', *American Cinematographer*, Feb. 1984, p. 73

Flowers, A. D., 'Mechanical special effects for *1941*', *American Cinematographer*, Dec. 1979, p. 1220

Foster, Frederick, 'Mattes, miniatures and meticulous cinematography', *American Cinematographer*, March 1950, p. 82

Fulton, John P., 'Staging miniature fires for amateur defense films', *American Cinematographer*, Dec. 1942, p. 1220

Gentleman, Wally, 'Voyage in miniature', *American Cinematographer*, May 1964, p. 264

Hammeras, Ralph, 'An American cameraman in American studios', *International Photographer*, June 1935, p. 20. Review of contemporary American special-effects miniature work

Harmer, Paul R., 'Glass, miniature and projection combined', *International Photographer*, Nov. 1934, p. 12

Harrington, Clifford V., 'Japan's master of monsters', *American Cinematographer*, August 1960, p. 488

Harrison, Bob, 'Battle scenes and model shots', *American Cinematographer*, August 1963, p. 472

Haskins, Byron, 'Miniatures for 16 mm defense films', *American Cinematographer*, March 1942, p. 116

Hilchey, Eugene, 'Special effects outside the camera', *American Cinematographer*, Nov. 1965, p. 725

Hitchins, Alfred B., 'A method for using miniatures or models for the introduction of extra detail in motion pictures', *Transactions SMPE*, No. 15: October 1922, p. 41

Hitchins, Alfred B., 'Miniatures and models for motion picture use', *American Cinematographer*, Nov. 1922, p. 13

Hoult, Robert L., 'Making movie miniatures look realistic', *American Cinematographer*, Oct. 1960, p. 598

Hutchins, G. F., 'Dimensional analysis as an aid to miniature cinematography', *International Photographers Bulletin*, Oct. 1929, p. 9. See also Hutchins, 'Dimensional analysis as an aid to miniature cinematography', *Journal SMPE*, April 1930, p. 377

Jahraus, Don, 'Making miniatures', *American Cinematographer*, Nov. 1931, p. 9

Jein, Gregory, 'The mini-world of *1941*', *American Cinematographer*, Dec. 1979, p. 1216

Jennings, Gordon, 'A boom for operating miniature airplanes', *American Cinematographer*, July 1942, p. 297

Jennings, J. D., 'How miniatures are photographed', *American Cinematographer*, June 1934, p. 60

Kellino, Roy, 'Photographing of models', *Cine Technician*, Sept.–Oct. 1943, p. 97

Kershner, Glenn R., 'Miniatures and puppets used in religious films', *American Cinematographer*, July 1947, p. 262

Korda, Vincent, 'Why overlook the set miniature?', *American Cinematographer*, Dec. 1941, p. 560

Lee, Nora, 'Modelmaking for *Return of the Jedi*', *American Cinematographer*, June 1983, p. 87

Loring, Charles, 'The use of miniatures in 16 mm films', *American Cinematographer*, July 1955, p. 412

Loring, Charles, 'How to use miniatures for "big" production value in low budget filming', *American Cinematographer*, April 1966, p. 260

Maginot, Mike and Turner, George, 'The art of the movie miniature', *American Cinematographer*, Oct. 1982, p. 1010

Matza, Joe, 'Magicam', *American Cinematographer*, Jan. 1975, p. 35

Matza, Joseph L. and Gale, John C., 'Magicam – The process and production techniques', *Journal SMPTE*, Oct. 1977, p. 728

McCune, Grant, 'Models for *Firefox*', *American Cinematographer*, Sept. 1982, p. 922

McHugh, Tim and Leilani, 'Shooting miniature effects for the year 2020', *Millimeter*, April 1982, p. 75

Meddings, Derek, 'Creating mechanical models and miniatures for *The Spy Who Loved Me*', *American Cinematographer*, Feb. 1979, p. 187

Meddings, Derek, 'Two worlds in miniature', *American Cinematographer*, Jan. 1979, p. 48

Mercer, Ray, 'Monsters and miniatures', *American Cinematographer*, Dec. 1959, p. 747

Munson, Brad, 'Greg Jein – miniature giant', *Cinefex*, No. 2, August 1980, p. 24

O'Brien, Willis, 'Miniature effects shots', *International Photographer*, May 1933, p. 38

Rowan, Arthur, 'Miniatures in motion picture production', *American Cinematographer*, Sept. 1952, p. 386

Scot, Darrin, 'Wizardry in special effects', *American Cinematographer*, April 1963, p. 218

Seldon, Nicholas, 'Gulliver in Hollywood: the world of movie miniatures', *American Cinematographer*, Nov. 1983, p. 87

Stine, Clifford, 'The *Earthquake* miniatures', *American Cinematographer*, Nov. 1974, p. 1334

Swarthe, Robert, 'Of miniatures, mattes and magic', *American Cinematographer*, Jan. 1983, p. 38

Tasker, Ann, 'Ray Harryhausen talks about his cinematic magic', *American Cinematographer*, June 1981, p. 38

Turner, George E., 'Photographic effects for *The Winds of War*', *American Cinematographer*, Feb. 1983, p. 51

Voigtlander, Ted, 'Filming a battle – in miniature', *American Cinematographer*, August 1941, p. 376

Walker, Vernon, 'Use of miniatures in process background', *American Cinematographer*, August 1934, p. 154

Waxman, Harry, 'Artificial clouds in third dimension', *Cine Technician*, July–August 1946, p. 86. A method for introducing three-dimensional cloud effects into miniature sets

Composite cinematography, miscellaneous

Anderson, Howard, 'Dual photography matter of timing', *International Projectionist*, Jan. 1942, p. 16

Anderson, Howard, 'Dual roles in pictures', *International Photographer*, March 1942, p. 3

Anonymous, 'Actors now argue with selves via Movietone', *American Cinematographer*, July 1929, p. 37

Anonymous, 'Mosfilm process photography', *Cine Technician*, August–Sept. 1937, p. 109

Anonymous, 'New photographic process is launched', *American Cinematographer*, August 1926, p. 23. Explanation of the Handschiegl composite process

Baker, Friend F., 'Inventor describes his process', *International Photographer*, Oct. 1932, p. 4. Description of the Baker composite process

Battison, John H., 'Trick effects in TV commercial films', *American Cinematographer*, Dec. 1951, p. 502

Brautigam, Otto, 'Double exposures of the early days', *American Cinematographer,* Sept.–Oct. 1922

Dunning, Carroll, 'Some problems related to composite photography', *American Cinematographer,* June 1929, p. 9

Kelley, William V. D., 'Trick photography', *Transactions SMPE,* No. 27: Jan. 1927, p. 128

Stull, William, 'The Dieterich process for composite photography', *American Cinematographer,* March 1933, p. 9

Stull, William, 'Multiple exposure cinematography in sound pictures', *American Cinematographer,* Dec. 1929, p. 4. See also Stull, 'Multiple exposure cinematography in sound pictures', *Journal SMPE,* March 1930, p. 318

Zeper, Roy, 'How still camera can aid "freeze-action" lineups', *American Cinematographer,* Sept. 1960, p. 543

Special-effects cinematography for particular productions

Abbott, L. B., 'Creating the special effects for *Tora, Tora, Tora', American Cinematographer,* Feb. 1971, p. 138

Abbott, L. B., 'Magic for the 23rd century', *American Cinematographer,* June 1976, p. 642. Special-effects work on the production of *Logan's Run*

Allen, Leigh, 'Filming a trip to the moon', *American Cinematographer,* Feb. 1950, p. 46. The production of George Pal's *Destination Moon*

Anderson, Howard, 'Out-of-this-world effects for *Star Trek', American Cinematographer,* Oct. 1967, p. 714

Anderson, Margo, 'Spectacular visual effects for *Damnation alley', American Cinematographer,* Nov. 1977, p. 1182

Andorfer, Greg, 'The special visual effects of *Cosmos', American Cinematographer,* Oct. 1980, p. 1010

Anonymous, 'Backlit effects and animation for *Tron', American Cinematographer,* Oct. 1980, p. 1010

Anonymous, 'Biggest stage on earth devoted entirely to special process work', *American Cinematographer,* April 1929, p. 20. The special-effects stage at Warner Brothers Studios

Anonymous, 'Combined techniques in visual effects', *American Cinematographer,* August 1963, p. 474. Special-effects work of the Canadian Film Board studios on particular productions

Anonymous, 'Fantastic *Dr. Cyclops', International Photographer,* March 1940, p. 17

Anonymous, '*King Kong* – A wonder in celluloid', *International Photographer,* March 1933, p. 34

Anonymous, 'Movie Magic', *National Geographic World,* June 1980, p. 10. Special-effects work on the production of *The Empire Strikes Back*

Anonymous, 'Multiple-image technique for *The Boston Strangler', American Cinematographer,* Feb. 1969, p. 200

Anonymous, 'Peter Ellensha: designer for Disney', *Horizon,* Sept. 1979, p. 60

Anonymous, 'Photographic special effects "Emmy" award for *The Time Tunnel', American Cinematographer,* July 1967, p. 478

Anonymous, 'Process technique', *International Photographer,* Dec. 1940, p. 8. Special-effects work on the Warner Brothers production of *The Sea Wolf*

Anonymous, 'Schoedsack tells of making *Dr. Cyclops', American Cinematographer,* April 1940, p. 158

Anonymous, 'Some tricks of the moving picture maker', *Scientific American,* June 26, 1909, p. 476. Special-effects work on the 1909 J. Stuart Blackton/Albert E. Smith/Vitagraph production of *The Princess Nicotine*

Anonymous, 'Special effects', *International Photographer,* Feb. 1955, p. 5. The production of George Pal's *Conquest of Space*

Arbogast, Roy, 'Of vampires, castles and mechanical bats', *American Cinematographer,* June 1979, p. 572. Special-effects work on the 1978–1979 production of *Dracula*

Auslender, Leland, 'The Birth of Aphrodite', *American Cinematographer,* Sept. 1971, p. 868. Optical distortion effects used on an experimental film

Blinn, Dr. James, F., Cole, Pat, and Kolhase, Charles E., 'Computer magic for *Cosmos', American Cinematographer,* Oct. 1980, p. 1018

Blalack, Robert, 'How the world looks through the eyes of (cinematic) wolves', *American Cinematographer,* Nov. 1981, p. 1130. Special-effects work on the production of *Wolfen*

Blalack, Robert and Roth, Paul, 'Composite optical and photographic effects for *Star Wars*', *American Cinematographer*, July 1977, p. 706

Bonifer, Michael, 'A specially effective man', *American Cinematographer*, Jan. 1980, p. 56. The work of mechanical-effects supervisor Danny Lee on *The Black Hole*

Bowie, Les (interview), 'Mattes and composites for *Superman*', *American Cinematographer*, Jan. 1979, p. 52

Brown, Garrett, 'Steadicam plates for *Return of the Jedi*', *American Cinematographer*, June 1983, p. 76

Brown, H. J., '*Cosmos* cinematography', *American Cinematographer*, Oct. 1980, p. 1006. Work on the production of *Cosmos*

Carpenter, Lynn, 'Creature design for *Return of the Jedi*', *American Cinematographer*, June 1983, p. 70

Cruickshank, Art, 'Photographing miniatures on a massive scale', *American Cinematographer*, Jan. 1980, p. 48

Dow, James, 'The Magicam miniatures constructed for *Star Trek – the Motion Picture*', *American Cinematographer*, Feb. 1980, p. 153

Draper, William V., 'Photography of *1 000 000 B.C.*', *International Photographer*, March 1940, p. 6

Draper, William, 'Topper tipoffs', *International Photographer*, August 1937, p. 18. Effects work on the Hal Roach production, *Topper*

Dryer, David (interview), '*Blade Runner*: special photographic effects, *American Cinematographer*, July 1982, p. 692

Duncan, Pamela, '*Silent Running*', *Cinefex*, No. 8, April 1982, p. 36

Dunn, Linwood G., 'Creating film magic for the original *King Kong*', *American Cinematographer*, Jan. 1977, p. 64

Dunn, Linwood G., 'Effects and titles for *West Side Story*', *American Cinematographer*, Dec. 1961, p. 736

Dunn, Linwood G., 'Getting the most out of special effects', *The Cinemeditor*, Spring 1964, p. 9

Dunn, Linwood G., 'The "Mad, Mad" world of special effects', *American Cinematographer*, March 1965, p. 160. Special-effects work on the Stanley Kramer production of *It's a Mad, Mad, Mad, Mad World*

Dunning, Carroll, 'Typical problems in process photography', *Journal SMPE*, May 1929, p. 298. The solution of production problems through the application of various effects techniques

Dykstra, John, 'Miniature and mechanical special effects for *Star Wars*', *American Cinematographer*, July 1977, p. 702

Dykstra, John, 'Special effects for *Firefox*', *American Cinematographer*, Sept. 1982, p. 912

Dykstra, John, 'Special effects for *Silent Running*', *American Cinematographer*, July 1972, p. 756

Dykstra, John (interview), 'Star Trekking at Apogee with John Dykstra', *Cinefex*, No. 2, August 1980, p. 50. Visual effects on the production of *Star Trek – The Motion Picture*

Dykstra, John (interview), 'Very special effects for *Star Trek – The Motion Picture*', *American Cinematographer*, Feb. 1980, p. 144

Edlund, Richard, 'Creating the special visual effects for *Raiders*', *American Cinematographer*, Nov. 1981, p. 1106

Edlund, Richard (interview), 'Of ice planets, bog planets, and cities in the sky', *Cinefex*, No. 2, August 1980, p. 4. Visual effects on the production of *The Empire Strikes Back*

Edlund, Richard, 'Special visual effects for *The Empire Strikes Back*', *American Cinematographer*, June 1980, p. 552

Eisenberg, Adam, 'Low tech effects – *The Right Stuff*', *Cinefex*, No. 14, Oct. 1983, p. 4

Eisenberg, Adam, 'Waging a four-minute war', *Cinefex*, No. 15, Jan. 1984, p. 28. Description of production work on the television-film feature, *The Day After*

Eisenberg, Adam, Muren, Dennis and Ralston, Ken, 'Jedi journal', *Cinefex*, No. 13, July 1983, p. 4. A journal of effects work conducted on the Lucas production of *Return of the Jedi*

Ellenshaw, Harrison, 'Creating the matte paintings for *The Empire Strikes Back*', *American Cinematographer*, June 1980, p. 582

Ellenshaw, Harrison (interview), 'Making the unreal real with matte paintings', *American Cinematographer*, Jan. 1980, p. 70. Special-effects work on *The Black Hole*

Ellenshaw, Peter (interview), 'Designing a deep space world for *The Black Hole*', *American Cinematographer*, Jan. 1980, p. 28

Ferren, Bran, 'Creating special visual effects for *Altered States*', *American Cinematographer*, March 1981, p. 236

Field, Roy, 'The ultimate in optical illusions', *American Cinematographer*, Jan. 1979, p. 56. Work on the production of *Superman*

Field, Roy and Iles, Tony, 'Modern techniques of optical trick cinematography', *American Cinematographer*, Sept. 1979, p. 892. Work on the production of *Superman*

Fielding, Raymond, 'Special visual effects for *One From the Heart*', *American Cinematographer*, Jan. 1982, p. 30

Fisher, Bob, 'Magical matte paintings for *The Wiz*', *American Cinematographer*, Nov. 1978, p. 1078

Flowers, A. D. 'Mechanical special effects for *1941*', *American Cinematographer*, Dec. 1979, p. 1220

Ford, Freddie, 'Man with a movie camera', *Cine Technician*, Jan.–Feb. 1939, p. 158. Experiences of the author in solving production problems by applying special-effects techniques

Fox, Donald, 'The making of *Omega*', *American Cinematographer*, May 1970, p. 412

Fulton, John P., 'How we made *The Invisible Man*', *American Cinematographer*, Sept. 1934, p. 200

Gentleman, Wally, 'Horror effects enhance television film', *American Cinematographer*, January 1966, p. 44. Special-effects work on the Canadian National Film Board production of *The Banquet of the Dead*

Gentleman, Wally, 'The Moon in a Teacup', *Industrial Photographer*, May 1963, p. 48

Gentleman, Wally, 'Special photographic effects as an aid to low-budget production', *Journal SMPTE*, July 1962, p. 487

Gentleman, Wally, 'Visual effects as cinematic art form', *American Cinematographer*, Jan. 1982, p. 32

Gentry, Ric, 'John Dykstra on *Firefox*', *Millimeter*, Sept. 1982, p. 121

Gentry, Ric, 'Special visual effects: *The Exorcist* to *Tron*', *Millimeter*, Dec. 1983, p. 53

Glennon, James, 'Location photography for *Return of the Jedi*', *American Cinematographer*, June 1983, p. 74

Goldner, Orville and Turner, George E., 'The making of the original *King Kong*', *American Cinematographer*, Jan. 1977, p. 60

Gow, John, 'Electricity as applied to special effects', *Cine Technician*, Nov.–Dec. 1950, p. 188

Greenberg, R., 'Building unique special effects for *Xanadu*', *American Cinematographer*, August 1980, p. 820

Hammond, David, 'Conceiving the persona of King Kong – in two sizes', *American Cinematographer*, Jan. 1977, p. 42

Hansard, Bill, 'Creating front projection effects for *Black Sunday*', *American Cinematographer*, August 1977, p. 832

Harvey, Herk and Lacey, Charles, 'Systematic control for special effects in 16 mm production', *American Cinematographer*, March 1956, p. 162

Haskin, Byron, '"Special effects" and wartime production', *American Cinematographer*, March 1943, p. 89

Henderson, Scott, 'How special effects brought Elliot to life on screen', *American Cinematographer*, Oct. 1977, p. 4036. Description of optical printing and traveling-matte work by Eustace Lycett on Walt Disney's production of *Pete's Dragon*

Heutschy, Vic and Ross, Ron, '*War of the Worlds*', *International Photographer*, July 1953, p. 16. Production of the George Pal fantasy film

Hill, George, 'Effects department', *Cine Technician*, Jan.–Feb. 1948, p. 22. Description of a visit by British special-effects worker George Hill to the RKO special-effects department

Hume, Alan, 'Cinematography for *Return of the Jedi*', *American Cinematographer*, June 1983, p. 73

Jackman, Fred, '"Comedy kicks" require courage and skill", *American Cinematographer*, Dec. 1922, p. 5. Experiences of a special-effects cinematographer

Jein, Gregory, 'The mini-world of *1941*', *American Cinematographer*, Dec. 1979, p. 1216

Jennings, Gordon, 'Special-effects and montage for *Cleopatra*', *American Cinematographer*, Dec. 1934, p. 350

Johnson, Brian (interview), 'Through the galaxy from ice planet to bog planet', *American Cinematographer*, June 1980, p. 558. Special-effects work on the production of *The Empire Strikes Back*

Kennard, David, 'On location for *Cosmos'*, *American Cinematographer*, Oct. 1980, p. 1014

Lee, Nora, 'Effects art direction for *Return of the Jedi'*, *American Cinematographer*, June 1983, p. 78

Lee, Nora, 'Modelmaking for *Return of the Jedi'*, *American Cinematographer*, June 1983, p. 86

Lee, Nora, 'Motion control for *Blue Thunder'*, *American Cinematographer*, May 1983, p. 58

Lewell, John, 'One eye at a time', *American Cinematographer*, July 1983, p. 69. Production on *Jaws 3-D*

Lightman, Herb A., 'Cameraman becomes the "Star" of *Fantastic Voyage*, The', *American Cinematographer*, Feb. 1966, p. 98

Lightman, Herb A., 'Cinematographic magic for *A Stolen Life'*, *American Cinematographer*, June 1946, p. 196

Lightman, Herb A., 'Producing the special photographic effects for *Voyage to the Bottom of the Sea'*, *American Cinematographer*, Sept. 1961, p. 532

Loring, Charles, 'Emmy awards for *Voyage to the Bottom of the Sea'*, *American Cinematographer*, July 1966, p. 470

Lowell, Allen, 'Matte effects for *Return of the Jedi'*, *American Cinematographer*, June 1983, p. 81

Lycett, Eustace, 'Screen magic from *Snow White* to *The Black Hole'*, *American Cinematographer*, Jan. 1980, p. 52. An interview with optical printing supervisor Lycett at Walt Disney Studios

Mandell, Paul, 'Altered states of *Altered States*, The', *Cinefex*, No. 4, April 1981, p. 32

Mandell, Paul, 'Making miracles the hard way', *American Cinematographer*, Dec. 1983, p. 42. The work of John Fulton on numerous Universal and Paramount Films

Mandell, Paul, 'Parting the Red Sea (and other miracles)', *American Cinematographer*, April 1983, p. 46. Special-effects work on the 1956 production of *The Ten Commandments*. See also follow-up letter from Paul Mandell, *American Cinematographer*, July 1983, p. 7

Mandell, Paul, '*Poltergeist* – stilling the restless animus', *Cinefex*, No. 10, Oct. 1982, p. 4

Mandell, Paul, 'Stop-frame fever, post-animation blues', *Cinefex*, No. 12, April 1983, p. 28. Stop-frame work with miniatures on the productions of *The Howling*, *Q*, *The Thing*, *The Hunger*, and *Krull*

Martinelli, Ezo A., 'Photographing *The Invisible Man'*, *American Cinematographer*, July 1975, p. 774

Mayer, John, '*Radio Rocket Boy* and how it was filmed', *American Cinematographer*, Oct. 1973, p. 1270

McHugh, Tim and Leilani, 'Shooting miniature effects for the year 2020', *Millimeter*, April 1982, p. 75. Special effects on the production of *Blade Runner*

Meddings, Derek, 'Creating mechanical models and miniatures for *The Spy Who Loved Me'*, *American Cinematographer*, Feb. 1979, p. 187

Meddings, Derek, 'Two worlds in miniature', *American Cinematographer*, Jan. 1979, p. 48. Work on the production of *Superman*

Milrad, Abe, 'Special visual effects for the Concord – *Airport '79'*, *American Cinematographer*, August 1979, p. 780

Munson, Brad, '*Brainstorm* Getting the cookie at the end', *Cineflex*, No. 14, Oct. 1983, p. 26

Munson, Brad, '*Something Wicked This Way Comes* – adding the magic', *Cineflex*, No. 12, April 1983, p. 4

Muren, Dennis (interview), 'Effects photography for *The Empire Strikes Back'*, *American Cinematographer*, June 1980, p. 572

Murton, Peter (interview), 'Of vampires, castles and mechanical bats', *American Cinematographer*, June 1979, p. 572. Special-effects work on the 1978–1979 production of *Dracula*

Nicholson, Bruce, 'Composite optical photography for *The Empire Strikes Back'*, *American Cinematographer*, June 1980, p. 562

O'Dell, Chris, 'Location shooting for KCET's *Cosmos* – India, Egypt, Germany, Austria, Czechoslovakia and England', *American Cinematographer*, Oct. 1980, p. 1009

Oyster, David, '*Cosmos* cinematography', *American Cinematographer*, Oct. 1980, p. 1006

Parks, Peter D., 'High-speed blood and worms: Oxford scientific film meets Pink Floyd', *American Cinematographer*, Oct. 1982, p. 1028. Special-effects work for the production of *The Wall*

Patterson, Richard, 'Making *The Invisible Woman'*, *American Cinematographer*, April 1983, p. 42

Patterson, Richard, 'Producing and directing *Return of the Jedi*', *American Cinematographer*, June 1983, p. 66

Patterson, Richard, 'Special effects for *Airplane II – The Sequel*', *American Cinematographer*, March 1983, p. 63

Patterson, Richard, 'Special effects for *Jaws 3-D*', *American Cinematographer*, July 1983, p. 64

Perisic, Zoran, 'Flying with Superman', *American Cinematographer*, Sept. 1979, p. 882

Rand, Gary, 'The special mechanical effects', *American Cinematographer*, Nov. 1974, p. 1306. Work on the production of *Earthquake*

Reynolds, Norman, 'Art direction for *Return of the Jedi*', *American Cinematographer*, June 1983, p. 69

Robinson, Glen, 'Constructing a 42-foot superstar', *American Cinematographer*, Jan. 1977, p. 51. Mechanical effects for the 1976 production of *King Kong*

Sammon, Paul M., 'Mach 5 effects – the apogee of *Firefox*', *Cinefex*, No. 10, Oct. 1982, p. 40

Sammon, Paul M., 'Turn on your heartlite – inside *ET*', *Cinefex*, No. 11, Jan. 1983, p. 4

Samuelson, David W., 'British entry wins UNIATEC Film Technology Grand Prix', *American Cinematographer*, Feb. 1979, p. 186. Production work on *The Spy Who Loved Me* is honored

Savage, Golda, 'Producing *Battle Star: Galactica* with a galaxy of special effects experts', *Millimeter*, Sept. 1978, p. 28

Scot, Darrin, 'Movie magic for *the Magic Sword*', *American Cinematographer*, March 1962, p. 158

Seawright, R. and Draper, W. V., 'Photographic effects in the feature production *Topper*', *Journal SMPE*, Jan. 1939, p. 60

Seldon, Nick, 'Gulliver in Hollywood: the world of movie miniatures', *American Cinematographer*, Nov. 1983, p. 87

Shay, Don, '*Blade Runner* – 2020 foresight', *Cinefex*, No. 9, July 1982, p. 4

Shay, Don, 'Clash of the (foot-tall) titans', *Cinefex*, No. 5, July 1981, p. 20

Shay, Don, 'Creating an alien ambience', *Cinefex*, No. 1, March 1980, p. 34. Special visual-effects design on the production *Alien*

Shay, Don, 'David Dryer – *Never Say Never Again*', *Cinefex*, No. 15, Jan. 1984, p. 4

Shay, Don, 'Jedi journal', *Cinefex*, No. 13, July 1983, p. 4. Description of work on the production of *Return of the Jedi*

Shay, Don, 'Outland', *Cinefex*, No. 4, April 1981, p. 4

Shay, Don, 'Willis O'Brien – creator of the impossible', *Cinefex*, No. 7, Jan. 1982, p. 4. Production of *The Lost World*, *King Kong* and *Mighty Joe Young*

Shay, Don, 'Wrath of God, the – and other illusions', *Cinefex*, No. 6, Oct. 1981, p. 62. Special visual effects for *Raiders of the Lost Ark*

Shay, Don and Sammon, Paul, 'Shadow and substance', *Cinefex*, No. 14, Oct. 1983, p. 50. A discussion of effects work on the production of *Brainstorm*

Sher, Lanny, 'Creating the electronic special effects for *The Invisible Man*', *American Cinematographer*, July 1975, p. 782

Slifer, Clarence W. D., 'Creating visual effects for *G.W.T.W.*', *American Cinematographer*, August 1982, p. 788. The production of *Gone With the Wind*

Smith, Alvy Ray, 'The Genesis demo', *American Cinematographer*, Oct. 1982, p. 1038. Computer graphics effects for *Star Trek II*

Sorensen, Peter, 'Tronic imagery', *Cinefex*, No. 8, April 1982, p. 4. Visual effects in the Walt Disney production of *Tron*

Stengler, Mack, 'Camera tricks that build "production value"', *American Cinematographer*, August 1941, p. 380

Stevens, G. R., 'Independent frame – an attempt at rationalization of motion picture production', *Journal SMPTE*, November 1951, p. 434. Integration of 'unit sets' and background projection to cut production costs and time

Stull, William, '*Dr. Cyclops* in two counts in hall of fame', *American Cinematographer*, May 1940, p. 220

Stull, William, 'Improvising camera tricks', *American Cinematographer*, Dec. 1934, p. 346

Sullivan, Tom, 'Matte work for *The Blue and the Gray*', *American Cinematographer*, March 1983, p. 40

Swarthe, Robert, 'Creating special visual effects for *Radio Rocket Boy*', *American Cinematographer*, Oct. 1973, p. 1338

Swarthe, Robert, 'Of miniatures, mattes and magic', *American Cinematographer*, Jan. 1982, p. 38. Effects work on the production of *One From the Heart*

Trumbull, Douglas, 'Creating special effects for *2001: A Space Odyssey*', *American Cinematographer*, June 1968, p. 416

Trumbull, Douglas, 'Creating the photographic special effects for *Close Encounters*', *American Cinematographer*, Jan. 1978, p. 72

Trumbull, Douglas, 'Into the v'ger maw with Douglas Trumbull', *Cinefex*, No. 1, March 1980, p. 4

Trumbull, Douglas, '"Slit-scan" process, the', *American Cinematographer*, Oct. 1969, p. 998. A description of the optical techniques employed to produce a psychedelic efect for Kubrick's *2001*

Turner, George, 'Creative realism for *The Day After*', *American Cinematographer*, Feb. 1984, p. 56

Turner, George, 'Effects photography for *Return of the Jedi*', *American Cinematographer*, June 1983, p. 89

Turner, George, 'Making the *Flash Gordon* serials', *American Cinematographer*, June 1983, p. 56

Turner, George, 'Photographic effects for the *Winds of War*', *American Cinematographer*, Feb. 1983, p. 51

Turner, George and Lee, Nora, '*Spacehunter* – adventures in the forbidden zone in 3-D', *American Cinematographer*, July 1983, p. 56

Vanderbilt, Scott, '*Caveman* – the real stars', *Cinefex*, No. 5, July 1981, p. 54

Van der Veer, Frank, 'Composite scenes for *King Kong* using the blue-screen technique', *American Cinematographer*, Jan. 1977, p. 56

Veilleux, 'Warp speed and beyond', *American Cinematographer*, Oct. 1982, p. 1032. Special effects for *Star Trek II*

Veze, Robert, '*Blue Thunder*', *American Cinematographer*, May 1983, p. 54

Wade, Louise, 'Optical effects for *Return of the Jedi*', *American Cinematographer*, June 1983, p. 95

Wellman, Harold, '*King Kong* – then and now', *American Cinematographer*, Jan. 1977, p. 66

Wells, Richard, 'Dreaming to scale', *American Cinematographer*, Oct. 1980, p. 1048. Magicam techniques and miniatures in the production of *Cosmos*

Wells, Richard, 'Four-in-one filming', *American Cinematographer*, Oct. 1980, p. 1044. Special effects for the production of *Cosmos*

Whitlock, Albert, 'Reincarnating an 800-foot giant superstar', *American Cinematographer*, Jan. 1976, p. 38. Production on *The Hindenberg*

Whitney, John Jr., 'Creating the special effects for *Westworld*', *American Cinematographer*, Nov. 1973, p. 1477

Effects filters

Anonymous, 'Scheibe's effect filters', *International Photographer*, March 1937, p. 23

Anonymous, 'Scheibe works and plays, too', *American Cinematographer*, Dec. 1940, p. 557

Anonymous, 'Do it yourself special effects', *American Cinematographer*, Sept. 1964, p. 518. Image fragmentation effects produced by the use of an optical device mounted in front of the camera lens

Browning, Irving, 'The diffusion disc', *American Cinematographer*, March 1946, p. 98

Harrison, Hartley, 'Special effect use of filters', *American Cinematographer*, June 1933, p. 51; July 1933, p. 91, Sept. 1933, p. 170; Oct. 1933, p. 215

Mascelli, Joseph V., 'Licking contrast problems with ND filters', *American Cinematographer*, April 1959, p. 228

Oster, Emil, 'Device for producing variable diffusion effects', *American Cinematographer*, Feb. 1937, p. 52

Scheibe, George, 'Effects filters', *International Photographer*, Dec. 1937, p. 9

Scheibe, George, 'Filters for special effects', *American Cinematographer*, April 1934, p. 486

Scheibe, George, 'Fog effect filters', *International Photographer*, March 1939, p. 13

Sparkhul, Theodor, 'How one cinematographer secures variable diffusion', *American Cinematographer*, August 1937, p. 328

Day-for-night cinematography

Allen, Leigh, 'They do it with infra-red', *American Cinematographer*, Oct. 1949, p. 360

Anonymous, 'Day-for-night shots', *American Cinematographer*, Jan. 1961, p. 36

Anonymous, 'Grabbing night effects in daytime', *American Cinematographer*, August 1939, p. 370

Clarke, Charles G., 'How to film night scenes in daylight', *American Cinematographer*, May 1966, p. 334

Clarke, Charles G., 'Shooting night effects in daytime', *American Cinematographer*, Dec. 1956, p. 735

Dyer, Elmer G., 'Filming infra-red night effects in the air', *American Cinematographer*, May 1941, p. 214

Dyer, Elmer G., 'Flying high with infra-red', *Agfa Motion Picture Topics*, May–June 1939, p. 5

Edouart, A. Faricot, 'Production night-effects with Agfa's fundamentally new type of infra-red film', *American Cinematographer*, March 1937, p. 96

Hough, G. W. and Leahy, W., 'Infra-red negative as applied to special-effects photography', *Journal SMPE*, Sept. 1937, p. 326

Keene, George T., 'Simulated night photography using color reversal films', *Journal SMPTE*, Oct. 1961, p. 795

Kelley, W. Wallace, 'Making modern night-effects', *American Cinematographer*, Jan. 1941, p. 11

Meyer, Herbert, 'Infra-red versus Panchromatic types', *American Motion Picture Topics*, Jan.–Feb. 1938, p. 5

Miller, Virgil, 'Filter factors for daytime night-effects', *American Cinematographer*, March 1942, p. 107

Stout, Archie, 'Dramatic pictorialism with infra-red film', *American Cinematographer*, August 1948, p. 265

Patents

Anonymous, 'The Dawley patent', *American Cinematographer*, April 1929, p. 4

Dunning, Carroll H., 'Patents vs. patents vs. practice', *American Cinematographer*, April 1929, p. 18

Elgabri, Ali Z., 'A bibliography of special-effects patents'. (Monograph). Columbus: Dept. of Photography and Cinema, The Ohio State University (1969)

Fleischer, Max, 'Letter to the Editor: historical note on composite production of motion pictures', *Journal SMPTE*, April 1960, p. 263

Hineline, H. D., 'Composite photographic processes', *Journal SMPE*, April 1933, p. 283

Stull, William, 'Producers pool composite process patents', *American Cinematographer*, Nov. 1936, p. 461

Theisen, Earl, 'In the realm of tricks and illusions', *International Photographer*, June 1934, p. 8

Wall, E. J., 'Some patents for trick photography', *Transactions SMPE*, No. 30: August 1927, p. 328

Wallace, Ernest L., 'Patents as related to photography', *American Cinematographer*, March 1929, p. 25. Description of the Dawley patent

Biography

Anonymous, 'Close-ups: Paul Lerpae, special effects first cameraman', *International Photographer*, Sept. 1939, p. 21

Anonymous, 'Co-operative research laboratory needed', *International Photographer*, Jan. 1941, p. 8. Interview with special-effects technician Larry Butler

Anonymous, 'Horsley heads universal special effects department', *American Cinematographer*, Dec. 1945, p. 417

Anonymous, 'Jackman returns to business', *American Cinematographer*, April 1937, p. 137. Description of the work of special-effects expert Fred Jackman and his independent effects organization

Anonymous, 'Ray Mamme's inventions', *International Photographer*, June 1933, p. 17. Biographical sketch of MGM effects expert Ray Mamme and a description of the processes which he developed

Anonymous, 'Roach's Mr. Young', *International Photographer*, Dec. 1937, p. 18. A review of the work of Frank Young of Hal Roach Studios

Anonymous, 'Teague', *International Photographer*, July 1937, p. 18. An account of the activities of George Teague, freelance effects worker, specializing in rear projection

Anonymous, 'Veteran trick cameraman passed on', *International Photographer*, May 1948, p. 14. Obituary and description of the work of Fred A. Dobson

Anonymous, 'Wizard of miniatures', *International Photographer*, March 1940, p. 16. Biographic sketch of Frank William Young of Hal Roach Studios

Black, Hilda, 'Aces of the camera: John P. Fulton, A.S.C', *American Cinematographer*, Dec. 1945, p. 415

Blanchard, Walter, 'Aces of the camera, XVIII: Farciot Edouart, A.S.C.', *American Cinematographer*, June 1942, p. 256

Blanchard, Walter, 'Unseen camera aces: Linwood Dunn, A.S.C.', *American Cinematographer*, July 1943, p. 254

Blanchard, Walter, 'Unseen camera aces: Maximillian Fabian A.S.C.', *American Cinematographer*, June 1943, p. 210

Bonifer, Michael, 'A specially effective man', *American Cinematographer*, Jan. 1980, p. 56. Danny Lee of Walt Disney Studios

Boscoe, W. G. Campbell, 'Aces of the camera: Irving Reis, A.S.C.', *American Cinematographer*, Oct. 1946, p. 351

Boscoe, W. G. Campbell, 'Aces of the camera: Jerome (Jerry) Ash, A.S.C.', *American Cinematographer*, April 1946, p. 115

Boscoe, W. G. Campbell, 'Unseen aces of the camera: Hans (Koney) Koenekamp, A.S.C.', *American Cinematographer*, Jan. 1944, p. 12

Cavalcanti, Alberto, 'A pioneer', *Sight and Sound*, Summer 1938, p. 55. Description of the career of British special-effects cinematographer Edward Charles Rogers

Culhane, John, 'The remarkable visions of Peter Ellenshaw', *American Film*, Sept. 1979, p. 18

Engel, Robert, 'A close encounter with Doug Trumbull', *Technical Photography*, Jan. 1975, p. 36

Fielding, Raymond, 'Norman O. Dawn: pioneer worker in special effects cinematography', *Journal SMPTE*, Jan. 1963, p. 15

Fleet, Roe, 'Aces of the camera: Lloyd Knechtel, A.S.C.', *American Cinematographer*, June 1947, p. 206

Fox, Jordan, 'Roy Arbogast', *Cinefex*, No. 5, July 1981, p. 42

Hachem, Samir, 'Bo Gehring: thinking in fast forward', *Millimeter*, Sept. 1983, p. 93

Harryhausen, Ray (interviewed by Vic Cox), 'Ray Harryhausen – acting without the lumps', *Cinefex*, No. 5, July 1981, p. 4

Jackman, Fred, 'Comedy "kicks" require courage and skill', *American Cinematographer*, Dec. 1922, p. 5. Experiences of a special-effects cameraman

Johnson, Grady, 'Special photographic effects magic', *American Cinematographer*, Dec. 1947, p. 431. An interview with effects expert Gordon Jennings of Paramount Studios

Kains, Maurice, 'Hot points', *International Photographer*, June 1930, p. 130. Review of the work of Lloyd Knechtel, head of special cinematographic effects at R.K.O.

Kallis, Stephan A. Jr., 'Motion picture "Magic" demonstrated in Boston', *American Cinematographer*, Feb. 1972, p. 188. Description of a lecture on special visual effects given by Linwood Dunn

Mandell, Paul, 'Making miracles the hard way: John R. Fulton, A.S.C.', *American Cinematographer*, Dec. 1983, p. 42

Munson, Brad, 'Greg Jein – miniature giant', *Cinefex*, No. 2, August 1980, p. 24

Shay, Don, 'Photographs and memories – Ralph Hammeras', *Cinefex*, No. 15, Jan. 1984, p. 50

Shay, Don, 'Special visual effects – Robert Swarthe', *Cinefex*, No. 11, Jan. 1983, p. 50

Shay, Don, 'Willis O'Brien – creator of the impossible', *Cinefex*, No. 7, Jan. 1982, p. 4

Spielberg, Steven, 'The unsung heroes: or credit where credit is due', *American Cinematographer*, Jan. 1978, p. 68. The work of special-effects workers on *Close Encounters of the Third Kind*

Tasker, Ann, 'Ray Harryhausen talks about his cinematic style', *American Cinematographer,* June 1981, p. 556

Turner, Susan, 'Dennis Muren: tracing special effects through one man's career', *Millimeter,* Sept. 1980, p. 91

Witty, Susan, 'The masters of special effects', *GEO,* June 1983, p. 42. The work of selected contemporary special-effects workers

Bibliographies

Fielding, Raymond, 'Special effects cinematography: a bibliography', *Journal SMPTE,* June 1960, p. 421

Pixilation techniques

Benson, Harold, 'Pixilation – New idea in movie making', *American Cinematographer,* Nov. 1954, p. 568

Gerber, Sophia P., 'Making cartoons out of people', *Science Digest,* Feb. 1963, p. 28

McLaren, Norman, 'Pixilation', *Canadian Film News,* Oct. 1953, p. 3

McLaren, Norman, 'Pixilation', *International Photographer,* March 1954, p. 18

Witherell, William R., 'Pixilation – new technique with commercial possibilities', *American Cinematographer,* July 1962, p. 412

Electronics and computer applications in special-effects cinematography

Anonymous, 'Automatic camera effects system (ACES), The', *American Cinematographer,* Jan. 1980, p. 60. Description of the motion-control system developed at Walt Disney Studios

Anonymous, 'Computer research and development as Lucasfilm', *American Cinematographer,* August 1982, p. 773

Anonymous, 'Disney's new matte scan system', *American Cinematographer,* Jan. 1980, p. 68

Blinn, Dr. James, Cole, Pat and Kolhase, Charles, 'Computer magic for *Cosmos*', *American Cinematographer,* Oct. 1980, p. 1018

Champlin, Chuck Jr., 'The electronic optical printer', *American Cinematographer,* April 1983, p. 76

Dupy, O. L., 'A motion repeating system for special effect photography', *Journal SMPTE,* March 1950, p. 290

Holm, Wilton, 'The new electronic composite photography and image modification system (ECP & IM)', *American Cinematographer,* April 1975, p. 424

Katz, Cynthia, 'Faerie tale theatre', *Videography,* June 1983, p. 25. The use of glass shots, miniatures, matte shots, and the Ultimatte process on a video production for the Showtime Cable Network

Lee, Nora, 'Motion control', *American Cinematographer,* May 1983, p. 60

Lee, Nora, 'Motion control, Pt. II', *American Cinematographer,* June 1983, p. 44

Lee, Nora, 'Motion control for *Blue Thunder*', *American Cinematographer,* May 1983, p. 58

Mendrala, James A., 'Filming 14 TV monitors simultaneously without shutter bar, roll bar or visible splice line', *American Cinematographer,* Feb. 1979, p. 154

Patterson, Richard, 'Electronic special effects', *American Cinematographer,* Oct. 1972, p. 1160

Patterson, Richard, 'Ultimatte', *American Cinematographer,* Oct. 1982, p. 1041

Richardson, Marc A., 'A dream in the making', *Cinefex,* No. 12, April 1983, p. 50. The work of the motion-control group, Dream Quest

Sher, Lanny, 'Creating the electronic special effects for *The Invisible Man*', *American Cinematographer,* July 1975, p. 782

Smith, Alvy Ray, 'Special effects for *Star Trek II*: the Genesis demo – instant evolution with computer graphics', *American Cinematographer,* Oct. 1982, p. 1038

Sorenson, Peter, 'Computer imaging – an apple for the dreamsmiths', *Cinefex,* No. 6, Oct. 1981, p. 4

Miscellaneous

Arnold, Alan, '"O Pioneers!" or "Inside ILM"', *American Cinematographer*, June 1980, p. 554

Elkins, Merry, 'San Francisco's special effects', *Millimeter*, Sept. 1982, p. 112

Hachem, Samir, 'Space operas, special effects and the summer of '83', *Millimeter*, Sept. 1983, p. 78

La Zare, Howard, T., 'Progress report: motion pictures/special effects', *Journal SMPTE*, April 1983, p. 91

Marks, James, 'Getting (and holding) it together in the wild and wacky world of special effects', *American Cinematographer*, April 1979, p. 372

Takahashi, Tama, 'The 1980-81 assistant camera training program: special effects', *American Cinematographer*, Oct. 1981, p. 1010

Travkin, B. T., 'Chemical mixtures for creating special effects cinematography', *American Cinematographer*, August 1974, p. 962

Index